Palgrave Studies in Risk and Insurance

Series Editor
Maurizio Pompella
Università di Siena
Siena, Italy

Palgrave Studies in Risk and Insurance explores leading research in the fields of risk and insurance, alternative risk transfer and structured finance and insurance. It reflects on the convergence of insurance and financial markets over the last two decades. It offers insight into the areas of risk theory and insurance economics, and offers a special focus on cross-diagonal and market risk transfers. The series covers a range of related topics, including financial and pure risk securitization, structured finance and innovation, the engineering of insurance policies and risk transfer between banks and insurance companies. The collection represents some of the most up to date and innovative content currently available in risk and insurance.

More information about this series at
http://www.palgrave.com/gp/series/15815

Christopher L. Culp · Andria van der Merwe
Bettina J. Stärkle

Credit Default Swaps

Mechanics and Empirical Evidence on Benefits, Costs, and Inter-Market Relations

palgrave
macmillan

Note

1. For full disclosure, I have known Chris for about 15 years. He is a good friend and coauthor in a few projects on options and credit risk. We have also worked together in several cases for the consulting firm Compass Lexecon. Moreover, as an interesting turn of events, Andria was a student of mine at Chicago Booth, and I was happily surprised when I learnt she was working closely with Chris. Bettina is the newer addition to the group, and I had the pleasure to be working with her as well more recently. Still, whoever knows me also knows that I do not let friendship and work bias my views. I would have rather not have agreed to write this foreword to their book if I thought the book was not worthy.

Christopher L. Culp · Andria van der Merwe
Bettina J. Stärkle

Credit Default Swaps

Mechanics and Empirical Evidence on Benefits, Costs, and Inter-Market Relations

palgrave
macmillan

Christopher L. Culp
Johns Hopkins University
Baltimore, MD, USA

Bettina J. Stärkle
Compass Lexecon
Chicago, IL, USA

Andria van der Merwe
Johns Hopkins University
Baltimore, MD, USA

ISSN 2523-8221 ISSN 2523-823X (electronic)
Palgrave Studies in Risk and Insurance
ISBN 978-3-030-06580-5 ISBN 978-3-319-93076-3 (eBook)
https://doi.org/10.1007/978-3-319-93076-3

Cover illustration: opico, iStock/Getty Images Plus
Cover design by Thomas Howey

Printed on acid-free paper

This Palgrave Macmillan imprint is published by the registered company Springer Nature Switzerland AG
The registered company address is: Gewerbestrasse 11, 6330 Cham, Switzerland

Additional Praise for *Credit Default Swaps*

"This is the definitive book on CDS. The book is well written, so that it is a pleasure to go through it, but it will also serve as a valuable reference book. It is rigorous, but readers will be impressed by the authors' unusually strong institutional knowledge. This knowledge is particularly useful in making sense of today's regulations for CDS. The book addresses all the important issues that anybody interested in CDS should know about."

—René M. Stulz, Everett D. Reese *Chair of Banking and Monetary Economics and Director of the Dice Center for Research in Financial Economics, Ohio State University*

"In a critical discussion of the mechanics of CDS products and a comprehensive review of the literature to which they are major contributors, Culp, van der Merwe, and Stärkle address the informational role of CDSs, their supply, the cost of credit, risk sharing, speculation, spillovers on related markets, and potential distortions in the monitoring of borrowers. Credit Default Swaps is a must-read by researchers in academia and industry, regulators, and policy makers involved with CDS products."

—George M. Constantinides, Leo Melamed *Professor of Finance, Booth School of Business, The University of Chicago*

"This is the definitive summary of everything we know about CDS—academic theory, empirical evidence, operational details and economic effects. The book is clear and even-handed, suitable as a comprehensive introduction as well as an authoritative reference work."

—Aaron Brown, *Author and 2011 Global Association of Risk Professionals Risk Manager of the Year*

For my parents, Lindalu and Johnny Lovier.
—CLC

For my parents, Frans and Amanda van der Merwe.
—AvdM

For Kyle and my family, Diana, Christian, David, and Andrea Stärkle.
—BJS

Foreword

I am glad Chris, Andria, and Bettina wrote this book.[1] I really am. The reason is simple: We need clarity about Credit Default Swaps ("CDSs"). We need clarity about their functioning, we need clarity about their regulatory framework, but most importantly, we need clarity about their role in financial markets and, more broadly, in the whole economy. That is, are CDSs useful for something? Do we learn anything from them? Do they achieve the goals of risk transfer that they—like all derivatives—were invented for? Are they good or not for society overall?

The stance of the book is great: Let the data speak. That is, rather going over the arcane analytics and the details of CDS pricing, let's take an unbiased view of the existing empirical literature, organize it by using existing theoretical frameworks, and discuss the costs and benefits of CDSs. The collective expertise of Chris, Andria, and Bettina on CDS markets makes this book an authoritative reference on the subject, and its non-technical nature and detailed prose make it accessible to all types of readers. I thoroughly enjoyed reading (and learning from) this book, and I encourage anyone with the slightest interest in the subject to read it as well.

Like many other observers and contributors to finance, I was taken aback by the unraveling of the financial crisis of 2007–2008 and especially by the suffering it generated to the population as the US economy plummeted into what goes by the name "the Great Recession." Much has been written about the causes of the financial crisis, and researchers are still debating to this day. CDSs have been pointed at as one of the financial vehicles partly responsible for the financial crisis. Books have been written about them, and even movies have been made about them. CDSs have become a sort of super villain. But they are still around today—albeit in a smaller market—and the question is why. Why isn't the villain behind bars? Why are they still in circulation today?

As many financial instruments, CDSs serve multiple roles. Their main financial purpose is to allow market participants to transfer an important source of risk—default risk—from one counterparty to another. If I hold, for instance, Italian sovereign bonds and I am worried about a potential default of Italy (I am not, by the way), I can buy insurance against such an event by purchasing credit default swap protection on Italy. Of course, an alternative would simply be to sell the Italian bonds. But purchasing insurance is normally more efficient than an outright sale of the underlying, as corporate and sovereign bonds tend to be rather illiquid and expensive to trade. In doing so, however, CDS coupon rates—i.e., the insurance premiums—also reveal investors' beliefs about the future prospects of a firm or a country, as well as their willingness to take the risk of default. If insurance is very expensive, for instance, it means that the prospects for the underlying bond are not good, or that investors providing the insurance want to be handsomely compensated for providing such insurance.

CDS rates are thus not only an insurance-like instrument to transfer risk from those who hold risky debt (institutional investors, banks, and so on) to those who want it (other institutional investors, hedge funds, and so on), but they aggregate and reflect dispersed information about the worthiness of the underlying company or sovereign and, as importantly, the size of the risk premium that market participants require to provide insurance. This information may be very valuable to market participants. However, because of the commingling of investors' beliefs about default and the risk premium they require, the information contained in CDSs is often misunderstood by non-sophisticated market participants, media, and policy makers.

Indeed, while CDSs are indeed instruments designed to provide insurance about some underlying risk, standard statistical arguments to determine the insurance premium do not hold for CDSs. In the life insurance business, for instance, the critical characteristic of the underlying risks—peoples' deaths—is that they are uncorrelated with each other. My death is uncorrelated with Chris's, even if we are about the same age. This means that an insurance company can determine the expected loss from insuring a large number of different people with a great deal of precision. The life insurance premium is just the amount required to cover such a precisely estimated expected loss.

Unfortunately, this critical diversification argument does not hold for the entities underlying CDSs. A firm's default is not uncorrelated with other firms' defaults. The data strongly suggest that defaults occur in waves: Many firms "die" at the same time. The reason is simple—firms' survivals depend on common economic conditions, such as the business cycle or the health of financial markets (for instance, the willingness of banks or lenders to rollover companies' debts). Therefore, insuring corporate bonds or sovereigns is far more risky than insuring uncorrelated events, such as individuals' deaths or, to some extent, property values. As an example, an insurance company would never just insure home properties in Florida. The reason is that there are common factors—hurricanes—that can destroy all properties in Florida. It is thus critical for an insurance company to insure also many other properties that are not affected by hurricanes in Florida. Geographic diversification becomes critical.

For CDSs, geographical diversification has little bearing. It helps, but it has a minimal impact. The reason is that in an integrated global market, economic shocks to one side of the globe can reverberate to another part of the globe. Thus, probabilities of defaults tend to move together. They are hard to diversify. That's why CDS rates not only reflect the probability of default of the underlying firms or countries, but they also reflect an important risk premium component. Indeed, even if investors may be diversified in their investments, they would still require a risk premium to insure against the defaults of companies or countries, because defaults most likely occur in bad economic times—exactly when these investors may suffer losses from other investments, such as stocks or housing.

The commingling of default probabilities and risk premiums makes it hard to decipher the information contained in CDS spreads. If a sovereign CDS spread increases, for instance, it is hard to say whether it is due to the country's economic prospects or simply the increase in the premium that investors require to provide insurance. Indeed, some empirical research shows that over 50% of the variation in emerging markets' sovereign CDS spreads has little to do with events in the countries themselves, but they rather depend on events that are very far away. If investors suffer losses in a US stock market crash, for instance, most likely they will be less able to provide insurance to the sovereign bonds of emerging economies, and thus CDS rates of such countries may increase with no fault to the countries themselves. Even if an emerging economy is doing well, its insurance premium may increase for such global reasons.

This discussion brings me back to this book. The empirical evidence on CDSs has been growing steadily over the last 20 years. Moreover, the market for CDSs went through a series of changes both before and especially in the aftermath of the 2007–2008 financial crisis. There is a ton of material out there, and it is just daunting to make sense of it all. This book took up this daunting task and for this reason is very valuable as it provides both a precise account of the various types of CDSs (there are many), their markets, their regulatory framework, and it especially discusses their pros and cons, both theoretically and empirically.

Part I of the book is a nice, instructive read about the types of CDSs, their purposes, and their structures. The book clearly draws on the authors' vast knowledge of these markets, and they include the discussion of several real cases to make their points as concrete as possible. For instance, a CDS must pay in case of a company default. But what is "default"? The matter turns out to be much more complicated than one may think, because there are many events at the company level that may deemed "default events" by some people and not so by some others. By going through some real cases and discussing the arguments made by opposing parties, the reader immediately gauges the difficulties of the issue itself.

I was especially intrigued by the discussion of the "strategic default" cases, in which a party may strategically default (even if it has money to pay the debt) in order to make another related party—who bought a large quantity of CDS—richer as it would receive the insurance from the CDS seller. Is strategic default a real "default event" that should trigger the payment of the CDS? An interesting question.

Part II and Part III of the book discuss the benefits and the costs of CDSs, first from a theoretical perspective (Part II) and then from an empirical perspective (Part III). As mentioned already, the authors refrain from going over the analytics of both theoretical and empirical arguments, but provide terse descriptions of the arguments made in the existing literature for benefits and costs. The reading is actually quite instructive. There are many benefits, and many costs, that even experts in this market may not have thought about. For instance, I mentioned earlier two clear benefits of CDS, namely risk transfers and information aggregation. But there are potentially other, less-obvious benefits of CDS, such as the relaxation of borrowing constraints for some parties or their increase in bargaining power during lending negotiations.

But clearly, there are also costs, potentially big costs. CDSs may induce excessive lending, and their lack of transparency (before the crisis especially) may induce fragility in credit markets. The reason is that while the risk sharing may indeed make the credit market more resilient to individual entities' shocks (the default of even a big company should not affect the economy if such cost is divided across many lenders), it may make the credit market more rigid and more fragile to large shock, such as the melting of the housing market in 2008. In addition, such side bets on defaults may induce some market manipulation and strategic defaults, as mentioned earlier.

The discussion of the empirical evidence is equally informative. There is a lot to take in, as the empirical literature is vast. But Chris, Andria, and Bettina do an excellent job in classifying the evidence into benefits and costs by using their earlier theoretical discussion.

One notable feature of the book is that Chris, Andria, and Bettina do not attempt any personal opinions on the theories or empirical findings. They state what the theoretical and empirical literature says by going over paper by paper. And then they leave it at there that. There is never any "in conclusion, CDSs are good" or "in conclusion, CDSs are bad" statement. They just state the arguments and the evidence in what appears a neutral and unbiased manner.

This unbiased view that is taken in the book however may make some readers a bit unhappy, as there is no final conclusion. Are CDS friends or foes? Or both? We started from this question, and the answer is laid out in the 200+ pages of this book. But at the end of the day, after having reviewed the opposite arguments, each reader may just reach a different conclusion.

Chicago, IL, USA
April 2018

Pietro Veronesi, Ph.D.
Roman Family Professor of Finance
and Robert King Steel Faculty Fellow
The University of Chicago
Booth School of Business

Note

1. For full disclosure, I have known Chris for about 15 years. He is a good friend and coauthor in a few projects on options and credit risk. We have also worked together in several cases for the consulting firm Compass Lexecon. Moreover, as an interesting turn of events, Andria was a student of mine at Chicago Booth, and I was happily surprised when I learnt she was working closely with Chris. Bettina is the newer addition to the group, and I had the pleasure to be working with her as well more recently. Still, whoever knows me also knows that I do not let friendship and work bias my views. I would have rather not have agreed to write this foreword to their book if I thought the book was not worthy.

Preface

Credit Default Swaps ("CDSs") are types of derivatives contracts with cash flows and values derived from the credit quality of one or more underlying reference borrowers or credit-sensitive assets. Apropos to the inclusion of our volume in the *Palgrave Studies on Risk and Insurance* series, CDSs are classic risk transfer instruments that facilitate the shifting of credit risk from one party to another.

The primary types of CDS contracts include single-name CDSs (based on the credit risk of a single borrower—a.k.a "reference entity" or "reference name"), multi-name CDSs (based on the credit risk of more than one reference name or an index of reference entities), and asset-backed CDSs (based on the credit risk of specific securities—usually asset-backed securities ("ABSs"), including mortgage-backed securities ("MBSs") and securities issued as a part of collateralized debt obligations ("CDOs").

The single-name CDS market expanded rapidly from 2002 through 2007. Growth in single-name CDS notional amounts outstanding, however, slowed after the eruption of the global credit market crisis that suddenly spread from US subprime mortgage-related credit markets to numerous other fixed-income markets in August 2007 and during the Eurozone sovereign debt crisis in 2010 and 2011.

Despite deliberate efforts by the International Swaps and Derivatives Association ("ISDA")—the primary trade association that represents the interests of dealers and end users in derivatives executed outside the confines of organized financial exchanges (a.k.a. over-the-counter ("OTC") derivatives)—and other market participants, the single-name CDS market has shifted from stagnating growth to contraction and has shrunk substantially in recent years. Other CDS products such as single-name loan-only CDSs ("LCDSs") and asset-backed CDS ("ABCDSs") have also languished since the credit crisis. The only constituent of the global CDS marketplace that has experienced sustained market activity to date is the market for CDS index products based on North American and European corporate credit risk.

Motivation for and Scope of the Book

A February 4, 2016, story in the *Financial Times* stated that single-name CDSs "are experiencing renewed growth after a long period of decline."[1] Yet, an article in the *Financial Times* just four months later stated that "[i]nvestors … have all but lost the ability to buy a … single-name credit default swap."[2] Such cognitive dissonance makes it difficult to assess the state of the single-name CDS market based solely on popular media accounts, and, indeed, the data indicate that neither of those two extremes is entirely accurate.

There is little doubt that the single-name CDS market has shrunk appreciably and has been plagued with controversy in recent years. Among the most frequently cited reasons for the decline in single-name CDS activity is the series of sweeping changes to the global financial regulatory framework that have been (and continue to be) implemented following the crisis. Three of the most significant changes that have impacted CDSs include the revised Basel Accord (i.e., Basel III), which significantly increases the capital costs of trading certain single-name CDSs, as well as the ban in the E.U. on short selling using single-name CDSs (i.e., buying CDSs without owning an obligation of the reference entity), and also the mandated clearing of some CDSs by central counterparties ("CCPs") under the Dodd–Frank Wall Street Reform and Consumer Protection Act("Dodd-Frank") in the USA and the European Market Infrastructure Regulation ("EMIR") in the E.U. The first two regulatory reforms have had a decidedly chilling impact on single-name CDS trading. In addition to regulatory changes, the relatively low default rates on corporate debt during recent years has also suppressed the demand for lenders exposed to the credit risk of borrowers to use CDSs for risk transfer purposes and thus has contributed to a relative lack of interest in CDSs as a hedging instrument.

The third regulatory reform (i.e., mandated clearing) thus far only has applied to multi-name CDS index products and has not had a direct impact on single-name CDSs as of the date of this publication. Indeed, trading volume for index CDS products subject to mandatory clearing has not abated since the advent of the applicable regulations.

One possible explanation for declines in trading volume and notional amounts outstanding for certain non-index CDSs is that in their original form (i.e., before the implementation of new post-crisis market practices), CDSs might have been inherently defective. Indeed, some contend (despite a lack of any significant empirical evidence) that single-name CDSs "caused" the credit crisis and Eurozone sovereign debt crisis.

Although some of the issues and controversy surrounding CDSs are subjective and qualitative, the majority of such issues are empirically testable. Examples of empirical questions that can help explain the value (or lack thereof) of CDSs include the following:

- What information is contained in CDS spreads about the credit risk of underlying borrowers? In particular, do CDSs convey valuable and useful information about the likelihood and severity of a borrower experiencing an adverse credit event over the life of a CDS contract?
- Do CDSs enable lenders to manage their credit risk more efficiently, or do they instead incentivize and facilitate additional credit risk-taking by lenders?
- Does the availability of CDSs to lenders result in attenuated monitoring of the credit risks of their borrowers either at the inception of loans to borrowers underlying single-name CDSs or on an ongoing basis?
- Do CDSs impact the supply and/or cost of credit to borrowers on which CDSs are traded and, if so, what exactly is the nature of that impact?
- Does the ability for a lender to a reference entity to hedge its exposure with CDSs give rise to "empty creditors" (i.e., creditors that eliminate their credit exposure to borrowers but retain their control rights), and, if so, do those empty creditors prematurely and inefficiently force ailing firms into bankruptcy instead of negotiating restructurings that would allow the reference entity to remain in operation with an enterprise valuation in excess of ailing firms' liquidation values?

- Do CDS spreads lead or lag corresponding debt, equity, and options markets in processing and reflecting new information about borrowers?
- How has the introduction of CDS trading impacted the volatility, liquidity, and informational efficiency of related equity, debt, and options markets?
- What economic factors drive the differences between credit spreads for a reference entity as reflected in CDSs as compared to credit spreads implied by the entity's cash bonds?
- Are CDSs a source of heightened interconnectedness and potential systemic risk in the banking and financial systems?
- Do CDSs contain information that can be used by policy makers to improve their quantitative measurements of systemic interconnectedness?
- What information can be observed from index CDS products as distinct from single-name and asset-backed CDS products?

Since the advent of CDS trading in the 1990s, a large academic literature has evolved that examines all of the above issues and more. The purpose of this book is to provide a survey of that literature and to summarize the empirical evidence on CDSs and the impact of CDS trading on related markets in order to try and elucidate the true economic benefits and costs of these derivatives products. In addition, we review the mechanics of corporate and sovereign single-name CDSs, LCDSs, multi-name and index CDSs, and asset-backed CDSs ("ABCDSs") to ensure that this book is a comprehensive reference work on CDS products.

Our book is an outgrowth and expansion of a research initiative that was originally commissioned by ISDA in which we were requested to prepare a review of the empirical academic literature (only) on single-name CDSs for the purpose of providing a better understanding of the benefits and costs of single-name CDSs based both on theory and the extant empirical evidence. Our study was published in September 2016 by ISDA and as a working paper in the *Studies in Applied Finance* working paper series at the Johns Hopkins Institute for Applied Economics, Global Health, and the Study of Business Enterprise (Culp et al. 2016a, b).

Some portions of this book overlap with our original study for ISDA. Nevertheless, this book expands our initial research project in several important ways. First, we have included in Part I more detailed discussions of the mechanics of various CDS products in addition to single-name CDSs, such as multi-name and index CDSs, LCDSs, and ABCDSs. Although certain products—namely LCDSs (see Chapter 3) and ABCDSs (see Chapter 5)—are no longer actively traded and do not represent significant constituents of the current global credit derivatives marketplace, we include chapters that describe these CDS products, both because of their historical relevance and the potential for these products to be revitalized in the future.

Second, we have expanded our review of the empirical academic literature to include studies based on CDS data that are not limited to single-name CDSs and that now include empirical academic research based on other types of CDS products—index CDSs, in particular.

Finally, we have updated our literature review of the empirical academic articles on single-name CDSs to ensure that our book is current with the latest empirical academic studies as of April 2018.

Target Audience

We anticipate that this book will be primarily of interest to researchers involved with CDSs who work at banks, hedge funds, pension plans, other asset managers, regulators, and policy makers, all of whom may benefit from a comprehensive review of the mechanics of the various types of CDSs and the empirical evidence regarding the benefits, costs, and inter-market relations of CDSs. In addition, the combination of our discussion of the mechanics of various CDS products together with our review of the relevant empirical academic literature should make this a suitable textbook for an advanced M.B.A. and/or Ph.D.-level course on credit derivatives. Finally, those already familiar with the global CDS marketplace may find this work to be a valuable reference on the mechanics and empirical academic literature on CDSs.

Structure of the Book

Our book is divided into three distinct parts. In Part I, we explain the mechanics of the primary types of CDS products that characterize the CDS marketplace. Chapter 1 presents a broad overview of CDSs and aggregate market activity. Chapters 2 through 5 explore the mechanics and details of single-name CDSs, single-name LCDSs, multi-name and index CDSs, and ABCDSs, respectively. Chapter 6 concludes Part I with a discussion of how CDS transactions are executed and/or cleared by CCPs.

In Part II Chapters 7 and 8, we explain the potential benefits and costs of CDSs, respectively. Part II is a purely conceptual section of the book that helps frame the empirical issues explored in Part III regarding the testing of the CDS benefit and cost hypotheses articulated in Chapters 7 and 8.

Part III of the book presents our survey of the academic empirical literature on the benefits, costs, and inter-market relations of single-name, multi-name, and asset-backed CDSs. In Chapter 9, we review the academic literature on the informational content of CDS spreads—specifically, the information contained in CDS spreads regarding default probabilities and loss-given-default ("LGD") rates for the underlying reference entities. We also discuss how the literature decomposes CDS spreads into expected credit loss and risk premium components, where the latter is demanded by protection sellers to bear both unexpected credit risk and non-credit risks such as market liquidity risk. We further review how single-name CDS spreads and/or changes in those spreads can provide useful information regarding certain events and announcements related to underlying reference entities (e.g., ratings actions, earnings announcements, and public policy actions such as bailout and bail-in initiatives).

Chapter 10 summarizes the existing academic research on how the availability of single-name CDSs impacts both lenders to reference entities underlying traded CDSs and the reference entities themselves. We evaluate the literature on the influence of single-name CDSs on the availability and supply of credit to reference entities, reference entity borrowing costs, and the credit and credit risk management decisions of lenders.

In Chapter 11, we review the academic literature on the relations between single-name CDSs and other related financial products and markets, including the bonds and equities issued by reference entities underlying single-name CDSs. In particular, we consider which market is the primary source of price discovery for the revelation of new information about the reference entities underlying single-name CDSs, the implications of the introduction of CDS trading on the liquidity and volatility of related bond and stock markets, and the differences between the credit spreads on a reference entity as reflected in single-name CDSs versus cash bonds issued by the same reference entities (i.e., the "CDS-bond basis").

Chapter 12 reviews the academic literature on the systemic risk aspects of CDSs. We specifically review the literature on CDS cross-market correlations, how CDSs can give rise to interconnectedness across financial institutions, and how CDS spreads can be used to measure systemic interconnectedness, spillover effects, and relations between sovereign CDS spreads and the financial condition of local banking systems.

The book also includes two appendices. In Appendix A, we explain in detail the methodology that we used to select the various articles that we defined for the universe of our survey of the academic empirical literature that is discussed in Part III of the book. Appendix B shows three tables that are too long for inclusion in the text. Tables B.1 and B.2 summarize the ISDA determination events and auctions for single-name CDSs and LCDSs, respectively. Table B.3 provides details of the underlying data sources and samples on which all of the empirical papers surveyed in Part III are based. (Note that Table B.3 does not summarize the data on which *we* rely, but rather the data on which the studies we review in the book rely.) In addition, a list of frequently used abbreviations or acronyms and their definitions is included in the front matter of the book following the Table of Contents and the List of Figures and Tables.

Related Work

Ours is certainly not the only book on CDSs. Standard treatments of CDS products and markets can be found in Gregory (2003), Chaplin (2010), Bomfim (2015), Chacko et al. (2016), and elsewhere. All of these books are useful product (and in some cases modeling) references and worthy of being on interested researchers' bookshelves, but none comprehensively review the empirical evidence on the benefits and costs of CDSs. Conversely, the studies that minimize discussion of CDS product mechanics and focus on reviewing the empirical literature on the benefits and costs of CDSs are the excellent surveys by Augustin et al. (2014, 2016).[3]

None of the above books or studies, however, contain *both* detailed discussions of the mechanics of CDS products *and* a comprehensive and current review of the empirical academic literature on the benefits and costs of CDSs. In this context, our treatise fills a void and presents an integrated and thorough discussion of the mechanics of the primary CDS products and the evidence from the empirical academic literature on the benefits and costs and inter-market relations of CDSs.

Acknowledgements

We have benefitted (individually and collectively) from numerous conversations with various people that have helped inform our knowledge of CDS products and markets and have enabled us to obtain data for the analyses we present in this book. We particularly wish to thank Aaron Brown, George Constantinides, Audrey Costabile, Natalie Calloway, George Cassidy, John Cochrane, Paul Forrester, Steve Kennedy, Andrea Neves, Mark New, Janusz Ordover, Fred Quenzer, Harris Rothman, Pietro Veronesi, Vonda Versical, and Debbie Zimmermann for their comments on and assistance with earlier drafts. We are especially grateful to our research assistant, Charmaine Alcain, who diligently and meticulously audited every chapter of the book and all of our data to ensure the accuracy of our figures, tables, and references. We are also grateful to Clarus Financial Technology for providing us with access to CDS data on an academic fee-discounted basis. Finally, we thank Tula Weis and Ruth Noble at Palgrave for their capable and patient assistance in the editing and production of this book, and, especially, Maurizzio Pompella for inviting us to contribute to this Palgrave series.

All of the above individuals and organizations are, of course, blameless for any remaining errors or omissions. The opinions expressed herein are ours alone and are not necessarily the opinions of any of the organizations with which we are affiliated (including Compass Lexecon, with which all three authors are affiliated) or those organizations' other professionals, affiliates, clients, and/or customers.

Disclosure

We gratefully acknowledge the financial support of ISDA in providing a financial honorarium to us for the completion of the White Paper on which this book is based (Culp et al. 2016a, b). Our research expenses exceeded the amount received as an honorarium from ISDA, however, and we therefore did not earn any *net* compensation for the ISDA-sponsored White Paper.

All three of us occasionally provide consulting services on many of the issues explored in this book. We nevertheless represent that this is not a work for hire on behalf of any of our consulting clients, and none of our opinions and analyses in this book were impacted by any commercial considerations.

Chicago, IL, USA

Christopher L. Culp
Andria van der Merwe
Bettina J. Stärkle

Notes

1. P. Stafford and J. Rennison, "Credit Default Swaps Activity Heats Up," *Financial Times* (February 4, 2016).
2. J. Rennison and M. Childs, "Debt Traders Miss Credit Default Swaps as Losses Loom," *Financial Times* (June 9, 2016).
3. For more targeted surveys, see Das and Hanouna (2006) (emphasizing the literature on the difference between CDS spreads and credit spreads on bonds) and Griffin (2014) (emphasizing the relation between CDS spreads and accounting information).

References

Augustin, P., M. G. Subrahmanyam, D. Y. Tang, and S. Q. Wang. 2014. "Credit Default Swaps: A Survey". *Foundations and Trends in Finance* 9, nos. 1–2

Augustin, P., M. G. Subrahmanyam, D. Y. Tang, and S. Q. Wang. 2016. "Credit Default Swaps: Past, Present, and Future." *Annual Review of Financial Economics* 8, no. 10.

Bomfim, A. N. 2015. *Understanding Credit Derivatives and Related Instruments.* 2nd ed. New York, NY: Academic Press.

Chacko, G., A. Sjöman, H. Motohashi, and V. Dessain. 2016. *Credit Derivatives: A Primer on Credit Risk, Modeling, and Instruments.* Old Tappan, NJ: Pearson FT Press.

Chaplin, G. 2010. *Credit Derivatives: Trading, Investing and Risk Management.* 2nd ed. Hoboken, NJ: Wiley.

Culp, C. L., A. van der Merwe, and B. J. Stärkle. 2016a. Single-Name Credit Default Swaps: A Review of the Empirical Academic Literature." *International Swaps and Derivatives Association Study* (September).

Culp, C. L., A. van der Merwe, and B. J. Stärkle. 2016b. "Single-Name Credit Default Swaps: A Review of the Empirical Academic Literature." *Johns Hopkins Institute for Applied Economics, Studies in Applied Finance*, no. 11 (September).

Das, S. R., and P. Hanouna. 2006. "Credit Default Swap Spreads." *Journal of Investment Management* 4, no. 3 (Third Quarter).

Gregory, J. (ed.). 2003. *Credit Derivatives: The Definitive Guide.* London: Risk Books.

Griffin, P. A. 2014. "The Market for Credit Default Swaps: New Insights into Investors' Use of Accounting Information?" *Accounting & Finance* 54, no. 3.

Contents

Part III Empirical Evidence on the Benefits, Costs, and Inter-Market Relations of CDSs

About the Authors

Christopher L. Culp, Ph.D. specializes in structured finance, derivatives, insurance/reinsurance, credit risk and credit markets, and risk management. He is a Research Fellow at the Johns Hopkins Institute for Applied Economics, Global Health, and the Study of Business Enterprise and the Co-Director of the Institute's *Studies in Applied Finance* working paper series, an Adjunct Professor at the Swiss Finance Institute and Universität Bern, and he was an adjunct member of the faculty at The University of Chicago Booth School of Business from 1998–2013, where he taught M.B.A.-level courses on derivatives, structured finance, and insurance. He is the author of *Structured Finance and Insurance* (John Wiley & Sons, 2006), *Risk Transfer: Derivatives in Theory and Practice* (John Wiley & Sons, 2004), *The ART of Risk Management* (John Wiley & Sons, 2002), and *The Risk Management Process* (John Wiley & Sons, 2001), and the co-editor of *Corporate Aftershock: The Public Policy Lessons from the Collapse of Enron and Other Major Corporations* with William Niskanen (John Wiley & Sons, 2003) and *Corporate Hedging in Theory and Practice* with Merton H. Miller (Risk Books, 1999).

Dr. Culp provides consulting services and testimonial expertise on his areas of specialization through his firm Financial Economics Consulting, Inc., and Compass Lexecon, respectively. He is a member of the Federal Reserve Bank of Chicago's Working Group on Financial Markets and is currently or was formerly a member of the editorial advisory boards of *Derivatives Quarterly* (co-managing editor), *FMA Online, Futures Industry* magazine, the *Journal of Applied Corporate Finance*, the *Journal of Risk Finance*, and the *Journal of Structured Finance*.

Culp earned his Ph.D. with a concentration in finance from The University of Chicago's Booth School of Business and his B.A. in economics (Phi Beta Kappa and with general and departmental honors) from The Johns Hopkins University. He resides in Chicago, IL, and Bern, Switzerland.

Andria van der Merwe, Ph.D. specializes in fixed-income and credit markets and market microstructure, including liquidity, high-frequency trading, spoofing, and market manipulation. She is a Research Fellow at the Johns Hopkins Institute for Applied Economics, Global Health, and the Study of Business Enterprise and was previously an Adjunct Professor at the Illinois Institute of Technology, where she taught graduate-level courses on fixed-income asset pricing and modeling. She is the holder of three USA patents, has been published in several internationally renowned journals, and is the author of *Market Liquidity Risk: Implications for Asset Pricing, Risk Management and Financial Regulation* (Palgrave Macmillan, 2015).

Dr. van der Merwe is a Senior Vice President at Compass Lexecon, where she provides both consulting and testimonial expertise in matters involving securities and derivatives class action litigation, regulatory investigations and proceedings, trading disputes including market manipulation, and cryptocurrency and distributed ledger (e.g., blockchain) technologies. Before joining Compass Lexecon, she served as a Director of Portfolio Management at the Federal Home Loan Bank of Chicago, where she developed as well as executed trading strategies in fixed-income markets, including debt, derivatives, and securitized products.

Dr. van der Merwe earned her Ph.D. in electrical engineering with concentrations in signal processing and applied mathematics from The Ohio State University and an M.B.A. with concentrations in finance, econometrics, and accounting from The University of Chicago's Booth School of Business. She resides in Chicago, IL.

Bettina J. Stärkle, M.Sc. specializes in derivatives and structured finance, securities and financial markets, corporate valuation, and corporate governance. She is a Senior Economist with Compass Lexecon. Her experience covers a variety of industries, including fixed-income securities and financial services, insurance, energy, and media. Ms. Stärkle previously worked in the Swiss banking industry, and she holds an M.Sc. in business administration with concentrations in finance and accounting from the University of Bern. She resides in Chicago, IL.

Abbreviations and Acronyms

ABCDS	Asset-Backed CDS
ABS	Asset-Backed Security
APD	Arbitrage-Pricing Difference
BIS	Bank for International Settlements
bp/bps	Basis point/basis points
CBOT	Chicago Board of Trade
CCP	Central Counterparty
CDO	Collateralized Debt Obligation
CDS	Credit Default Swap
CLO	Collateralized Loan Obligation
CSA	Credit Support Annex
CTD	Cheapest-to-Deliver
DC	Determinations Committee (ISDA)
ECB	European Central Bank
EDF	Expected Default Frequency
EFSF	European Financial Stability Facility
EMEA	Europe, Middle East, and Africa
EMIR	European Market Infrastructure Regulation
FINRA	Financial Industry Regulatory Authority
FSB	Financial Stability Board
FSOC	Financial Stability Oversight Council
FV	Face Value
ICE	InterContinental Exchange
IMF	International Monetary Fund
ISDA	International Swaps and Derivatives Association
LBO	Leveraged Buyout

LCDS	Loan-Only CDS
LGD	Loss-Given-Default
LIBOR	London Interbank Offered Rate
OECD	Organisation for Economic Co-operation and Development
PAUG	Pay-As-You-Go
PPDM	Primary Price Discovery Market
SOE	State-Owned Enterprise
SRO	Standard Reference Obligation
SSRN	Social Science Research Network
TBTS	Too Big to Save
TRACE	Trade Reporting and Compliance Engine

List of Figures

List of Tables

PART I

The CDS Market and Product Mechanics

CHAPTER 1

Overview of CDS Products and Market Activity

In a CDS, a party known as the protection purchaser (a.k.a. buyer) makes one or more payments to a counterparty known as the protection seller. In return, the protection seller commits to make a payment to the protection buyer following the occurrence of any adverse credit event occurring at the underlying reference entity, entities, or security underlying the CDS. In this chapter, we provide a basic overview of the universe of CDS products and the aggregate activity in the CDS marketplace.

1.1 Primary CDS Product Types

At a high level, we can categorize CDS products based on the source of the credit exposure underlying a CDS from which the cash flows and value of the CDS are derived. From that perspective, there are three main types of CDS products: (i) single-name CDSs; (ii) multi-name CDSs; and (iii) asset-backed CDSs. These three CDS product types are discussed briefly in the sections below and in more detail in Chapters 2 and 3, 4, and 5, respectively.

1.1.1 Single-Name CDSs

In a *single-name CDS*, the cash flows and value of the CDS are based on the credit quality of a single entity, such as a corporation, sovereign, or municipality.[1] In credit derivatives parlance, such a "reference name" (a.k.a. "name" or "reference entity") refers to a legal entity that borrows

C. L. Culp et al., *Credit Default Swaps*, Palgrave Studies in Risk and Insurance, https://doi.org/10.1007/978-3-319-93076-3_1

by issuing debt securities or entering into bank loans that expose lenders to at least some credit risk, such as the risk of a partial or total default on a required interest or principal payment. The specific liabilities of the reference entity underlying a single-name CDS may include all or most of the debt securities issued by the reference entity (see Chapter 2), or, in the case of loan-only CDSs ("LCDSs"), a specific set of loans or a loan facility outstanding at the reference name (see Chapter 3).

1.1.2 Multi-Name CDSs

In a *multi-name CDS*, the value and cash flows of the CDS are based on the credit risk of more than one underlying reference name. Multi-name CDSs can generally be classified as either portfolio/basket CDSs or index CDSs. In the case of index CDSs, the underlying reference portfolios comprised of multiple reference entities can either be based on whole portfolios or tranched portfolio exposures.

1.1.2.1 Portfolio and Basket CDSs

The most basic form of a multi-name CDS is a contract for which the protection purchaser is compensated for credit-related losses on any/all reference entities in the underlying reference portfolio. For example, a portfolio CDS based on a specific basket of 100 bonds—each of which has a par amount of \$1000—provides as much as \$100,000 of protection to the CDS protection purchaser, which is paid out when all 100 bonds default with no actual/expected recovery amounts. If the actual/expected recovery amounts (see Sect. 2.1.5 of Chapter 2 for a discussion of the distinction between the two) are not zero, the protection purchaser of such a whole-portfolio receives compensation upon the occurrence of adverse credit events on each and every underlying reference name based on the par values and actual/expected recovery rates of the borrowings underlying the reference names in the portfolio CDS.

Such portfolio CDSs, however, can be very expensive because the protection purchaser is paying for protection from the risk of adverse credit events on potentially all of the names in the reference portfolio. As such, many multi-name CDSs are tailored to the risk management needs or investment objectives of protection purchasers. Specifically, protection purchasers often choose to purchase protection on a subset of the names in the reference portfolio or on a subset of the total underlying credit-related losses. By reducing the scenarios and/or amounts payable by protection sellers to protection purchasers, such tailored multi-name basket CDSs are generally less expensive than full protection purchased on all names in the reference portfolio.

Portfolio and basket CDSs are discussed in more detail in Sect. 4.1 of Chapter 4.

1.1.2.2 Index CDSs

An index CDS has cash flows and a value tied to the credit risk of an index or portfolio of multiple reference entities that satisfy certain criteria articulated by the index provider. Index CDSs may have cash flows that are either based on the entire value of an index or the values of an index over specific ranges of losses in index values (the latter of which is discussed in Sect. 1.1.2.3).

In a traditional or whole-portfolio index CDS, the protection purchaser makes periodic payments to the protection seller (including perhaps an up-front payment) in return for payments from the protection seller based on declines in the value of the underlying index (resulting, e.g., from credit events occurring at one or more of the underlying reference names). Index CDSs can be based either on multiple reference names or multiple reference assets (as discussed in Chapters 4 and 5, respectively).

As a simple illustrative example, suppose an index CDS is based on the values of senior debt securities (or single-name CDSs on the corresponding reference name issuers) of 100 different reference entities, each of which issues $1000 in a single class of bonds. Suppose further that the initial value of the index is 100, the notional amount of an index CDS based on that initial index value is $100,000, and (by necessity) the multiplier that determines the cash flows on the index CDS is $1000. For each one-point decline in the index, the protection purchaser receives $1000. The maximum payout on such a CDS—which is sufficient to cover defaults with no expected or actual recoveries on *all* the underlying bonds—is $100,000.

1.1.2.3 Tranched Index CDSs

Unlike a whole-portfolio index CDS, a tranched index CDS enables credit protection purchasers to buy protection on specific tranches (from the French word meaning "slices") of the underlying index. These tranches are usually specified based on the amount of cumulative default losses or declines in value in the underlying index and reference portfolio.

For the same reference portfolio described in the previous subsection for a traditional whole-portfolio index CDS, suppose now that two tranched CDSs are offered, each of which has a notional amount of \$50,000 and an index multiplier of \$1000. Both CDSs are based on the same index and reference portfolio. The subordinated tranched CDS is exposed only to losses on the underlying index of up to \$50,000 (i.e., declines of as much as 50% in the index), whereas the protection purchasers in the senior tranched index CDS are compensated only for more than a 50% decline in the index (i.e., losses of greater than \$50,000 resulting from declines in the index times the multiplier).

A numerical example may be useful to distinguish the traditional and tranched index CDSs using the above reference portfolio and tranching scheme. Specifically, suppose the index declines by 10% from 100 to 90. The protection seller in the traditional index CDS makes a payment and realizes a loss of \$10,000—i.e., 10% of the notional amount of the CDS. On the tranched index CDSs, the junior tranche CDS protection seller absorbs the entire \$10,000 loss, which is 20% of the notional amount of the contract. The senior tranched index CDS protection seller, however, is unaffected. Protection sellers on the senior tranche of the reference index only experience losses when the index declines by at least 50% (at which point protection sellers have paid the maximum amounts to junior CDS protection purchasers).

Index and tranched index CDSs are explained in greater depth in Sects. 4.2 and 4.3 of Chapter 4, respectively.

1.1.3 Asset-Backed CDSs

The third CDS product type is a CDS based on the credit quality of a specific underlying asset or security. Unlike single-name CDSs that are related to a potentially large number of securities or loans issued by a single reference entity and multi-name CDSs that are based on a universe of securities or loans issued by two or more reference names, the credit exposure on which the cash flows and value of an asset-backed CDS are based is determined by the cash flows and/or value of the single specific underlying reference asset or security.

Asset-backed CDSs ("ABCDSs") are fundamentally distinct from single-name and multi-name or index CDSs in several important ways.

First, the legal entity that issues the security on which an ABCDS is based is generally a finite-lived "special purpose entity" ("SPE")—i.e., trusts or corporations established to facilitate a structured financing transaction that are not actively managed and have no independent operating business mandate.

Second, to match the often-complex cash flows of the underlying asset-backed securities ("ABSs") on which ABCDSs are usually based, ABCDSs generally allow for two-way payments between protection buyers and sellers. Protection purchasers may be required to reimburse protection sellers in certain circumstances when the cash flows or value of the underlying reference security recovers after first experiencing a decline. This is distinct from single-name and multi-name CDSs in which the only payments that protection purchasers must make to protection sellers are the "premium" payments for the credit protection.[2]

The mechanics and cash flows of ABCDSs and their distinctions vis-à-vis single- and multi-name CDSs are discussed in Chapter 5.

1.2 Aggregate Market Activity

The two sections below show CDS notional amounts outstanding (and year-over-year growth rates in notional amounts) and trades per day by CDS product type. More detailed discussions of product-specific CDS market activities are included in Chapters 2 through 6.

1.2.1 CDS Notional Amounts Outstanding

1.2.1.1 Single-Name, Multi-Name, and Index CDSs

Figure 1.1 shows semi-annual dollar-equivalent notional amounts (as of end-June and end-December) of all single-name, multi-name, and index CDSs outstanding with reporting dealers from December 2004 through June 2017. These amounts include all dealers reporting to the Bank for International Settlements ("BIS") across all countries and currencies. Figure 1.2 presents annual percentage growth rates in CDS notional amounts outstanding—i.e., the percentage change in notional amounts outstanding from the same period in the prior year.[3]

As Figs. 1.1 and 1.2 both illustrate, CDS notional amounts experienced explosive growth from end-December 2004 through end-December 2007. The average year-over-year growth rate over this period was

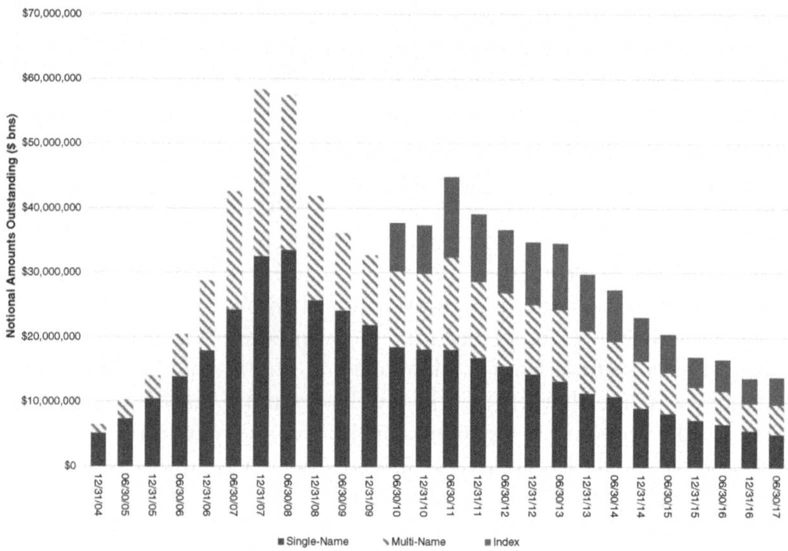

Fig. 1.1 Notional amounts of CDSs outstanding by type, 2004H2–2017H1 (*Note* Index CDS amounts outstanding were not separately reported prior to 2010H1. *Source* BIS)

107%, and total CDS notional amounts outstanding grew by just over 810%. Multi-name CDSs accounted for a relatively larger proportion of the expansion of CDS markets from 2004 through 2007 with an average annual notional growth rate of 165% as compared to an average 84% growth rate in single-name CDSs.

In August 2007, the US subprime mortgage lending crisis unexpectedly erupted into a global credit market crisis.[4] The CDS market was not immune from the disruptive impacts of the outbreak of the credit crisis. As Fig. 1.2 demonstrates, year-over-year growth rates in CDS notional amounts declined from end-December 2007 through end-June 2009 and remained negative for both single- and multi-name CDSs through end-June 2010.

Single-name CDSs experienced a more sustained period of declining market activity (measured by notional amounts outstanding) than multi-name and index CDSs. Annual growth rates in notional amounts outstanding for both single-name and multi-name CDSs first became negative as of end-December 2008. Multi-name CDS activity experienced a brief rebound from end-June 2010 through end-December

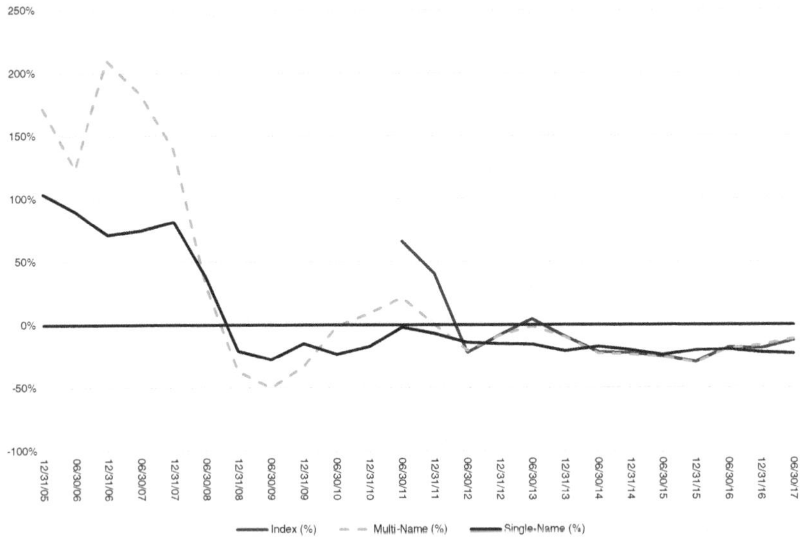

Fig. 1.2 Annual growth rates in CDS notional amounts outstanding, 2005H2–2017H1 (*Note* Index CDS amounts outstanding were not separately reported prior to 2010H1. *Source* BIS)

2011, and annual growth rates in multi-name notional amounts have been volatile (varying between positive and negative) since. Notional amounts of single-name CDSs, by contrast, have continued to contract at varying year-over-year rates since growth rates first became negative in December 2008. From end-June 2011 through end-June 2017, single-name, multi-name, and index CDSs experienced percentage declines in notional amounts outstanding of 72, 68, and 66%, respectively.

Figures 1.1 and 1.2, however, must be interpreted with some caution. Over the last decade, swap market participants have been increasingly reliant on portfolio compression services to eliminate redundant positions and reduce unnecessary credit exposures. In a typical portfolio compression service, participants submit trades to a compression service provider (e.g., Markit/Creditex or TriOptima), which then evaluates and compares potentially offsetting trades. Any identified offsetting trades are then terminated legally and voluntarily (assuming all involved counterparties agree) and replaced with economically equivalent bilateral trades. The net cash flows and risk exposures on the compressed bilateral trades are identical to the original portfolio, but the gross notional amounts and numbers of trades can be reduced significantly through this compression process.[5]

The increased usage of portfolio compression services creates the false impression that the CDS market has contracted by more than the underlying data indicate. Especially for multi-name CDS index products for which portfolio compression has been the most popular, some of the shrinkage in notional amounts in recent years (i.e., the cross-hatched columns and dashed line in Figs. 1.1 and 1.2) is attributable to compression.

1.2.1.2 Single-Name Corporate and Sovereign CDSs, LCDSs, and ABCDSs

Figure 1.3 shows the weekly gross notional amounts outstanding in single-name CDSs based on corporate and sovereign reference names and single-name LCDSs compared to ABCDSs from October 2008 through October 2015. (Note that notional amounts of LCDSs and ABCDSs are shown on the right vertical axis.) As Fig. 1.3 demonstrates, the market

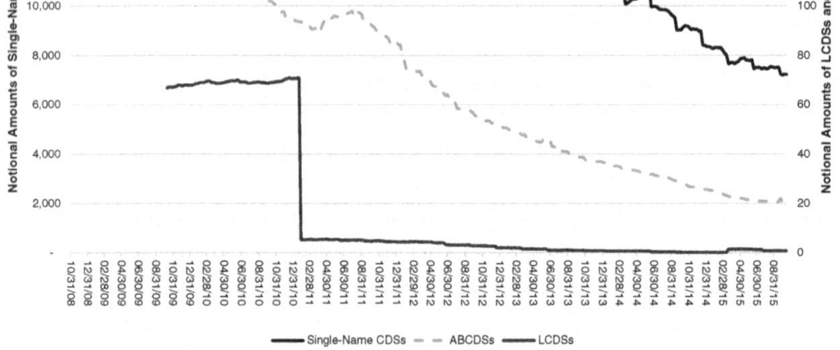

Fig. 1.3 Weekly gross notional amounts of single-name and ABCDSs outstanding, 10/31/2008–10/16/2015 (*Source* BIS)

for single-name CDSs is orders of magnitude larger than the markets for ABCDSs and LCDSs. For the week ending October 9, 2009, when the ABCDS market was at its high water mark level, the gross notional amount of ABCDSs outstanding was still only one percent of the gross notional amount of single-name CDSs outstanding.

Like Figs. 1.1 and 1.2, Fig. 1.3 shows a significant decline in gross notional amounts of all three types of CDSs in the period from October 2008 through October 2015. Single-name CDSs are still relatively significant (i.e., roughly $7.2 trillion in gross notional outstanding for the week ending October 16, 2015) despite the pronounced decline from earlier periods, whereas ABCDS and LCDS markets have significantly contracted or virtually disappeared (respectively) in recent times.

1.2.2 CDS Trading Activity

Whereas notional amounts outstanding indicate the total amount of protection purchases (and, in aggregate, the corresponding total amount of protection sales) on any given date, notional amounts do not indicate how "active" or "liquid" the markets for different CDS products have been. To examine trading activity and market liquidity, we show in Fig. 1.4 the total number of trades per week in both single-name and index CDSs from October 31, 2008, through December 29, 2017.

Figure 1.4 illustrates that index CDS trading volume declined by 52% from the week ending October 31, 2008, to the week ending December 25, 2009, or put differently, the number of trades per week declined from 301,963 to 144,293. Thereafter, weekly trading volume in CDS index products remained roughly level around an average of 159,996 trades per week.

Despite the unfolding of the credit crisis, single-name CDS trading volume remained relatively stable around a brisk 2,065,387 average volume per week from the week ending October 31, 2008, through the week ending March 16, 2012. But after March 16, single-name CDS trading volume began to decline steadily. Average weekly trading volume from the week ending March 23, 2012, through the week ending December 29, 2017, was only 1,301,491 trades—i.e., down 73.5% over the period.

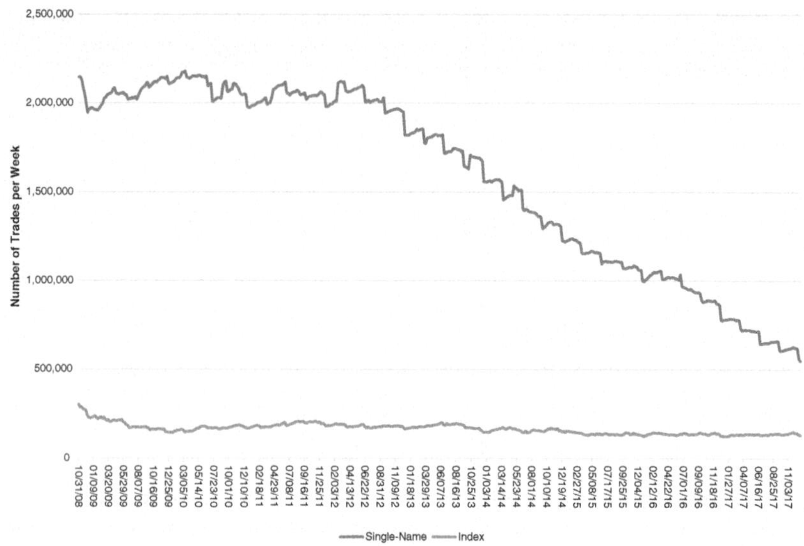

Fig. 1.4 CDS trading volume by product type, 10/31/2008–12/29/2017 (*Note* The data reflects trades reported to the DTCC or Bloomberg swap data repositories. *Source* ISDA Swapsinfo.org)

Notes

1. Other economic variables (e.g., liquidity and counterparty risk) may also impact the value of the cash flows on single-name CDSs, but the product is designed primarily to reflect changes in the perceived credit quality of the underlying reference entity.
2. Mark-to-market payments based on changes in current premium values are an exception.
3. We note that notional amounts outstanding do not accurately reflect the capital at risk in the underlying transactions because the notional principal amount is never actually exchanged by the counterparties. Nevertheless, notional amounts are an industry-standard metric for tracking market activity despite being an inaccurate depiction of actual capital at risk.
4. See, e.g., Brunnermeier (2009), Gorton (2010), and Culp (2018) for further discussions of the causes and timing of the credit crisis.
5. See *generally*, ISDA, "Interest Rates Derivatives: A Progress Report on Clearing and Compression," *ISDA Research Note* (February 2014).

References

Brunnermeier, M.K. 2009. Deciphering the Liquidity and Credit Crunch 2007–2008. *Journal of Economic Perspectives* 23 (1) (Winter).

Culp, C.L. 2018. A Review of the Academic Literature on the Causes and Evolution of the Credit Crisis. *Johns Hopkins Institute for Applied Economics, Global Health, and the Study of Business Enterprise—Studies in Applied Finance* (24) (April).

Gorton, G.B. 2010. *Slapped by the Invisible Hand: The Panic of 2007*. Oxford: Oxford University Press.

CHAPTER 2

Single-Name CDSs

A single-name CDS is a financial instrument—specifically, a type of credit derivatives contract—that has cash flows and a market value derived from the credit quality of a single specified underlying reference name/entity. Single-name CDSs can be based on a variety of different types of reference entities. The two most prominent types of reference names are private corporations (both financial and non-financial) and sovereigns. In addition, single-name CDSs can be based on municipals, state-owned enterprises ("SOEs"), or other individual types of debt securities issuers.

The reference entity obligations that determine the exact cash flows or securities to be exchanged upon the occurrence of a defined credit event for a single-name CDS are generally limited to bonds. A different segment of the single-name CDS universe includes loan-only CDSs or LCDSs that are based on loan obligations of the individual reference name underlying a given single-name CDS. In this chapter, we focus only on single-name CDSs based on debt securities issued by reference entities. In Chapter 3, we separately discuss LCDSs based on loan tranches and facilities.

The terms of a single-name CDS transaction are set forth in a pro forma master agreement together with any credit support annex and

C. L. Culp et al., *Credit Default Swaps*, Palgrave Studies in Risk and Insurance, https://doi.org/10.1007/978-3-319-93076-3_2

the confirmations of individual transactions executed pursuant to a governing master agreement and credit support annex. The ISDA master agreements and ISDA credit support annex ("CSA")—together with the ISDA Credit Derivatives Definitions—are the most common documentation for single-name CDSs.[1]

The significant economic terms of a single-name CDS contract specified in the underlying documentation include the following: (i) name or legal entity identifier ("LEI") of the underlying reference entity; (ii) stated legal maturity (a.k.a. "tenor") of the CDS contract during which credit protection is in force for the protection purchaser; (iii) required payments by the protection buyer to the protection seller; (iv) credit events experienced by the underlying reference name that give rise to an obligation from the protection seller to the protection buyer; (v) the method of settlement for any obligations between protection buyers and sellers arising following the occurrence of a credit event at the underlying reference entity; and (vi) conditions that securities must satisfy to be deliverable under any physically settled CDSs after a credit event occurs.

Privately negotiated, bilateral CDS transactions first emerged in the last half of the 1990s.[2] By 2004, market participants were already considering the practicability and desirability of clearing certain CDSs through central counterparties ("CCPs") in an effort to reduce counterparty-specific, bilateral credit and settlement risks.[3] (See Chapter 6 for a more detailed discussion of CDS clearing by CCPs and certain mandated trade execution provisions for a few specifically designated CDS products.)

To accommodate potential CCP clearing of CDSs, market participants began an effort to standardize certain significant economic terms of CDS contracts. The ultimate result was a series of changes implemented by ISDA and major CDS market participants beginning in 2009, which resulted in a more homogenous and standardized CDS product. Those initiatives involved changes in CDS contracts, trading conventions, and clearing and are henceforth collectively referred to as the "2009 Standardization Initiatives."

The significant contract terms for single-name CDSs (i.e., terms (i)–(vi) as defined above) and the impact of the 2009 Standardization Initiatives on those terms and conventions are discussed in Sect. 2.1 below. Section 2.2 then presents several "case studies" of selected potential and actual credit events that created discussion and/or confusion in the marketplace.

2.1 Standard Single-Name CDS Terms and Conventions

2.1.1 Underlying Reference Name

The single-name CDS market and its activity can be viewed in two distinct ways: by the *type* of underlying reference entity or the *risk* of the reference name underlying the single-name CDS. The next two subsections summarize recent single-name CDS activity along those two dimensions.

2.1.1.1 Market Composition by Type of Underlying Reference Entity
The market activity of single-name CDSs is frequently described by reference entity type to distinguish between CDSs based on financial corporations, non-financial corporations, and sovereigns. Figure 2.1 shows gross notional amounts outstanding of single-name CDSs from end-December 2004 through end-June 2017 by type of reference entity as reported to the BIS.

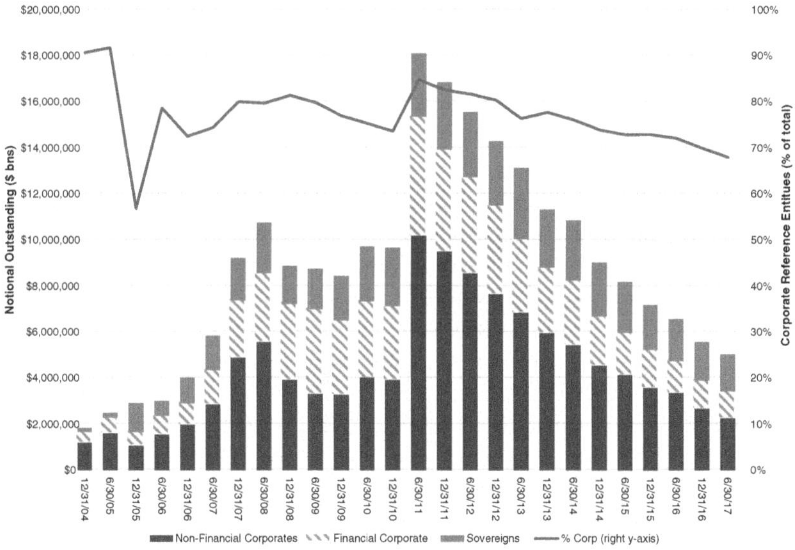

Fig. 2.1 Notional amounts outstanding on single-name CDSs by type of reference name, 2004H2–2017H1 (*Source* BIS)

More specifically, the dark-shaded bars in Fig. 2.1 show notional amounts outstanding of single-name CDSs based on non-financial corporate reference names, and the light-shaded cross-hatched bars reflect notional amounts outstanding for financial institution reference entities. The light-shaded solid bars, in turn, reflect notional amounts outstanding of CDSs based on sovereign debt. The solid line indicates the proportion of all single-name CDSs outstanding based on corporate (i.e., non-governmental) reference entities over the time period.

As Fig. 2.1 indicates, single-name CDSs based on corporate debt accounted for an average of 77% of the total notional amount of all single-name CDSs outstanding over the period. CDSs based on non-financial corporate debt experienced a significant spike in activity in 2011H1, which is consistent with increased hedging activity in response to the significant increase in perceived corporate default risk at the time. Since then, although sovereign debt remains a smaller segment of the single-name CDS market, sovereign CDSs have accounted for a growing proportion of single-name CDS notional amounts outstanding.

For the period from July 2010 to July 2012, Berg and Streitz (2016) analyze trading volume for sovereign CDSs on a weekly basis across 57 sovereigns. They conclude that the five largest CDS markets during that period (measured based on net notional amounts reported to the Depository Trust Clearing Corp.'s Swap Data Repository) were Italy, France, Germany, Brazil, and Spain.

2.1.1.2 Market Composition by Credit Risk of Underlying Reference Entity

We can also analyze the composition of the single-name CDS market based on the relative credit risk of underlying reference entities based on the ratings of the debt issued by those reference names. Figure 2.2 summarizes the credit ratings of reference entities on which single-name CDSs were based for the semi-annual periods from end-December 2004 through end-June 2017.

From 2004H2 through 2006H2, the proportion of single-name CDSs based on investment-grade borrowers (i.e., reference entities rated BBB-/Baa3[4] or above) declined significantly, even though actual notional amounts of CDSs on such entities rose from 2005 through 2006H2. The reason was the explosive growth in single-name CDSs based on speculative-grade (i.e., BB+/Ba1 and below) and unrated borrowers through 2007. As Culp (2013) and Culp and Forrester (2013, 2015) explain, the

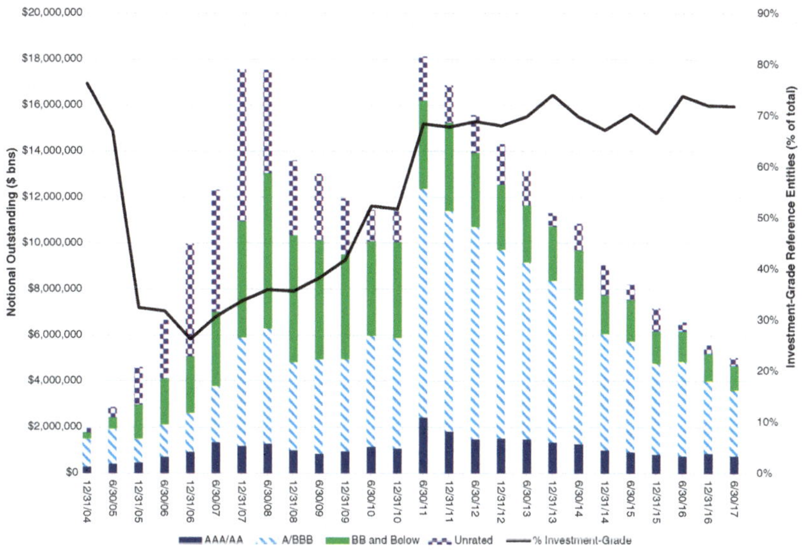

Fig. 2.2 Notional amounts outstanding on single-name CDSs by credit rating of reference name, 2004H2–2017H1 (*Source* BIS)

increased demand for CDSs based on speculative-grade and unrated borrowers during this period was not indicative of increases in underlying default rates in speculative-grade borrowers, but rather was largely driven by the demand from collateralized loan obligation ("CLO") managers and high-yield bond funds to *sell* credit protection on leveraged debt during a period of low interest rates and credit spreads, which had fueled a significant leveraged buyout boom at the time.[5] See the related discussion in Chapters 3 and 6.

In 2007H1, when instability in US subprime mortgage markets first began to impact subprime mortgage-backed securities, total notional amounts of CDS protection sold on investment-grade entities began to rise, whereas total protection sold on unrated entities began to decline gradually beginning in 2007H2. As the mortgage crisis spilled over first into US leveraged finance markets (as discussed in Culp 2013, 2018) and, in August 2007, to broader global credit markets, total notional amounts of credit protection sold on unrated entities contracted dramatically and continued a generally declining trend through the end of 2011.

As of 2017H1, less than 10% of the single-name CDS notional amount outstanding was accounted for by unrated reference entities.

Since the end of 2010, the proportion of single-name CDSs based on investment-grade reference entities (shown in Fig. 2.2 with a black line) rose dramatically. Over the same period, the total notional amount of single-name CDSs outstanding has fallen. This inverse relationship is unsurprising—viz., as perceptions of the credit risk of below investment-grade reference entities have declined, so, too, has the amount of single-name CDS activities.

2.1.2 Maturity/Tenor

The stated legal maturity date of a single-name CDS contract reflects the last date on which credit protection is in force for the protection purchaser. In other words, the maturity date of a CDS is the date on which the credit protection purchased by the protection purchaser and the contingent credit event-based protection payment obligations of the protection seller expire. The maturity of a CDS does not necessarily depend on the maturity of the securities issued by the reference entity.

The tenor of a CDS contract is its time to maturity as of the initial effective trade date. Even before the 2009 Standardization Initiatives, most single-name CDS tenors were annual with the most popular tenor being five years. The calendar dates of CDS contract maturities were not formally standardized until the 2009 Standardization Initiatives, by which time the market standard coalesced around CDS maturity dates of March 20th, June 20th, September 20th, and December 20th (known collectively as standard maturity dates). For example, a one-year single-name CDS on reference entity XYZ Corp. with a trade date of February 17, 2016, would have a maturity date of March 20, 2017, under the 2009 Standardization Initiatives.

Figure 2.3 shows the remaining time to maturity (as distinct from original tenors when the CDSs were first executed) for all single-name CDSs outstanding from end-December 2004 through end-June 2017. Five years remains the most popular tenor for *new* CDS transactions, and, not surprisingly, CDSs with one to five years remaining to maturity have regularly accounted for the largest proportion of single-name CDSs outstanding.

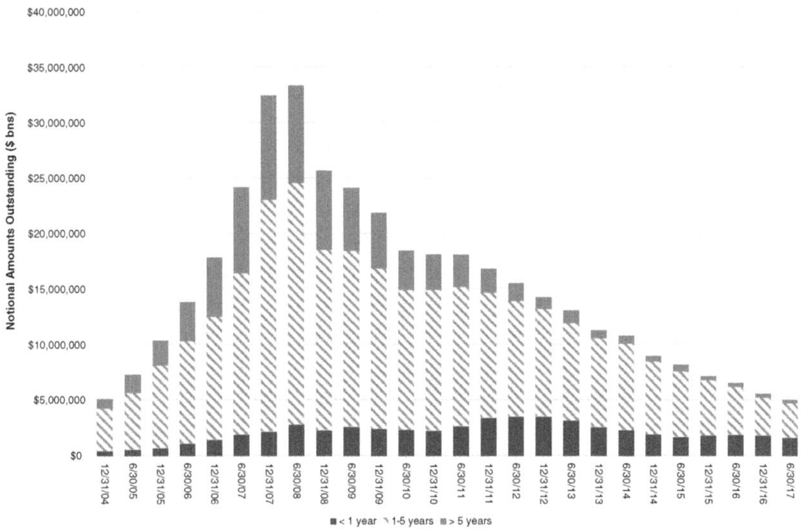

Fig. 2.3 Notional amounts outstanding on single-name CDSs by remaining time to maturity, 2004H2–2017H1 (*Source* BIS)

2.1.3 Coupon/Spread/Premium

In a single-name CDS, the credit protection purchaser must pay a contractually specified and fixed coupon (also known as a spread[6]) periodically over the life of the contract to the protection seller. The contractually specified fixed coupon rate on a single-name CDS is also often referred to as the premium because the payment by protection purchasers is analogous to (albeit not the same as) premiums paid for insurance.

For an "at-market" CDS contract (i.e., a CDS contract with a coupon set on the trade date to reflect current market conditions), the coupon rate is the spread over the London Interbank Offered Rate ("LIBOR") that equates the present value of fixed coupon payments paid by the protection purchaser to the discounted expected payments from the protection seller pursuant to the occurrence of a credit event. In an efficient market with no transaction costs, heterogeneous information, counterparty risk, or illiquidity issues, the coupon on the CDS should be the same as the spread over LIBOR in any comparable floating-rate debt issued by the reference entity.

Single-name CDS coupon rates are fixed on the trade dates of CDS transactions and do not vary over the lives of CDS contracts. If the perceived credit risk of the reference entity changes during the life of the CDS contract—as it surely will, at least to some degree—then the *market value* of that CDS and the mark-to-market credit spread will fluctuate accordingly. For example, suppose a single-name CDS based on reference entity XYZ Corp. has a one-year tenor and a contractual coupon rate of 100 basis points ("bps"), which was at-market on the trade date.[7] If XYZ Corp. is downgraded shortly into the life of the CDS, investors in a new CDS following the downgrade with a maturity date identical to the original CDS would require a higher coupon to compensate for the heightened perceived credit risk of XYZ Corp.—say, e.g., 125 bps. With a then below-market contractual coupon rate of 100 bps, the original CDS will trade below its par value. Although some single-name CDS counterparties are required to post collateral and true up the value of their contracts to current running market spreads, the coupon rate itself remains fixed for the tenor of the CDS.

Following the 2009 Standardization Initiatives, standardized CDS coupon payments began to emerge that were and are still made by protection buyers to sellers quarterly on March, June, September, and December 20th.[8] Standardized CDS coupons are quoted on an annualized basis, and the actual payment amount is computed using the notional amount of the CDS contract and an Actual/360 day-count convention. The actual payment, moreover, is based on an accrual period that begins with the previous standardized coupon payment date and ends with the current coupon payment date minus one day (except for the last coupon payment, which is based on an accrual through the final stated legal maturity date). If a credit protection buyer purchases CDS protection in the middle of a quarter, for example, the first coupon payment is in arrears and based on an accrual period from the last standard coupon payment date (i.e., not the actual trade date). In other words, the protection buyer must pay for coverage from the previous standard coupon date even when the trade date occurs later.

Consider, for example, the aforementioned one-year single-name CDS on XYZ Corp., and suppose that the counterparties agree to a 100 basis point ("bp") annualized coupon as of the February 17, 2016, trade date. The first coupon payment date is due on March 21, 2016 (i.e., the Monday following Sunday, March 20, 2016), and is based on an accrual period from Monday, December 21, 2015 (i.e., the coupon payment

Table 2.1 Coupon payments for a one-year CDS on XYZ Corp. with a 100 bp coupon and $25 mn notional amount

	Accrual period begins	*Accrual period ends*	*Coupon payment date*	*Actual days*	*Coupon payment amount*
1st Coupon	12/21/2015	3/20/2016	3/21/2016	90	$62,500
2nd Coupon	3/21/2016	6/19/2016	6/20/2016	90	$62,500
3rd Coupon	6/20/2016	9/19/2016	9/20/2016	91	$63,194
4th Coupon	9/20/2016	12/19/2016	12/20/2016	90	$62,500
5th Coupon	12/20/2016	3/19/2017	3/20/2017	89	$61,806

date for the standard 2015Q4 coupon payment), through March 20, 2016 (i.e., the day before the 2016Q1 standard coupon payment date). The standard coupon dates and corresponding amounts payable by the protection buyer to the protection seller in this exemplar transaction (with an assumed notional amount of $25 million) are shown in Table 2.1.

The 2009 Standardization Initiatives included an effort to shift CDSs toward standard coupon rates in order to promote the ease with which CDSs could be cleared by CCPs (as discussed further in Chapter 6). These standard coupons vary by geographical region. For example, single-name CDSs based on North American corporate and sovereign reference entities generally have standard coupon rates of either 100 bps or 500 bps per annum for investment-grade and high-yield reference names, respectively.

In practice, very few CDSs have at-market coupon rates of either exactly 100 bps or 500 bps on their trade dates. As a result, credit protection buyers usually make upfront payments to protection sellers (or vice versa depending on whether the at-market credit spread is above or below the standard coupon rate) that reflect the difference in the present values of cash flows on the CDS valued using the standard coupon rate and the current market-based running spread, as well as any accrued coupons.[9]

2.1.4 Credit Events

The basic concept of a credit event—i.e., an adverse development in a reference entity's financial condition and creditworthiness that exposes its lenders to heightened credit risk—has not changed since single-name

CDSs first began trading in the mid-1990s. The specific definitions of different scenarios that give rise to credit events (and the process by which determinations are made as to when credit events occur) are articulated in ISDA's *Credit Derivatives Definitions* ("Definitions"). In response to various issues concerning the credit events experienced by specific reference entities (some of which are discussed in Sect. 2.2 below) and in the aftermath of the credit crisis, ISDA (in coordination with market participants) has made several significant revisions to its *Credit Derivatives Definitions*. We review the most important of these revisions in the sections below.

2.1.4.1 The 1999 and 2003 Definitions

The original 1999 ISDA *Credit Derivatives Definitions* (the "*1999 Definitions*") specify six types of credit events which, if experienced by a reference entity, will trigger corresponding single-name CDS payments by protection sellers to buyers[10]:

- *Bankruptcy*: The reference entity becomes insolvent or admits in a regulatory, judicial, or administrative proceeding that it is insolvent;
- *Obligation Acceleration*: One or more obligations of the reference entity (with an aggregate amount equal to or in excess of a specified "Default Requirement" threshold) become due and payable before their scheduled payment dates as a result of an event of default or default-like condition (excluding "Failure to Pay" events);
- *Obligation Default*: One or more obligations of the reference entity (with an aggregate amount equal to or in excess of the Default Requirement) are *capable of being declared* due and payable before their scheduled payment date(s) as a result of an event of default or default-like condition;
- *Failure to Pay*: The reference entity fails to make a required payment when and where it is due on one or more of its obligations (following the expiration of a contractually specified grace period);
- *Repudiation/Moratorium*: The reference entity (or a governmental authority) disaffirms, rejects, disclaims, repudiates, or challenges the validity of one or more obligations (equal to or in excess of the Default Requirement) or imposes a moratorium on the payment of one or more obligations (equal to or in excess of the Default Requirement), provided that the reference entity has experienced a failure-to-pay or restructuring event (without regard to the Default

Requirement) on or prior to the repudiation/moratorium "evaluation date"; or

- *Restructuring*: The reference entity restructures one or more obligations (including through an "Obligation Exchange"—i.e., a mandatory transfer of securities, obligations, or assets) equal to or in excess of the Default Requirement as a result of any of the following and provided that the following were the direct or indirect result of a deterioration in the reference entity's credit quality: (i) reductions in accrued or payable interest; (ii) reductions in principal payable or premiums payable on redemption dates; (iii) deferrals of interest or principal repayment dates; (iv) changes in the priority/subordination of an obligation; or (v) changes in the currency denomination of interest and/or principal payments to an impermissible currency.

In 2003, ISDA released a revised version of its *Credit Derivatives Definitions* (the "*2003 Definitions*").[11] Among the changes to the 1999 credit events reflected in the *2003 Definitions* were refinements to the definitions of the bankruptcy, repudiation/moratorium, and restructuring credit events.

For single-name CDSs, restructuring events have presented market participants with some significant challenges over the years, both for corporate and sovereign reference entities. These challenges have involved both the definition of a restructuring credit event (mainly an issue for sovereign reference entities) and the obligations deliverable under physically settled CDSs following a restructuring event (primarily an issue for corporate reference entities). Some of these issues are discussed in Sect. 2.2, and the more general topic of eligible deliverable obligations is discussed in Sect. 2.1.6.

For sovereign CDSs, the three primary triggering events are failure-to-pay, repudiation/moratorium, and restructuring.[12] Historically, the most prevalent credit event triggering sovereign CDSs is restructuring (Pan and Singleton 2008; Longstaff et al. 2011; Das et al. 2012). The definition of a sovereign restructuring event, however, has evolved in the ISDA documentation over time as specific sovereign defaults have highlighted issues about which market participants desired clarification. In particular, the restructurings of Argentine sovereign debt in 2001 and Greek sovereign debt in 2012 (see Sects. 2.2.1 and 2.2.2 below, respectively) resulted in disputes over the meaning of restructuring events, and both events precipitated revisions in the *2003 Definitions*.

One change in the *2003 Definitions* occurred following the announcement in November 2001 by the Argentine Republic ("Argentina") of its plan to voluntarily restructure $95 billion of its $132 billion in outstanding debt by exchanging the $95 billion in 15% bonds for bonds with interest rates capped at seven percent.[13] For the reasons explained in Sect. 2.2.1 below, uncertainties arose regarding single-name sovereign CDSs with Argentina as a reference name based on language in the 1999 Definitions involving an "Obligation Exchange." In response to the uncertainties surrounding the settlement of Argentine sovereign CDSs, the 2003 Definitions redefined a restructuring credit event to be based solely on the occurrence of any of the six events defined in the 1999 Definitions as long as such events bind all holders of any obligations to the restructuring and eliminated any references to an "Obligation Exchange."

2.1.4.2 The 2009 "Big Bang Protocol" and Supplement to the 2003 Definitions

As part of the 2009 Standardization Initiatives, ISDA redefined the means by which a credit event is determined. Prior to the 2009 Standardization Initiatives, a protection purchaser typically notified its counterparty when it believed a credit event had occurred at the underlying reference entity. In the event of a dispute between counterparties, the documentation of the transaction and the facts of the circumstances were subject to the determination of a court.

In consultation with market participants and various regulatory agencies, ISDA implemented the 2009 Standardization Initiatives by promulgating the *2009 ISDA Credit Derivatives Determinations Committees, Auction Settlement and Restructuring Supplement to the 2003 ISDA Credit Derivatives Definitions* (the "*2009 Amendments to the 2003 Definitions*"),[14] more commonly known as the "Big Bang Protocol." Specifically, the Big Bang Protocol resulted in three significant changes to single-name CDS contract terms: (i) the creation of "determinations committees" ("DCs") for each major geographical region together with the definition of the roles and responsibilities of DCs and corresponding changes in CDS documentation; (ii) the incorporation of common "look-back" provisions for credit and succession events; and (iii) the introduction of "Auction Settlement" as a default method settling single-name CDSs. Components (i) and (ii) of the Big Bang Protocol are discussed below, and the third component is discussed in Sect. 2.1.5.2

later in this chapter. As of its April 8, 2009, effective date, over 2000 market participants opted to adhere to the Big Bang Protocol.[15]

In prong (i) of the Big Bang Protocol, adherents to the protocol agree that instead of counterparties to a CDS making determinations about the occurrence of a credit event bilaterally, the appropriate geographical DC will make such determinations instead. DCs are established on a geographical basis (based on the domicile of the reference entity at issue) and include DCs for the Americas, Asia Ex-Japan, Europe/Middle East/Africa ("EMEA"), and Japan. Each DC consists of up to 10 voting swap dealer members, five voting non-dealer members, and up to three consultative non-voting members (two dealers and one non-dealer). Dealer members are selected annually based on their firms' CDS trading volumes from the previous year, and non-dealer members are selected at random from a pool of buy-side firms with CDS activity in excess of specified minimum transaction volume thresholds.

DCs may accept requests from eligible market participants (including non-members of ISDA) to consider whether or not a credit event has occurred at a particular reference entity. If an eligible market participant petitions the DC under its own name and asks the DC to determine whether or not a credit event has occurred, at least one member of a DC must accept the question before the issue is put to the DC for a vote. "General interest" questions may also be submitted to a DC in which the submitter does not disclose its name. Such questions must be accepted by at least two members of the DC before the whole DC considers whether or not a credit event has occurred.

Apart from their responsibilities for determining the occurrence of credit events, DCs also decide whether or not an auction will be held to determine final CDS settlement values and which obligations are eligible for submission in the auction. We discuss this further in Sect. 2.1.5.3.

Prong (ii) of the Big Bang Protocol—i.e., the creation of a common look-back provision—is intended to deal with the basis risk to which traders were previously exposed in the event that they purchased and sold credit protection on the same reference entity on different dates. Prior to the Big Bang Protocol, credit protection began for the purchaser one day after the CDS trade date *T*. For example, a CDS on XYZ Corp. purchased on April 26, 2016, would go into effect on April 27, 2016. If the protection purchaser subsequently decided to reverse out its protection purchase—say, on May 1, 2016—the protection sale went into effect on May 2, 2016. If a credit event occurred anytime from April

27th through May 2nd, the protection purchase was in force, but the protection sale was not. As such, seemingly offsetting exposures did not actually offset and gave rise to basis risk for users of single-name CDSs engaged in risk transfer and hedging.

To address this concern, the Big Bang Protocol specifies that CDS protection is in force at *T-60* for credit events.[16] This modification of CDS documentation was intended to help promote fungibility across individual CDSs transactions by eliminating the basis risk arising from any "stub period" occurring between the initial protection purchase (sale) in-force date and the in-force date for a subsequent protection sale (purchase) hedge or reversal of the original protection purchase (sale). Market participants refer to the rolling 60-day look-back period for credit events as their "statute of limitations."[17]

2.1.4.3 The 2014 Definitions

On February 21, 2014, ISDA published a new and substantively revised version of its *Credit Derivatives Definitions* (the "*2014 Definitions*"). The new definitions reflected a number of substantive changes to the *2009 Amendments to the 2003 Definitions.*

First, the *2014 Definitions* added "governmental intervention" as a new credit event that a reference entity might experience. Such a triggering event occurs when an announcement or action by a governmental authority results in any of the following for obligations in excess of the Default Requirement threshold:

- Changes in creditors' rights so as to cause:
  - Reductions in interest payable or accrued;
  - Reductions in principal or premiums payable upon redemption;
  - Postponements or deferrals of interest payable or accrued and/or principal/premium payable beyond the originally scheduled dates; or
  - Changes in the priority (seniority) of an obligation that results in an increased depth of subordination;
- Expropriation (i.e., any event that mandatorily changes the beneficial holder of an obligation);
- Mandatory cancelation, conversion, or exchange of an obligation; or
- Any other event that has an analogous effect to the above events.

The governmental intervention trigger was included in the *2014 Definitions* to address forced "bail-ins" of creditors—i.e., situations in which governmental authorities force creditors to participate in a bail-out of a distressed firm. For example, the Dutch Ministry of Finance nationalized SNS Reaal bank on February 1, 2013,[18] which resulted in the expropriation of the bank's subordinated debt. Under the *2003 Definitions* and *2009 Amendments to the 2003 Definitions*, significant uncertainty existed as to whether a mandated debtor bail-in qualified as a restructuring event.[19] The new triggering event eliminates any such ambiguities and explicitly defines governmentally mandated creditor bail-ins as a credit event that will trigger corresponding single-name CDSs.

Second, the *2014 Definitions* allow counterparties in a single-name CDS to elect "Financial Reference Entity Terms" in a confirmation, which separates credit event determinations for governmental intervention and restructuring events that impact CDSs based on senior and subordinated obligations of the reference entity differently. In the case of SNS Reaal, the expropriation of subordinated debt resulted in all CDSs on SNS Reaal being triggered under the restructuring event even though the senior debt holders of SNS Reaal were unaffected by the intervention.[20] Under the *2014 Definitions*, if counterparties opt for Financial Reference Entity Terms, a governmental intervention or restructuring event that affects subordinated debt but *not* senior debt will not trigger protection payments on corresponding senior single-name CDSs.

Third, the credit events experienced by SNS Reaal, Argentina and Greece highlighted issues associated with mandatory exchanges of debt that persisted even with the elimination of the term "Obligation Exchange" in 2003 (see Sects. 2.2.1 and 2.2.2). After the determination that SNS Reaal had experienced a credit event following the expropriation of its subordinated debt holders, *all* of the single-name CDSs on SNS Reaal obligations were triggered. The DC determined that the final value of CDSs referencing SNS Reaal would be determined by auction settlement at a final auction price that included *only* senior obligations (because the subordinated debt had been expropriated) despite the fact that senior obligations were unaffected by the mandatory expropriation of subordinated debt. As a result, CDSs referencing the SNS Reaal entity were settled at prices that were too high relative to the actual expected recovery rates on the expropriated subordinated debt.

To address the various problems associated with mandatory debt exchanges, the *2014 Definitions* introduced the concepts of an "Asset Package Delivery" and an "Asset Package Credit Event." For Financial Reference Entities, these provisions allow credit protection buyers in physically settled single-name CDSs to deliver a portfolio of assets resulting from the exchange of "Prior Deliverable Obligations" or "Package Observable Bonds."

Finally, the *2014 Definitions* introduce the concept of a "Standard Reference Obligation," which we discuss in more detail in Sect. 2.1.6.

2.1.5 Settlement Methods

Credit protection purchasers in single-name CDSs have historically been compensated following the occurrence of a credit event at the underlying reference entity in one of three ways: (i) physical settlement; (ii) cash settlement; or (iii) auction settlement. We discuss these three settlement methods below.

2.1.5.1 Physical Settlement

Historically, physical settlement has been the most prevalent CDS settlement method. In a physically settled CDS, the protection buyer must deliver any eligible deliverable obligation (see Sect. 2.1.6) to the protection seller in return for a cash payment by the protection seller equal to the notional amount of the swap (in turn equal to the par value of the deliverable obligation(s)). In that situation, a protection buyer that initially owns the underlying XYZ Corp. obligation receives the par amount of that obligation (assuming it matches the notional amount of the CDS) and neither benefits from any subsequent improvements in the recovery rate expected by market participants at the time nor suffers any losses arising from later declines in the recovery rate. Instead, the protection seller in the CDS bears that risk and return potential. If the protection seller holds the bond until the bankruptcy trustee makes a final distribution of assets (which is not usually the case) and the final recovery rate exceeds the expected recovery rate reflected in the market price of the bond at the time of the CDS settlement, the protection seller will be better-off *ex post* than if it had entered into an otherwise identical cash-settled CDS. But if the final recovery rate is below the expected recovery rate reflected in bond prices at the time of the CDS settlement, the protection seller will be worse-off *ex post* for electing physical rather than cash settlement.

Beginning in 2005, market participants began to express concerns with the physical CDS settlement process. As long as the total amount of CDS credit protection sold is less than the amount of underlying deliverable obligations corresponding to that CDS—as is generally the case for sovereign CDSs—physical and cash settlement (discussed in Sect. 2.1.5.2) should not generate significantly different payments by credit protection sellers to buyers. Yet, a credit protection purchaser in a CDS need not own any obligation of the reference entity underlying the CDS and may instead be using the position to take a short position on the credit risk of the reference entity. When the notional amount of credit protection sold for a given reference entity significantly exceeds the amount of actual debt issued by that reference entity and deliverable into single-name CDSs based on that entity, problems can arise.

A classic "short squeeze" occurs when market participants establish a short position using a physically settled derivatives contract based on an asset that participants do not own at the time in order to try and benefit from subsequent price declines in the underlying asset. To realize any economic benefits from such price declines, however, the trader must eventually acquire the asset in order to deliver it to its counterparty. When the underlying supply of the asset is less than the amount of derivatives based on that asset, traders that have open positions when the single-name CDS contract matures are forced to buy the underlying deliverable obligation in the spot market. Knowing that such "naked shorts" cannot realize the benefits of their derivatives transactions unless they acquire the underlying asset, the actual holders of the asset may "squeeze" those shorts and sell the underlying asset for more than what it is actually worth.

For example, suppose XYZ Corp. experiences a credit event at a time when it has a total amount of debt equal to $100 million that could be eligible for delivery into physically settled CDSs but that a total of $500 million notional in physically settled CDSs is outstanding. To take the most extreme case, suppose the holders of XYZ Corp.'s $100 million debt have not purchased CDS protection, so that the purchasers of all $500 million in notional CDS protection have "naked" short positions—i.e., they do not own an XYZ Corp. debt instrument at the time they purchase credit protection and thus cannot receive a protection payment from their CDS counterparties without acquiring XYZ Corp. debt in the secondary bond market. For the protection purchaser in a naked physically settled short CDS position, the delivery of an eligible

XYZ Corp. bond will result in a payment of 100% of the par value of an eligible XYZ Corp. obligation. Such a credit protection purchaser thus would potentially be willing to pay up to 99.99% of the par value of such securities in the secondary market. Yet, if protection purchasers do indeed bid up the price of the underlying $100 million in available securities, the result will be that the price of the XYZ Corp. obligations may be well above the actual expected recovery rate on XYZ Corp. The artificially higher prices on XYZ Corp. bonds driven by the demand from naked short CDS purchasers for deliverable securities thus may impose losses on hedgers that have purchased cash-settled CDS protection.

In 2005, market participants expressed concern that short squeezes could create basis risk for counterparties using CDSs to hedge their actual credit exposures to underlying reference entities. For example, when Delphi Corp. ("Delphi") declared bankruptcy in 2005, the firm had about $5.2 billion in par value of bonds and loans outstanding but had an estimated $28 billion of single-name CDSs. From one week prior to Delphi's bankruptcy filing to one week after, weekly trading volume increased from about $1.5 billion to more than $3 billion. As a percentage of the total par amount of Delphi obligations outstanding, weekly trading volume grew from roughly 75% to over 150% between the week prior to and after Delphi's bankruptcy filing. The secondary market price of Delphi's bonds following its bankruptcy filing, moreover, reached a peak in the low 70s, despite that Delphi bonds traded below that level for about three months prior to the bankruptcy.[21]

2.1.5.2 Cash Settlement

Although rarely used historically and virtually nonexistent in recent years, a second CDS settlement mechanism is cash settlement, which involves a single payment by the protection seller to the protection buyer equivalent to the notional amount of the CDS less the *expected* recovery value. The expected recovery amount reflects the ability of the CDS protection purchaser to receive subsequent payments on the underlying reference entity's debt from its bankruptcy trustee (or the equivalent).

The actual recovery of a bondholder is, of course, determined well after (sometimes many years later than) the occurrence of the credit event on which the corresponding CDS is based. As such, cash-settled CDSs generally rely on the market price of a bond at the time of CDS settlement (which should, in principle, equal the market-based expected recovery value) or a pre-specified recovery rate as fraction of par value based on the credit rating of the reference entity and/or historical recovery data.

For example, suppose a credit protection purchaser that owns a $1 million face value bond issued by XYZ Corp. enters into a $1 million notional CDS on XYZ Corp. in which the protection payment from the seller to the buyer is based on the market-determined expected recovery rate (i.e., the price of an obligation of XYZ Corp.) on the final settlement date of the CDS. Suppose that the market price of a representative XYZ Corp. bond on the CDS settlement date is 40 (implying a 40% expected recovery rate). In that case, the protection seller must make a payment of $600,000 to the protection purchaser (i.e., the par value of $1 million less expected recovery of $400,000). In such a cash-settled CDS, the protection purchaser locks in the market-based expected recovery rate (i.e., 40%) as of the CDS settlement date.

If in this example the bankruptcy court eventually distributes more than 40% to XYZ Corp. bondholders—say, e.g., 50%—then the CDS protection purchaser that also owns the bond will actually experience a net gain—i.e., $600,000 received from its CDS protection seller counterparty plus $500,000 received upon surrender of the actual bond to the bankruptcy trustee, resulting in a total of $1.1 million received on a $1 million hedged bond investment. Conversely, if a determination by the bankruptcy trustee concludes that the recovery rate is less than 40%—say, e.g., 30%—then the CDS protection buyer that owns the bond will be under-compensated for its actual losses. It will receive $600,000 from its CDS counterparty but will only receive $300,000 from the bankruptcy trustee, resulting in a net loss of $100,000 *vis-à-vis* the $1 million par value of the XYZ Corp. bond it owned.

2.1.5.3 Auction Settlement

To address potential problems arising from short squeezes in bonds deliverable into physically settled CDSs and imperfections in cash settlements arising from predetermined recovery rates, ISDA introduced a third CDS settlement method in 2005 called auction settlement. The auction settlement essentially converts physically settled CDSs into cash-settled CDSs *and* defines the price at which cash settlement occurs through a rule-bound auction mechanism for the bonds underlying the defaulting reference entity.

Following the occurrence of a credit event, buyers and sellers of single-name CDS protection can choose to agree to a protocol provided by ISDA that entitles those counterparties to convert physically settled CDSs to auction-settled contracts for which the final settlement payment from the protection seller to the buyer was cash settled in an amount equal to the notional amount of the CDS less the final auction price of the reference entity's deliverable obligation (as opposed to some measure of the expected recovery rate in pure cash-settled CDSs).

The final auction price is determined based on a two-stage process. In the first stage, the main participants are dealers that have committed to place minimum bids or offers along with any bids/offers for physical settlement at the final price. Those stage one bids and offers establish an initial market midpoint ("IMM") price, which is a constraint on the final auction price. In stage two, limit orders from customers of dealers are added to the original stage one limit orders to arrive at a stage two auction price that clears the total net open interest. If the stage two auction price falls within a specified range (known as the "cap") of the IMM, the stage two auction price is the final auction price. If the stage two auction price is greater than the IMM plus the cap (for auctions in which the first-stage net open interest for physical settlement at the final auction price is for a purchase of the bonds), the final auction price is set to the IMM plus the cap. Conversely, if the net first-stage open interest is for a sale of the bonds, the final auction price is limited by the IMM minus the cap. The IMM and cap are intended to prevent large off-market limit orders from being submitted in an effort to manipulate the price.[22] Manipulation is also discouraged by the imposition of a penalty for off-market submissions in stage one.

In 2009, prong (iii) of the Big Bang Protocol hardwired CDS documentation to specify auction settlement as the default settlement method provided that the relevant DC (as described in Sect. 2.1.4.2) concludes that there is a sufficient amount of CDSs outstanding to justify an auction. For reference entities with either a small amount of total outstanding debt or with total face values of debt well above the DC's estimate of total CDS protection bought and sold, the DC may choose not to hold an auction, in which case the settlement method chosen by counterparties in the master agreement and trade confirmations will remain in force.

Another common occurrence when a reference entity has a significant quantity of senior debt but only a small amount of subordinated debt is for a DC to hold a senior CDS auction but not a subordinated CDS auction, in which case the subordinated CDSs revert to settlement through their fallback mechanism (i.e., almost always physical).

A list of all single-name CDS auctions held from 2009 (following the 2009 Standardization Initiatives) through 2017 is shown in Table B.1 in Appendix B. Sovereign reference entity determinations and auctions are indicated with italics in Table B.1. There were four sovereign default events during the period: the Hellenic Republic in 2012, the Argentine Republic in 2014, the Republic of Ukraine in 2015, and Bolivarian Republic of Venezuela in 2017. (The Republic of Ecuador experienced a credit event in early 2009 prior to the implementation of the 2009 Standardization Initiatives.) The remaining 67 DC event determinations shown in Table B.1 involved single-name CDSs with corporate or SOE reference entities.

Helwege et al. (2009) analyzed the results of 43 CDS auctions from 2005 through 2009 in order to evaluate how well final auction prices approximate expected recovery rates implied by cash bond market transactions. They find that final auction prices are generally very close to cash bond prices on the day before and the day of a CDS auction. The authors also report that the cash price of the bond on the date of the occurrence of the credit event is a good predictor of the final auction price (with the exceptions of Lehman Brothers and Washington Mutual) and thus conclude that the bond market was generally effective in providing price discovery prior to the CDS auction. Notably, the authors do not explicitly consider whether or not CDS auctions play price discovery roles for post-auction cash bond trading.

Coudert and Gex (2010) reviewed the results of 27 senior CDS auctions from 2005 through 2009. They find that the difference between the secondary market price of a defaulted bond and the final CDS auction price declines from the date of the credit event through the date of the auction. Examining secondary market bond prices on the date the CDS auction is *settled* (which is several days after the CDS final auction price is determined), the authors find significant differences between secondary market prices on the settlement date and final auction prices. In most cases, secondary market prices rose (in some cases significantly) from the auction date to the settlement date. Similar results of undervaluations of bond prices in the CDS auction are documented in many of the other studies reviewed below.

Chernov et al. (2013) examined 26 CDS auctions involving US corporate reference entities between 2006 and December 2011. The authors compare the final auction prices to market prices of the bonds traded in the secondary market and reported through the Trade Reporting and Compliance Engine ("TRACE") maintained by the Financial Industry Regulatory Authority ("FINRA"). Their evidence indicates that the bonds analyzed were undervalued in the CDS auctions by six percent on average on the dates of the auctions, and that the amount of undervaluation is directly related to the total amount of bonds exchanged in stage two of the auctions—i.e., the larger the net open interest, the greater the underpricing of the bonds in the auction on average.

Lieu (2011) also compared CDS auction prices to cash bond prices obtained from TRACE for 23 auctions involving US corporate in 2008 and 2009. Unlike Chernov et al. (2013), Lieu (2011) does not analyze mispricings on the auction date but rather examines the price discovery role of the auction and its impact on secondary market trading in the five days subsequent to the auction. His results suggest that CDS auctions play an important role in price discovery and that auction prices are generally fair despite a slight increase in bond prices on average following the auction date. (The latter result is consistent with Chernov et al. (2013), whereas the former is not.) At odds with the price discovery role Lieu (2011) finds being played by the CDS auction; however, he also documents a significant increase in bond price volatility after an auction than in the pre-auction five-day window. His finding that post-auction trading volume is significantly higher than pre-auction volume suggests that the higher post-auction volatility may be the result of new market participants trading the bonds after the direct and indirect offers from auction participants have been satisfied.

Gupta and Sundaram have written two studies of CDS auction performance. In Gupta and Sundaram (2015a), the authors analyzed 22 CDS auctions from 2008 through 2010. Like Lieu (2011), the authors focus on the price discovery auction and confirm the results in Lieu (2011) that CDS auctions play a critical role in providing information to market participants for post-auction price formation in the cash market. In fact, the authors find that when the final auction price is taken into consideration, no pre-auction price or volume information at all helps explain post-auction secondary market prices—i.e., all of the information on which post-auction trading is based is driven by the auction process. Gupta and Sundaram (2015a) also report that final auction prices are biased despite being informative. They attribute the pricing bias primarily to a combination of "winner's curse" issues influencing order placement, strategic bidding related to the size of bidders' net CDS positions, and illiquidity in the secondary bond market.

In Gupta and Sundaram (2015b), the authors evaluated 30 CDS auctions from November 2006 through December 2013 to examine the extent of any mispricings between the CDS auction final price and the pre- and post-auction cash market prices of the bonds. They report a systematic underpricing of bonds in CDS auctions where the net open interest is on the sell side and a systematic overpricing of bonds in auctions dominated by buy orders. Although they estimate that an arbitrageur could earn as much as 15% by exploiting these mispricing patterns, they also attribute that return to a liquidity risk premium compensating arbitrageurs for illiquidity in the underlying bond market.

Most of the studies of CDS auctions have two major common conclusions. First, CDS final auction prices have tended to be biased (often on the side of undervaluing the underlying bonds). Second, the auction process is a critical component in the price discovery process for post-auction cash bond trading. Many of the studies, moreover, attribute pricing differences around auctions to illiquidity in the underlying bonds.

2.1.6 *Deliverable Obligations for Single-Name CDSs with Physical or Auction Settlement*

Prior to the 2009 Standardization Initiatives, the debt obligations issued by a reference entity that were deliverable in a physically settled CDS were specified in the original transaction documentation. After the implementation of the 2009 Standardization Initiatives, the applicable DC applies the conditions contained in market-standard documentation to the available bonds in order to determine which bonds qualify for physical delivery and trading in the CDS auction. Eligible market participants are entitled to submit proposed obligations for the DC to consider, and such market participants may also submit objections to the DC regarding the inclusion of certain obligations on the deliverable obligations list.

For most reference entities, any plain vanilla debt can be delivered in the CDS auction or by the protection purchaser in a physically settled CDS, usually subject to a maximum maturity of 30 years and to the constraint that subordinated debt cannot be delivered to satisfy the requirements of a senior CDS. As such, the CDS protection purchaser holds a cheapest-to-deliver ("CTD") option that drives the pricing of the corresponding CDS contract. In other words, the market-based spread on a single-name CDS is based not only on the credit risk of the underlying reference entity, but also on the probability that the protection seller will receive the lowest possible valued deliverable obligation (e.g., long-dated, high-duration, subordinated bonds) in lieu of less-risky deliverable securities (e.g., short-term, low-duration, senior debt).

For single-name CDS auctions involving restructuring credit events, moreover, the deliverable obligations are often constrained by the contractual maturities of the underlying bonds and CDSs. This can give rise to auctions for different "buckets" of obligations issued by the reference entity as defined by the insolvency proceedings. For example, in the auction for Northern Rock (Asset Management) PLC ("NRAM") held on February 2, 2012, the EMEA DC elected to hold two auctions. In making this determination, the DC classified NRAM's senior and subordinated obligations into four maturity buckets, in which the obligations in buckets one, two, three, and four had approximately 2.5, 5, 7.5, and 10 years to maturity, respectively. The DC decided to hold auctions for Buckets 1 and 2, in which senior and subordinated obligations within the covered maturities were deliverable. The DC opted not to hold auctions for the longer-dated maturity buckets, presumably because of the low number of deliverable obligations—viz., Buckets 1 and 2 included 355 transactions, whereas Buckets 3 and 4 only included 22 transactions.

In the *2014 Definitions*, ISDA also introduced the concept of a standard reference obligation ("SRO"). Although deliverable obligations under single-name CDSs are not limited exclusively to SROs, the SROs for a reference entity (published by ISDA periodically for frequently traded CDSs) are a minimum subset of deliverable obligations. In any physically settled CDSs, the protection buyer is contractually obligated to deliver the SRO to the protection seller before the latter makes a payment to the former. SRO designations are intended to further reduce the basis risk associated with the CTD option and to promote consistent pricing across CDS contracts.

Similarly, for LCDSs, Markit Group publishes lists of deliverable obligations, which we discuss further in Chapter 3.

2.2 Selected Credit Event Determinations

Given the large number of credit event determinations since the inception of the single-name CDS market, relatively few incidents have occurred that have called into question either the *Definitions* or the credit event determination process. But there have been some notable exceptions, which we discuss below.

2.2.1 The Argentine Republic (2001)

In November 2001, Argentina announced a plan to voluntarily restructure \$95 billion of its \$132 billion in outstanding debt by exchanging the \$95 billion in 15% bonds for bonds with interest rates capped at seven percent.[23] Argentina claimed that because the bond exchange was voluntary it did not constitute a restructuring event and dedicated tax revenues had been earmarked to cover the interest payment obligations on the new bonds. Rating agencies and analysts disagreed, however, and contended that Argentina's declining tax revenues were insufficient to support the old bonds and, hence, that any investor not swapping old bonds for news ones would be subject to an even greater risk. As such, the rating agencies and many analysts claimed that the proposed debt swap was de facto involuntary (Pollack 2003).

Based on two sovereign CDS transactions outstanding with JPMorgan as its counterparty, HBK Master Fund LP ("HBK") provided JPMorgan in December 2001 written notice that it believed a restructuring event had occurred on Argentine sovereign debt underlying its CDSs in which HBK was the credit protection purchaser. Under the 1999 Definitions, the definition of a restructuring depended heavily on the definition of an "Obligation Exchange," defined as "the mandatory transfer (other than in accordance with the terms in effect as of the later of the Trade Date or date of issuance of the relevant Obligation) of any securities, obligations, or assets to holders of Obligations in exchange for such Obligations."[24] JPMorgan responded to HBK that a restructuring event had *not* occurred because the Argentine restructuring was a voluntary one and, as such, no Obligation Exchange had taken place. HBK responded that, regardless of whether any *actual* Obligation Exchange had occurred, the exchange constituted a restructuring event because it triggered a reduction in principal and interest and a deferral of the maturity dates on the Argentine sovereign debt (Collins and Sackmann 2003; Pollack 2003). Eternity Global Master Fund Limited ("Eternity") filed a similar lawsuit against JPMorgan.[25]

Both the HBK and Eternity lawsuits resulted in drawn-out litigation and generated significant controversy among market participants about the term Obligation Exchange in the definition of a restructuring event in the Definitions. As a result, the *2003 Definitions* eliminated the term Obligation Exchange from the definition of a restructuring event. Under the *2003 Definitions*, a restructuring credit event was defined solely based on the occurrence of any of the six events defined in the *1999 Definitions* as long as such events bind all holders of any obligations to the restructuring.

2.2.2 The Hellenic Republic (2012)

The determination process and revised restructuring event guidelines adopted in the *2003 Definitions* and the Big Bang Protocol's *2009 Amendments to the 2003 Definitions* were tested during the European sovereign debt crisis with respect to the debt obligations of the Hellenic Republic (i.e., Greece). Public recognition of Greece's financial difficulties moved under the microscope in October 2009, when the newly elected federal government announced that previous statistics had badly understated the actual amounts of Greek sovereign debt and the sovereign's deficit. Following several months of continuing bad news from Greece regarding its economic condition and public-sector spending, several of the rating agencies downgraded Greek sovereign debt. By April 2010, spreads on Greek sovereign debt had risen to as much as nine percent higher than otherwise-similar German sovereign bonds.[26]

In May 2010, E.U. country leaders agreed to a comprehensive "bailout" package that involved increased lending to Greece (conditional on certain fiscal reforms), the creation of a European Financial Stability Facility ("EFSF") to provide up to €440 billion in loans to troubled E.U. sovereigns and the authorization of the European Central Bank ("ECB") to engage in secondary purchases of troubled E.U. sovereign debt to help reduce yields and stabilize the markets. The May 2010 intervention by Eurozone leaders did indeed stabilize the market, but only briefly. By mid-2011, the situation in Greece (as well as several other E.U.

countries) had deteriorated even further. By the summer of 2011, many market participants anticipated that the Hellenic Republic's sovereign debt was rapidly becoming (or had already become) unsustainable unless substantial additional public-sector assistance was provided.[27]

On July 21, 2011, leaders of the Eurozone countries convened and agreed on another set of reforms and rescue measures designed to provide an additional estimated €109 billion to the Hellenic Republic. This time, the rescue package called for a combination of public-sector loans from the EFSF and International Monetary Fund ("IMF") together with contributions from the private sector. Of the total €109 billion in additional planned bailout funds, €37 billion was expected to come from *voluntary* private-sector involvement ("PSI")—specifically, through voluntary agreements by Greek creditors to exchange their existing debt for new debt issued on terms more favorable to Greece.[28]

By October 2011, many market participants, politicians, and commentators believed that even the reforms proposed in the July 2011 summit would be insufficient to ensure the sustainability of Greek sovereign debt without significant additional reforms, including substantial PSI.[29] The official statement following the E.U. summit on October 26, 2011, thus included the following "invitation": "[W]e invite Greece, private investors and all parties concerned to develop a voluntary bond exchange with a nominal discount of 50% on notional Greek debt held by private investors."[30] Although large investors in Greek debt (e.g., German banks) were subject to pressure from their local regulators (known as "moral suasion") to accept this invitation from the E.U., non-E.U. investors in Greek debt (e.g., US banks and asset managers) were skeptical of the proposal.[31]

Leading up to and immediately following the October 2011 E.U. summit, numerous market participants had already informally questioned whether the latest proposed reforms would constitute a restructuring event under the ISDA *Credit Derivatives Definitions* and determinations process. Such concerns and questions had become so frequent leading up to the *July* 2011 summit that ISDA published a "Greek Sovereign Debt Q&A" on July 8, 2011. On October 27, 2011, ISDA updated its Q&A and stated the following:

> The determination of whether the Eurozone deal with regard to Greece is a credit event under CDS documentation will be made by ISDA's EMEA [DC] when the proposal is formally signed and if a market participant

requests a ruling from the DC. Based on what we know, it appears from preliminary news reports that the bond restructuring is voluntary and not binding on all bondholders. As such, it does not appear to be likely that the restructuring will trigger payments under existing CDS contracts. In addition, it is important to note that the restructuring proposal is not yet at the stage at which the ISDA Determinations Committee would be likely to accept a request to determine whether a credit event has occurred.[32]

On February 21, 2012, the ministers of finance for the Eurozone countries issued a statement, indicating that an agreement had been reached with Greece that, consistent with the broad goals of the October 2011 E.U. summit, would involve an exchange of existing debt for new debt with a face value of about 53.5% of the nominal amount of the original debt.[33] On February 23, 2012, the Greek parliament enacted the "Greek Bondholder Act" to provide for the voluntary redemption of bonds on those terms. On February 24, 2012, the Hellenic Republic Ministry of Finance issued a statement, indicating that it had approved the terms of invitations for such debt exchanges to private-sector investors outside the USA and issued a statement in which it said:

Under the collective action procedures introduced by the Greek Bondholder Act, the proposed amendments will become binding on the holders of all the Republic's Greek-law governed bonds issued prior to 31 December 2011 identified in the act of the Ministerial Council approving the PSI invitations, if at least two thirds by face amount of a quorum of these bonds, voting collectively without distinction by series, approve the proposed amendments.[34]

On the same day as the Hellenic Republic Ministry of Finance's statement, the ISDA DC responsible for deciding whether a restructuring event had occurred for Greece—i.e., the EMEA DC[35]—received its first question, which was submitted by HBK Capital Management (i.e., the same fund manager that sued JPMorgan regarding the Argentine restructuring event). The DC agreed to accept the question on February 28, 2012,[36] and to resolve the question by February 29, 2012.[37] The question posed by HBK to the EMEA DC was as follows:

Does the announcement of the passage by the Greek parliament of legislation that approves the implementation of an exchange offer and vote providing for collective action clauses ("CACs") that impose a "haircut amounting to 53.5%"…constitute a Restructuring Credit Event in accordance with Section 4.7 of the [*2009 Amendments to the 2003 Definitions*] because (i) the [ECB] and National Central Banks benefitted from "a change in the ranking in priority of payment" as a result of the Hellenic Republic exclusively offering them the ability to exchange out of their "eligible instruments" prior to the exchange and implementation of the CACs, thereby effectively "causing the Subordination" of all remaining holders of eligible instruments, and (ii) this announcement results directly or indirectly from a deterioration in the creditworthiness or financial condition of the Hellenic Republic?[38]

Before the DC issued its answer to the first question, it received a second question on February 29, 2012.[39] This question, submitted by Bracebridge Capital LLC, raised related concerns:

> Does (i) the agreement that has been reached between the Hellenic Republic and a number of private sector holders of Greek debt…exchange the Designated Securities for new securities…; (ii) the enactment of [the Greek Bondholder Act] and (iii) the statement by the Ministry of Finance of the Hellenic Republic on 21 [sic.] February 2012…constitute a Restructuring Credit Event in accordance with Section 4.7 of the [*2009 Amendments to the 2003 Definitions*] because (i) a reduction in the amount of principal or premium payable at maturity or at scheduled redemption dates of the Designated Securities has been agreed between the Hellenic Republic and *a sufficient number of holders of the Designated Securities to bind all holders of the Designated Securities* and (ii) this agreement results directly or indirectly from a deterioration in the creditworthiness or financial condition of the Hellenic Republic? [emphasis added][40]

On March 1, 2012, the EMEA DC issued a statement that "it had not received any evidence of an agreement which meets the requirements of Section 4.7(a) of the [*2009 Amendments to the 2003 Definitions*] and therefore based on the facts available to it, the EMEA DC unanimously determined that a Restructuring Credit Event has not occurred…."[41] For the first question, all 15 of the DC's voting members agreed that "the specific fact pattern…does not satisfy…the definition of Subordination as set out in the [*2003 Definitions*] and therefore a Restructuring Credit Event has not occurred…."[42] For the second question, the DC provided no additional details.

> On March 6, 2012, however, the Hellenic Republic Public Debt Management Agency announced that if the Republic receives sufficient consents to the proposed amendments of the Greek law governed bonds identified in the [February 24, 2012] invitations for the amendments to become effective, it intends…to declare the proposed amendments effective and binding on *all* holders of these bonds. Consequently, all obligations of the Republic to pay holders of those bonds any amount on account of principal will be amended to permit the Republic to discharge these obligations in full by delivering to the holders of the amended bonds on the settlement date the consideration described in the invitations. [emphasis added][43]

In other words, if enough market participants accepted the voluntary request from the Hellenic Republic to exchange their existing debt for new debt at lower face values and/or on less-favorable terms, Greece intended to impose those new terms on *all* bondholders—even those which did *not* consent to the proposed exchange.

On March 9, 2012, the Hellenic Republic Ministry of Finance announced that of the roughly €177 billion in outstanding sovereign Greek debt governed by Greek law and eligible for voluntary exchange under the Greek government's invitations, investors in approximately €152 billion (face value) in Greek debt had consented to and tendered for the proposed debt exchange. Accordingly, the Hellenic Republic advised that it intended "to accept the consents received and amend the terms of *all* of its Greek law governed bonds, including those not tendered for exchange pursuant to the invitations, in accordance with the terms of the Greek Bondholder Act. [emphasis added]"[44] In other words, on March 9, 2012, the Hellenic Republic declared its intention to impose reductions of principal on *all* holders of enumerated Greek sovereign debt instruments, even if investors did not consent, thus rendering the restructuring involuntary.

Also on March 9, 2012 (i.e., the same date as the announcement by the Hellenic Republic Ministry of Finance), UBS submitted a question to the EMEA DC, asking whether or not a restructuring credit event had occurred in the Hellenic Republic as a result of the latest statements by the Greek government. The DC accepted the question the same day and also reached a determination that same day (by unanimous consent of all 15 members) that Greece's latest actions did constitute a restructuring credit event as defined in *2009 Amendments to the 2003 Definitions*.[45]

2.2.3 Noble Group Ltd. (2017)

On June 16, 2017, the heavily leveraged Hong Kong-based commodities trading firm Noble Group Ltd. ("Noble") entered into an agreement that, among other things, secured a 120-day extension on its obligations to a syndicate of Asian, European, and US banks on a US$2.03 billion senior secured revolving credit facility known as the Noble Americas Borrowing Base Facility ("BBF").[46]

Noble's announcement of the restructuring of its BBF created significant uncertainty in single-name CDS markets as to whether a restructuring event had occurred under the *2009 Amendments to the 2003 Definitions* and the *2014 Definitions*.[47] On June 19, 2017, the ISDA Asia Ex-Japan DC received a general interest inquiry that questioned whether Noble's extension of the effective maturity of its BBF constituted a restructuring event under the 2003 and 2014 Definitions.[48] On June 22, 2017, the Asia Ex-Japan DC announced that it needed additional time to gather and review more information before making a determination.[49] On July 24, 2017, the DC convened again to consider the Noble question and once more announced that it needed additional time and information to make a determination.[50] And on August 1, 2017, the Asia Ex-Japan DC convened once more and announced in more detail that it still lacked sufficient information to reach a determination. Specifically, the DC indicated that it did not have documentation regarding the terms of Noble's BBF or Noble's guaranty of that facility, and the Committee requested that any market participant in possession of such information (provided it was public) should submit it to the DC by August 4th in anticipation of an additional DC meeting on August 7th.[51]

On August 9, 2017, the Asia Ex-Japan DC finally dismissed the question it had received on the grounds of insufficient documentation. Significantly, the DC noted that, under the governing DC rules, its dismissal of the question did not constitute a DC resolution as to whether a restructuring event had or had not occurred at Noble.[52]

Under the various rules related to the 2009 Standardization Initiatives and *2014 Definitions*, an 80% supermajority vote of the DC is required to dismiss a question without making a determination, and that is what occurred in early August 2017 vis-à-vis the general interest restructuring question for Noble.[53] As current ISDA CEO and former chairman of the CFTC Scott O'Malia explained:

> Market participants crave certainty, and so the lack of public information on the Noble loan and guarantee has created confusion and frustration in the market. The rules do allow the DCs to dismiss a question…and provide for the bilateral triggering of contracts in the event a question is dismissed. Now, people can argue that a different outcome would have been preferable, but they can't argue that the potential for a dismissal isn't set out in the rules as they stand.[54]

On August 23rd and 24th, JPMorgan and BNP Paribas (respectively) submitted additional questions to the Asia Ex-Japan DC, questioning whether a restructuring event occurred at Noble on or around June 17th.[55] The BNP Paribas question for the DC included the following explanatory language:

> Whilst the [August 9th] dismissal of the DC Question did not constitute a DC Resolution, there is now uncertainty generally as to how to interpret Sections 1.32 and 4.7(a) in the light of the approach and challenges described by the DC Statement when seeking to determine the Credit Event. For the purposes of Section 10.2 of the [2014 Definitions], we respectfully request a DC Resolution in respect of this question. This is so that market stability and integrity and safe and efficient derivatives markets can be maintained. The credit derivatives market now generally requires certainty as to the treatment of Credit Event Notices describing a Restructuring Credit Event relating to Noble Group Limited where…the Unavailable Documentation cannot be obtained or provided.[56]

The ongoing uncertainty in the market for single-name CDSs on Noble resulted in numerous submissions by protection purchasers to CDS protection sellers for claims related to a credit event at Noble. More than $1.2 billion of CDSs on Noble were outstanding at the time.[57] Disputes over CDSs based on Noble included highly sophisticated CDS market participants on both the protection purchase and sale sides—e.g., protection purchasers including Goldman Sachs, Nomura, and various hedge funds submitted claims to CDS protection sellers including JPMorgan and BNP Paribas.[58]

On August 30, 2017, the ISDA Asia Ex-Japan DC convened again and determined that the "Settlement Suspension Provisions" in the *2009 Amendments to the 2003 Definitions* and the *2014 Definitions* applied as of that date.[59] Those provisions enable the DC to activate a "suspension period" in which "the [relevant CDS counterparties] are not obliged to, nor are they entitled to, take any action in connection with the settlement of any relevant Credit Derivative Transaction."[60] In other words, the ISDA DC froze the ongoing efforts of CDS protection purchasers on the Noble Group to reach bilateral settlement agreements with their protection seller counterparties until the Asia Ex-Japan DC had reached a final determination regarding the possible Noble restructuring event.[61]

The DC finally took the outstanding requests off the table in a statement issued on September 19, 2017. The Asia Ex-Japan DC explained its decision to dismiss the questions posed by both JPMorgan and BNP Paribas as follows based on the lack of underlying documentation for the Noble BBF facility at issue:

> For the avoidance of doubt, the effect of the DC Resolution in respect of the Rephrased Noble Interpretation Question is that any purported Notice of Publicly Available Information that does not contain a copy, or a description in reasonable detail, of Publicly Available Information that is sufficient to confirm whether the relevant guarantee of Noble Group Limited is a Qualifying Guarantee shall be invalid and ineffective, and no further action is required by the parties in response to such notices in relation to the relevant 2014 Transaction or Updated 2003 Transaction....
>
> For the avoidance of doubt, the DC Resolution in respect of the Rephrased Noble Interpretation Question is concerned only with the interpretation of Section 1.34 of the 2014 Definitions and Section 3.6 of the Updated 2003 Definitions (as applicable) in the context of the Rephrased Noble Interpretation Question and, accordingly, only applies to the delivery of a Notice of Publicly Available Information for the purpose of bilaterally triggering a 2014 Transaction or Updated 2003 Transaction (as applicable) in respect of which Noble Group Limited is the Reference Entity. In particular, the DC Resolution in respect of the Rephrased Noble Interpretation Question has no application to the submission of Potential DC Issues to the DC Secretary, nor to the DC's ability to commence deliberations in respect thereof, pursuant to Section 2.1 of the DC Rules in the future.
>
> In light of the DC Resolution in respect of the Rephrased Noble Interpretation Question, the DC determined that answering the Noble Credit Event Question was unlikely to have any relevance and therefore Resolved to dismiss the Noble Credit Event Question.[62]

In the end, the relevant ISDA DC was unable to make a definitive determination as to whether a restructuring event occurred at Noble because of a lack of public documentation about Noble's BBF facility. The Noble event controversy is therefore not an indictment of the ISDA determinations process, but rather an important illustration of the need for market participants to document credit events adequately for a DC, including by providing the underlying loan facility documents at issue.

2.2.4 *Blackstone-Hovnanian (2017–2018)*

In 2013, Blackstone Alternative Asset Management ("BAAM")—the largest discretionary investor in hedge funds and an affiliate of the Blackstone Group LP ("Blackstone")[63]—purchased credit protection using single-name CDSs on the Spanish gaming company Codere S.A. BAAM was also a lender to Codere and allegedly agreed to roll over and extend a $100 million revolving credit facility in exchange for Codere agreeing to make interest payments on certain bonds a few days late, thus triggering CDSs with the Codere reference name and apparently generating significant profits for Blackstone.[64]

As we discuss in Chapters 8 and 10 (Sects. 8.2.5 and 10.2.5), the question of whether or not "strategic defaults"—actual or merely threatened—adversely impact borrowers (and their shareholders) that are also reference names of single-name CDSs purchased by borrowers, is a hotly contested question with relatively scant empirical evidence. Critics of strategic default contended that the purchases of CDS credit protection on a reference entity by a firm that is also a lender to that reference entity may seek to force the reference borrower to default in order to maximize the lender/protection purchaser's total profits (across both its loans and CDS protection purchases) at the expense of the market value of the borrowing firm.

The apparent strategic default by Codere in 2013 for the benefit of Blackstone seems to lend some legitimacy to this concern about the incentive effects of lenders holding open single-name CDSs protection positions on financially constrained borrowers. On the other hand, some believe that strategic default—or the threat thereof—can provide an important disciplining mechanism to pressure troubled firms into accepting debt restructuring packages and avoiding bankruptcy, thereby leading to a higher market value of a borrowing firm.

In 2017 and 2018, a more contentious and controversial case brought the issue of strategic defaults much further into the spotlight. The sections below discuss this case in more detail.[65] We note that this matter remains the subject of both controversy and litigation at the time of our writing, and we base all of our discussion on publicly available documents that were available to us as this book went to press.

2.2.4.1 The July 2017 Secured Hovnanian Debt Restructuring

In early 2017, market participants were expressing concerns that New Jersey-based and Delaware-domiciled homebuilding and mortgage-financing firm Hovnanian Enterprises, Inc. ("Hovnanian") might be unable to repay or refinance at least some of its secured and unsecured debt due between 2018 and 2020. As a result, CDS spreads on Hovnanian rose substantially in response to these concerns.

In July 2017, Hovnanian announced its intention to refinance $75 million of senior secured second-lien 10% notes due in 2018, $145 million of 9.125% senior secured second-lien notes due in 2020 and $577 million of 7.25% senior secured first-lien notes due in 2020. The outstanding debt was retired with the proceeds from a new issuance of $840 million of new senior secured notes due in 2022 and 2024. In particular, the new senior secured notes were backed by collateral senior to all other collateral pledged to back Hovnanian's other secured debt (apart from a senior secured $75 million term loan, to which the new senior secured notes' collateral was subordinate). The new notes consisted of $440 million 10% senior secured notes due in July 2022 (the "Secured 10% Notes") and $400 million senior secured 10.5% notes due in July 2024 (the "Secured 10.5% Notes").[66] (The types of and distinctions between different loan facilities are discussed in Sect. 2.1 of Chapter 3.) The refinancing is depicted graphically in Fig. 2.4.

Markets responded favorably to the refinancing, and CDS spreads on the Hovnanian reference name declined to about two percent per annum.[67] The refinancing was completed on July 27, 2017.[68]

2.2.4.2 Rumors of an Unsecured Hovnanian Debt Restructuring

Soon after the refinancing of its secured debt was completed, Hovnanian announced that it was also seeking to refinance $369 million of its *unsecured* notes with maturity dates in 2019. As of December 28, 2017, Hovnanian's outstanding unsecured debt included $132,546,000

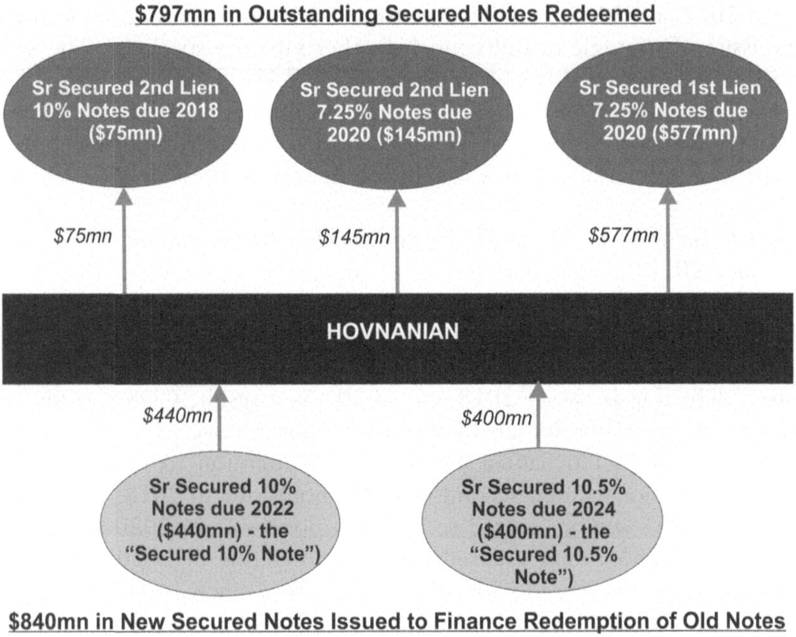

Fig. 2.4 The July 2017 Hovnanian secured debt refinancing

of 7% senior notes due January 2019 (the "Unsecured 7% Notes") and $235,961,000 of 8% senior notes due in November 2019 (the "Unsecured 8% Notes"). New concerns about Hovnanian's liquidity profile and ability to repay its debts began to show up in the CDS market in mid-September 2017. Some market participants even voiced concerns that Hovnanian would default on more than $50 million of debt principal repayments due on December 1, 2017, which it did not.[69]

As of October 2017, a reported $668 million in net notional principal protection had been purchased on Hovnanian in the CDS market. By mid-November 2017, rumors were reported in the press that Hovnanian was discussing a refinancing package with Blackstone Group LP's GSO Capital Partners ("GSO") which would involve a credit event that would trigger CDSs on Hovnanian's reference name.[70] Not surprisingly, Hovnanian CDS spreads rose from just over four percent in late October to 16.12% in mid-November.[71] One fund in particular—Solus Alternative Asset Management ("Solus")—sent a letter on November

29, 2017, to the board of directors of Hovnanian that it believed GSO's refinancing proposal was a disguised effort to generate profits on GSO's Hovnanian CDS protection purchases.[72] Solus had sold about $260.5 million in net notional credit protection through CDSs based on the Hovnanian reference name.[73]

2.2.4.3 The December 2017 Unsecured Hovnanian Debt Refinancing

On December 28, 2017, Hovnanian announced that it had completed a refinancing package with GSO that would raise up to $362.5 million in funds for Hovnanian. Figure 2.5 graphically depicts this refinancing, which included the following agreements[74]:

- An unsecured term loan provided by GSO to Hovnanian with up to $212.5 million in principal, a tenor of nine years (i.e., maturing in 2027), and an interest rate of 5% per annum;
- A senior secured first-lien revolving credit facility provided by GSO to Hovnanian with up to $125 million in drawn principal, an interest rate equal to the volume-weighted average yield over the previous 30 days on the Senior 10.5% Notes minus 0.5%, and a tenor of two years with a provision that unpaid drawn balances

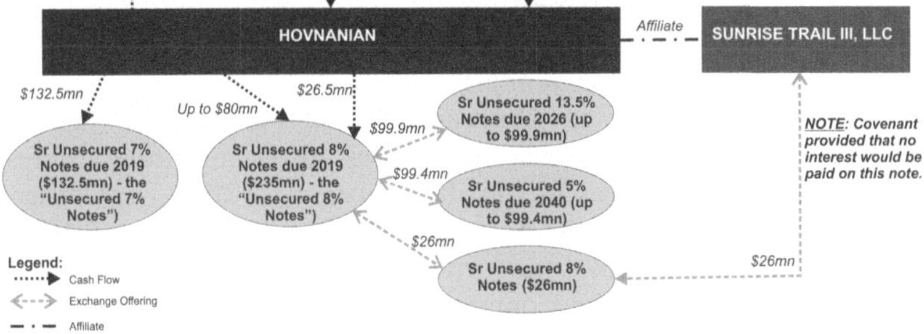

Fig. 2.5 The December 2017 Hovnanian unsecured refinancing with Blackstone/GSO

as of December 28, 2019, would automatically be converted into a three-year term loan; and

- An agreement by GSO to purchase $25 million in additional Senior 10.5% Notes to be issued by Hovnanian with the same terms as the Senior 10.5% Notes issued as part of the July 2017 refinancing.

Hovnanian planned to use the proceeds of these new credits as follows[75]:

- Refinance $132.5 million of the Unsecured 7% Notes (i.e., the entire outstanding balance at the time) using the proceeds of the unsecured term loan;
- Refinance up to $185 million in the Unsecured 8% Notes through an exchange offering consisting of the following:

  - $26.5 million in cash;
  - Up to $99.9 million of newly issued unsecured 13.5% notes maturing in 2026;
  - Up to $99.4 million of newly issued unsecured 5% notes maturing in 2040; and
  - The purchase by a Hovnanian affiliate of $26 million in Unsecured 8% Notes due in 2019.

In addition, the $185 million exchange offering included a guarantee by GSO to commit up to $80 million (financed through the unsecured term loan) to refinance Unsecured 8% Notes that were not surrendered by investors in the exchange offering. The exchange offering was also subject to a minimum total participation requirement of $140 million and did not change the relative priority of any outstanding notes. The notes to be retired, new securities and loans to be issued, and the exchange offering are depicted in Fig. 2.5.

In order to refinance its Unsecured 7 and 8% Notes as desired, Hovnanian had to amend the indentures governing those Notes. Accordingly, Hovnanian sent on December 28, 2017, a Consent Solicitation to holders of the Secured 10% Notes and Secured 10.5% Notes seeking their approval to amend those Note indentures "to eliminate the restrictions on the Company's ability to purchase, repurchase, redeem, acquire or retire for value [the Senior 7% Notes] and [Senior 8% Notes] and refinancing or replacement indebtedness in respect thereof contained in the indenture governing the Notes."[76] Investors were obliged to respond to the Consent Solicitation by January 12, 2018, and any investors that gave their consent to the proposed amendment were compensated with $2.50 per $1000 of principal.[77] As an investor in the Secured 10% Notes and Secured 10.5% Notes, GSO agreed to provide its consent to the proposed amendment as part of a "Support Agreement" executed by Hovnanian and GSO as part of Hovnanian's refinancing package.[78]

A majority of investors in the Secured 10.5% Notes gave their consent to the proposed amendment by the January 12th deadline, but responses from a majority of investors in the Secured 10% Note were not received.[79] The consents to the proposed amendment provided included consent by GSO on all of its Secured 10.5% Note holdings, which some reports suggest was as much as $126.8 million—i.e., above the majority required for the proposed amendment and leaving Hovnanian just about 10% shy of its $140 million minimum.[80]

On January 16, 2018, Hovnanian extended its Consent Solicitation deadline through January 22nd and also increased the consideration it would give to investors that consented to the proposed amendment from $2.50 to $5.00 per $1000 of principal on the Secured 10% Notes.[81] By January 22nd, Hovnanian still had not received the required majority consent to amend the indenture as proposed for the Secured 10% Notes, and, as such, the indenture for those Notes remained unchanged.[82]

The refinancing package and related agreements between Hovnanian and GSO also included an unusual additional agreement. As noted above, Hovnanian agreed as part of the refinancing that one of its affiliates would purchase $26 million in Unsecured 8% Notes. Hovnanian affiliate Sunrise Trail III, LLC ("Sunrise"), ultimately purchased the $26 million in Unsecured 8% Notes (the "Purchased 8% Notes"). But, pursuant to the terms of the exchange offering and the indenture governing the new unsecured 13.5 and 5% notes, Hovnanian agreed: (i) not to redeem, cancel, retire, purchase, or acquire any Purchased 8% Notes prior to their stated maturity; or (ii) make any required interest payments on the $26 million in Purchased 8% Notes prior to the stated maturity date of those Notes in 2019.[83]

In other words, Hovnanian and GSO agreed as part of the Hovnanian-GSO December 2017 refinancing package that no interest would be paid on the $26 million of Purchased 8% Notes held by Hovnanian's Sunrise affiliate. Payments to other bondholders on the Unsecured 8% Notes, however, would be made as required.[84]

Under the terms on which Hovnanian and GSO agreed, Hovnanian's failure to pay its Sunrise affiliate interest on the Purchased 8% Notes could constitute (barely) a trigger event under the prevailing ISDA Definitions, thereby enabling GSO to deliver any eligible Hovnanian bonds to its credit protection sellers in exchange for par repayments. Following the executed December 2017 refinancing transactions, GSO could then deliver the relatively cheap unsecured 5% notes and generate substantial profits on its CDS positions.

2.2.4.4 Litigation-Related Controversy

In its December 28, 2017, disclosures of the details of its refinancing package with GSO, Hovnanian indicated its recognition that this aspect of the refinancing package exposed the firm to potential litigation risk:

> We understand that the non-payment of interest on such Purchased 8.0% Notes may result in the occurrence of a "credit event" under certain [CDS] contracts entered into by third-parties, resulting in significant monetary exposure for those entities that sold such credit default swaps. Although we are not a party to any of these [CDS] contracts, we and our officers and directors may become subject to legal proceedings, and review from the Securities and Exchange Commission, Commodity Futures Trading Commission and other regulatory bodies, regarding the occurrence, or anticipated occurrence, of such "credit event." In addition, certain third parties have threatened legal action against us if we proceed with certain refinancing transactions, which may include all or a portion of the Transactions. Such litigation exposure and regulatory review may cause harm to our reputation and adversely affect our ability to access debt and other financing markets or make doing so more costly in order to refinance our existing debt or finance our operations in the future.[85]

In early January 2018, Solus sued both GSO and Hovnanian for allegedly manipulating the CDS market based on Hovnanian's debt.[86] In the complaint, the Plaintiff contended:

> Hovnanian's default is entirely avoidable and does not reflect its financial distress. Indeed, Hovnanian has nearly half a *billion* dollars of cash on its balance sheet available to meet the interest obligation. Rather, the sole purpose of Hovnanian's agreement to engage in a sham default is to deliver windfall gains to GSO on its CDS by engineering an artificial "credit event."[87]

Market participants reacted adversely to the lawsuit because of the uncertainty it created in the single-name CDS marketplace regarding how CDS markets and documents handle strategic defaults—an already contentious and ambiguous issue as discussed further in Chapters 8 and 11. One market participant said, "I would definitely recommend that [ISDA's] working groups look to find a solution to prevent strategies like this."[88] Another market participant voiced the following opinion:

> [L]ast week [Solus] sued [Hovnanian], its chief executive officer and chief financial officer, and GSO....The problem is that Hovnanian really isn't doing anything to Solus. Solus wrote some CDS on Hovnanian, but Hovnanian wasn't a party to that CDS and has no obligations to Solus under it. So the lawsuit consists of a lot of hand-waving and shouting about fraud....Hovnanian isn't defaulting, fraudulently or otherwise, on a payment owed to Solus; it's not forcing Solus to buy any bonds, rigged or otherwise. Solus's objection is strangely aesthetic: Hovnanian's new bonds are so ridiculous that they just shouldn't be allowed to exist.[89]

Solus sought to block the Hovnanian restructuring with an injunction barring the Hovnanian debt exchange with GSO, but, on January 29, 2018, US District Court judge the Hon. Laura Taylor Swain said that she would not stop Hovnanian from refinancing its debts because it did not endanger the CDS market's very existence (as Solus claimed) and that any harm to Solus could be calculated as damages if a later court ascertained that Solus had been harmed.[90]

Indeed, even the CEO of GSO, Bennett Goodman, subsequently indicated that, although he thinks the Solus lawsuit is without merit, he believes in this context that "[i]f people want to change the rules that are written in black and white because they think it makes for a more effective market structure, we are all for it."[91] Judge Swain, moreover, charged the marketplace—and ISDA in particular—with correcting the problem underlying this controversy. The Court found that

> [A]ny proliferation of engineered defaults that did occur could likely be mitigated by actions on the part of ISDA. ISDA, whose membership is comprised of CDS market participants, has a process in place to study and approve modifications to its standard documentation, definitions, and Master Agreement that could change the definition of a failure to pay event. [Former ISDA CEO Robert Pickel] testified that ISDA's mechanisms would be insufficient to confront the threat of cleverly engineered

> defaults because CDS market participants and the ISDA Determinations Committee require the certainty of a bright-line rule, and that prohibiting engineered defaults would require a subjective inquiry into a Reference Entity's intent when defaulting....The Court is not, however, persuaded that ISDA is so powerless to act in an effective way with respect to the effect of intentional defaults on the CDS market, given the numerous proposals to prohibit such engineered defaults, as to require an injunction by this Court to prevent irreparable damage to the CDS marketplace.[92]

2.2.4.5 The April 2018 Second Hovnanian Restructuring

During the first few months of 2018, CDS protection sellers have reportedly attempted to block GSO's strategic default by bidding up the new below-market bonds issued by Hovnanian to prices that would make GSO's triggering of its CDSs uneconomic—i.e., the bonds intended to be CTD have been bid up enough that they might not be CTD and the CTD bonds would be priced high enough to attenuate significantly GSO's intended windfall on its CDS protection purchases.[93]

In April 2018, Hovnanian proposed an additional restructuring of some of its senior debt. Specifically, Hovnanian announced an exchange offering on April 6, 2018, for any and all of its outstanding $440 million Senior Secured 10% Notes maturing in 2022 and its $400 million outstanding of the Secured 10.5% Notes maturing in 2024. Both notes were issued as part of the exchange offerings in the July 2017 refinancing. Under the proposed exchange offer, a minimum of $150 million in the Secured 10 and 10.5% Notes would be exchanged for 125% of the face value of the bonds surrendered in the exchange in new senior secured notes due in April 2047 and paying a 3% coupon per annum.[94] On April 13th, Hovnanian amended the terms of its exchange offer such that participating bondholders would receive new bonds with 140% of the face value of the surrendered bonds.[95] On April 19th and 23rd, moreover, Hovnanian twice extended the early tender deadline from April 19th to April 20th and then from April 20th to April 23rd, respectively.[96] In another amendment filed on April 24th, Hovnanian reduced the minimum of Secured 10 and 10.5% Notes which would need to be tendered from $150 million to $50 million and extended the early tender deadline once more from April 23rd to April 27th, 2018. The final expiration of the exchange offer is May 3, 2018.[97]

As a result of the long maturities and deep discounts to par of the new proposed notes, the estimated market value of those notes is about 35 cents on the dollar. As Sridhar Natarajan of Bloomberg News commented, "Such an offering could only be designed for one type of investor: those who, like GSO, have bought insurance against a default."[98]

Even Hovnanian recognizes the possibility that the new notes issued in the April 2018 exchange offering could be CTD notes, which, at such a deep discount to par, could yield significant profits if deliverable into triggered CDSs. Hovnanian also offers the following caveat in its April 6th *Form 8-K* filing:

> If ISDA determines that there will be a CDS auction in connection with a "credit event" due to the Issuer's failure to pay interest on the Purchased 8.0% Notes, ISDA will also determine which of our debt instruments are "deliverable obligations" in such an auction for settlement and determination of the final auction price. We have no involvement in any of these ISDA determinations or the auction itself. Therefore, we cannot predict whether the New Notes will be determined to be "deliverable obligations" and what, if any, impact they may have on the settlement and final pricing determination. However, there is the potential for an adverse impact to those entities who sold CDS if the New Notes were to be deliverable in any such auction.

2.2.4.6 Proposed "Fixes" to Strategic Defaults like Hovnanian

On April 11, 2018, the ISDA Board of Directors issued a statement concerning "narrowly tailored credit events" such as Hovnanian. The ISDA Board's statement includes the following language:

> Whether any specific narrowly tailored arrangements meet the definition of a credit event under the ISDA Credit Derivatives Definitions will be determined by one of five regional Credit Derivatives Determinations Committees (DCs)....Under the DC rules, a determination can only be made based on publicly available information submitted to the DC. This information is then analyzed against the criteria for credit events within the ISDA Credit Derivatives Definitions to determine whether a credit event has occurred. The credit event determination process does not allow the DC to make subjective decisions, or to consider the intent or good faith of the parties that put in place the arrangements leading to a potential credit event. This ensures the process is objective and predictable, and decisions can be made quickly.
>
> We believe that narrowly tailored defaults, those that are designed to result in CDS payments that do not reflect the creditworthiness of the

> underlying corporate borrower (the reference entity in the CDS), could negatively impact the efficiency, reliability and fairness of the overall CDS market. We have therefore instructed the ISDA staff, as part of its ongoing dialogue with the market, to consult with market participants and advise the Board on whether further amendments to the ISDA Credit Derivatives Definitions should be considered.[99]

Several specific "fixes" have been proposed by commentators and market participants. First, some have suggested an increase in the minimum threshold amount for a failure-to-pay triggering event from its current $1 million to $5 or $10 million.[100] The failure of Hovnanian to pay interest to its Sunrise affiliate on the 8% 2019 note would have been above $1 million but below $5 million. In other cases, however, the $5 and $10 million thresholds might be too small relative to the potential benefits to CDS protection purchasers on a strategic default.

A second potential solution would be to limit the maturities of securities deliverable into triggered CDSs. By eliminating very long-dated securities (such as those contemplated in the April 2018 Hovnanian proposed restructuring), the likelihood of securities with deep discounts to par being delivered into CDS auctions or settlements would be greatly minimized. Modification of the ISDA *Definitions* to restrict maturities deliverable into CDSs, moreover, is not unprecedented. In 2000, lenders to the insurance company Conseco agreed to restructure Conseco's debt including some very long-dated maturities. In turn, many of those lenders with large CDS hedges made considerable profits by delivering the new deeply discounted debt into the triggered CDSs. As a result of the controversy generated over Conseco's auction, ISDA introduced a "modified" restructuring provision in 2001 that required all bonds surrendered by protection sellers pursuant to a restructuring event to be 60 months or less to maturity.[101]

Given the fundamental nature of single-name CDSs as risk transfer instruments, a third possibility would be to include a new provision in the *Definitions*, requiring that any triggering event be associated with the deterioration in some measure of the financial condition or creditworthiness of the reference entity (such as is already included in the restructuring event). As noted in the excerpt from the ISDA *Press Release* above, however, the ISDA determinations process does not permit DCs to engage in subjective credit assessments for directly observable credit events (e.g., failure to pay) or to evaluate the intent of the parties that led to the potential credit event. Modifying the *Definitions* to include creditworthiness as an explicit factor for DCs to consider even for observable triggers thus could impede the time it takes for DCs to make determinations, thus giving rise to uncertainties and undermining at least some of the risk transfer value of single-name CDSs.

The outcome of this matter, as well as any potential changes in the ISDA documentation, is likely to have a large impact on the future value of single-name CDSs. As of this writing, no determination has been made about Hovnanian (and the DC has not, to our knowledge, accepted any questions), the Solus case remains in ongoing litigation, and the specific actions that ISDA will take to address such "narrowly tailored credit events" are still unknown. Interested readers are recommended to follow the case.

Notes

1. As we discuss in Chapter 6, most index CDSs are now centrally cleared and are subject to new documentation tailored for cleared CDSs.
2. See G. Tett, *Fool's Gold* (New York: Free Press, 2009), at 3–71.
3. Tett, op. cit., at 157–60.
4. The rating before the slash indicates the rating frameworks of Standard and Poor's and Fitch, for which BBB—is the lowest investment-grade rating. The rating after the slash uses the lexicon from Moody's Investors Service, for which Baa3 denotes the lowest investment-grade rating.
5. A CLO is a structure in which a special-purpose entity issues tranched debt instruments to finance either the purchase of loans or the collateralized sale of credit protection on loans using CDSs. For a general discussion, see C. L. Culp, *Structured Finance and Insurance* (Hoboken, NJ: Wiley, 2006) and Chapter 5 of this book.
6. The term "spread" is used because the CDS spread is analogous to the spread over LIBOR on a floating-rate bond issued by the reference entity underlying the CDS.
7. A basis point is equal to 1/100th of a percentage point. For example, 100 bps is equivalent to one percentage point.
8. Unless otherwise specified in the transaction documentation, if the 20th falls on a weekend or holiday, the payment is due on the first business day following the 20th.
9. Market participants can also still negotiate a specific coupon rate by entering into two CDSs with different notional amounts that result in the desired blended coupon rate. For example, if a firm wishes to buy

credit protection on XYZ Corp. with a net exposure of $15 million at a 75 bp coupon rate for one year, the firm can buy protection on a $15.9375 million notional amount at the standardized 100 bp spread and simultaneously sell protection on a $937,500 notional amount at the standardized 500 bp coupon, which results in a net exposure of $15 million notion protection purchased at the effective cost of 75 bps.

10. ISDA, *1999 Credit Derivatives Definitions* (hereinafter "*1999 Definitions*"), at §§4.1–4.9.
11. ISDA, *2003 Credit Derivatives Definitions* (hereinafter "*2003 Definitions*").
12. ISDA, *Greek Sovereign Debt FAQ* (March 19, 2012).
13. *BBC News*, "Argentina Announces Debt 'Default' Plan" (November 2, 2001).
14. ISDA, *2009 Credit Derivatives Determinations Committees, Auction Settlement and Restructuring Supplement to the 2003 ISDA Credit Derivatives Definitions* (July 14, 2009) (hereinafter "*2009 Supplement to the 2003 Definitions*").
15. ISDA, "ISDA Announces Successful Implementation of 'Big Bang' CDS Protocol; Determinations Committees and Auction Settlement Changes Take Effect," *ISDA News Release* (April 8, 2009).
16. The Protocol further indicates that CDS protection is in-force at *T-90* for succession events, which are defined in the 2003 Definitions with respect to non-Sovereign reference entities as "an event such as a merger, consolidation, amalgamation, transfer of assets or liabilities, demerger, spin-off or other similar event in which one entity succeeds to the obligations of another entity, whether by operation of law or pursuant to any agreement." *2003 Definitions*, op. cit., at §2.2(b).
17. Markit, *The CDS Big Bang: Understanding the Changes to the Global CDS Contract and North American Conventions* (March 13, 2009).
18. Ministerie van Financiën, *Letter to the Chairman of the Second Chamber of Parliament of the States General RE: Nationalisation of SNS Reaal* (February 1, 2013).
19. Linklaters, "Credit Supernova: ISDA Publishes 2014 Credit Derivatives Definitions," *Client Memorandum* (February 2014).
20. Linklaters, op. cit.
21. J. Batterman and E. Rosenthal, "Delphi, Credit Derivatives, and Bond Trading Behavior After a Bankruptcy Filing," *Fitch Ratings Credit Policy Special Report* (November 28, 2005).
22. Markit/Creditex, *Credit Event Auction Primer* (February 2010).
23. *BBC News*, "Argentina Announces Debt 'Default' Plan" (November 2, 2001).
24. *1999 Definitions*, op. cit., at §4.9.

25. *Eternity Global Master Fund Limited v. Morgan Guaranty Trust*, 375 F.3d 168 (2004).
26. See, e.g., Zettelmeyer et al. (2013).
27. See, e.g., International Monetary Fund, "Greece: Fourth Review Under the Stand-by Arrangement and Request for Modification and Waiver of Applicability of Performance Criteria," *IMF Country Report No. 11/175* (July 2011).
28. Council of the European Union, *Statement by the Heads of State or Governments of the Euro Area and EU Institutions* (July 21, 2011).
29. See, e.g., Zettelmeyer et al. (2013) and IMF, *Greece: Debt Sustainability Analysis* (October 21, 2011) at http://folk.uio.no/hmehlum/2310h2011/troika_greece_dsa.pdf (last visited April 27, 2018).
30. Council of the European Union, *Euro Summit Statement* (October 26, 2011).
31. See, e.g., C. Whittall, "Dealers Reassess Value of Sovereign CDS After Greece Plan," *International Financing Review* (October 28, 2011).
32. ISDA, *Greek Sovereign Debt Q&A (Update)* (October 27, 2011).
33. "Euro-Area Finance Ministers' Statement on Greek Bailout: Text," *Bloomberg* (February 21, 2012).
34. Hellenic Republic, Ministry of Finance, *Press Release* (February 24, 2012).
35. The voting members of the EMEA DC at the time were as follows: Bank of America Merrill Lynch, Barclays, BlueMountain Capital, BNP Paribas, Citadel Investment Group, Credit Suisse, D. E. Shaw Group, Deutsche Bank, Elliott Management Corporation, Goldman Sachs, JPMorgan Chase Bank, Morgan Stanley, PIMCO, Societe Generale, and UBS. See ISDA, *EMEA Determinations Committee Decision* (March 1, 2012) (hereinafter "Greece DC Decision").
36. http://dc.isda.org/cds/the-hellenic-republic/ (last visited April 27, 2018).
37. ISDA, "ISDA Determinations Committee: The Hellenic Republic," *News Statement* (February 27, 2012).
38. http://dc.isda.org/cds/the-hellenic-republic/ (last visited April 27, 2018).
39. http://dc.isda.org/cds/the-hellenic-republic-2/ (last visited April 27, 2018).
40. http://dc.isda.org/cds/the-hellenic-republic-2/ (last visited April 27, 2018).
41. Greece DC Decision, op. cit.
42. Id.
43. Hellenic Republic, Public Debt Management Agency, *Press Release* (March 6, 2012).

44. Hellenic Republic, Ministry of Finance, *Press Release* (March 9, 2012).
45. ISDA, *EMEA Determinations Committee Decision* (March 9, 2012).
46. ISDA, *Asia Ex-Japan Determinations Committee* (June 19, 2017). See also, e.g., F. Bermingham, "Struggling Noble Group Secures Debt Extension Relief," *Global Trade Review* (June 20, 2017).
47. See, e.g., E. Orr, J. Blas, and J. Farchy, "Noble Group's $2 Billion Loan Deal Prompts Default-Swap Question," *Bloomberg* (June 19, 2017), and BNP Paribas, *Question Submitted to Asia Ex-Japan DC* (August 24, 2017).
48. ISDA, *Asia Ex-Japan Determinations Committee* (June 19, 2017).
49. ISDA, *Asia Ex-Japan Determinations Committee* (June 22, 2017).
50. https://dc.isda.org/cds/noble-group-limited/ (last visited April 27, 2018).
51. Id.
52. ISDA, *Asia Ex-Japan Determinations Committee Statement* (August 10, 2017).
53. S. O'Malia, "Some Thoughts on Noble," *DerivatiViews* (August 30, 2017).
54. Id. See also A. Scurria, "Home Builder Accused of Default Swap Scheme with Blackstone Unit," *Wall Street Journal* (December 2, 2017).
55. J. P. Morgan Chase Bank, N.A., *Question Submitted to the Asia Ex-Japan Determinations Committee* (August 23, 2017), and BNP Paribas, *Question to the Asia Ex-Japan Determinations Committee* (August 24, 2017).
56. BNP Paribas, *Question to the Asia Ex-Japan Determinations Committee* (August 24, 2017).
57. R. Smith and D. Sheppard, "World's Biggest Banks Square Off Over Noble Credit Default Swaps," *Financial Times* (August 27, 2017).
58. Id.
59. ISDA, *Asia Ex-Japan DC Statement* (August 30, 2017).
60. *2014 Definitions*, op. cit., at §10.1.
61. R. Smith, "ISDA Freezes Attempts to Settle Noble CDS," *Financial Times* (August 30, 2017).
62. ISDA, *Asia Ex-Japan DC Statement* (September 19, 2017).
63. https://www.blackstone.com/the-firm/asset-management/hedge-fund-solutions-(baam) (last visited April 27, 2018).
64. M. Levine, "Blackstone Made Money on Credit-Default Swaps with This One Weird Trick," *Bloomberg* (December 5, 2013).
65. Despite the details provided, our discussion is nevertheless simplified. The actual details of the case are beyond the scope of our discussion here.
66. Hovnanian Enterprises, Inc., "K. Hovnanian Enterprises, Inc. Announces New Senior Notes Offering," *Press Release* (July 11, 2017),

and Hovnanian Enterprises, Inc., *Form 8-K* (December 28, 2017), at Exhibit 10.1 ("Support Agreement").

67. Moody's Investors Service, "Moody's Rates Hovnanian's Secured Notes Caa2, Changes Outlook to Stable," *Rating Action* (July 11, 2017), and S. Natarajan, K. Burton, and L. Abramowicz, "A High-Stakes Hedge Fund Battle Erupts Over Hovnanian Debt," *Bloomberg* (November 15, 2017).
68. Hovnanian Enterprises, Inc., "K. Hovnanian Enterprises, Inc. Announces Expiration of Tender Offers for Certain of Its Senior Secured Notes and Satisfaction and Discharge of Indentures Relating Thereto," *Press Release* (July 27, 2017).
69. Scurria, op. cit.
70. Memorandum Opinion and Order Denying Motion for Preliminary Injunction, *Solus Alternative Asset Management LP v. GSO Capital Partners LP* et al. (S.D.N.Y.), No. 18 CV 232 (LTS-BCM) (January 29, 2018) ("*Solus v. GSO* Preliminary Injunction Ruling"), at 7, Natarajan, Burton, and Abramowicz, op. cit., and Scurria, op. cit.
71. Natarajan, Burton, and Abramowicz, op. cit.
72. Scurria, op. cit.
73. *Solus v. GSO* Preliminary Injunction Ruling, op. cit., at 6.
74. Hovnanian Enterprises, Inc., *Form 8-K* (December 28, 2017), at Exhibit 10.2 ("Commitment Letter").
75. Hovnanian Enterprises, Inc., *Form 8-K* (December 28, 2017), at Exhibit 99.5 ("Hovnanian Presentation").
76. Hovnanian Enterprises, Inc., *Form 8-K* (December 28, 2017), at Exhibit 99.3 ("Consent Solicitation").
77. Consent Solicitation, op. cit.
78. Support Agreement, op. cit.
79. Hovnanian Enterprises, Inc., "K. Hovnanian Enterprises, Inc. Announces Expiration of Consent Solicitation for Its 2024 Notes and Extension of Expiration Date and Amendment for the Consent Solicitation for Its 2022 Notes," *Press Release* (January 16, 2018).
80. Complaint, *Solus Alternative Asset Management LP v. GSO Capital Partners LP* et al. (S.D.N.Y.), No. 18 CV 232 (LTS-BCM) (January 11, 2018) ("*Solus v. GSO* Complaint"), at ¶54.
81. Hovnanian Enterprises, Inc. (January 16, 2018), op. cit.
82. Hovnanian Enterprises, Inc., "K. Hovnanian Enterprises, Inc. Announces Expiration of Consent Solicitation for Its 2022 Notes," *Press Release* (January 23, 2018).
83. Hovnanian Enterprises, Inc., *Form 8-K* (December 28, 2017), at Exhibit 99.1 ("Litigation Disclosure").
84. *Solus v. GSO Complaint*, op. cit., at ¶57. See also *Solus v. GSO Preliminary Injunction Ruling*, op. cit., at 8.

85. Litigation Disclosure, op. cit.
86. *Solus v. GSO* Complaint, op. cit.
87. *Solus v. GSO* Complaint, op. cit., at ¶8.
88. C. Davis, "Blackstone-Hovnanian CDS Deal Revives Credit Rules Debate," *Risk* (December 22, 2017).
89. M. Levine, "Not Everyone Appreciates CDS Creativity," *Bloomberg* (January 18, 2018).
90. M. Childs, "Judge Denies Injunction Request for Fancy CDS Transaction," *Barron's* (January 29, 2018). See also M. Childs, "Trigger Warning: The Latest Battle Over CDS," *Barron's* (January 27, 2018).
91. S. Natarajan and E. Schatzker, "GSO's Goodman Backs Closing CDS Loophole that His Firm Mastered," *Bloomberg* (March 9, 2018).
92. *Solus v. GSO* Preliminary Injunction Ruling, op. cit., at 9–10.
93. See, e.g., M. Levine, "More Hovnanian!" *Bloomberg* (April 10, 2018).
94. Hovnanian Enterprises, Inc., *Form 8-K* (April 6, 2018).
95. Hovnanian Enterprises, Inc., *Form 8-K* (April 13, 2018).
96. Hovnanian Enterprises, Inc., *Form 8-K* (April 19, 2018), and Hovnanian Enterprises, Inc., *Form 8-K* (April 23, 2018).
97. Hovnanian Enterprises, Inc., *Form 8-K* (April 23, 2018, and filed April 24, 2018).
98. Levine (April 10, 2018), op. cit.
99. ISDA, "Board Statement on Narrowly Tailored Credit Events," *Press Release* (April 11, 2018).
100. H. Bartholomew, "Fixing CDSs: Lots of Patches, No Magic Wand," *Risk* (April 20, 2018).
101. Id.

References

Berg, T., and D. Streitz. 2016. Determinants of the Size of the Sovereign Credit Default Swap Market. *Journal of Fixed Income* 25 (3) (Winter).

Chernov, M., A.S. Gorbenko, and I. Makarov. 2013. CDS Auctions. *Review of Financial Studies* 26 (3) (March).

Collins, J.P., and P.J. Sackmann. 2003. Assessing the Legal and Regulatory Environment for Credit Derivatives. Paper Presented at the ABA Annual Meeting, Section of Business Law, Commercial Financial Services Forum: A Structured Finance Trio (August).

Coudert, V., and M. Gex. 2010. The Credit Default Swap Market and the Settlement of Large Defaults. *Economie Internationale* 3 (123).

Culp, C.L. 2013. Syndicated Leveraged Loans During and After the Crisis and the Role of the Shadow Banking System. *Journal of Applied Corporate Finance* 25 (2) (Spring).

Culp, C.L. 2018. A Review of the Academic Literature on the Causes and Evolution of the Credit Crisis. *Johns Hopkins Institute for Applied Economics, Global Health, and the Study of Business Enterprise—Studies in Applied Finance* (24) (April).

Culp, C.L., and J.P. Forrester. 2013. U.S. Structured Finance Markets: Recent Recovery, Post-Crisis Developments, and Ongoing Regulatory Uncertainties. *Journal of Structured Finance* 18 (4) (Winter).

Culp, C.L., and J.P. Forrester. 2015. Have Pre-Crisis Levels of Risk Returned in U.S. Structured Products? Evidence from U.S. Subprime Auto ABS, CLOs, and Insurance-Linked Securities Markets. *Journal of Structured Finance* 21 (1) (Spring).

Das, U.S., M.G. Papaioannou, and C. Trebesch. 2012. Sovereign Debt Restructurings 1950–2010: Literature Survey, Data, and Stylized Facts. IMF Working Paper WP/12/203 (August).

Gupta, S., and R.K. Sundaram. 2015a. Inventory Effects, the Winner's Curse, and Bid Shading in Credit Default Swap Auction Outcomes. *Journal of Derivatives* 23 (2) (Winter).

Gupta, S., and R.K. Sundaram. 2015b. Mispricing and Arbitrage in CDS Auctions. *Journal of Derivatives* 22 (4) (Summer).

Helwege, J., S. Maurer, A. Sarkar, and Y. Wang. 2009. Credit Default Swap Auctions. Federal Reserve Bank of New York Staff Report No. 372 (May).

Lieu, A. 2011. An Analysis of Credit Default Swap Auctions and Distressed Bond Markets. Working Paper (April).

Longstaff, F.A., J. Pan, L.H. Pedersen, and K.J. Singleton. 2011. How Sovereign Is Sovereign Credit Risk? *American Economic Journal: Macroeconomics* 3 (2) (April).

Pan, J., and K.J. Singleton. 2008. Default and Recovery Implicit in the Term Structure of Sovereign CDS Spreads. *Journal of Finance* 63 (5) (October).

Pollack, E.R. 2003. Assessing the Usage and Effect of Credit Derivatives. Paper Presented to Harvard Law School International Finance Seminar (April).

Zettelmeyer, J., C. Trebesch, and M. Gulati. 2013. The Greek Debt Restructuring: An Autopsy. *Economic Policy* 28 (75) (July).

CHAPTER 3

Loan-Only CDSs

Prior to 2006, firms that wished to buy or sell credit protection on loans (as opposed to debt securities) made by reference entities used traditional single-name CDSs. For lenders wishing to manage the credit risk of actual loans to reference entities, however, purchasing protection on loan exposures with single-name CDSs gave rise to certain basis risks, especially for "leveraged loans" to below investment-grade borrowers. For example, high-yield ("HY") debt securities are generally unsecured, whereas typical leveraged loans are senior secured instruments with much higher recovery rates than HY debt. Hedging a leveraged loan exposure with a traditional single-name CDS based on deliverable HY bond obligations thus gave rise to potentially large basis risks resulting from (among other things) different recovery rates in the bonds deliverable into the CDS vis-à-vis the leveraged loans being hedged.

In June 2006, ISDA first introduced a master agreement for the documentation of loan-only CDSs. Like traditional single-name CDSs, LCDSs are also single-name CDS products based on a single reference entity. Unlike CDSs, however, LCDSs are specifically tailored to the loan facilities and obligations of the reference entities underlying those LCDSs.

Since the introduction of the ISDA LCDS template, LCDS markets in the USA and Europe have never accounted for a significant proportion of notional amounts outstanding or trading volume in the global CDS marketplace. (see Fig. 1.3). Not surprisingly, the empirical academic literature surveyed in Part III of this book contains only a handful

C. L. Culp et al., *Credit Default Swaps*, Palgrave Studies in Risk and Insurance, https://doi.org/10.1007/978-3-319-93076-3_3

of articles that use LCDSs as the basis for empirical studies of CDSs. Nevertheless, LCDSs have a "cult following"—mainly by participants in the leveraged loan market (both lenders/investors and borrowers)—and thus warrant some discussion.

Most LCDSs are based on broadly syndicated leveraged commercial and industrial ("C&I") loans. We thus begin this chapter in Sect. 3.1 with a review of the syndicated leveraged loan market, its primary financial instruments, and the evolution of certain of those into a relatively commoditized market. Section 3.1 provides a background for the discussion in Sect. 3.2 of this chapter of how certain terms of single-name LCDSs differ materially from single-name CDSs as discussed in Chapter 2. In addition, Sect. 3.1 provides background for certain discussions of the empirical academic literature in Part III—not because studies are based on LCDSs, but rather because many research papers (especially in Chapter 10) are based on bank loans, syndications, and other concepts defined in Sect. 3.1 below.

3.1 The Syndicated Leveraged Loan Market

The leveraged finance market includes borrowings by below investment-grade corporations or borrowing instruments (bonds or loans) that are themselves rated below investment-grade. In the nomenclature of credit rating agencies Standard and Poor's ("S&P"), Moody's Investors Services ("Moody's"), and Fitch Ratings ("Fitch"), HY bonds and leveraged loans or their issuers are considered as part of the leveraged finance market if they are rated no higher than BB+, Ba1, or BB+, respectively.

Leveraged financings in the bond market involve the issuance of HY debt (f.k.a. "junk bonds"), which may be senior or subordinated and are generally unsecured. In contrast, a leveraged loan is a loan—usually senior and secured—made to a corporation that has a below investment-grade credit rating or a loan-specific rating of below investment-grade. Leveraged loans are generally used to finance mergers and acquisitions, leveraged buyouts ("LBOs"), debt restructurings, and other highly leveraged transactions.

Figure 3.1 shows the total issuance of US HY bonds and leveraged loans from 1993 through end-September 2017. Annual loan issuance is shown on the left-hand *y*-axis in billions of dollars, where the dark-shaded bars reflect leveraged loan issuance and the lighter-shaded bars indicate HY bond issuance. The dashed black line corresponds to the

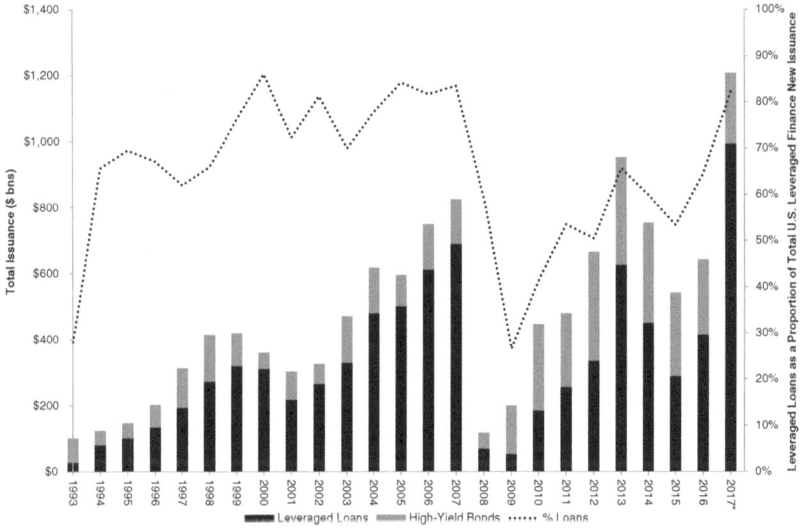

Fig. 3.1 US leveraged financings, 1993–2017 (*Note* *2017 data is through end September 2017. *Source* Thomson Reuters LPC)

right-hand *y*-axis, which indicates the annual percentage of US leverage financings raised through leveraged loans (as opposed to HY bonds). In all but three of the 25 years shown in Fig. 3.1 (i.e., 1993, 2009, and 2010), leveraged loans accounted for more than 50% of US leveraged financings. In six of the 25 years shown in Fig. 3.1, moreover, leveraged loans represented over 80% of the total US leveraged finance market.

3.1.1 Syndication and Loan Facilities

Syndicated loans involve a group of bank lenders (known as a syndicate) that collectively agree to provide financing to a corporate borrower on common terms through a facility that is designed, structured, and administered by one or more arrangers and managed by a lead arranger. The process by which a newly funded leveraged loan is distributed to non-arranger syndicate members and/or outside investors is known as syndication. The syndication process is the equivalent of the "primary market" for the sale of C&I loans and loan participations.

Like the investment banking underwriting business model, the loan syndication business model is based on two different types of commitments between syndicates and borrowers. In firm-commitment syndication, the syndicate members guarantee to fund the loan to the borrower on the strength of its balance sheet and creditworthiness. If broad syndication of the loan is not possible by the closing date (e.g., because of insufficient demand), the syndicate members generally fund the loan and absorb the unsyndicated portion on their balance sheets, which they usually try to sell again later either in the secondary loan market or to an affiliated entity such as an asset-backed commercial paper conduit.[1] By contrast, in best-efforts syndication, the syndicate members may either refuse to fund the deal or substantially restructure it if their best efforts to syndicate the loan fail.

A "broadly syndicated" leveraged loan facility generally contains multiple types of loans or tranches and is usually inaccessible for small or middle-market borrowers. Loan facilities with tranches of $250 million or more are typically broadly syndicated to a number of banks (in contrast to directly originated loans from a single bank to a small or middle-market borrower). A broadly syndicated leveraged loan facility generally contains four significant components or tranches: asset-based revolving credit facilities, term loans, letter-of-credit facilities, and bridge loans (Miller 2007).

3.1.1.1 Revolving Credit Facilities

In the 1980s and early 1990s, leveraged loans extended by banks were primarily originated by arrangers and were syndicated on a "pro rata" basis. In other words, bank syndicate members agreed to accept a certain proportion of each loan tranche (including proportional interest and principal payments) in return for providing a ratable amount of the funding.

One of the main components of the pro rata portion of a syndicated leverage loan facility has historically been an asset-based revolving credit facility ("revolver"). A revolver or asset-based lending ("ABL") revolver functions like the corporate equivalent of a secured credit card. A borrower is charged a commitment fee on the entire limit on the ABL revolver's credit line, but the borrower only incurs interest on actual drawn amounts. Principal can be repaid on revolvers any time and can later be redrawn (perhaps multiple times) until the stated maturity date of the ABL revolving credit facility. Revolvers are usually senior and secured by the borrower's receivables or inventories.

In some cases, a syndicated leveraged loan facility may also include an unsecured line of credit which functions like a traditional (i.e., unsecured) credit card. Like an ABL revolver, a line of credit has a limit, a maturity date, a commitment fee, and an interest rate payable by the borrower on drawn outstanding balances. Lines of credit may be senior or junior and are unsecured. Interest rates on drawn balances by leveraged borrowers thus are typically considerably higher than interest rates on drawn senior, secured ABL revolver balances—so much so that unsecured lines of credit are often not included in syndicate leverage loan facilities.

3.1.1.2 Term Loans

Specifically, a senior secured loan with a fixed maturity date (usually six or seven years after closing) with periodic interest payment dates is known as a term loan. Interest on term loans is typically floating based on an interest rate index like LIBOR plus a credit spread that is fixed on the closing date. The proceeds of a term loan are usually drawn on the closing date and can be prepaid without penalty. Unlike revolvers, however, once a term loan is prepaid the proceeds cannot later be redrawn.[2]

In the 1980s and early 1990s, another significant pro rata tranche of typical syndicated leveraged loan facilities was the Term Loan A ("TLA"). TLAs are fixed-tenor term loans that were required to be fully drawn upon the closing of the loan facility, had periodic coupon payments (usually based on a fixed credit spread above a floating reference rate index like LIBOR), had no prepayment penalties, could not be redrawn if prepaid, and included often-aggressive principal amortization schedules.

Beginning in the early 1990s, syndicate members began to sell tranches of loans or loan participations to non-bank institutional investors. Such investors were primarily interested in loan tranches that were fully funded at closing, senior and secured, had medium-term fixed maturities, could not be redrawn if prepaid, and had bullet principal repayments at maturity with little or no principal amortization. As such, TLAs were of little interest to non-bank investors, largely because of their principal amortization schedules. Thus was born the Term Loan B ("TLB"), which has all of the characteristics desired by non-bank investors.[3] TLBs are the loan market analogues to senior, secured floating-rate bonds.

Term loans (especially from 2008 onwards) may also contain call protection provisions. Call protection specifies that borrowers cannot prepay the loan without penalty over a certain period of time. For example, a TLB with a one-year period of call protection and a 1% penalty rate can only be prepaid by the borrower in the first year of the loan if 101% of the principal is repaid. This example is typical. For the most part, call protection is usually for one year and includes a 1% penalty rate *if* call protection is included at all.

TLBs thus resemble coupon bonds with floating-rate coupons, seniority in capital structure, collateral based on some or all of the assets of the borrower, and possibly call protection analogous to callable bonds. Unlike TLAs, moreover, TLBs had little or no principal amortization and thus had much more predictable cash flows than TLAs.

TLBs and other tranches of a syndicated leveraged loan facility that are meant to be sold to non-bank investors (preferably through the primary syndication market, but also in the secondary market) are known as "institutional" leveraged loan tranches. Unlike pro rata tranches of leveraged loan facilities that are syndicated ratably to syndicate members but not sold to market participants outside the syndicate, institutional tranches of syndicated leveraged loan facilities are *not* intended to be retained by syndicate member lenders.

In other words, institutional tranches of syndicated leveraged loan facilities represent loans originated by bank syndicate members to leveraged borrowers that syndicate member banks do not wish to retain on their balance sheets and intend to sell to non-syndicate investors. TLBs and other institutional loan tranches are thus the originate-and-distribute ("O&D") component of syndicated leveraged loans, whereas pro rate tranches constitute the originate-and-hold ("O&H") segment—see Chapter 5 for further discussion of the O&D and O&H concepts.

3.1.1.3 Letters of Credit

A letter of credit ("L/C") is a financial guarantee made by a bank on behalf of the corporate borrower that the borrower can pledge to a third party as a performance guarantee on an obligation. If the borrower defaults on the obligation, the third-party obligee may draw on the L/C from the issuing bank to cover the defaulting borrower's payment obligation.[4] Many typical leveraged loan facilities include a senior secured

L/C facility in which the borrower can direct lenders to post L/Cs with the borrower's obligees.

L/C facilities are difficult to syndicate to non-banks and thus are typically pro rata tranches of a leveraged loan facility. In particular, many third parties have credit limits on banks that include any L/Cs posted by those banks on behalf of their borrowers. Third parties reliant on borrower L/Cs thus are reluctant to have the issuing bank sell its L/C obligations to another firm that might or might not be a bank and might or might not be equally creditworthy. In addition, third-party obligees of borrowers rely on being able to contact the L/C provider *quickly* to rectify non-payments by borrowers and thus dislike the possibility that they may need to track "who owns the L/C facility" across multiple potential banks or investors.

3.1.1.4 Bridge Loans

Leveraged financings by borrowers usually include a contemplated issuance of HY debt as a part of the leveraged transaction. Unlike leveraged loans, HY debt is often more time-consuming to market and issue. As such, syndicated leveraged loan facilities (especially when connected with explicit highly leveraged transactions like LBOs) usually contain a bridge loan tranche that is a relatively short-term loan facility intended to provide interim financing for borrowers until a HY bond issuance can be placed (the proceeds of which are used to retire the bridge loan).

Like term loans, bridge loans can typically be drawn only on the closing date for the facility and cannot be redrawn once repaid. Bridge loans often have tenors of at most one or two years, and the proceeds of bridge loans are intended to be repaid by the proceeds of a subsequent HY bond issuance. The terms of a bridge loan usually closely mimic the planned terms of the future HY bond offering. If a bridge loan matures and the borrower has not yet successfully issued HY debt, the bridge loan generally converts into a TLB, often at a higher interest rate.

For example, suppose a \$100 million one-year bridge loan is included in a syndicated leveraged loan facility with an interest rate of 250 basis points ("bps") above three-month LIBOR. The bridge loan is intended to cover the one year it could take to arrange a \$100 million HY debt offering on substantially similar terms. If the planned \$100 million HY bond issuance has not occurred within one year, the bridge loan might convert to a six-year \$100 million TLB with a coupon rate of 300bps over three-month LIBOR. Once the intended \$100 million HY debt issuance is successfully offered to the market, the $100 million in issuance proceeds on that debt will be used to prepay the new TLB.

Although not as common as TLBs, bridge loans are sufficiently standardized and bond-like, so that bridge loan tranches may be institutional tranches that are sold to third parties (as well as syndicate members).

3.1.2 *The Commoditization of the Leveraged Loan Market*

In the 1990s, the leveraged loan market experienced significant increases in standardization and commoditization that fostered growing liquidity and secondary market trading (i.e., the trading of loans or loan participations after the initial syndication). In 1995, the Loan Syndications and Trading Association ("LSTA") was formed as a trade association dedicated to advancing the efficiency and liquidity of the floating-rate corporate loan asset class. LSTA has been for the leveraged loan market what ISDA has been for the over-the-counter derivatives market. Some of the significant contributions of the LSTA to the commoditization of the leveraged loan market include the creation of a pricing service for marking secondary loans to market, the development of standardized documentation for loan-related transactions, the promulgation of a Code of Conduct, the creation (with S&P) of the S&P/LSTA Leveraged Loan Index, and facilitating the assignments of CUSIPs (a unique nine-character alphanumeric code to identify securities) to loan tranches.

The commoditization of the institutional tranches of leveraged loan facilities was also greatly facilitated by the introduction of explicit credit ratings for institutional loan tranches. S&P began to rate institutional loan tranches in 1996, and the proportion of leveraged loans rated by the rating agencies has increased steadily since then.

Following the Asian crisis of 1997 and the Russian ruble crisis of 1998, leveraged loan market participants also began to change the way that institutional loans were sold. Prior to 1998, arrangers of leveraged loans engaged in "price talk" with potential investors and then priced the various loan facilities based on a credit spread and fees that arrangers believed would clear the market. If the credit spread was too high, the syndication would be oversubscribed. If the credit spread was too low, the syndication would be undersubscribed and arrangers would either be left with undesirably large holdings (in firm-commitment syndications) or the loan syndication would fail (in best-efforts syndications).

Beginning in 1998, loan commitment letters began to include the possibility for arrangers to use "market flex" in loan syndications involving institutional loan tranches. In a typical market-flex arrangement, syndicate members may change the credit spread over LIBOR that borrowers will ultimately pay to lenders in response to demand based on a specified range around the target interest rate on which the borrower agrees. "Upward flex" occurs when arrangers receive insufficient interest from investors at the target spread and the credit spread over LIBOR must be raised, and "downward flex" occurs when a loan is oversubscribed at the target spread and syndicate members can reduce the spread paid by borrowers in consequence. Standard market-flex language in loan commitment letters also permits arrangers to shift loan amounts between the tranches (say, by reducing the size of the TLB and increasing the size of the TLA).

In addition, market participants in both the derivatives and syndicated leveraged loan markets began to develop a more standardized process for defining reference entities and their related loan obligations. Unlike debt securities, loan tranches do not have specific identifiers like CUSIPs, nor were all reference entities assigned a unique borrower identification code prior to 2009. In 2009, Markit Group began to promulgate a reference entity database ("RED") that defined standard reference obligations for reference entities with traded CDSs and LCDSs. The proliferation of the use of RED codes further facilitated the commoditization of leveraged loan markets.[5]

As a result of the above changes to the documentation, syndication process, and secondary market trading of leveraged loans (especially institutional tranches), the leveraged loan market experienced a significant increase in secondary market liquidity and standardization beginning in the late 1990s that led to a period of sustained growth and the replacement of HY bonds with leveraged loans as the main source of US leveraged finance (see Fig. 3.1). Prior to that point, non-bank investors faced significant challenges in becoming lenders to corporations on C&I loans. But as the leveraged loan market commoditized, the traditional O&H banking model of originating C&I loans and holding them to maturity rapidly gave way to an increasingly successful O&D model. As a result, leveraged loans became increasingly integrated and dependent upon non-bank institutional investors in the so-called non-bank shadow banking system (Culp 2013; Culp and Forrester 2013, 2015; Culp and Neves 2017).

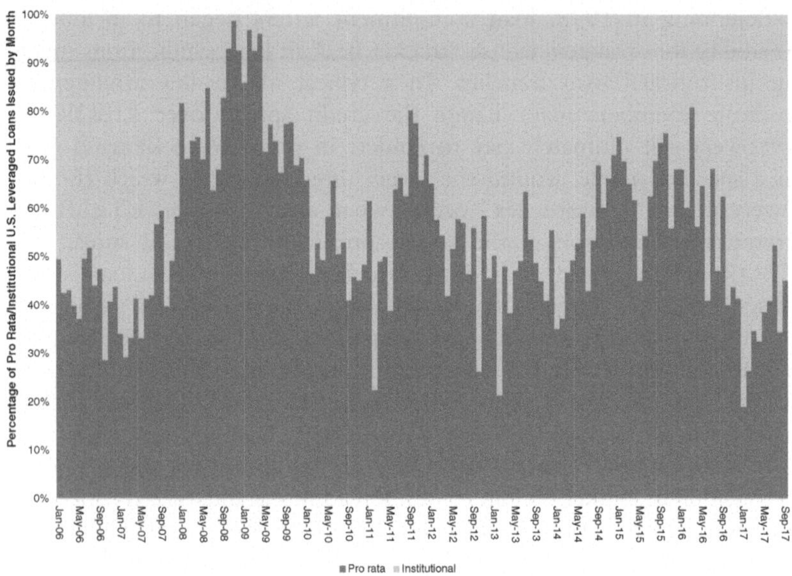

Fig. 3.2 Pro Rata vs. Institutional US leveraged loan issuance, 01/2006–09/2017 (*Source* Thomson Reuters LPC)

Figure 3.2 presents the monthly proportion of total US leveraged loan issuance for pro rata and institutional syndicated leveraged loan tranches from 2006 through end-September 2017. Before disruptions in US subprime mortgage and mortgage-related ABS markets began to impact leveraged finance markets in the summer of 2007, most months shown in Fig. 3.2 demonstrate that more than half of new US leveraged loan tranches were institutional. From late 2007 through 2009 (as discussed further below), institutional issuance of US leveraged loans contracted sharply, and, as Fig. 3.2 demonstrates leveraged lending by syndicate members on pro rata facilities took up the slack during that period when institutional syndicated leverage loan tranche issuance virtually disappeared. In more recent periods, non-banks and non-syndicate purchasers of leveraged loan tranches (especially TLBs) once again account for the majority of funds provided to leveraged borrowers.

3.2 Distinctions Between LCDSs and CDSs

As discussed earlier, prior to the introduction of ISDA's LCDS documentation in 2006, credit protection sellers and purchasers focused on loan-specific obligations of reference entities used single-name CDS contract documentation for any desired loan-only credit protection purchases and sales. That led to various complications, including the following: basis risk arising from hedging a loan exposure with a traditional CDS priced to CTD bonds with different seniorities, coupons, and recovery rates; problems with being potentially unable to provide an eligible deliverable obligation to settle a physically or auction-settled CDSs; mismatches between traditional CDS with fixed tenors and notional amounts with loan prepayments; and more.

Beginning with the introduction of the LCDS ISDA documentation in 2006, such firms had an alternative to traditional single-name CDSs that address most of these problems. LCDSs are conceptually similar to single-name CDSs in many ways: both are single-name CDSs based on individual reference entities; both have coupon rates that are fixed at the inception of the contracts; and both are triggered by specific credit events occurring at the underlying reference entity. The important distinctions between single-name CDSs and LCDSs are discussed in the sections below.

3.2.1 Triggering Credit Events

Like single-name CDSs based on bonds issued by reference names, LCDSs are triggered by most of the same credit events specified in the corresponding ISDA *Definitions*. Those triggering credit events include the insolvency of the reference entity and a failure to pay (generally on obligations of $1 million or more) by the reference entity on its direct and guaranteed obligations (including loans, as well as bonds). Unlike single-name CDSs, however, LCDSs on US reference names are *not* triggered by restructuring events, whereas LCDSs on E.U. reference entities *are* triggered by restructurings.

In addition, following the 2009 Standardization Initiatives, the 2010 revised ISDA LCDS documentation distinguishes between "succession" and "refinancing" events. Under the *2003 Definitions*, if a succession event occurs (e.g., merger, spin-off, consolidation, amalgamation, etc.), the new reference entity replaces the original reference entity underlying an LCDS contract. Such events did not always apply to related refinancings—e.g., if a new entity drew down a referenced loan in order to pay down a corresponding loan outstanding at the previous reference entity, then the underlying reference loan need not be replaced.

Under the revised 2010 LCDS definitions, a "refinancing event" includes the following: (i) a refinancing that redeems, repays, or otherwise discharges all or any portion of the original reference entity's obligations under the LCDS using the proceeds of new loan drawdowns or the issuance of bonds that is not an affiliate of the reference entity; (ii) a refinancing in which all or part of the original obligations have been redeemed, repaid, discharged in full, or in which the assets securing the original obligations have been repurchased through the proceeds from drawdowns on new loans or the issuance of bonds that is not an affiliate of the reference entity; (iii) repayments or discharges of obligations that cease to secure outstanding obligations and instead secure new financings; (iv) a refinancing in which the reference entity is no longer an obligor to the previous entity and where all original obligations are replaced with different obligors; and (v) any other refinancing that has similar effects as in (i)–(iv) in which the redemption or original loans are not financed by the original reference entity (Schulte Roth & Zabel, LLP 2010).

In addition, the revised ISDA documentation requires that a law firm (not an ISDA DC) must determine whether a succession or refinancing event has occurred. Table B.2 in Appendix B summarizes single-name LCDS determination events from March 2009 through December 2017.

3.2.2 *Coupon/Spread*

Under the original ISDA master agreement for LCDSs published in June 2006 as well as ISDA's amended documentation for LCDSs published in May 2007, payments between LCDS counterparties were based entirely on privately negotiated, bilateral terms. The protection purchaser paid a coupon or spread payment periodically (usually quarterly) to the protection seller that was contractually fixed on the LCDS trade date. In return, the protection seller had a contingent liability (see Sect. 3.2.3) to the protection purchaser following the occurrence of a credit event at the underlying reference entity.

Alternatively, in some cases, the credit protection purchaser would pay a cash amount based on an up-front spread based on the difference between a standardized coupon rate and the actual mark-to-market credit spread for the underlying reference entity. Thereafter, the protection purchaser would pay a "running spread" to account for changes in the mark-to-market value of the credit protection purchase vis-à-vis the initial fixed spread.

More specifically, following the 2009 Standardization Initiatives, LCDSs—like standard single-name CDSs—began to trade with standardized coupons. For North American reference entities, those standard coupons were 100, 250, and 500 basis points above the reference floating rate (e.g., LIBOR). Protection purchasers thus were required to pay points up front to compensate protection sellers (or vice versa) for any up-front differences between standard coupon rates and market-based coupon rates. This 2009 change in market practices resulted in virtually all LCDSs being written based on standardized coupons with an up-front payment and periodic marking to market to the then-current coupon rate.

In addition, some market participants began to execute zero-coupon LCDSs in which counterparties chose to make upfront cash payments in lieu of any interim coupon payments. In such cases, protection purchasers paid protection sellers an upfront payment based on standardized coupon rates and a recovery rate assumption over the expected life of the swap (Schulte Roth & Zabel, LLP 2010).

3.2.3 Deliverable Obligations and Settlement Methods

Under the original 2006 ISDA LCDS master agreement, LCDSs could be settled either physically or in cash. In a physically settled LCDS, the protection purchaser is obliged to deliver an eligible senior secured first-lien loan to the protection seller with a par amount equal to the notional amount of the LCDS, in exchange for which the protection purchaser would receive a cash payment from the protection seller equal to the notional amount of the loan/CDS. In a cash-settled LCDS, by contrast, the protection seller need not own nor deliver an eligible loan and would receive a cash payment equal to the notional amount of the LCDS minus the "market price" of the underlying loan tranche outstanding at the reference entity borrower.

Like single-name CDSs, loan-only CDSs have cash flows and values that are derived from a single reference entity. In contrast to single-name CDSs, however, LCDSs typically have deliverable obligations or cash-equivalent valuations based *only* on certain loan facility tranches. Eligible loans for delivery/settlement are limited to senior secured first-lien loans outstanding at the reference entity borrower as determined by a poll of LCDS dealers. The polls are administered by Markit Group, and Markit provides a list of all reference names and corresponding deliverable obligations through its "Syndicated Secured List." Markit also provides a list of substitute deliverable reference obligations.

Although most LCDSs are based on TLB tranches, other tranches can be and have been included in LCDS deliverable obligations. For example, the LCDS auction pursuant to the 2015 credit event at Caesar's Entertainment Operating Company, Inc., included an approximate total of \$5.345 billion in four TLB tranches and about \$100.3 million in a revolver tranche as eligible deliverable obligations into triggered LCDSs.[6] Similarly, the LCDS auction pursuant to July 1, 2009, default date of Lear Corporation included one \$1bn term loan and two tranches of revolvers with \$821.7 million and \$467.5 million limits, respectively.[7]

In the May 2007 amended master agreement for LCDSs, ISDA specified auction settlement as a hard-wired default settlement method following the occurrence of a credit event (see Sect. 2.1.5.3 in Chapter 2). For counterparties opting into LCDS default protocols, LCDS settlement obligations from protection sellers to protection purchasers are based on the notional amount of the LCDS less the auction-based price of the underlying deliverable loan obligation. Counterparties in LCDSs, however, may still opt for physical settlement through assignments of LCDSs or indirect participation in LCDS auctions, as well as by opting out of the default protocol.

For LCDSs in which counterparties opt for physical settlements, such settlements are typically governed by a "Physical Settlement Rider" and "Market Standard Indemnity" amendment to the LCDS confirmation, both of which are published by the LSTA. Under the Physical Settlement Rider, both counterparties agree to standardized settlement timelines on a non-negotiable basis. Under the Market Standard Indemnity amendment to LCDS conformations, counterparties agree to accept underlying loan documentation on the assumption that it is market-standard documentation and thus incorporates any non-LSTA credit-specific provisions that are otherwise consistent with market-standard loan documentation (Grady 2007). The routine attachment of LSTA's two documentation supplements to the standard ISDA LCDS master agreement and confirmations is yet another example of LSTA's effort to commoditize and integrate syndicated leveraged loan markets with related LCDS markets.

3.2.4 Early Terminations and Bullet LCDSs

3.2.4.1 Pre-2010 Legacy LCDSs

Most LCDSs reference the term loan tranches of corresponding syndicated leveraged loan facilities. As discussed in Sect. 3.1 of this chapter, term loans can generally be prepaid without penalty and, in practice, often are prepaid without penalties or call protection.

Traditional single-name CDSs are non cancellable and have constant notional principal amounts. As a result, hedging a TLA or TLB with a single-name CDS exposes a hedger to significant basis risk—i.e., as the underlying term loan amortizes or prepays, the protection buyer becomes over-hedged vis-à-vis the underlying loan. To help mitigate this basis risk, LCDSs used to include cancellation provisions that permit protection purchasers to extinguish their outstanding LCDSs under certain circumstances. In the event of a cancellation, no cash flows are exchanged between the protection purchaser and seller apart from accrued premium from the last coupon payment date through the date of the cancellation.

Legacy LCDSs based on US reference entities were subject to a substitution clause that limited the ability of purchasers to terminate their open LCDSs prior to maturity. Specifically, following significant paydowns of all underlying deliverable obligations on Markit's Syndicated Secured List, Markit updated its poll of dealers to ascertain whether appropriate replacement loans are available, and, if so, the underlying deliverable obligations for the corresponding LCDS contracts were revised to include such substitutes as the relevant deliverable obligations. If not, the LCDSs could be cancelled. In the E.U., by contrast, LCDSs generally could be paid down after material prepayments of all underlying deliverable reference loans regardless of any attempt to replace the paid-down loan tranche with a substitute (Duncan 2006).

3.2.4.2 Post-2010 and Bullet LCDSs

Following the implementation of the 2009 Standardization Initiatives, LCDSs based on North American reference names are no longer cancellable. Instead, the original legacy LCDS documentation template was replaced with a new documentation templated for so-called Bullet LCDSs.[8] As discussed in the previous section, legacy LCDSs in the US permitted either party to terminate the LCDS agreement if no deliverable loan tranches had been available for delivery in the previous 30 days.

Based on the uncertainty associated with when borrowers would prepay their loans, many market participants complained that the early termination feature of legacy LCDSs was too difficult to value and led to reduced liquidity. As a result, the new Bullet LCDS documentation (published by ISDA in April 2010) disallows early terminations and specifies single maturities for bullet principal repayments regardless of the underlying loans.[9] In other words, Bullet LCDSs remain outstanding with the same original notional amount until the expiration of the LCDS, regardless of whether or not any deliverable loan tranches remain outstanding. (Schulte Roth & Zabel, LLP 2010)

Notes

1. Loan commitment letterssometimes contain a material adverse change ("MAC") clause that lets banks escape their commitment to fund the loan if conditions in the loan syndication market have deteriorated significantly. Such "Market MAC" clauses are distinct from (and less common than) traditional credit MAC clauses that are based on unexpected deteriorations in the financial conditions of borrowers. Unless Market MAC clauses contain precise definitions; however, they often just serve as an invitation for disputes or litigation.
2. Some leveraged loan facilities also include a delayed-draw term loan, which is a term loan used to finance acquisitions or asset/equipment purchases (and hence which are often known as acquisition/equipment lines).
3. Leveraged loan facilities may have multiple institutional TLB tranches. In some cases, they are referred to as different numbered tranches of the TLB (e.g., TBL-1, TLB-2, and TLB-3), whereas in other facilities, they are called TLB, TLC, TLD, etc.
4. Upon the drawdown of an L/C by an obligee of the borrower, the provider of the L/C enjoys the equivalent of "subrogation rights"—i.e., the issuer of the L/C (and not the borrower on whose behalf the L/C has been written) is entitled to recovery rights from the obligee.

5. See, e.g., Markit Group Ltd., *Markit RED: A Primer* (May 2009).
6. ISDA, *2015 Caesars Entertainment Operating Company, Inc.: First Lien Loans LCDS and Bullet LCDS Auction Settlement Terms* (February 17, 2015).
7. ISDA, *LCDS Auction Settlement Terms for Lear Corporation First Lien Loans* (July 17, 2009).
8. J. Lu and J. Grady, "Bullet LCDs: A New Direction for the U.S. Loan Credit Default Swap Product," *Richards Kibbe & Orbe LLP* (June 24, 2010).
9. ISDA, *Bullet Syndicated Secured Loan Credit Default Swap: Standard Terms Supplement* (April 5, 2010).

References

Culp, C.L. 2013. Syndicated Leveraged Loans During and After the Crisis and the Role of the Shadow Banking System. *Journal of Applied Corporate Finance* 25 (2) (Spring).

Culp, C.L., and J.P. Forrester. 2013. U.S. Structured Finance Markets: Recent Recovery, Post-Crisis Developments, and Ongoing Regulatory Uncertainties. *Journal of Structured Finance* 18 (4) (Winter).

Culp, C.L., and J.P. Forrester. 2015. Post-Crisis Developments in U.S. Leveraged Loans and CLOs. *BNA's Banking Report* (August 24).

Culp, C.L., and A.M.P. Neves. 2017. Shadow Banking, Risk Transfer, and Financial Stability. *Journal of Applied Corporate Finance* 29 (4) (Fall).

Duncan, A. 2006. Loan-Only Credit Default Swaps: The March to Liquidity. *Commercial Lending Review* (September–October).

Grady, J. 2007. Introduction to U.S. LCDS and LCDX. *Advanced Swaps & Other Derivatives in 2007.* New York, NY: Practising Law Institute.

Miller, S. 2007. Basic Loan Structures. In *The Handbook of Loan Syndications and Trading*, ed. A. Taylor and A. Sansone. New York: McGraw-Hill.

Schulte Roth & Zabel, LLP. 2010. ISDA Publishes New Bullet LCDS Documentation. *Alert* (April 8).

CHAPTER 4

Multi-Name and Index CDSs

Whereas Chapters 2 and 3 focused on CDS products based on single reference names, in this chapter we explore the mechanics of multi-name CDSs, which derive their value from the creditworthiness of two or more reference entities. These multi-name CDSs include portfolio and basket CDSs, index CDSs, and tranched index CDSs. Some of these CDS products are essentially similar to single-name CDSs—apart from the fact that the underlying is a reference portfolio or index comprised of multiple entities—whereas other multi-name CDSs depend significantly on the correlations between prospective defaults of the underlying reference names.

4.1 Portfolio and Basket Multi-Name CDSs

4.1.1 Portfolio CDSs

The most basic type of multi-name CDS is a whole portfolio CDS ("portfolio CDS") that functions almost exactly like a single-name CDS except that the protection buyer is covered if *any or all* reference names in the underlying reference portfolio experience a credit event. For example, if an asset manager owns 100 bonds and seeks to hedge the risk of incurring credit-related losses on any or all 100 bonds, it can (i) enter into 100 distinct single-name CDSs on all 100 reference entities, or (ii) execute a single multi-name portfolio CDS based on the 100 reference names that issued the 100 bonds. Despite the obvious need for the two

C. L. Culp et al., *Credit Default Swaps*, Palgrave Studies in Risk and Insurance, https://doi.org/10.1007/978-3-319-93076-3_4

strategies to be sufficiently similar to avoid obvious arbitrage opportunities, there are some important mechanical differences between strategies (i) and (ii).

4.1.1.1 Coverage Period

One of the differences between a portfolio CDS and a single-name CDS is that the portfolio CDS is not extinguished upon the occurrence of a credit event at a single reference entity, whereas the single-name CDS is. For a CDS constructed to provide protection on a whole portfolio, it would be nonsensical for the transaction to terminate after the occurrence of just one event. Instead, coverage for the specific reference entity that has experienced a credit event terminates under the portfolio CDS (and the notional amount of the portfolio CDS is reduced accordingly), but protection coverage remains ongoing and in force for all other reference entities that have not experienced a credit event to date.

In other words, to ensure that strategies (i) and (ii) defined above do not create obvious arbitrage opportunities, the occurrence of a credit event at a reference entity underlying a portfolio CDS (as in strategy (ii)) is generally treated the same way (in the context of triggering credit events) as if the protection purchaser of all reference entities in the reference portfolio had purchased protection through 100 individual constituent single-name CDSs.

4.1.1.2 Settlement Mechanisms

The somewhat obvious problem of settling portfolio CDSs based on auction protocols is the difficulty of unbundling individual underlying reference entity credit events from the whole portfolio. Especially because the occurrence of a credit event at a single reference portfolio constituent does not trigger the extinguishment of the entire portfolio CDS, auctions are essentially intractable, as are physical settlements on individual reference entities that are constituents of the CDS portfolio. Settlements pursuant to credit events on portfolio CDSs thus are typically in cash and resemble pay-as-you-go settlements (as discussed in Chapter 5) except that portfolio CDS cash settlements are generally one way from protection sellers to purchasers. The total notional amount of the portfolio CDS is then reduced by the par amount of the defaulting reference name.

4.1.1.3 Costs of Portfolio CDSs—the Whole Versus the Sum of the Parts

Portfolio CDSs provide comprehensive credit risk transfer for owners of whole portfolios of credit-sensitive assets wishing to hedge the credit risks of each constituent reference name in the portfolio, but, not surprisingly, they are relatively expensive. Firms wishing to hedge the credit risk of an entire portfolio or take a position on that same reference portfolio, after all, are free to go into the market and purchase individual single-name CDSs on all the reference names of interest. A market participant that wants to purchase full credit protection on a specific portfolio through a single bespoke whole portfolio CDS usually has one of two objectives in mind: (i) The credit protection purchaser lacks the operational capability or acumen to purchase each constituent CDS on its own and values the "bundling services" provided by the protection seller in a whole portfolio CDS; or (ii) single-name CDSs are not traded or are too illiquid on some (perhaps many) of the constituent reference names and the protection buyer thus needs a dealer to bundle the liquid and illiquid names together in the same risk-transfer agreement.

In either case, the protection seller is unlikely to want to retain the risk of the portfolio protection sale and thus will either purchase offsetting single-name CDSs or hedge its protection exposure in the cash bond, repo, or loan market. Regardless, the result will almost always be a higher cost for the protection purchaser. Not surprisingly, portfolio CDSs thus are relatively uncommon, bespoke, and customized transactions designed to meet the specific needs of particular protection purchasers that are willing to pay a premium for bundled protection.

Indeed, in many situations, if a protection purchaser (seller) wants a short (long) position in an entire portfolio of reference names, the firm will opt to use a total return swap ("TRS") in lieu of a portfolio CDS. A total return swap is a non-CDS type of credit derivatives contract that differs from a portfolio CDS in two important ways: (i) on a gross cash flow basis, both legs of a TRS include a financing component (e.g., LIBOR) and (ii) the credit protection purchaser and seller agree to two-way payments in which the protection purchaser is reimbursed by the protection seller for declines in the reference portfolio value (measured in some objective manner on which both parties agree) ***and*** the protection seller is paid by the protection purchaser for any increases in the reference portfolio value (Culp and Neves 1998a, b).

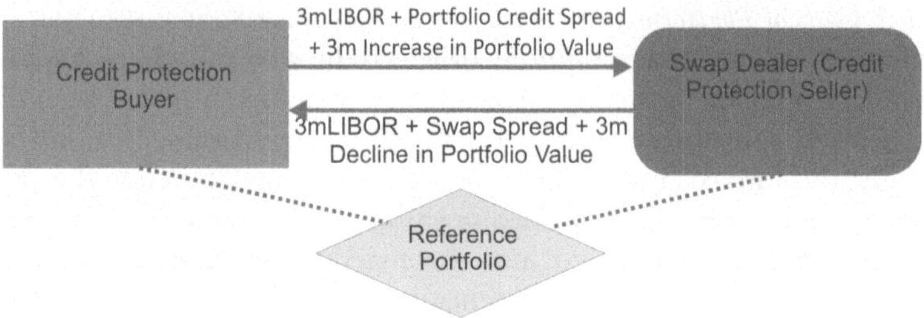

Fig. 4.1 Total return swap with quarterly settlements

Figure 4.1 illustrates the typical periodic (e.g., quarterly) cash flows on a TRS with a financing reference index of 3mLIBOR. The credit protection purchaser owes payments to the protection buyer every quarter equal to the notional amount of the transaction multiplied by 3mLIBOR plus the portfolio credit spread (e.g., the weighted-average coupon income on the assets in the reference portfolio) plus any increase in the market value of the portfolio over the previous three months. Conversely, the protection seller must make quarterly payments to the protection purchaser with a value equal to the notional amount of the TRS multiplied by 3mLIBOR plus the TRS spread (fixed at the inception of the transaction) plus any declines in the market value of the reference portfolio over the previous three months.

If an asset originator or manager owns a reference portfolio of assets and wishes to divest its economic exposure to both the risk and return of that portfolio, a TRS accomplishes that. A portfolio CDS, by contrast, enables the owner of a credit-sensitive asset portfolio to purchase default protection without having to surrender potential increases in the value of the portfolio. Yet, many market participants wishing to transfer *all* of the credit risk of a particular portfolio are content to surrender the potential upside, as well, if a net cost savings can be realized. Although a TRS on a given reference portfolio is more expensive than purchases of individual single-name CDSs on each constituent name in the reference portfolio, a TRS is likely to be cheaper than a whole portfolio CDS because the protection purchaser is giving up the profit potential on the portfolio, whereas the portfolio CDS protection purchaser is not.

4.1.2 *Nth-to-Default Basket CDSs*

For risk managers and correlation traders, one way to reduce the premium cost of multi-name CDS protection is to enter into contracts with multi-name reference portfolios that only pay off to credit protection purchasers in specific scenarios. Instead of buying full credit protection on all reference names in the reference portfolio, the credit protection purchaser in more stylized multi-name basket CDSs can purchase protection more selectively at a cost that is below full protection on credit events occurring at all entities in the reference portfolio.

One popular structured multi-name basket CDS is an *Nth-to-Default* CDS, which can significantly facilitate hedgers' and speculators' desires to enter into a transaction based on a given multi-name reference portfolio with a more tailored payoff structure and a reduced premium. Specifically, in such a transaction, the credit protection purchaser receives compensation (via physical or cash settlement) upon the occurrence of the *Nth* credit event in the underlying reference entity basket.

Perhaps the most common *Nth-to-Default* Basket CDS is a *First-to-Default* ("FTD") basket CDS, which requires the protection seller to compensate the protection purchaser for the first reference entity's default in the reference portfolio. After the first default of *any* name in the reference entity portfolio, the contract is extinguished; the protection seller provides no ongoing protection, nor does the protection buyer owe any subsequent premium payments. These types of multi-name CDSs are useful when a firm hedging or speculating on a credit portfolio *expects* one default but is not sure which reference entity in the portfolio will be that first-defaulting reference name and thus cannot manage its risk by purchasing protection with a single-name CDS or LCDS based on a specific reference name.

More sophisticated applications of *Nth-to-Default* Basket CDSs than the simple FTD basket CDSs involve protection purchasers and sellers that have uncertainties about exactly how many reference entities might experience credit events in a portfolio without any *ex ante* expectations about the order in which particular name(s) in the reference portfolio will default. For example, consider a commercial bank with a portfolio of 100 loans with differing principal amounts to 100 distinct reference entity borrowers. The bank's risk manager may conclude that the *expected* (i.e., average) losses on the portfolio are based on the presumptive occurrence of a credit event on 10 of the 100 reference names in the portfolio. The bank thus sets aside loan-loss reserves and capital to cover the expected losses corresponding to credit events on 10 of the 100 loans in the reference portfolio (without knowing which of the 100 loans may default).

The bank in this example, however, may remain concerned about the potential for above-expected losses by an 11th borrower. Yet, it would be unnecessarily costly and inefficient from a regulatory capital standpoint for the bank to set aside the entire expected loss on the 11th marginal loan in the reference portfolio. So, instead, the bank could purchase credit protection using an *11th-to-Default* Basket CDS that compensates the lender for any losses arising from a credit event occurring at the 11th lender in the reference portfolio. That CDS pays the lender nothing for losses arising from the 1st through 10th defaults (which have already been reserved) or the 12th and additional defaults (which the lender considers improbable). But the swap enables the lender to manage the risk of the 11th reference name in the specified portfolio without incurring the costs of setting aside capital for a full loss reserve against the 11th reference name.

Apart from the above obvious applications of *Nth-to-Default* Basket CDSs as applications for risk management, these types of multi-name CDSs are also popular investments for market participants wishing to bet on the correlations of defaults within a specific reference portfolio (Lucas and Thomas 2003; O'Kane et al. 2003).

4.1.3 Excess-of-Loss Basket CDSs

Another variant of bespoke multi-name CDSs with tailored payoff profiles and lower premiums than whole-portfolio CDSs is an excess-of-loss ("XOL") basket CDS. In a typical XOL CDS, a reference portfolio is defined that consists of specific reference entities (and sometimes specific loans, bonds, and other assets). Most features of XOL CDSs are similar to those of single-name CDSs. The main differences are the triggers, payment amounts, and settlement mechanisms.

In particular, the trigger that determines when and how much XOL CDS protection sellers must compensate protection purchasers for XOL CDSs is based on the *cumulative losses* on the underlying reference portfolio. Whereas on *Nth*-to-Default CDSs, payments from credit protection sellers to purchasers are based on the specific loss (i.e., principal less actual/expected recovery) on the defaulting *Nth* reference obligation, payments by protection sellers to protection buyers on XOL CDSs are triggered by and based on total, aggregate losses on the underlying reference portfolio as a whole.

XOL CDSs are akin in XOL reinsurance contracts (Culp 2006). In a typical XOL CDS (or reinsurance) contract, the protection seller makes payments to the protection purchaser based on cumulative losses on a defined reference portfolio. Contractual payouts for such contracts are based on the following terms:

- The *attachment point* is the amount of cumulative losses on the reference portfolio that have been realized before the credit protection seller must begin to make payments to the protection purchaser;
- The *coverage amount* is the maximum payment amount owed by the credit protection seller to the protection buyer (akin to an insurance policy limit); and
- The *exhaustion point* is the amount of cumulative losses on the reference portfolio that has been realized when the credit protection seller is no longer obliged to make any additional payments.

Although CDSs are not insurance or reinsurance products because protection purchasers need not have an insurable interest in the reference portfolio (i.e., need not own any of the assets in the underlying reference portfolio), the attachment point can still be viewed as a type of risk retention or deductible for the protection purchaser. In other words, because the protection purchaser does not receive payments for losses on the reference portfolio from zero up to the attachment point, any realized losses in that "first-loss layer" are absorbed by the credit protection purchaser.

In typical XOL parlance, an *A* XS *B* CDS contract requires the credit protection seller to make payments of up to the coverage amount *A* once a total of *B* losses have been realized on the reference portfolio and the CDS has reached its attachment point. The exhaustion point for the CDS is $(A + B)$. For example, a 100 XS 500 credit protection agreement would reimburse the protection purchaser in an XOL CDS for any losses from \$500 million up to \$600 million, resulting in a coverage amount of \$100 million. The maximum potential \$100 million payout to credit protection purchasers thus is only triggered after at least \$500 million in losses on the reference portfolio have already been realized.

Figure 4.2 illustrates a hypothetical probability distribution of cumulative losses on a given reference portfolio (Panel (a)) and corresponding risk-based tranches (Panel (b)) that might be used to define several different XOL CDSs on this particular reference portfolio. For illustrative purposes, Panel (a) also indicates the ratings that might apply to each tranche based on a rating agency's estimates of the risks of losses on the reference portfolio corresponding to each tranche.

For the hypothetical reference portfolio and cumulative loss distribution depicted in Fig. 4.2, five risk-based tranches are shown. The riskiest tranche is the residual tranche, which is typically unrated and corresponds to the first-loss retention (i.e., deductible) that a protection purchaser might be required to retain if seeking to transfer the credit risk of an entire reference portfolio to one or more swap dealers using XOL CDSs (as discussed in Chapter 5). In the example, the first-loss risk retention is 10% of the value of the reference portfolio.[1] The two junior or mezzanine tranches in Fig. 4.2 correspond to the 5 XS 10 and 5 XS 15 cumulative loss layers. The senior tranche, in turn, corresponds to the 5 XS 20 cumulative loss layers.

Figure 4.2 also depicts a "super-senior" tranche corresponding to the 75 XS 25 cumulative loss layer. In the pre-crisis period from 2005

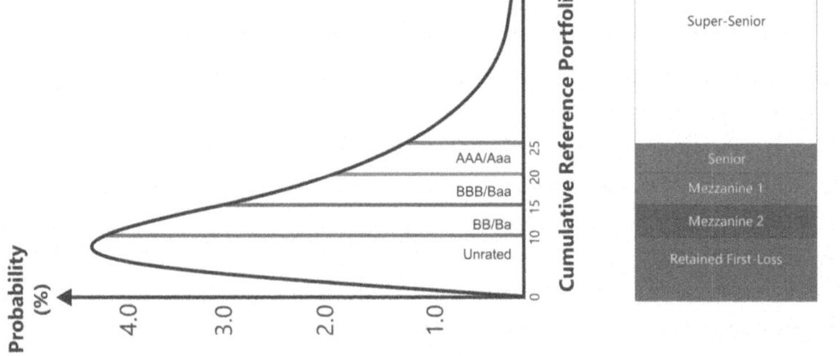

Fig. 4.2 Hypothetical loss distribution and risk-based tranches for XOL CDSs

through 2007, it was especially common for large dealer banks arranging structured products to provide super-senior XOL CDSs as protection on the lowest-risk (and, at the time, viewed as better than AAA/Aaa) portions of a reference portfolio. Specifically, a typical bank wishing to transfer the risk of a given reference loan portfolio might have entered into three XOL CDSs in this example: (i) a 10 XS 10 subordinated CDS to protect any losses in the two mezzanine tranches (possibly funded through the issuance of securities based on the credit quality of the assets in this tranche); (ii) a 5 XS 20 senior CDS to protect any losses in the senior tranche (again possibly funded by the issuance of securities); and (iii) a super-senior CDS based on the 75 XS 25 loss layer to provide catastrophic risk protection against cumulative losses on the reference portfolio of above 25%. The protection purchaser in this example would retain the first-loss 10 XS 0 layer and thus would absorb all losses from zero up to 10%.

As Chapter 5 explains in further detail, a protection purchaser likely would pre-fund the potential losses in the junior and senior tranches by issuing securities based on the credit risk of the two mezzanines and one senior tranche. Prior to the credit crisis, the super-senior XOL CDS was generally unfunded—i.e., not backed by a securitization and thus a general unsecured obligation of the protection seller. Protection purchases using XOL CDSs corresponding to this super-senior tranche cost only a few basis points prior to 2008, but the value of that protection was dependent on the creditworthiness of the super-senior CDS counterparties and their ability to post collateral to cover mark-to-market losses on super-senior CDSs.

4.2 Index CDSs

The multi-name CDSs discussed in the previous Sect. 4.1 are examples of bespoke credit risk transfer instruments that were designed to facilitate risk transfer on particular reference portfolios. In this section, we examine standardized credit risk transfer instruments in the form of index CDSs—i.e., CDSs with cash flows based on the value of an underlying index of the aggregate creditworthiness of multiple reference entities defined on a standardized basis.

Popular index CDS contracts are based on index values calculated and distributed by IHS Markit (f.k.a. Markit Group). Index CDS contracts available to trade using Markit's index values generally have common features, all of which are explained in the sections below.

4.2.1 *Underlying Reference Portfolios*

Each Markit index CDS specifies a portfolio of underlying reference entities based on the regional location of reference names included in the index, the relative risk and/or rating(s) of the reference entities, and the type of issuer (i.e., corporate, sovereign, and municipal). For each index, Markit specifies in detail the criteria that included reference names must satisfy. For example, the CDX.NA.IG Markit index is based on a reference portfolio including 125 of the most liquid investment-grade North American corporate reference entities, and the CDX.NA.HY index has a reference portfolio comprised of the 100 most liquid (in the single-name CDS market) North American corporate reference entities rated below investment-grade.[2] Table 4.1 summarizes the various reference portfolios and indices published by Markit that correspond to traded index CDS products.

In defining the reference portfolios underlying each index, Markit generally applies an equal weighting across reference entities. To ascertain the "most liquid" reference names, Markit creates a weekly liquidity list based on trades reported to the Depository Trust Clearing Corp.'s Swap Data Repository. Eligible reference names for inclusion in the index are drawn from the liquidity list subject to additional criteria.[3] Once all reference entities have been identified for inclusion in an index, Markit selects specific reference entities for inclusion in each index based on a well-defined set of selection criteria.

4.2.2 *Index Series and Roll Dates*

For all indices published by Markit to which index CDSs settle, the reference portfolios are redefined on discrete "roll dates" that occur every six months. On each roll date, a new series of the index is published based on the new reference portfolio. The various reference portfolios underlying each index are re-calibrated by Markit based on various factors, such as changes in the ratings of constituent reference entities.

Some indices roll on predetermined dates (e.g., the CDX.NA rolls every March and September), whereas other indices roll based on a determination by Markit from a poll of dealers in the index. The value of

Table 4.1 Markit indices available for index CDS trading

Underlying asset	*Type of issuer*	*Region*	*Markit index*	*Sub-indices*
Bonds	Sovereign	Global	iTraxx SovX	• Western Europe • CEEMEA[a] • G7[b] • Global Liquid IG[c]
	Corporate	Emerging Markets	CDX.EM	• EM Whole • EM Diversified
		North America	CDX.NA	• IG[c] • IG[c] High Volatility • Crossover[d] • HY[e]
		Europe	iTraxx Europe	• Main • High Volatility • Financials Sr and Sub • Non-Financials
		Asia	iTraxx Asia	• Japan Main • Japan High Volatility • Asia Ex-Japan IG[c] • Asia Ex-Japan HY[e] • Australia
	Municipal	USA	MCDX	
Loans	Corporate	USA	LCDX	
		Europe	iTraxx LevX	• Senior • Junior
ABS	SPE	USA	ABX	Subprime Home Equity Loans
			CMBX	Commercial Mortgage Loans

Notes [a]Central & Eastern Europe, Middle East, and Africa
[b]Canada, France, Germany, Italy, Japan, the UK, and the United States
[c]IG indicates investment-grade (rated BBB-/Baa3 or above)
[d]Crossover indicates reference entities with one investment-grade rating and one or more below-investment-grade ratings (or no ratings) across the three major credit rating agencies
[e]HY indicates high yield, below investment-grade
Source Chaplin (2010)

a new series on each roll date is based on the then-current CDS spreads that price the new series of the index to par.

The on-the-run ("OTR") series for a given index is the most recently listed index. Off-the-run ("OFTR") indices are indices that remain listed and calculated for CDS trading purposes but are based on older reference portfolios and par coupon rates. Most liquidity in index CDS trading is based on the OTR index, and OFTR indexed CDSs rapidly lose liquidity following the series rollovers that results in an old OTR index becoming the most recent OFTR index. Nevertheless, trading in the most recent OFTR index remains relatively vigorous for some time following the index series roll dates, as discussed later in Chapter 6.

4.2.3 *Pricing and Settlement*

Index values are not based on the actual values of the debt obligations of the underlying entities in the reference portfolios. Instead, index values are calculated based on the single-name CDSs spread for those reference entities in the index.

On each roll date, a fixed coupon for the index is defined that prices the reference portfolio to par. Thereafter, a "running spread" is calculated that marks the reference portfolio to market each day and generates corresponding cash flows between protection purchasers and sellers based on deviations between the current running spread and the up-front fixed coupon. Like a futures contract, index CDSs are marked-to-market and resettled in cash each day. Index CDS transactions may include an up-front payment that reconciles the index to current underlying weighted single-name CDS spreads, as well as ongoing mark-to-market payments based on changes in the value of the CDS-derived index.

4.3 Tranched Index CDSs

For certain index CDSs, Markit also provides calculations and valuations for corresponding tranched index CDS products. Tranched index CDSs are constructed in the same way that XOL CDSs are constructed as explained in Sect. 1.3 of this chapter. Specifically, Markit calculates index values corresponding to pre-defined cumulative loss tranches on which tranched index CDSs are available for trading.

For example, the TABX is a tranched index based on Markit's ABX. HE index which in turn is based on ABCDSs on tranches of subprime home equity loans. Under the standard terms of the TABX, credit protection purchasers and sellers can execute tranched index CDS contracts based on specified attachment and exhaustion points to tailor their risk management and investment objectives.[4]

Notes

1. As we discuss in Chapter 5, post-crisis regulations require a minimum 5% risk retention by securitizers. In Fig. 4.2, the risk retention tranche corresponds to a horizontal retention under the post-crisis regulations.
2. Markit, *Markit CDX High Yield and Markit CDX Investment Grade Index Rules* (August 2016).
3. Id.
4. Markit, *ABX Transactions: Standard Terms Supplement* (January 19, 2006).

References

Chaplin, G. 2010. *Credit Derivatives: Trading, Investing, and Risk Management*. Hoboken, NJ: Wiley.

Culp, C.L. 2006. *Structured Finance and Insurance*. Hoboken, NJ: Wiley.

Culp, C.L., and A.M.P. Neves. 1998a. Credit and Interest Rate Risk in the Business of Banking. *Derivatives Quarterly* 4 (4) (Summer).

Culp, C.L., and A.M.P. Neves. 1998b. Financial Innovations in Leveraged Commercial Loan Markets. *Journal of Applied Corporate Finance* 11 (2) (Summer).

Lucas, D., and A. Thomas. 2003. Nth to Default Swaps and Notes: All About Default Correlation. In *Credit Derivatives: The Definitive Guide*, ed. J. Gregory. London: Risk Books.

O'Kane, D., et al. 2003. Guide to Exotic Credit Derivatives. Lehman Brothers.

CHAPTER 5

Asset-Backed CDSs

In Chapters 2 and 3, we discussed CDSs based on specific single reference entities. In Chapter 4, we reviewed the markets for portfolio, basket, and index (whole and tranched) CDS products based on the creditworthiness of multiple reference entities. In this chapter, we discuss a third type of CDS product that is not triggered by a credit event at one or more specific reference *entities* but is instead triggered by credit events associated with specific assets or securities. Such ABCDSs enable firms to purchase and sell protection on the cash flows and values of specific assets, which are typically issued through the structured financing process.

Asset-backed CDSs ("ABCDSs") are almost always based on a structured finance product or ABS—i.e., a security issued by a special purpose entity ("SPE") such as a trust or corporation with a tax-friendly domicile that is formed solely for the purpose of facilitating a planned structured financing.[1] To understand ABCDSs, one must first understand the structured financing process and the major types of structured securities on which ABCDSs are most often based. We thus begin this chapter in Sect. 5.1 with a background discussion of structured finance and the general nature of structured products. In Sect. 5.2, we then discuss the main types of ABSs on which ABCDSs were based during the heyday of those products—i.e., RMBSs and mortgage-related (often home equity loan-based) ABSs, as well as CDOs. In Sect. 5.3, we explain why single-name CDSs based on specific ABSs did not work well under the ISDA *2003 Definitions*. Section 5.4 summarizes ISDA's solution to

C. L. Culp et al., *Credit Default Swaps*, Palgrave Studies in Risk and Insurance, https://doi.org/10.1007/978-3-319-93076-3_5

that problem and describes the pay-as-you-go ("PAUG") template for ABCDSs based on ABS and CDO tranches.

ABCDS volumes and notional amounts outstanding grew rapidly following the introduction by ISDA of an ABCDS Master Agreement in June 2005. After the U.S. subprime mortgage market collapse and the subsequent implosion of subprime-backed mortgage-based securities and CDOs based on subprime ABSs that began in 2007, the popularity of ABCDSs waned rapidly and significantly. As of today, there is little or no trading in ABCDSs.

The sudden disappearance of ABCDSs following the outbreak of the credit crisis, however, is not an indictment of the design of the PAUG template for ABCDS products generally. Indeed, there is no inherent "design flaw" in the PAUG template for ABCDSs that would inhibit the return of these products to the global credit derivatives marketplace.

The academic empirical literature of ABCDSs primarily analyzes the ABX index, which we introduced briefly in Chapter 4. Empirical analyses utilizing ABX data are almost exclusively intertwined with the literature on the causes, timing, and consequences of the credit crisis—a literature that merits a book unto itself and is simply too voluminous for us to review here. Although by no means unimportant, we exclude much of the crisis-related academic literature involving the ABX from our literature review presented in Part III not for lack of relevance but purely to maintain the focused scope of our treatise.

5.1 Structured Finance and ABSs

Structured finance can be broadly defined as the process by which market participants raise capital and/or manage risk by the issuance of structured products whose cash flow attributes are engineered to satisfy the specific needs of the sponsor/originator and/or the demands of target investors. Perhaps the most popular form of structured financing is a securitization in which a securities issuer sells debt (known as securitized products) to raise funds that are then used to finance the purchase of assets from or (in a "synthetic securitization") sell credit protection (using CDSs) to the current owner of those assets.[2]

The cash flows on the securitized products are collateralized by the cash flows on the purchased assets or low-risk debt combined with coupon income on CDS protection sales. Securitizations and securitized products can be distinguished along at least two dimensions:

(i) motivation of the sponsor/originator of the transaction and (ii) execution method (i.e., "cash" vs. "synthetic"). At the center of either such type of securitization, moreover, is the issuer of the securitized products and the purchaser of the underlying assets or seller of credit protection on such assets known as an SPE.

5.1.1 *Special Purpose Entities*

An SPE plays a crucial role in most securitizations by functioning as the issuer of the securitized products (i.e., ABSs) that are collateralized by the cash flows on the collateral purchased by the SPE in cash securitizations or the residual value of the interest and CDS credit protection coupon payment receivables less any CDS payments by the SPE to protection purchasers in synthetic securitizations. For most securitizations, the SPE has no operating business mandate and simply acts as a transformer of assets or credit exposures into cash flows for ABSs issued to acquire those exposures. Most SPEs formed for securitizations, moreover, are finite-lived—i.e., once all the liabilities are repaid, the SPE unwinds and self-liquidates.[3]

An SPE is usually organized either as a corporation or an indenture trust. The exact form depends on a wide variety of commercial, legal, tax, accounting, and regulatory considerations. In addition to standard SPE organizational forms (including limited liability companies and business trusts formed in tax- and legal-friendly domiciles), some of the other most popular forms of SPEs include the following:

- *Special purpose corporation*: Usually a special purpose finance subsidiary of a corporation or a licensed (re-)insurance company that plans to issue new securities;
- *Master trust*: Can issue multiple series of securities backed by a common asset pool—very useful if the sponsor or originator wishes later to "recharge" the collateral pool with new assets;
- *Owner trusts*: Formed to hold pooled non-revolving assets;
- *Grantor trusts*: Passive tax vehicles that can issue a single class of securities or senior and subordinated classes of pass-through securities backed by a common asset pool, but tranching of cash flows by maturity or time is not allowed;
- *Regulated investment companies*: Special companies that issue securities for investment management purposes; and

- *Investment trusts (including real estate investment trusts)*: Assets may include cash, mortgage loans, debt securities (other than those issued by the owner of the trust), pass-through certificates, and the like.

5.1.2 Types of Securitizations

The sponsor or originator of an asset securitization is the institution that perceives a need or opportunity to raise funds and/or manage its risks. Securitizations can be distinguished along two dimensions: (i) the economic motivation for the transaction and (ii) the mechanics of risk transfer for the underlying collateral pool.

5.1.2.1 Motivations for Securitizations

There are two typical motivations to initiate a securitization. First, so-called "balance-sheet" securitizations are motivated either by (i) the desire of an asset originator (e.g., a mortgage or C&I lender) to sell certain credit-sensitive assets, thereby monetizing those assets (i.e., converting future receivables into their current cash equivalents) and reducing its credit exposure to its borrowers going forward, or (ii) the desire of an asset originator to retain the originated assets on its balance sheet while eliminating all or most of its ongoing credit exposure to the underlying pool of assets.

Second, so-called "arbitrage" securitizations do not typically involve an asset's originator and instead involve open market purchases or credit protection sales of the assets to be securitized by a collateral manager that is unaffiliated with the assets' originators. Arbitrage securitizations are essentially transactions that are designed solely for investment management purposes—i.e., to generate performance-based and management fees for the collateral manager in return for providing investors in the securitized products a desirable risk/return tradeoff.

5.1.2.2 Mechanics of Risk Transfer in Securitizations

Securitizations can also be distinguished based on the execution method by which the SPE issuer of the securitized products acquires the credit risk of the underlying assets that investors in the securities products agree to accept as a risk transfer in return for appropriate compensation. "Cash" securitizations involve the actual purchase of securities, loans, or other assets either from an originator (or an affiliate of the originator) using the proceeds from the issuance of securitized products collateralized by the assets acquired by the SPE.

Alternatively, "synthetic" securitizations do not require the SPE issuer of securitized products to purchase the underlying assets collateralizing the securitized products. Instead, the SPE invests the proceeds of the securitized product issuance in low-risk assets (e.g., Eurodollar time deposits yielding a LIBOR interest rate) and sells credit protection to the originator or current third-party owner of the assets in the open market. The CDS or LCDS protection single-name sales or multi-name protection sales are collateralized with the proceeds of the securitized product issuance that is invested in low-risk assets. In the event of no defaults on the underlying collateral, investors receive the low-risk (e.g., LIBOR) interest on the invested proceeds of the securitized product issuance *plus* the CDS or LCDS coupon payments by the asset's originator or current owner(s). If the underlying securities experience depletions of cash flows or reductions in value (subject to the CDS or LCDS documentation), then securitized product bondholders receive less interest and/or principal according to the seniority and terms of their bond investments.

Most securitizations involve the issuance of tranched securitized products, such that investors in more junior tranches experience losses resulting from declines of the cash flows or market values of the collateral before more senior tranches are affected. For example, subprime-based RMBSs can experience reduced cash flows and declines in value when delinquency and foreclosure rates on the underlying loans rise, which, in turn, reduce the cash flows and values of the RMBS collateral. Investors in more junior RMBS tranches will experience losses before investors in more senior tranches. As we discuss in more detail below, moreover, securitizations typically include additional credit enhancements (beyond subordination) to protect investors in the most senior tranches of securities from declines in the cash flows on or values of the underlying collateral that secures the senior securities.

5.2 Typical ABSs

Since the late 1970s, most mortgage bankers have relied more on the capital markets than on direct borrowings as a source of funds for their mortgage originations.[4] Through the process known as securitization, mortgage bankers bundle loans they have originated into portfolios and sell those loan portfolios to investors through the issuance of new securities whose cash flows are collateralized by the underlying loan pool.[5] The cash proceeds received by originators through securitizations are used to finance the ongoing production of new loans.

The mortgage securitization process ushered in a new era of mortgage banking in which originators moved away from an "originate-and-hold" ("O&H") business model toward the "originate-and-distribute" ("O&D") model (as discussed in Chapter 3, Sect. 3.1 for the syndicated leveraged loan market).[6] In the O&D model, originators needed to depend less on retail depository liabilities and interbank borrowings to finance their mortgage loans because the loans could instead be sold in a securitization. O&D mortgage banking also provided balance sheet and regulatory capital relief for banks by allowing them to diversify and securitize their loan exposures, thereby enabling banks to comply more easily with extant regulatory capital requirements.[7]

Mortgage originators do not, however, completely eliminate their credit exposures to borrowers through securitizations. Most originators retain their mortgage servicing rights and thus have a continuing interest in the ongoing payments by borrowers on the underlying mortgage portfolio. In addition, originators typically retain the residual interests in mortgage securitizations so that originators in balance-sheet securitizations remain exposed to the risks of poor performance on the mortgage loans they originated and sold. Even after securitizing a loan portfolio, originators thus generally have strong ongoing incentives to monitor the underlying securitized loans to try and ensure that they will remain performing loans.[8]

Residential mortgage securitizations can be used by originators to raise medium- or long-term funds, as well as short-term funds. The former are generally used by originators to facilitate new loan originations, whereas short-term mortgage-related securitizations (mainly through mortgage-based asset-backed commercial paper conduits) are primarily used by originators to finance their mortgage warehouses—i.e., mortgages that have been originated and funded but that have not yet been sold through a long-term securitization.

The widespread and successful issuance of RMBSs by mortgage originators to raise funds and manage loan credit risks facilitated the issuance of ABSs by originators of *non*-mortgage assets to achieve similar fund-raising and risk transfer need. Popular forms of non-mortgage collateral have included auto loans and leases, credit card receivables, and student loans etc.

Figure 5.1 shows the annual issuance of all major ABSs by collateral types (excluding mortgage-related ABSs and CDOs, which we discuss in the following two subsections) from 1985 through 2017. As Fig. 5.1 indicates, the most popular underlying collateral for ABSs issued in the USA has historically included auto loans and leases, credit card receivables, and student loans.

5.2.1 *RMBSs and Home Equity Loan-Backed ABSs*

The new securities issued in a medium- or long-term securitization of residential mortgage loans are known as mortgage-related ABSs.[9,10] Particularly popular through mid-2007 were ABSs based on home equity loans ("HELs"), which were backed both by first- and second-lien HELs and home equity letters of credit ("HELOCs") and included loans to borrowers across a range of credit qualities.

RMBSs are classified as either "Agency" or "private-label" based on whether the interest and principal payments to RMBS investors are guaranteed by a government sponsored enterprise ("GSE"). In typical

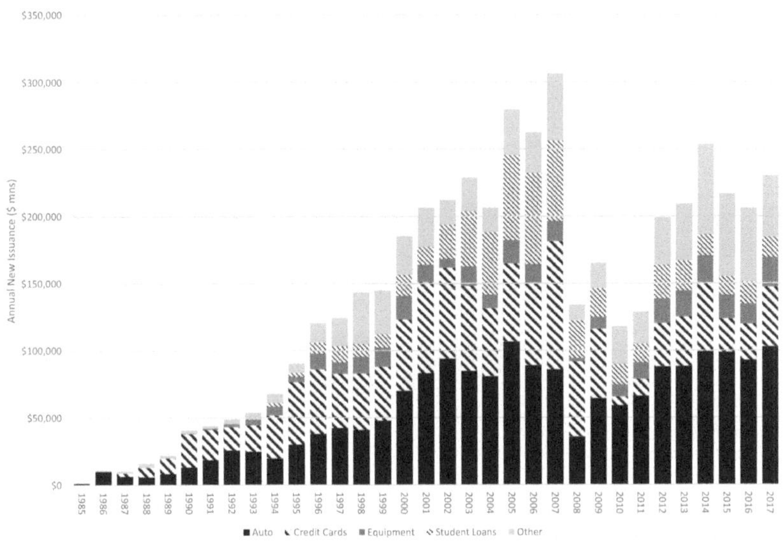

Fig. 5.1 Annual US ABS issuance by collateral type (excluding mortgage-related ABSs and CDOs), 1985–2017 (*Source* SIFMA)

Agency securitizations,[11] a mortgage banker sells a portfolio of "conforming" loans eligible for sale to a GSE, which then creates RMBSs based on the acquired loan portfolio. The acquiring GSE also provides a guarantee to investors that it will cover any principal and/or interest shortfalls arising from defaults by the underlying mortgage borrowers. As a result, the primary risks to which investors in Agency RMBSs are exposed are interest rate and prepayment risks but not borrower default risks (which are borne by the GSE guarantor).

In a private-label mortgage-related ABS, by contrast, a mortgage originator sells a loan portfolio to an SPE instead of a GSE. The SPE raises the cash needed to purchase the loan portfolio by issuing new securities collateralized by the loan portfolio. Principal and interest received by the SPE on the loans finance principal and interest payments due to investors in the newly issued bonds.

Figure 5.2 depicts the cash flows and structure of a typical private-label RMBS. The encircled letters in Fig. 5.2 show the five simplified main

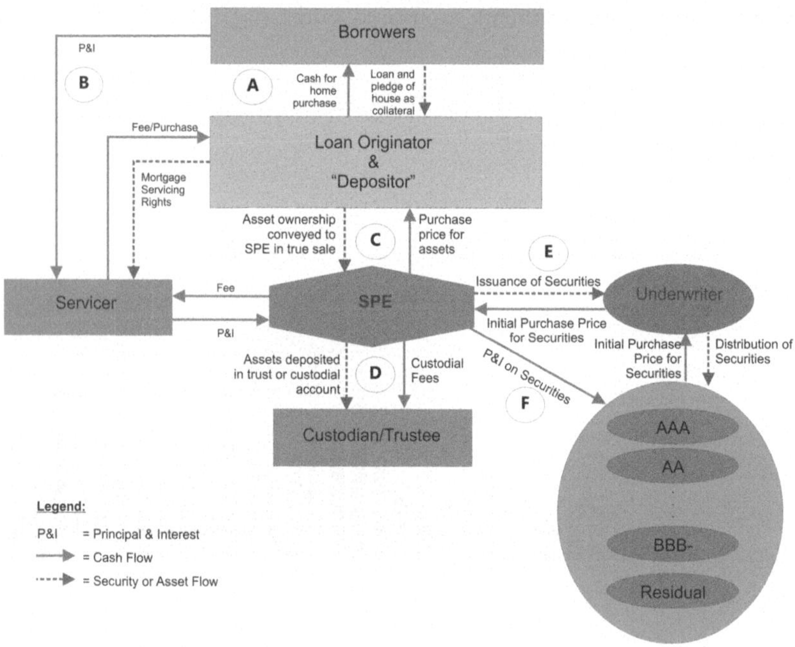

Fig. 5.2 Private-label RMBS securitization

components of the RMBS securitization process. Note that these steps are not necessarily chronological. In fact, in most cases all of the relevant documents governing the various components of a securitization are executed simultaneously. These five primary components are as follows:

- *A*: Loan originator provides cash to homeowners/borrowers who pledge the real estate to the originator as collateral for the mortgage loan.
- *B*: Loan originator conveys mortgage servicing rights to a servicer (often an affiliate of the originator) in exchange for cash (either the purchase price of the servicing rights or periodic fees). Periodic principal and interest ("P&I") payments on the loan are thereafter made by the borrower/homeowner to the servicer.
- *C*: The loan originator's "depositor" conveys the mortgage loan assets to an SPE in a "true sale," thereby removing the loans from the originator's balance sheet and transferring them to the SPE's. In exchange for selling the mortgage assets, the SPE remits a cash payment to the originator, which the originator uses to finance future loan originations. After the loans are purchased by the SPE, the servicer remits P&I payments on the underlying mortgage loans to the SPE (possibly in exchange for a servicing fee, depending on the arrangement between the servicer and the originator).
- *D*: The loan assets and documentation are transferred by the SPE to a custodian or trustee for safekeeping.
- *E*: Multiple tranches of RMBS securities are issued by the SPE (through an underwriter) to investors in exchange for cash. A first lien on the mortgage assets of the SPE is perfected for the benefit of bond investors, thereby securing investors' claim on the underlying real estate backing the mortgage loans in case of a default by the SPE on required P&I payments.
- *F*: Scheduled and unscheduled P&I payments are made by the SPE to the investors in the RMBS securities.

Unlike Agency securitizations, private-label structures do not include a GSE guarantee that covers any principal or interest shortfalls arising from borrower defaults for the benefit of investors in the RMBS securities. As a result, investors in private-label RMBS are subject to the credit risk of the underlying loan portfolio, and they demand higher promised yields to compensate them for bearing that risk.

Virtually, all private-label mortgage-related ABSs involve the issuance of multiple classes of securities with claims of differing priorities on the same underlying loan portfolio. These different security classes are exposed to varying degrees of credit risk based on the depth of subordination of the security in the SPE's capital structure. Holders of more junior tranches bear the impact of defaults or declines in value in the underlying mortgages before investors in more senior tranches. The depth of subordination of a given tranche/class of securities relative to the amount of losses that will erode more subordinated tranches and any other credit enhancements is known as the over-collateralization ("O/C") of a given tranche—i.e., how much value must be eroded in the underlying mortgage collateral pool before investors in the tranche in question begin to experience losses as a percentage of all liabilities issued.

To keep incentives properly aligned between originators and investors, the originator historically retained the most deeply subordinated or "residual" tranche of the ABS issue. On October 22, 2014, the Office of the Comptroller of the Currency ("OCC"), Federal Deposit Insurance Corporation ("FDIC"), Securities and Exchange Commission ("SEC"), Federal Housing Finance Agency ("FHFA"), and the Department of Housing and Urban Development ("HUD") jointly announced a final "risk retention" rule for securitizations. Specifically, the Dodd-Frank Act mandated that securitizers (e.g., mortgage originators) must retain at least 5% of the credit risks of the assets backing the bonds issued in a securitization.[12] In brief, securitizers can accomplish this in any of four ways[13]:

- An eligible "horizontal" retention of one or more of the most subordinated tranches with a combined fair value of at least 5% of all the ABSs issued in the securitization;
- An eligible "vertical" retention of either (i) a single security entitling the securitizer to the same payments to be made to investors in each tranche or (ii) an interest in classes of tranched securities in proportion to the investor classes of those securities, where, in both cases, the 5% minimum is measured relative to the par values of the ABS tranches issued;
- Some combination of horizontal and vertical interests where the minimum 5% is calculated for the horizontal interest at fair value and for the vertical interest at par; and/or

- A cash reserve account funded by the securitizer and placed in trust in an amount equal to what the 5% horizontal interest would have been. If the total amount of defaults over the life of the securitization is less than the amount deposited in the cash reserve plus interest, the residual reverts to the securitization after all final payments to investors in ABSs have been paid.

Private-label mortgage-related ABSs generally also include a variety of other credit enhancements designed to provide further protections to investors in relatively more senior tranches from losses on the underlying mortgage collateral.[14] One such credit enhancement (especially popular in HEL and subprime-backed ABSs and RMBSs) is an O/C cushion between the value of the loan portfolio and the value of the MBS tranches. O/C can be created at the inception of the deal (e.g., through a funded cash reserve account as discussed above) and/or built up over time by diverting “excess spread” (i.e., surplus income earned on the mortgages after paying senior expenses and interest to senior tranche holders) into a reserve account.

Figure 5.3 shows annual issuance of US private-label mortgage-related ABSs based on the type of underlying mortgage loans backing the securities. Mortgage loans are classified by the perceived credit risk of the borrower, the quality of the real estate collateral, and the terms of the loan at the time of the mortgage origination. The nomenclature has changed following the adoption of post-crisis regulations, but prior to then, prime mortgage loans were considered the least risky and subprime loans the most risky, with Alt-A loans lying in between the two. As Fig. 5.3 illustrates, a surge in new issuance of mortgage-related ABSs backed by subprime/non-prime loans, Alt-A loans, and HELOCs occurred from 2002 through 2006.

When the US subprime (and eventually Alt-A) markets destabilized beginning in 2007, new issuance of private-label mortgage-related ABSs based on relatively risky collateral ground to a halt. From 2008 through 2017, no new private-label mortgage-related ABSs were issued based on HELOCs or junior-lien mortgage loans. From 2009 through 2015, moreover, mortgage-related ABSs backed by subprime/non-prime mortgage loans was below $500 million in most years (compared to a high watermark of $463.1 billion issued in 2006) and was non-existent in 2009, 2012, and 2013. By 2017, private-label mortgage-backed ABS

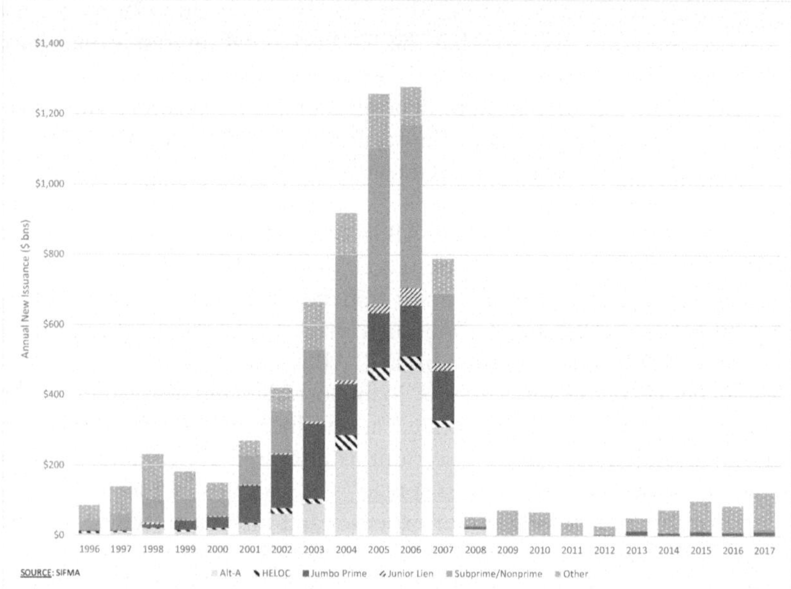

Fig. 5.3 Annual US private-label mortgage-related ABS issuance (*Source* SIFMA)

issuance increased to $5.66 billion—still a far cry from issuance levels from 2002 through 2007.

5.2.2 *CDOs*

CDOs are types of ABSs that are usually treated as a separate category of structured securities apart from ABSs because the CDO market is itself so diverse. Nevertheless, from an economic perspective, CDOs are indeed types of ABSs. Tranches or classes of securities issued through an SPE in a CDO can be based on various types of collateral, including the following:

- CDOs backed mainly by bonds are known as "traditional" CDOs or collateralized bond obligations ("CBOs");
- CDOs backed mainly by leveraged syndicated loans—typically Term Loan Bs (as discussed in Chapter 3)—are known as collateralized loan obligations ("CLOs");

- CDOs backed by ownership interests in private equity or other managed funds are called collateralized fund obligations ("CFOs");
- CDO tranches collateralized by ABSs are known as ABS CDOs or Structured Finance ("SF") CDOs; and
- CDOs known as CDO^2 deals include a significant amount of tranches from other CDOs in their collateral pools.

Figure 5.4 shows the annual US issuance of all types of CDOs from 1996 through 2017. Figure 5.5 shows the amounts outstanding of US-issued CDSs by category types from 1996 through 2017. All categories of CDOs saw increases in new issuance and amounts outstanding from 1996 through 2007. From 2002 through 2007, however, new issuances and amounts outstanding of ABS CDOs grew much more significantly than other types of CDOs. Over those years, traditional CDOs, CLOs, and ABS CDOs had a cumulative growth rate in total amounts outstanding of 64, 216, and 1104%, respectively.

The explosive growth of ABS CDOs from 2002 through 2007 was fueled by the purchases by CDO managers of subprime RMBSs and

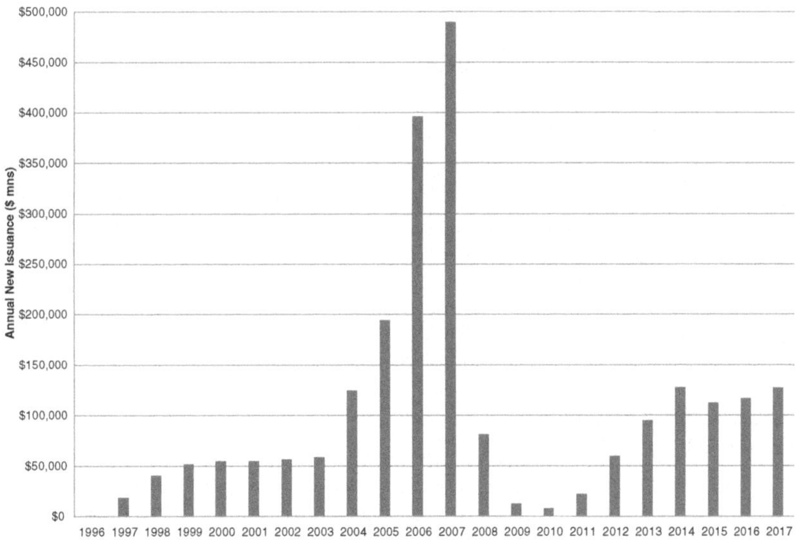

Fig. 5.4 Annual US new CDO issuance (all CDO categories), 1996–2017 (*Source* SIFMA)

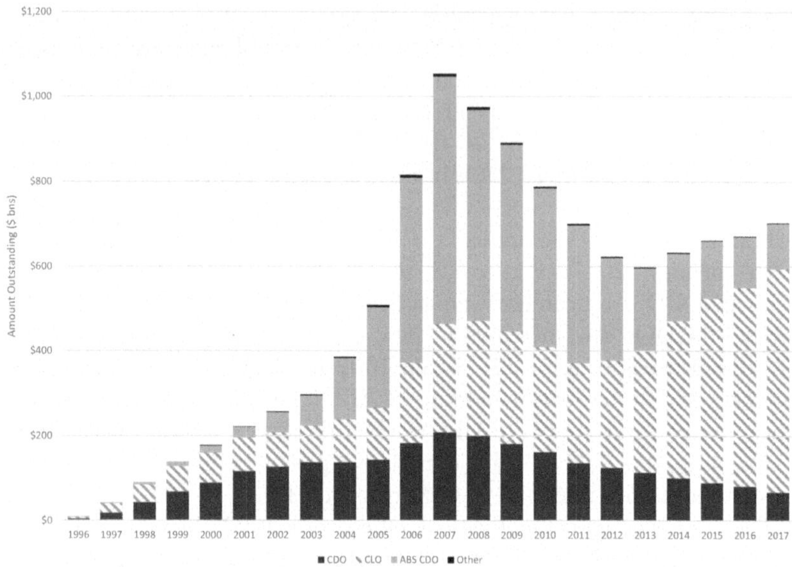

Fig. 5.5 US CDO amounts outstanding by CDO category, 1996–2017 (*Source* SIFMA)

mortgage-related ABSs and their repackaging the cash flows of those securities (along with other ABS based on non-mortgage collateral) into new securities by managers and sponsors of CDOs backed by ABSs. As the ABS CDO market evolved, two distinct categories of ABS CDOs emerged: high-grade ABS CDOs ("HG ABS CDOs") that typically issued securities collateralized by senior tranches of ABSs with ratings of AAA or AA; and mezzanine ABS CDOs ("Mezz ABS CDOs") backed predominantly by the mezzanine tranches of ABS offerings with ratings of BBB– or BBB. Like the RMBSs and ABSs that collateralize ABS CDOs, ABS CDO securities themselves are also tranched.

5.2.2.1 Cash ABS CDOs

In cash ABS CDOs, the ABS collateral investments are selected by a collateral manager and purchased by the SPE CDO issuer using the proceeds from the issuance of new securities by the SPE.[15] Fig. 5.6 depicts the cash flows on a typical cash ABS CDO. In many ways, it is very similar to the structure of the RMBS securitization shown in Fig. 5.2, but the differences are very important.

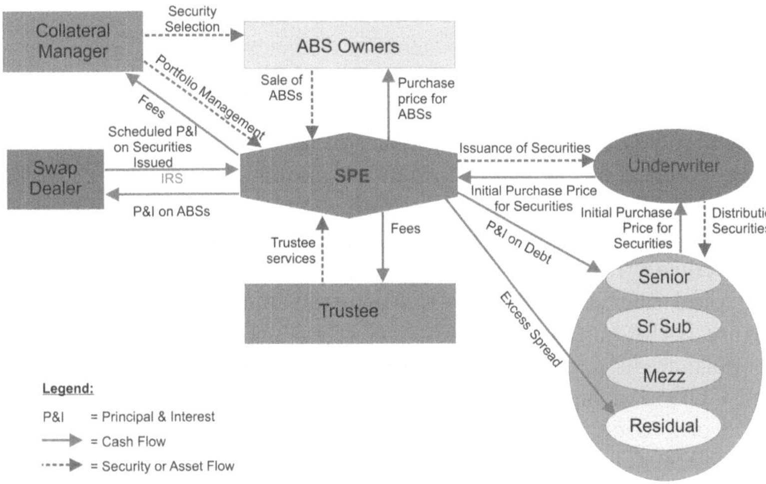

Fig. 5.6 Cash ABS CDO

First, no originator or original borrower is involved in a typical ABS CDO. Instead, a collateral manager selects the ABSs to be purchased in the secondary market from investors that own the already-issued ABSs. In return, collateral managers generally receive a fixed fee to cover their basic expenses (which are senior liabilities in the SPE's capital structure) and performance-based fees (that are subordinate in the SPE's capital structure) to align incentives.

Second, the most deeply subordinated residual tranche which functions like equity is now sold to an investor. Indeed, the successful arrangement of an ABS CDO in the period from roughly 2005 through 2008 required ABS CDO arrangers to identify the residual purchaser first because that was often the most difficult tranche to sell. Without a willing purchaser of the ABS CDO equity tranche, the ABS CDO deal on the whole was unlikely to close.

Third, ABS CDOs sometimes included an interest rate swap between the SPE and a swap dealer. Such swaps functioned as liquidity support mechanisms to ensure that regular periodic interest payments to CDO investors could be made even if cash flows on the ABS assets held by the SPE issuer occurred after corresponding cash outflows to investors. Such swaps did not provide credit enhancements—in the event of declines in the values of ABS collateral, the notional amount was typically reduced accordingly.

5.2.2.2 Synthetic ABS CDOs

In a synthetic ABS CDO, the SPE issuer of the ABS CDO securities sells credit protection on the obligations in the underlying reference portfolio using CDSs. The SPE then issues another set of securities, the interest and principal of which are based on the performance of the ABS collateral underlying the CDSs.

A typical synthetic ABS CDO is depicted in Fig. 5.7. Much of the structure is the same as the cash ABS CDO depicted in Fig. 5.6 with an important difference. In the synthetic CDO, the credit exposure to which CDO tranche investors are exposed is acquired through the sale of CDS protection to one or more credit protection purchasers (usually swap dealers). The assets of the SPE in a synthetic CDO consist of the proceeds from the issuance of the CDO tranches, which is then placed

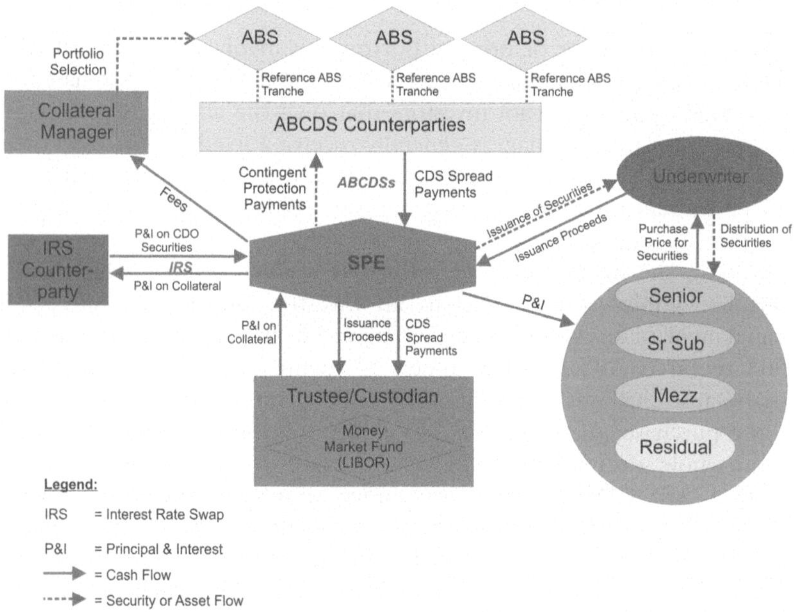

Fig. 5.7 Synthetic ABS CDO

in the hands of a trustee and invested in low-risk money market instruments such as Eurodollar time deposits. The collateral manager selects the underlying ABS collateral, but, instead of the SPE using the proceeds of the CDO securities to purchase the actual ABSs, the SPE enters into CDSs—typically ABCDSs—on the reference ABSs.

Whereas a lien on the ABS collateral is perfected for the benefit of bond investors in a cash CDO, a synthetic CDO involves both a first lien and second lien on the SPE's assets (i.e., the invested proceeds from the CDO tranche issuances). A first security interest (i.e., first lien) is perfected for the benefit of the CDS credit protection purchasers, and the second lien is perfected for investors in the classes of CDO securities. In the event that any payments are required to protection purchasers on the CDSs, the low-risk collateral is first liquidated to honor the SPE's protection sales. Bondholders have a claim on the low-risk collateral, but only on the amount that has not otherwise been used to finance CDS protection payments. In return for taking this risk, investors in tranches of the synthetic ABS CDO receive the interest earned on the cash collateral (e.g., LIBOR) plus the CDS premium received by the SPE from protection purchasers.

Following the collapse of US subprime mortgage-related ABS markets that began in 2007, new issuance of ABS CDOs (cash and synthetic alike) plummeted sharply, as indicated in Fig. 5.5. Indeed, as Fig. 5.4 demonstrates, new issuance of *all* categories of CDOs plunged as the credit crisis unfolded. New US CDO issuance fell from a 2007 high of $489.7 billion to a 2010 low of $8.1 billion—i.e., a roughly 98% decline.

5.3 Asset-Backed CDSs Under the *2003 Definitions*

As discussed in Chapter 2, single-name CDSs are triggered by six events under the *1999* and *2003 Definitions*: (i) bankruptcy of the reference entity; (ii) obligation acceleration; (iii) obligation default; (iv) failure to pay; (v) repudiation or moratorium; and (vi) restructuring. All of these provisions pose problems for CDSs based on SPE-issued ABSs. Although refinements in the ISDA Credit Definitions have addressed very specific issues in the single-name CDS market (as discussed in Chapter 2), these six specific credit events have proven to be robust and effective for CDSs based on specific individual reference entities (with the exception of narrowly defined credit events like Hovnanian).

Applying the six credit events in the *2003 Definitions* to CDSs based on ABSs (including CDO tranches), however, proved to be problematic. Prior to June 2005, when ISDA first began to provide standardized documentation for ABCDSs, market participants wishing to sell or purchase credit protection on particular ABS tranches generally relied on individualized, non-standard transaction documentation in a manner that did not run afoul of regulations (e.g., local insurance regulations).[16]

Two concerns were often expressed by market participants, especially as more and more market participants wanted to use CDSs to take a short position on subprime mortgage-related RMBSs and ABSs starting around 2004. Both concerns were based on beliefs that standard CDSs based on the *2003 Definitions* would not require protection sellers to make payments to protection purchasers even following the occurrence of an event that was adverse to the credit quality of an underlying ABS. We discuss those two concerns in more detail below.

5.3.1 SPE Issuers and Credit Events Under the 2003 Definitions

SPEs are formed as independent, bankruptcy remote entities. The activities in which SPEs are permitted to engage are generally extremely limited, with some SPEs (known as "qualifying SPEs" or "QSPEs") often being described as "brain dead." Even SPEs with some discretion have activities that are contractually limited to managing the assets and liabilities of the ABS or CDO within the confines of tight pre-defined investment policies, covenants, and the like. For example, most SPE-issued ABS-backed debt instruments contain covenants that obligate investors not to file for bankruptcy protection by placing an SPE issuer into involuntary bankruptcy but instead require that they rely on their perfected security interests in the SPE's assets (i.e., the ABS collateral) to claim preference payments.

The other five credit events under the *2003 Definitions* make equally little sense for an SPE inasmuch as the cash flows on an SPE's liabilities generally deal with default, acceleration, failure to pay, and the like in the deal documents through the seniority of payments in the structure's cash flow waterfall and related facility agreements. To take an obvious example, the failure to pay interest to a given class of ABS securities is not generally an event of default for an ABS unless it occurs on a legal maturity date.

For most ABS and CDO structures, the six standard credit events in the *2003 Definitions* thus did not necessary lead to the triggering of a CDS based on an SPE reference entity and thus did not provide protection sellers and purchasers with enough confidence to rely on CDSs for credit protection on ABSs issued by those reference entity SPEs.

5.3.2 Complications Arising from ABS Structures

As the discussion in Sects. 5.1 and 5.2 earlier in this chapter suggest, the nuances and details of any given ABS structure can be quite complicated. That does not necessarily mean that such structures and their tranches were difficult to understand, but rather that any given structure had various bells, whistles, and features embedded in the deal documents and cash flow waterfalls governing the allocation and distribution of cash flows that needed to be evaluated on a deal-by-deal basis—i.e., not the obvious recipe for governing CDSs based on such structures under the *2003 Definitions.*

For example, SPEs that acquire mortgage assets must determine when a performing mortgage becomes delinquent and ultimately impaired and how that affects a potential write-down of principal on outstanding ABS liabilities. Similarly, when performing mortgages become delinquent but are rapidly restored to performing, a previous write-down of principal may be written back up. Because the *2003 Definitions* rely on the triggering of a CDS upon the occurrence of a credit event, they are ill-equipped to handle this feature of ABSs—i.e., write-downs of principal are not necessarily credit events under the *2003 Definitions* despite being deleterious to the ABS tranche holder.

In addition, many ABSs are subject to the risk of temporary liquidity shortfalls when interest earned on the underlying collateral is insufficient in any given period to pay interest owed to ABS investors in that same period. This shortfall in "excess spread" (defined in Sect. 5.2 of this chapter) in many ABSs is allocated to specific tranches where it is accrued and earns interest until sufficient liquidity has been restored for its payment to those tranche holders. Some ABSs, however, have available funds caps ("AFCs") that limit investors' interest claims to the lower of the stated contractual interest rate or the rate specified in the AFC.

ABS CDOs, by contrast, typically address liquidity shortfalls in a different manner and do not rely on AFCs. Instead, SPE issuers of ABS CDO securities either enter into interest rate swaps to smooth temporary shortfalls in interest received vis-à-vis interest payable to investors or structure the mezzanine tranches to have paid-in-kind ("PIK") interest (which was also a common feature of many HY bonds in the leveraged finance market prior to the credit crisis). A PIK feature allows the SPE, upon the occurrence of a shortfall of the excess spread, to defer the interest payable to some or all mezzanine ABS CDO tranches by adding it to the outstanding principal on the CDO notes.

In both the ABS AFC and CDO PIK situations, it is possible that investors may not ultimately receive all of the interest payments they were promised. For example, if performance on the collateral steadily declines and interest payments fall, a shortfall in excess spread may *never* be rectified. In that case, an AFC would become binding on an ABS and PIKs would begin to occur on a CDO—both of which are signs of credit deteriorations in the collateral pool—without a credit event occurring under the *2003 Definitions* (Nolan and Dodson 2007).

The ISDA *Credit Definitions*, of course, are not the "end all be all" of CDSs on ABSs. In fact, ABS and CDO deal documents typically include a variety of triggers (e.g., interest coverage requirements and O/C requirements) designed to accelerate or terminate a structure early in order to protect investors in senior tranches. But without something tying such events to CDS triggers, the *2003 Definitions* are largely unworkable for CDSs on ABSs.

Yet another complication in using standard CDSs under the *2003 Definitions* for ABSs is related to "interest step-ups" that are contained in many mortgage-related ABSs (and HEL-based ABSs, in particular). In most historical HEL-based ABSs, the SPE issuer had the right but not the obligation to issue a clean-up call to retire all outstanding liabilities if the loan balance for the structure fell below, say, 10% of the original loan balance. If a clean-up call was not issued to retire the outstanding liabilities, then the interest rate on the ABS may be stepped up.

5.4 The ISDA PAUG Template

ISDA began to produce various forms of documentation specifically aimed at ABCDSs beginning in June 2005 and has made numerous revisions to its various ABS- and CDO-tailored CDS documentation since then (Whetten 2005; Nolan and Dodson 2007). The most innovative and prevalent new form of CDS documentation was ISDA's PAUG template.

A CDS documented with the ISDA PAUG template distinguishes between reversible and irreversible credit events that can adversely impact the value of the asset underlying an ABCDS. Reversible or "soft" credit events—known as "floating amount events"—are based on situations in which the cash flows of an ABS are *initially* affected adversely but that are potentially reversible. The floating amount events under the PAUG template include situations in which the notional principal of the underlying collateral backing the ABS (i) amortizes, (ii) is prepaid, (iii) is written down as a result of delinquencies or foreclosures, or (iv) defaults. Floating amount events also include any situations in which the cash flows on the ABS are reversed, resulting in negative floating-rate payments from the CDS protection purchaser back to the protection seller (in distinct contrast to single- and multi-name CDSs which, once triggered, are irreversible).

5.4.1 ABCDSs

Unlike single-name CDSs for which triggers are based on discrete credit events, ABCDSs documented with the PAUG template are designed to deal with non-triggering scenarios in which the credit quality of the underlying ABS has been adversely affected but that might be remediated in the future and thus do not cause a triggering event that forces the immediate redemptions of CDSs. The three main floating amount events under the PAUG ABCDS documents are as follows:

- *Write-Down Event:* A reduction of principal in an outstanding ABS security either based on an actual write-down of the corresponding ABS principal or an implied write-down resulting from the under-collateralization of a given tranche;
- *Principal Shortfall Event:* Failure of the SPE issuer to pay principal on an ABS tranche at maturity or in the event of the early termination of the ABS structure resulting in a liquidation of collateral; and
- *Interest Shortfall Event:* Contractual interest is not paid to investors in an ABS tranche resulting either from insufficient interest payments on the collateral pool or the binding of an AFC cap.

Importantly, the PAUG ABCDS template requires *two-way* payments between the credit protection seller and buyer for floating amount events. If any floating amount events resulting in a payment from the protection seller to the buyer are reversed in a subsequent period, the protection buyer must reimburse the protection seller. For example, if an interest shortfall on an ABS above the AFC is later recovered or if a principal write-down resulting, say, from delinquencies on the underlying assets are rectified with subsequent payments, and the principal is written-up, the protection purchaser must reimburse the protection seller under the PAUG CDS for those reversed cash flows arising from subsequent rectifications of floating-rate events.

In addition to floating amount events, the PAUG template for ABCDSs also provides credit protection purchasers with the option for early termination and physical settlement similar to single-name CDSs, albeit with different credit event triggers than defined in the *2003 Definitions.* Specifically, a protection seller in a PAUG ABCDS can deliver the whole amount of the underlying reference asset to the protection seller in exchange for the par amount of the reference asset after the occurrence of the following ABCDS-specific credit events: (i) principal write-down; (ii) failure to pay principal; or (iii) catastrophic downgrade. A catastrophic downgrade occurs when the reference asset is downgraded to Caa2/CCC or below or if a rating is withdrawn by one or more of the three main credit rating agencies (Fitch, Moody's, and S&P). The inclusion of a catastrophic downgrade event represented a major change from the credit events for reference entities underlying single-name CDSs, which were *not* triggered by a credit agency downgrade.

Figure 5.8 depicts the cash flows between ABCDS protection buyers and sellers for both floating amount and credit events.

ABCDSs also typically allow protection purchasers to decide whether or not to opt into any step-up provisions in the underlying ABS. Specifically, an ABCDS credit protection purchaser that opts into the step-up option can choose following a coupon step-up either to terminate the ABCDS early or remain in the ABCDS but paying a higher premium equivalent to the original premium plus the amount by which the ABS coupon was stepped up.

Alternatively, an ABCDS protection purchaser may opt out of the step-up provisions. If a clean-up call is issued (as discussed in Sect. 5.3.2 of this chapter), this ABCDS protection purchaser is indifferent. But if the clean-up call is issued and the coupon on the corresponding ABS steps up, the premium paid by the protection seller in the ABCDS is unchanged, thereby benefiting the protection purchaser at the expense of

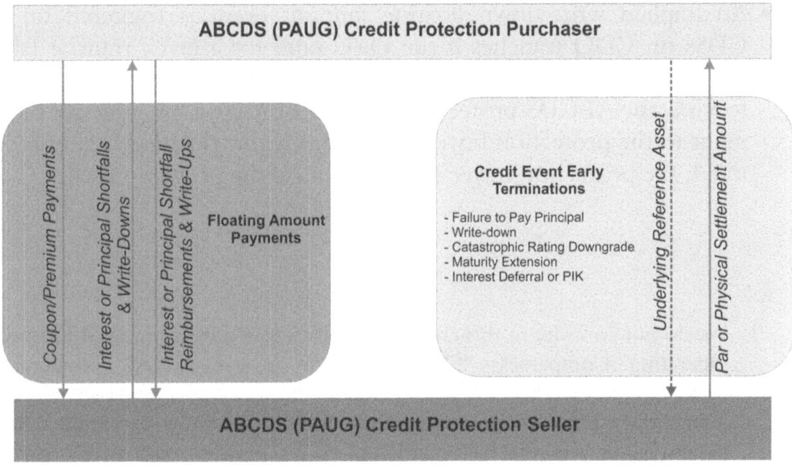

Fig. 5.8 Cash flows on ABCDS (PAUG template)

the protection seller. In that situation, ABCDS protection purchasers *do* care whether they have opted out of the step-up provisions or not.

5.4.2 CDSs on CDO Tranches

In 2006, ISDA introduced documentation for CDSs based on CDO tranches. Like the PAUG ABCDS template, the CDS on CDO tranche template is based on specific reference assets, the amortization schedule for those assets, and any interest shortfalls that constitute floating amount events. Unlike ABCDSs, however, CDSs on CDOs include a triggering event based on *implied* principal write-downs and not *actual* write-downs.

Although the ISDA template for CDSs on CDO tranches is mostly similar to the PAUG ABCDS documents, a few differences are worth noting[17]:

- When interest is not paid on time and PIK provisions of CDOs are triggered as a result of shortfalls in excess spreads, PAUG payments from protection sellers to buyers are immediately triggered. Physically settled credit events, however, require at least one year of consecutive shortfalls in excess spreads.

- An implied write-down floating amount event is triggered on a CDSs on CDO tranches if the O/C ratio for a given tranche falls below 100%. For example, if the O/C ratio on a given tranche falls to 95%, the ABCDS protection seller must make a 5% principal payment to the protection buyer. If the O/C ratio violation is later rectified, the protection buyer must reimburse the protection seller.

Notes

1. We do not consider in this chapter securities issued by Structured Finance Operating Companies ("SFOCs"), such as asset-backed commercial paper conduits or structured investment vehicles. Unlike most structured financings, SFOCs do not have finite lives, function as operating companies on an ongoing basis, and acquire collateral to back newly issued securities regularly.
2. For other types of structured financing transactions apart from securitizations, see Culp (2006).
3. Exceptions are ongoing securitization enterprises such as asset-backed commercial paper conduits and structured investment vehicles. To differentiate the securities issuers by such enterprises from SPEs, those issuers are usually referred to as structured finance operating companies ("SFOCs").
4. See, e.g., Financial Crisis Inquiry Commission, *Preliminary Staff Report: Securitization and the Mortgage Crisis* (April 7, 2010), and Adrian and Shin (2009, 2010).
5. See, generally Kravitt (1997) and Culp (2006).
6. See, e.g., Mizen (2008).
7. By giving banks access to a new source of funding and enabling them to manage their regulatory capital and credit risks more effectively, securitization promoted additional extensions of mortgage credit that might otherwise not have been possible. See, e.g., Loutskina (2011).
8. See, e.g., DeMarzo (2005), Demiroglu and James (2012), and Erel et al. (2014).
9. ABS can also be backed by non-mortgage collateral, including student loans, auto loans, and credit card receivables. See, e.g., Culp and Forrester (2013).
10. In some contexts, RMBS and mortgage-related ABS are distinct products. For example, securitized products based on first-lien, fixed-rate 30-year mortgages to prime borrowers are typically called RMBS, whereas

securities collateralized by subprime or home equity loans are generally classified as mortgage-related ABSs.

11. Beginning in 2013, Agency securitizations have started to change. See, e.g., Goodman et al. (2013). These very recent structures are not relevant to the issues explored in this book and are not discussed further herein.
12. Department of the Treasury—Office of the Comptroller of the Currency, Federal Reserve System, Federal Deposit Insurance Corporation, Federal Housing Finance Agency, Securities and Exchange Commission, and Department of Housing and Urban Development, "Credit Risk Retention—Final Rule," *Federal Register* 79, no. 247 (December 24, 2014).
13. For further discussion, see, e.g., Mayer Brown—Structured Finance Industry Group, "Credit Risk Retention Final Rule," *Regulatory Briefing Book* (November 2014), and Morrison Foerster, "A Closer Look at US Credit Risk Retention Rules," *Client Alert* (October 30, 2014).
14. See, e.g., Adelson and Bartlett (2004), Culp (2006), Gorton (2010), and Fabozzi et al. (2007).
15. During a "ramp-up" period when the ABS collateral is being assembled, the ABS may be acquired by the collateral manager and financed by a bank warehouse line or may be warehoused directly by the bank arranger of the CDO.
16. See, e.g., Forrester (2003).
17. For more details, see Flanagan et al. (2006).

References

Adelson, M., and E. Bartlett. 2004. Home Equity ABS Basics. *Nomura Fixed Income Research* (November 1).

Adrian, T., and H.S. Shin. 2009. Money, Liquidity, and Monetary Policy. *American Economic Review: Papers & Proceedings* 99 (2) (May).

Adrian, T., and H.S. Shin. 2010. The Changing Nature of Financial Intermediation and the Financial Crisis of 2007–09. *Federal Reserve Bank of New York Staff Report* (439) (March).

Culp, C.L. 2006. *Structured Finance and Insurance*. Hoboken, NJ: Wiley.

Culp, C.L., and J.P. Forrester. 2013. U.S. Structured Finance Markets: Recent Recovery, Post-crisis Developments, and Ongoing Regulatory Uncertainties. *Journal of Structured Finance* 18 (4) (Winter).

DeMarzo, P.M. 2005. The Pooling and Tranching of Securities: A Model of Informed Intermediation. *Review of Financial Studies* 18 (1): 1–35.

Demiroglu, C., and C. James 2012. How Important Is Having Skin in the Game? Originator-Sponsor Affiliation and Losses on Mortgage-Backed Securities. *Review of Financial Studies* 25 (11).

Erel, I., T. Nadauld, and R.M. Stulz. 2014. Why Did Holdings of Highly Rated Securitization Tranches Differ So Much Across Banks? *Review of Financial Studies* 27 (2).

Fabozzi, F.J., A.K. Bhattacharya, and W.S. Berliner. 2007. *Mortgage-Backed Securities*. Hoboken, NJ: Wiley.

Flanagan, C.T., et al. 2006. Introducing Default Swaps on CDOs. *JPMorgan Global Structured Finance Research* (July 28).

Forrester, J.P. 2003. Synthetic Resecuritizations: A Step Too Far? *Mayer Brown* (December).

Goodman, L.S., L. Yang, and B. Landy. 2013. The First GSE Risk-Sharing Deal: An Effective Risk Transfer Mechanism? *Journal of Structured Finance* 19 (3) (Fall).

Gorton, G.B. 2010. *Slapped by the Invisible Hand: The Panic of 2007*. Oxford: Oxford University Press.

Kravitt, J.H.P. 1997. Securitization. *The Financier* 4 (5) (December).

Loutskina, E. 2011. The Role of Securitization in Bank Liquidity and Funding Management. *Journal of Financial Economics* 100.

Mizen, P. 2008. The Credit Crunch of 2007–2008: A Discussion of the Background, Market Reactions, and Policy Responses. *Federal Reserve Bank of St. Louis Review* (September/October).

Nolan, A.R.G., and A.E. Dodson. 2007. Pay as You Go and Don't Forget Your Cap: Demystifying CDS of ABS. *Goodwin Procter LLP White Paper* (January 26).

Whetten, M. 2005. Synthetic ABS 101: PAUG and ABX.HE. *Nomura Fixed Income Research* (March 7).

CHAPTER 6

CDS Execution and Clearing Mechanisms

From the origins of CDS market activity in the late 1990s through about 2009, CDSs were dealer-centric and privately negotiated, bilateral contracts executed by two dealers or a dealer and a customer in which counterparties negotiated all significant terms (and could customize those terms fully) and relied on bilateral credit risk mitigation. Both dealer-to-dealer ("D2D") and dealer-to-customer ("D2C") transactions were negotiated primarily through voice brokers, request-for-quote inquiries from customers, or otherwise bilaterally using e-mails or instant electronic messaging systems. In other words, the early CDS market (across all major product types) was a decentralized, off-exchange and OTC, bilateral, and privately negotiated marketplace.

Beginning around 2005, innovations in both trade execution and clearing began to create shades of gray between the once-dichotomous categories of OTC and exchange-traded derivatives. In particular, an amorphous new category of derivatives known as "cleared swaps[1]" began to emerge. Cleared swaps are bilaterally negotiated, standardized OTC derivatives that are not executed on organized exchanges but that are subsequently cleared by a CCP.[2]

In the wake of the financial crisis that began in 2007, lawmakers and financial regulators throughout much of the world began to implement a coordinated overhaul of the financial regulatory framework. A significant aspect of the new regulatory apparatus involves the regulation of derivatives products, markets, and users—including CDSs. More specifically, in September 2009, the heads of state of the G-20 nations indicated their

C. L. Culp et al., *Credit Default Swaps*, Palgrave Studies in Risk and Insurance, https://doi.org/10.1007/978-3-319-93076-3_6

commitment to help build "a fundamentally stronger financial system than existed prior to the crisis."[3] One significant aspect of the G-20 proposal was the following:

> All standardized OTC derivative contracts should be traded on exchanges or electronic trading platforms, where appropriate, and cleared through central counterparties by end-2012 at the latest. OTC derivative contracts should be reported to trade repositories. Non-centrally cleared contracts should be subject to higher capital requirements.[4]

In 2011, the G-20 amended its initial recommendations and tasked the Basel Committee on Banking Supervision ("BCBS") of the BIS and the International Organization of Securities Commissions ("IOSCO") to develop a consistent set of minimum margin requirements for non-cleared swaps.[5] The expanded "G-20 Principles" thus can be summarized as follows:

- *Clearing*: All standardized OTC derivatives should be cleared by a CCP;
- *Execution*: All standardized OTC derivatives should be traded on regulated exchanges or recognized electronic execution platforms ("EEPs");
- *Reporting*: All OTC derivatives should be reported to a trade/data repository;
- *Margin*: Non-cleared OTC derivatives should be subject to a consistent set of minimum margin requirements; and
- *Capital*: Non-cleared OTC derivatives should be subject to higher capital requirements.

National regulators in North America, member countries of the E.U., several non-E.U. European countries (e.g., Switzerland), and some Asian countries have adopted various new legislation and/or regulations to transform their financial systems and regulatory regimes into markets and infrastructures that conform to the G-20 Principles. These changes have fundamentally redefined the global derivatives marketplace.[6]

Because the new regulatory framework has significantly impacted the market microstructure of CDSs, Sects. 6.1 and 6.2 below provide some background discussion of the new regulatory environment on CDS clearing and trade execution, current conventions, as well as a review of

CDS trading and clearing activity pursuant to the post-crisis regulations. Our emphasis is on the USA.

6.1 CDS Clearing[7]

All CDS contracts oblige both counterparties to make certain payments. For credit protection purchasers on non-PAUG single- and multi-name CDS contracts, such payments include up-front premium payments as well as ongoing coupon payments. For protection sellers on non-PAUG contracts, moreover, payments occur after the occurrence of credit events and depend on the elected method of settlement. Because no PAUG-based ABCDSs are currently cleared, we discuss only single-name and index CDSs in this chapter.

Clearing is the process by which payment obligations between two or more firms are computed (often using an applicable netting scheme), risk-reducing margin and collateral requirements are applied, related risk measures (e.g., value at risk) are calculated, and the like. Clearing by CCPs has been an integral component of exchange-traded derivatives for more than a century.[8] Derivatives that are cleared through CCPs expose traders only to the credit risk of the CCP itself and not to the credit risk of the original trading counterparty.

To protect the integrity of the marketplace, CCPs typically maintain strict safeguards and ample access to capital and liquidity. CCPs, moreover, have withstood the failures of various large market participants over time (e.g., Drexel Burnham Lambert, Barings, Refco, Lehman Brothers) and helped prevent the impact of those failures from spreading to other firms.

Prior to 2005, many banks active in the burgeoning CDS market were taken to task by regulators for having poor back-office support systems to support their CDS market activities. In September 2005, then-President of the Federal Reserve Bank of New York, Timothy Geithner, convened a meeting of the 14 largest banks during which the banks were strongly encouraged to modernize and update their back-office systems for CDS trade capture, reporting, and the like. Geithner also emphasized that the CDS marketplace needed (in his view) CCP clearing of CDS trades in order to mitigate counterparty credit risk and potential systemic risk issues arising from the possibility of contagion following the failure of a market participant with large amounts of open CDS positions (Tett 2009). Following the 2005 meeting of Geither with the major CDS dealers, the primary bank dealers began to explore solutions for the voluntary clearing of the most actively traded index CDSs (as discussed in Chapter 4).

In the wake of the global financial crisis that began in 2007, many regulators viewed the nature and role of CCPs and their successful track records as compelling reasons to believe that systemic risk could be reduced by shifting certain types of derivatives transactions out of the traditional bilateral OTC world and into the CCP-cleared environment. Regulators and legislators around the world, however, deemed that steps toward voluntary clearing of OTC derivatives like CDSs had not moved far enough and fast enough. As such, US and European legislators and regulators took a significant step and began to *mandate* CCP clearing for certain OTC derivatives, including certain CDSs.

6.1.1 USA

The USA was the first country to adopt sweeping new reforms of financial regulation with the passage of the Dodd-Frank Wall Street Reform and Consumer Protection Act ("DFA") by the US Congress on July 15, 2010, signed into law by President Obama on July 21, 2010. Title VII of the Dodd-Frank Act requires that all swaps not otherwise excluded by the CFTC be submitted for clearing to a CFTC-regulated CCP (or a CCP that is recognized by the CFTC but exempt from CFTC regulation).[9] CCPs must submit swaps they wish to clear for review and approval by the CFTC. In addition, the DFA requires the CFTC to perform its own independent assessment of specific swaps and classes of swaps that should be subject to the clearing mandate.

The US clearing mandate was implemented in 2013 on a phased-in basis and was fully in effect as of September 9, 2013. Table 6.1 shows the CDS products that were defined by the CFTC as subject to the US clearing mandate. Notably, none of these products have been alleged to have been either the underlying cause or the source of significant propagation of the credit crisis.

Subsequent implementation regulations and no-action letters issued by the CFTC exempt some CDS users and transactions from the US clearing mandate. Perhaps most importantly, certain "end users" of credit derivatives (i.e., firms that engage in CDSs for commercial or risk management purposes) are exempt from the mandated clearing requirement. In addition, certain transactions are exempt from the US clearing

Table 6.1 CDS products subject to the US CDS clearing mandate

	US reference names	*E.U. reference names*
Reference entities	Corporate	Corporate
Region	North America	Europe
Indices[a,b]	CDX.NA.IG CDX.NA.HY	iTraxx Europe iTraxx Europe Crossover iTraxx Europe HiVol
Tenors[a,b]	CDX.NA.IG: 3, 5, 7, 10 yr CDX.NA.HY: 5 yr	iTraxx Europe: 5, 10 yr iTraxx Europe Crossover: 5 yr iTraxx Europe HiVol: 5 yr
Tranched	No	No

Notes [a]Includes CDX.NA.IG 3 yr Series 15 and all subsequent series to date, CDX.NA.IG 5 yr Series 11 and all subsequent series to date, CDX.NA.IG 7 yr Series 8 and all subsequent series to date, CDX.NA.IG 10 yr Series 8 and all subsequent series to date, CDX.NA.HY 5 yr Series 8 and all subsequent series to date

[b]Includes iTraxx Europe 5 yr Series 10 and all subsequent series to date, iTraxx Europe 10 yr Series 7 and all subsequent series to date, iTraxx Europe Crossover 5 yr Series 10 and subsequent series to date. iTraxx Europe HiVol 5 yr Series 10 and all subsequent series to date

Source http://www.cftc.gov/idc/groups/public/@otherif/documents/ifdocs/clearingrequirementcharts.pdf

mandate based on *de minimus* swaps activity, inter-affiliate transactions, or trade-specific exemptions for block and package trades.

6.1.2 E.U.

The European Market Infrastructure Regulation ("EMIR") went into force on August 16, 2012,[10] and included a swap clearing mandate for E.U. member nations. The EMIR clearing mandate is generally comparable to the Dodd-Frank clearing mandate in the USA and was implemented in 2015 with a phased-in compliance period.

The responsibility for implementing the EMIR clearing mandate on an ongoing basis lies with the European Securities and Markets Authority ("ESMA"), the independent E.U. Authority charged with contributing "to safeguarding the stability of the European Union's financial system by enhancing the protection of investors and promoting orderly and stable financial markets."[11]

On October 1, 2015, the European Commission ratified two CDS products as subject to the clearing mandate under EMIR: (i) untranched iTraxx CDS index products based on Main European corporate reference names with 5-year tenors; and (ii) untranched iTraxx CDS index products based on Crossover European corporate reference names with 5-year tenors.[12]

6.1.3 *Market Activity*

From October 1, 2013, through December 31, 2017, a total of $38,770 billion in notional amounts of CDSs were cleared on CCPs. Of that total, 12.3% of cleared CDSs were single-name CDSs (i.e., $4761 billion), as compared to 87.7% of cleared index CDSs (i.e., $34,009 billion). Notably, all single-name CDSs cleared by CCPs were ***voluntarily*** cleared by the counterparties to those single-name CDS trades; no single-name CDSs were subject to a clearing mandate during this period either in the USA or the E.U.

Figures 6.1 and 6.2 show the notional amounts cleared of single-name CDS and index CDS transactions (respectively) by CCP

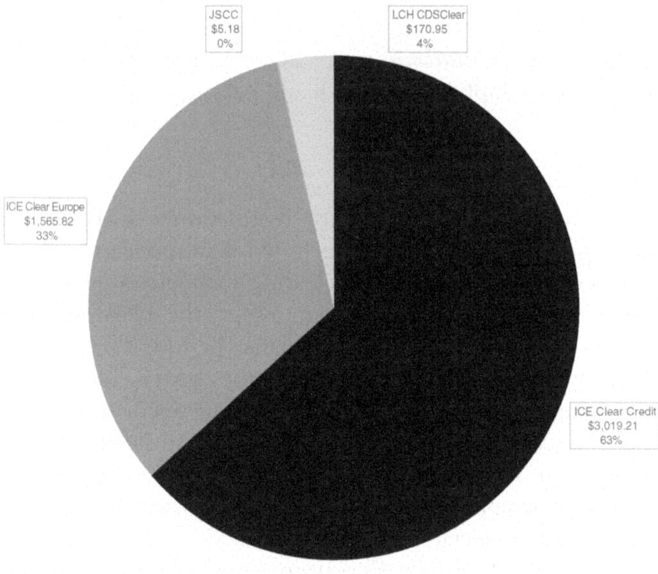

Fig. 6.1 Cleared single-name CDSs by CCP ($ bns notional), October 1, 2013–December 31, 2017 (*Source* Clarus Financial)

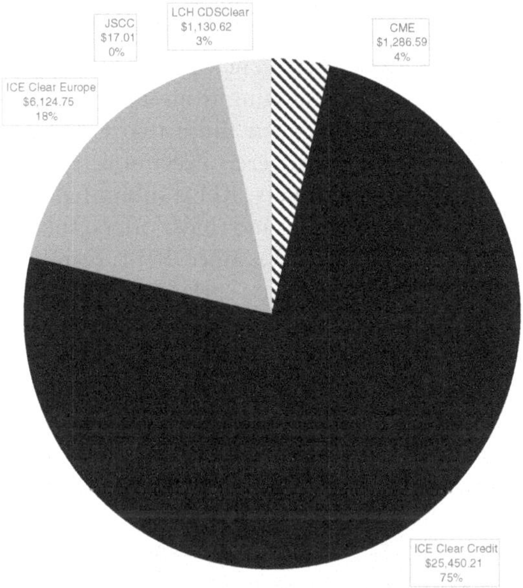

Fig. 6.2 Cleared index CDSs by CCP ($ bns notional), October 1, 2013–December 31, 2017 (*Notes* Cleared index CDSs include CDX.IG, CDX.HY, CDX.EM, iTraxx Crossover, iTraxx Europe, iTraxx Japan, iTraxx Asia, and iTraxx Australia. *Source* Clarus Financial)

from October 2013 through December 2017. As indicated by the data graphed in Fig. 6.1, ICE Clear Credit and ICE Clear Europe accounted for 96% of all single-name CDS clearing volume from October 2013 through December 2017. LCH CDSClear and the Japanese Securities Clearing Corporation ("JSCC") accounted for the remaining four percent of single-name CDS clearing volume during the period.

Figure 6.2 indicates the amounts and proportions of index CDSs cleared by CCPs in the October 2013 through December 2017 period. As is evident, ICE (including ICE Clear Credit and ICE Clear Europe) handles about 93% of all index CDS clearing, with CME accounting for four percent of the remaining volume. LCH's CDSClear facility then accounts for about three percent of CDS index clearing volume, with JSCC accounting for a tiny fraction of clearing volumes.

6.2 CDS Trade Execution

As noted earlier, CDS trades can generally be executed along a spectrum of market microstructures ranging from direct bilateral negotiation to full exchange trading. In between those two extremes are a variety of alternatives including voice-brokered execution, requests for quotes ("RFQs") submitted to single dealers, RFQs submitted to multiple dealers through execution platforms, and bids/offers submitted through central limit order books ("CLOBs"). Since 2014, certain CDS products are subject to regulations that mandate specific execution venues.

6.2.1 USA

Following the adoption of the DFA and the promulgation of related CFTC regulations, all CDSs for which clearing has been mandated are potentially subject to an execution mandate, which requires that certain CDSs be executed on CFTC-recognized swap execution facilities ("SEFs") or CFTC-recognized Designated Contract Markets ("DCMs"). SEFs are EEPs that provide trade execution platforms for both D2D and D2C transactions, whereas DCMs are comprehensive all-to-all organized derivatives exchanges.

EEPs that are required to register with the CFTC as SEFs must provide a minimum trading functionality—i.e., the SEF "must, at a minimum, offer trading services to facilitate Required Transactions by providing market participants with the ability to post both firm and indicative quotes on a centralized electronic screen accessible to all market participants who have access to the SEF."[13] SEFs are also subject to a wide range of additional regulatory and supervisory requirements.

Pursuant to CFTC regulations, SEFs are permitted to execute two types of transactions. First, "Required Transactions" are transactions involving swaps that *must* be executed on SEFs. Second, "Permitted Transactions" are transactions involving swaps that are not subject to the trade execution mandate but that a SEF may nevertheless choose to offer if it feels there is sufficient interest among its customers.[14]

In particular, Required Transactions include any CDS products for which any SEF or DCM has made an application to the CFTC and that the CFTC deems appropriate for designation as made-available-to-trade ("MAT"). If the CFTC approves an application by any SEF or DCM to classify a given product as MAT, then any trades involving that product (not subject to an exemption) must be executed on a SEF. The criteria that the CFTC requires a SEF or DCM to consider in making MAT applications include the following[15]:

- Whether there are ready and willing buyers and sellers;
- [T]he frequency or size of transactions on SEFs, DCMs, or of bilateral transactions;
- [T]he trading volume on SEFs, DCMs, or of bilateral transactions;
- [T]he number and types of market participants;
- [T]he bid/ask spread;
- [T]he usual number of resting firm or indicative bids and offers;
- [W]hether a SEF's trading system or platform or a DCM's trading facility will support trading in the swap; or
- [A]ny other factor that the SEF or DCM may consider relevant.

Three SEFs submitted determinations that certain CDS products were MAT: Bloomberg, MarketAxess, and Tradeweb. All three SEFs proposed that the CFTC designate the 5-year CDSs based on the CDX.NA.IG on-the-run ("OTR") series as MAT. MarketAxess and Tradeweb both also proposed that CDSs based on the most recent off-the-run ("OFTR") series of the CDX.NA.IG and iTraxx Europe also be designated as MAT. In addition, MarketAxess and Tradeweb proposed that 5-year CDSs based on the OTR and most recent OFTR series of the CDX.NA.HY and iTraxx Europe Crossover be designated as MAT.[16] Table 6.2 summarizes the CDS products that the CFTC ultimately agreed to certify as MAT—i.e., essentially all of the products proposed by the three SEFs that submitted CDS MAT determinations to the CFTC.

Table 6.2 CDS products subject to the US CDS MAT execution mandate

	US reference names	*E.U. reference names*
Reference Entities	Corporate	Corporate
Region	North America	Europe
Indices	CDX.NA.IG	iTraxx Europe
	CDX.NA.HY	iTraxx Europe Crossover
Tenors	CDX.NA.IG: 5 yr	iTraxx Europe: 5 yr
	CDX.NA.HY: 5 yr	iTraxx Europe Crossover: 5 yr
Series	OTR and First OFTR	OTR and First OFTR
Tranched	No	No

Source http://www.cftc.gov/idc/groups/public/@otherif/documents/ifdocs/clearingrequirementcharts.pdf

6.2.2 *E.U.*

The revised Markets in Financial Instruments Directive (known as "MiFID 2") and the related Markets in Financial Instruments Regulation ("MiFIR") delegate authority to ESMA for determining which types of derivatives are subject to mandatory execution requirements. Transactions subject to execution mandates include swaps subject to the EMIR clearing mandate that are made available to trade on a regulated exchange, multilateral trading facility ("MTF"), organized trading facility ("OTF"), or an equivalent platform outside the E.U.[17] ESMA, moreover, defines a minimum liquidity threshold for derivatives products that are deemed "sufficiently liquid" to be traded (by regulatory mandate) on a recognized MTF or OTF.

As of this writing, ESMA has determined that the same two CDS products subject to the EMIR clearing mandate are also subject to the venue execution mandate: (i) untranched iTraxx CDS index products based on Main European corporate reference names with 5-year tenors (both the current OTR series and the first OFTR series); and (ii) untranched iTraxx CDS index products based on Crossover European corporate reference names with 5-year tenors (both the current OTR series and the first OFTR series).[18]

6.2.3 *Market Activity*

Given the US and E.U. clearing and execution venue mandates, it is not surprising that almost all on-SEF trading of CDS products has been comprised of CDS index products and not single-name CDSs. From October 2013 through December 2017, a total of $29,418 billion notional of index CDSs were executed on a US SEF, as compared to $603 billion notional of non-index CDSs.

Figure 6.3 shows the total positions reported by US SEFs from October 2013 through December 2017 for all D2D CDS transactions (comprised almost entirely of CDS index products). Tullett Prebon and GFI evidently dominated the inter-dealer market, accounting for a combined notional amount of 82% of all CDS trades. ICAP and Tradition

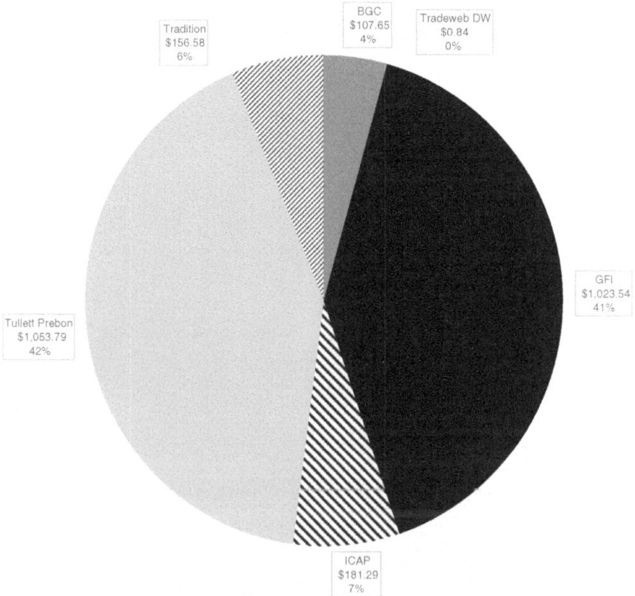

Fig. 6.3 On-SEF D2D US CDS Trades by SEF ($ bns notional), October 1, 2013–December 31, 2017 (*Notes* Includes all CDS product types and currency denominations. *Source* Clarus Financial)

accounted for 13% (notional) of CDS D2D trades executed on-SEF, with BGC and Tradeweb reflecting the remaining five percent.

Figure 6.4 shows the breakdown of CDS trades for D2C transactions across SEFs. The Bloomberg SEF platform obviously captures the vast majority of CDS transactions during the period, accounting for 81% of D2C CDS positions reported to the CFTC by recognized SEFs. Tradeweb is in second place, representing about 13% of D2C CDS trades over the October 2013 through December 2017 period. Finally, ICE and MarketAxess each account for about three percent of the remaining CDS activity over the period.

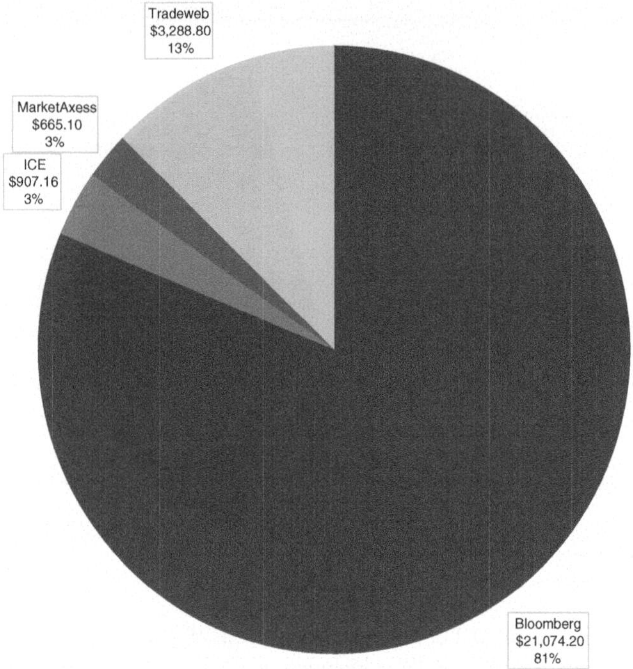

Fig. 6.4 On-SEF D2C US CDS Trades by SEF ($ bns notional), October 1, 2013–December 31, 2017 (*Notes* Includes all CDS product types and currency denominations. *Source* Clarus Financial)

Notes

1. "Swaps" in this context refers to essentially all OTC derivatives based on the definition of "swaps" in the US bankruptcy code following the 1990 amendments and US banking laws pursuant to the Financial Institutions Reform, Recovery, and Enforcement Act of 1989 and the Federal Deposit Insurance Corporation Improvement Act of 1991. From an economic perspective, many products captured under these legal definitions of "swaps" are either forward contracts or options and are not actually swaps.
2. For a review of the historical background and regulation of cleared swaps, see Culp (2010).

3. G-20, *Leaders' Statement—The Pittsburgh Summit* (September 24–25, 2009) (hereinafter "G-20 Pittsburgh Declaration"), p. 8.
4. G-20 Pittsburgh Declaration, op. cit., at 9. *See also* G-20, *Cannes Summit Final Declaration* (November 4, 2011) (hereinafter "G-20 Cannes Summit Declaration"), p. 5.
5. G-20 Cannes Summit Declaration, op. cit.
6. A review of the status of the implementation of these reforms as of April 2014 can be found in Financial Stability Board, *OTC Derivatives Market Reforms: Seventh Progress Report on Implementation* (April 8, 2014).
7. Some portions of Sects. 6.1 and 6.2 draw from Culp (2016) (writing about the post-crisis regulations governing interest rate derivatives).
8. For general discussions on the evolution and function of CCP clearing, see, e.g., Edwards (1984), Moser (1998), Kroszner (1999), Norman (2011), and Pirrong (2011).
9. Dodd-Frank Act §723(a)(3).
10. Regulation (E.U.) No. 648/2012 (July 4, 2012) (in force as of August 16, 2012) (hereinafter "EMIR").
11. https://www.esma.europa.eu/about-esma/who-we-are (last visited April 26, 2018).
12. Commission Delegated Regulation (EU) 2016/592 as of March 1, 2016, *Official Journal of the European Union* (April 19, 2016).
13. Commodity Futures Trading Commission, "Final Rule: Core Principles and Other Requirements for Swap Execution Facilities," *Federal Register* 78, no. 107, Part II (June 4, 2013), at 33483.
14. Id.
15. The eight criteria shown are quoted verbatim from Commodity Futures Trading Commission, "Final Rule: Process for a Designated Contract Market or Swap Execution Facility to Make a Swap Available to Trade, Swap Transaction Compliance and Implementation Schedule, and Trade Execution Requirement under the Commodity Exchange Act," *Federal Register* 78, no. 107, Part III (June 4, 2013), at 33612. The CFTC also states that "[u]nder the proposed rule, no single factor would be dispositive, as the DCM or SEF could consider any one factor or any combination of factors in its determination that a swap is available to trade." Id.
16. Bloomberg SEF LLC, *MAT Submission to the CFTC* (December 5, 2013), MarketAxess SEF Corporation, *MAT Submission to the CFTC* (October 30, 2013), TW SEF LLC, *MAT Submission to the CFTC* (October 28, 2013), and TW SEF LLC, *Clarification and Amendment of MAT Submission to the CFTC* (November 29, 2013).
17. Cleared swaps also must be sufficiently liquid to be subject to mandatory execution requirements.
18. Commission Delegated Regulation (EU) 2017/2417 as of November 17, 2017, *Official Journal of the European Union* (December 22, 2017).

References

Culp, C.L. 2010. OTC-Cleared Derivatives: Benefits, Costs, and Implications of the 'Dodd-Frank Wall Street Reform and Consumer Protection Act.' *Journal of Applied Finance* 20 (2).

Culp, C.L. 2016. Interest Rate Derivatives Products and Recent Market Activity in the New Regulatory Framework. In *Handbook of Fixed-Income Securities*, ed. P. Veronesi. Hoboken, NJ: Wiley.

Edwards, F.R. 1984. The Clearing Association in Futures Markets: Guarantor and Regulator. In *The Industrial Organization of Futures Markets*, ed. R.W. Anderson. Lexington: Lexington Books.

Kroszner, R.S. 1999. Can the Financial Markets Privately Regulate Risk?: The Development of Derivatives Clearinghouses and Recent Over-the-Counter Innovations. *Journal of Money, Credit and Banking* 31 (3), Part 2 (August).

Moser, J.T. 1998. Contracting Innovations and the Evolution of Clearing and Settlement Methods at Futures Exchanges. Federal Reserve Bank of Chicago Working Paper WP-98-26 (August).

Norman, P. 2011. *The Risk Controllers: Central Counterparty Clearing in Globalised Financial Markets*. Hoboken, NJ: Wiley.

Pirrong, C. 2011. The Economics of Central Clearing: Theory and Practice. ISDA Discussion Paper Series No. 1 (May).

Tett, G. 2009. *Fool's Gold*. New York: Free Press.

PART II

Potential Benefits and Costs of CDSs

CHAPTER 7

Potential Benefits of CDSs

There are four frequently noted potential benefits of single-name CDSs to their users and, in some cases, to other market participants: facilitating credit risk transfer; increasing the supply of loanable funds; providing opportunities for relatively lower-cost synthetic bond investments; and promoting price discovery and information aggregation. We discuss each of these potential benefits in this chapter.

7.1 Credit Risk Transfer

The classic rationale for CDSs (as with most other derivatives) is to provide a risk management solution for lenders to manage their credit exposures to borrowers. Prior to the advent of credit derivatives, there were mechanisms for firms to manage their corporate and sovereign credit exposures, but those credit risk transfer mechanisms were often inefficient, costly, and/or inaccessible to certain market participants. For example, bank lenders primarily managed and laid off their credit exposures to corporate borrowers through the loan syndication market and through the sale of loan participations on loan trading desks, as discussed in Chapter 3. Until the mid-1990s, however, the syndicated loan market was largely non-standardized and not easy for non-financial institutions to access except through loan or prime funds and early CLOs.

Asset managers and other investors in corporate and sovereign debt were limited to hedging in the cash bond markets, where a bond investor concerned about the credit risk of the bond issuer could either sell

C. L. Culp et al., *Credit Default Swaps*, Palgrave Studies in Risk and Insurance, https://doi.org/10.1007/978-3-319-93076-3_7

the bond or utilize repurchase agreements (repos) and reverse repos to construct synthetic bond forward contracts. The former option deprived the bond investor of any ongoing exposure to the issuer, and the latter alternatives were often prohibitively expensive and gave rise to significant basis risks.

The introduction of single-name CDSs fundamentally altered the availability of risk-sharing mechanisms by creating a new, more efficient product that enables market participants to customize their credit risk profile. Instead of being forced to sell a bond or loan investment or rebalance a whole portfolio, single-name CDSs present a more surgical and precise risk management tool (Duffee and Zhou 2001). In addition to facilitating more tailored credit risk transfer solutions, single-name CDSs are also more liquid and accessible to would-be hedgers than cash bond and loan markets.

The risk management applications of single-name CDSs can be classified into two distinct categories: (i) firms that purchase credit protection to cover future potential losses that would be realized following a credit event; and (ii) firms that acquire credit event protection using CDSs to hedge the risk of periodic changes in the market values of a reference entity's obligations resulting from changes in market participants' expectations of future potential adverse credit event-related losses and other market factors.

7.1.1 *Realized Default Risk*

The first category of hedgers relies on single-name CDSs for credit protection to cover realized losses following the occurrence of a credit event. These participants are generally unconcerned about interim changes in market expectations of the probability of default and/or expected recovery rates on the underlying reference entity. Although these hedgers must be attentive to funding liquidity risks arising from initial and variation margin, their main risk management objective is to protect themselves against an actual credit event, which could give rise to realized economic losses if unhedged.

For example, consider an asset manager that has invested in a large amount of bonds issued by XYZ Corp. If the asset manager believes that the market prices of XYZ Corp. bonds and CDSs referencing XYZ Corp. reflect an excessively optimistic view of the true default risk on XYZ Corp. obligations, the asset manager may keep its bond holdings and purchase what it perceives as relatively cheap protection against the risk of default-related losses on XYZ Corp. bonds. Changes in market perceptions of XYZ Corp.'s default risk can result in potentially significant volatility in the prices of the asset manager's holdings in actual XYZ Corp. bonds and CDSs and may present potentially significant funding requirements should the prices of XYZ Corp. bonds decline. Although the asset manager will have achieved its risk management objective of locking in the final value of its hedged bond position, it must pay close attention to the impacts of mark-to-market spread changes on its interim cash flows and funding liquidity.

Although often compared to bond insurance, CDSs differ from bond insurance in several important ways that are particularly relevant to hedgers. A typical indemnity credit insurance contract (e.g., bond or loan insurance that reimburses lenders for losses arising from a borrower default) provides a lender with a reimbursement of *actual losses* sustained following a default by the borrower (subject to a first-loss retention (a.k.a. deductible) and a policy limit). Because CDSs are based on a reference *entity* and not a specific individual security, there is some basis risk for a hedger that wishes to manage its credit exposure to a given firm using single-name CDSs. For example, suppose an investor purchases a short-term, senior bond issued by Firm ABC and also purchases an auction-settled CDS on reference entity ABC. The CDS spread will reflect the CTD option and, to the extent that Firm ABC also has significant amounts of longer-term and subordinated debt outstanding, the investor will pay a higher CDS coupon than suggested by the risk of the actual short-term senior obligation it holds. The final price in the CDS auction, moreover, will reflect the valuations of *all* of Firm ABC's outstanding deliverable debt, which could also result in Firm ABC receiving a lower payment from its protection seller counterparty than what the bond it holds is worth. The contract is thus not equivalent to an indemnity contract that reimburses actual losses and is not considered insurance.

7.1.2 Mark-to-Market Risk

The second category of hedgers uses single-name CDSs to manage their risk of actual economic losses or mark-to-market accounting losses (generating lower-quality and noisier earnings estimates) arising from interim changes in market expectations about the reference entity's probability of experiencing a credit event and or changes in the expected recovery rate following a credit event prior to the maturity of the CDS contract. Consistent with their risk management objectives, such CDS users can manage their risks by adopting appropriate "hedge ratios" (i.e., the proportions of CDS hedge positions vis-à-vis actual exposures to the reference entity). A typical hedge ratio will roughly match changes in mark-to-market values of CDS spreads (with opposite market directional exposure) to changes in the firm's corresponding risk exposure.[1]

7.2 Increased Supply of Loanable Funds

Financial institutions, including bank lenders to CDS reference entities, are major participants in the CDS market. If creditors selectively trade single-name CDSs linked to their borrowers, CDS positions can change the creditor–borrower relationship and play an important role in determining the borrower credit risk that defines the value of the CDSs and the likelihood of the borrowers experiencing a credit event that will trigger the CDSs. Because single-name CDSs enable creditors to hedge their credit exposures, moreover, CDSs (prior to Basel III) free up economic and/or regulatory capital that enables some lenders to increase the supply of credit either to the same underlying firm or more generally. Improved access to capital for borrowers, in turn, can increase their financial flexibility and resilience to financial distress. Cebenoyan and Strahan (2004) confirm that banks engaging in loan sales and other credit risk transfer mechanisms hold less capital, extend larger amounts of credit to relatively high-risk borrowers, and have lower overall risks and larger profits than other banks.

This gives rise to several empirical questions that we will examine in Chapter 10:

- To what extent do banks actually use single-name CDSs to hedge the credit risk of their borrowers?
- Does the use of CDSs by banks result in an increased supply of loanable funds to either the reference entities underlying the CDSs on which the bank has purchased protection or to other borrowers?
- Does the use of CDSs by banks lead to increased risk-taking by banks?

7.3 Synthetic Bond Investments

Unlike insurance, single-name CDSs do not oblige protection purchasers to own any of the underlying bonds issued by the reference entity. As such, single-name CDSs can be used by firms to take a position on the credit risk of the underlying reference entity either to add to or reduce/neutralize the same side of an existing bond position or to create a new credit exposure. Because single-name CDSs facilitate the standardized trading of underlying credit exposures, investors can usually achieve their desired economic exposure in the underlying bonds using CDSs as opposed to trading in fragmented, commoditized bond issues. The ability of investors to use CDSs as synthetic bond investments, moreover, indirectly benefits hedgers (all else equal) by bringing additional liquidity to the CDS market.

7.4 Price Discovery and Information Aggregation

A fourth manner by which single-name CDSs provide a benefit to market participants is through their role in information aggregation. Like other derivatives contracts, single-name CDS market prices (i.e., spreads) reveal market participants' expectations of the probability that the underlying reference entity will experience a credit event before the CDS contract matures and/or that the market-implied recovery rate and LGD will change. Even for firms that are not actively engaged in credit protection purchases or sales, market-determined CDS spreads still contain information that is potentially useful regarding market participants' expectations about the credit risk of reference entities underlying single-name CDS contracts with various maturities.

Note

1. See, e.g., P. Fage and X. Liu, "The Credit Default Swap—Bond Basis," *Credit Suisse Emerging Markets Sovereign Strategy* (August 15, 2002).

References

Cebenoyan, A.S., and P.E. Strahan. 2004. Risk Management, Capital Structure and Lending at Banks. *Journal of Banking & Finance* 28.

Duffee, G.R., and C. Zhou. 2001. Credit Derivatives in Banking: Useful Tools for Managing Risk? *Journal of Monetary Economics* 48 (1) (August).

CHAPTER 8

Potential Costs of CDSs

Single-name CDSs have potential costs that are also—like the potential benefits of CDSs—subject to empirical examination. The major potential costs that have been discussed in the literature are summarized below. Note that several of these potential costs have been analyzed extensively in the theoretical financial literature but have not been subject to significant empirical analysis.

8.1 Increased Risk-Taking and Diminished Monitoring by Banks

The widespread availability of single-name CDSs as credit risk transfer instruments can potentially give banks an incentive to assume greater risks in their lending portfolios. According to some, the easier it is for banks to protect themselves from the risk of borrower defaults, the more banks will have an incentive to originate larger and riskier loans. In other words, readily available credit risk transfer solutions can give rise to moral hazard and induce banks to make riskier lending decisions (see, e.g., Hakenes and Schnabel 2010). Similar criticisms have been leveled at mortgage lending as well as leveraged finance markets. In both of these markets, the O&D model of lending dominates the traditional O&H model as discussed in Chapters 3 and 5.

A related concern is that banks that hedge their credit risk exposures to borrowers will engage in insufficient monitoring of borrower credit

C. L. Culp et al., *Credit Default Swaps*, Palgrave Studies in Risk and Insurance, https://doi.org/10.1007/978-3-319-93076-3_8

risks—i.e., another form of moral hazard (see, e.g., Pennacchi 1988 generally; Morrison 2005 for a CDS-specific discussion). Monitoring involves screening borrowers *ex ante* in order to identify good credits and measure their risk and then following borrowers over the course of their loans in order to both prevent them from engaging in opportunistic and excessively risky behavior and to penalize them when they fail to meet contractual obligations. To the extent that bank lenders can hedge their borrower credit exposures on a relatively low-cost basis, single-name CDSs could attenuate banks' incentives to monitor the credit quality of borrowers and shift monitoring responsibilities to credit protection sellers with relatively less skill and expertise than lenders have.

The counter-argument, however, is that, to the extent the information about the credit risk of the reference entity reflected in CDS spreads is reliable, it may actually be a better source of information (even for the original bank lenders themselves) about the credit quality of borrowers than passive or even active borrower-specific credit risk monitoring.

Yet another similar concern is that CDSs can make it "too easy" for investors and banks to increase their credit risk exposures. The mere fact that the uses of single-name CDSs can sometimes lead to increased risk is not, however, an indictment of CDSs if the firms' managers and shareholders have a preference for greater risk-taking and the corresponding potential for higher returns. On the contrary, given that single-name CDSs enable firms to achieve their desired risk/return targets is an indication that single-name CDSs are effective in facilitating firms' specific risk management and investment objectives.

8.2 Empty Creditors, Negative Economic Interests, and Strategic Defaults

Concerns have been expressed that when debt holders in a company purchase too much credit protection through single-name CDSs but retain their voting rights, those firms may no longer have an incentive to renegotiate their debt or make concessions even when it is efficient for them to do so, thereby forcing the debtor into inefficient bankruptcy or liquidation (Hu and Black 2008a, b; Bolton and Oehmke 2011).

A more extreme version of this theory known as the "negative economic interest" problem is that hedged creditors may have an incentive to buy up a significant amount of a firm's debt, purchase protection in a much larger notional amount, and try and drive the firm into bankruptcy to make a net profit on its CDS protection purchases (Hu and Black 2008b). *The Economist* characterized this potential concern as follows: "By purchasing a material amount of a firm's debt in conjunction with a disproportionately large number of CDS contracts, rapacious lenders (mostly hedge funds) can render bankruptcy more attractive than solvency."[1] Examples of related phenomena are described in Sect. 2.2.4 of Chapter 2.

More specifically, single-name CDSs can potentially impact debtor–creditor relationships by enabling creditors to separate their control rights from their cash flow rights and risk exposures. Creditors that hedge their exposures with single-name CDSs can partially or fully eliminate their credit exposure to a borrower while retaining their rights to participate in discussions related to issues like bankruptcy, reorganization, restructuring, and the like.

One possible consequence of this separation is the creation of "empty creditors" that no longer have an economic interest in the efficient continuation of the debtor as a firm, which may lead such creditors to push the debtor into bankruptcy or liquidation even in situations when restructuring would be a more efficient solution. Some financial analysts and others have even raised concerns that CDS protection buyers could force a reference entity into bankruptcy in order to trigger a credit event under their CDS protection purchases, especially if the CDS documentation does not specify restructuring as a credit event (see, e.g., Pollack 2003).

Not all empty creditor theories, however, yield adverse implications for borrowers. In a frequently cited paper, Bolton and Oehmke (2011) develop a model to analyze how the increased bargaining power of creditors arising from the availability of single-name CDSs can have a positive impact on reference entity bankruptcy filings. Their model assumes that a firm issues debt to finance a positive net present value investment project and that some lenders choose to purchase CDSs. The model also assumes that the firm cannot credibly commit to pay out cash flows in the future. This "limited commitment" feature of the Bolton and Oehmke model results in the firm being unable to write enforceable financial contracts based on its uncertain future cash flows.

In the Bolton and Oehmke (2011) model, the firm may fail to make payments on its debt for either of two reasons: (i) the firm does not generate sufficient interim cash flows sufficient to cover its contractual interest payment obligations (a "cash flow default"); or (ii) the firm's cash flows are sufficient to service its debt, but the firm prefers to use the cash for internal purposes instead of repaying its creditors (a "strategic default"). When firms cannot credibly commit to repay their debt (e.g., when their cash flows are observable but not verifiable) and payments are not legally enforceable, firms may choose to default on their debt to divert cash flows to themselves even when the cash flows are sufficient to service their contractual debt payment obligations. The possibility of strategic defaults has been widely recognized as a problem arising from incomplete corporate debt contracts.[2] The risk that firms will engage in a strategic default increases the interest rate lenders will demand from such firms and reduces borrowers' debt capacities (Saretto and Tookes 2013).

A more recent and related concern is that large buyers of CDS protection may pressure reference entity borrowers to accept advantageous terms on restructured debt in return for strategic defaults that trigger CDS contracts, which generate large payoffs to lenders with significant CDS protection purchases (see Chapter 2, Sect. 2.2.4).

The ability of lenders to purchase credit protection with single-name CDSs, however, also gives creditors an advantage in distressed firm debt renegotiations and thereby attenuates the borrowers' incentives to engage in strategic defaults or debt renegotiations that are to the detriment of lenders. According to Bolton and Oehmke (2011), the existence of creditors with increased bargaining power resulting from their CDS hedges actually plays a useful role by increasing a firm's debt capacity—i.e., credit protection held by existing creditors may make them more willing to issue new debt to finance positive net present value investments, and the existence of hedged creditors with stronger bargaining power can also make other lenders more willing to extend more credit and at a lower rate. In other words, the availability of single-name CDSs can reduce the costs of contracting related to strategic defaults by improving the contracting technology and mitigating the limited commitment problem that firms face when making incomplete debt contracts.[3]

Kim (2013) explains that CDSs make up for incompleteness in some debt contracts by serving as a pre-commitment device that deters firms from strategic default. Firms with high strategic default incentives thus can be expected to experience relatively larger reductions in their corporate bond spreads following the introduction of CDSs. By giving more credibility to borrowers' commitments to repay their debt (assuming no cash flow default occurs), CDSs contribute to a reduction in the cost of corporate debt. Similar results by Saretto and Tookes (2013) confirm that the frictions CDSs introduce into renegotiation can reduce the risk of strategic default and hence increase debt capacity and/or lower the cost of debt. Salomao (2017) presents the related argument that reference entities underlying sovereign CDSs are associated with lower sovereign default probabilities, greater debt capacity, and lower borrowing costs because of enhanced bargaining power held by lenders given the restructuring provisions included in typical sovereign CDSs. Lee, Oh, and Yermack (2017) argue that the positive impact of CDS on debt capacity illustrated by Saretto and Tookes (2013) could be driven by important omitted factors such as corrected agency problems.

8.3 "Excessive" Volatility Arising from Speculation

The use of CDSs to replicate bond positions synthetically has been an important source of demand for single-name CDSs in the past, but has also been a significant source of controversy. As noted in the previous section, single-name CDS contracts are (by design) derivatives and not insurance contracts. As a result, the insurable interest doctrine does not apply to protection buyers and, as such, they are not obliged to own an underlying bond issued by the CDS reference entity. This investment activity thus is often described in the popular press as "speculation" or "uncovered selling" or "naked shorting."

A potential benefit of synthetic bond investors and speculators is, of course, the potential for added liquidity in the CDS marketplace. Greater liquidity benefits hedgers by reducing market liquidity risks. The presence of speculators also helps ensure that the information reflected in market prices is not biased toward either primarily optimistic or pessimistic investors.

Dating back to the earliest days of US futures regulation, however, many have held the belief that speculators can be a destabilizing influence and can cause an increase in market volatility not just in the derivatives product but also in the cash market underlying the derivatives product. For example, in 1947, President Harry S. Truman said:

> Another factor that contributes to high prices of food is gambling in grain. Grain prices naturally respond to the laws of supply and demand, but they should not be subject to the greed of speculators who gamble on what

may lie ahead in our commodity markets....I say this because the cost of living in this country must not be a football to be kicked about by gamblers in grain.[4]

Such beliefs persist today. For example, during the European sovereign debt crisis, numerous media, public policy, and political commentators blamed naked shorting in sovereign CDS markets for the seemingly excessive volatility on the prices and rates of European sovereign debt and for the decline in sovereign debt prices in the cash market. The European regulators' concerns escalated to a ban on naked shorting of sovereign debt through sovereign CDSs effective as of November 1, 2012. Excluded from the ban are protection purchasers that own the underlying bonds, have borrowed or arranged to borrow the underlying bonds, or had an arrangement with a third party confirming the source from which the deliverable bonds would be obtained.[5]

The empirical evidence does not provide support for regulators' concerns. For example, Duffie (2010) shows that the growth in the net open interest of CDSs on Eurozone countries that were perceived as potential default risks in 2010 was not particularly volatile, which indicates that most CDS protection purchases were buy-and-hold hedges and not short-term speculative attempts to "take a view" on those countries. Duffie (2010), moreover, finds no statistically significant relation between net changes in open sovereign CDS positions and weekly changes in the CDS coupon rates for Greece, Ireland, Italy, Portugal, or Spain. In fact, the empirical evidence indicates that the E.U. ban on the naked shorting of sovereign debt using sovereign CDSs adversely impacted the market by reducing liquidity (Duffie 2010; Pu and Zhang 2012; Silva et al. 2016) and interfering with price discovery (Ni and Pan 2011; Silva et al. 2016).

Related to concerns that single-name CDSs provide relatively low-cost and liquid instruments for speculators to take a view or make a synthetic investment in the underlying reference entity is the concern expressed by some that single-name CDSs may provide market participants with a mechanism to manipulate CDS prices in order to generate profits in related financial instruments (e.g., the reference entity's stocks or bonds). This concern is usually based on a perceived opacity in single-named CDS trading—i.e., a perceived lack of transparency in single-name CDSs makes cross-market manipulations harder for other market participants to detect and prevent (see, e.g., Anderson 2010; Brown 2010).

8.4 Systemic Risk

Although there is very little empirical evidence that single-name CDSs were either the proximate cause of the credit and Eurozone sovereign debt crises or that single-name or multi-name CDS markets stopped functioning during the crises, many still contend that single-name CDSs are a source of potential interconnectedness and systemic risk across financial institutions that could serve as a transmission mechanism for contagion in the event of a systemic financial disruption.[6] This concern has been the focus of both academic researchers and government regulators, such as the Financial Stability Oversight Council ("FSOC"). Some of these analyses are reviewed in Chapter 12.

Notes

1. "No Empty Threat: Credit-default Swaps are Pitting Firms Against their Own Creditors," *The Economist* (June 18, 2009).
2. See, e.g., Bolton and Scharfstein (1996) and Hart and Moore (1998).
3. For a somewhat different perspective, see Arping (2014).
4. H. H. Bakken, *Theory of Markets and Marketing* (Mimir Publishers, Inc., 1953).
5. Regulation (EU) No 236/2012 of the European Parliament and of the Council of 14 March 2012, *Official Journal of the European Union* (March 24, 2012).
6. Even before the outbreak of the crisis, some academic cautioned about the heightened interconnectedness to which single-name CDSs gave rise. See, e.g., Rajan (2006).

References

Anderson, R.W. 2010. Credit Default Swaps: What Are the Social Benefits and Costs? *Banque de France Financial Stability Review* (14) (July).

Arping, S. 2014. Credit Protection and Lending Relationships. *Journal of Financial Stability* 10 (February).

Bolton, P., and M. Oehmke. 2011. Credit Default Swaps and the Empty Creditor Problem. *Review of Financial Studies* 24 (8).

Bolton, P., and D.S. Scharfstein. 1996. Optimal Debt Structure and the Number of Creditors. *Journal of Political Economy* 104 (1) (February).

Brown, O.W. 2010. What Risks and Challenges do Credit Default Swaps Pose to the Stability of Financial Markets? *Banque de France Financial Stability Review* (14) (July).

Duffie, D. 2010. Is There a Case for Banning Short Speculation in Sovereign Bond Markets? *Banque de France Financial Stability Review* (14) (July).
Hakenes, H., and I. Schnabel. 2010. Credit Risk Transfer and Bank Competition. *Journal of Financial Intermediation* 19.
Hart, O., and J. Moore. 1998. Default and Renegotiation: A Dynamic Model of Debt. *Quarterly Journal of Economics* 113 (1) (February).
Hu, H.T.C., and B. Black. 2008a. Debt, Equity and Hybrid Decoupling: Governance and Systemic Risk Implications. *European Financial Management* 14 (4) (August).
Hu, H.T.C., and B. Black. 2008b. Equity and Debt Decoupling and Empty Voting II: Importance and Extensions. *University of Pennsylvania Law Review* 156 (3) (January).
Kim, G.H. 2013. Credit Default Swaps, Strategic Default, and the Cost of Corporate Debt. Working Paper.
Lee J., J. Oh, and D. Yermack. 2017. Credit Default Swaps, Agency Problems, and Management Incentives. NBER Working Paper 24064 (November).
Morrison, A.D. 2005. Credit Derivatives, Disintermediation, and Investment Decisions. *Journal of Business* 78 (2) (March).
Ni, S.X., and J. Pan. 2011. Trading Puts and CDS on Stocks with Short Sale Ban. Working Paper (December 7).
Pennacchi, G.G. 1988. Loan Sales and the Cost of Bank Capital. *Journal of Finance* 43 (2) (June).
Pollack, E.R. 2003. Assessing the Usage and Effect of Credit Derivatives. Paper Presented to Harvard Law School International Finance Seminar (April).
Pu, X., and J. Zhang. 2012. Sovereign CDS Spreads, Volatility, and Liquidity: Evidence from 2010 German Short Sale Ban. *The Financial Review* 47 (1).
Rajan, R.G. 2006. Has Finance Made the World Riskier? *European Financial Management* 12 (4).
Salomao, J. 2017. Sovereign Debt Renegotiation and Credit Default Swaps. *Journal of Monetary Economics* 90 (October).
Saretto, A., and H.E. Tookes. 2013. Corporate Leverage, Debt Maturity, and Credit Supply: The Role of Credit Default Swaps. *Review of Financial Studies* 26 (5) (May).
Silva, P.P., C. Vieira, and I.V. Vieira. 2016. The EU Ban on Uncovered Sovereign Credit Default Swaps: Assessing Impacts on Liquidity, Volatility, and Price Discovery. *Journal of Derivatives* 23 (4) (Summer).

PART III

Empirical Evidence on the Benefits, Costs, and Inter-Market Relations of CDSs

CHAPTER 9

The Informational Content of CDS Spreads

One of the most important and well-recognized aspects of the market-based price system is the informational role of prices (Hayek 1945). Prices that reflect all available information are essential in guiding and promoting efficient resource allocation across time and space. Financial asset prices, in particular, aggregate the information and expectations of a wide variety and number of market participants (see, e.g., Fama (1970, 1991).

Prices of derivatives contracts reflect market participants' information and expectations about the asset or reference rate underlying the derivatives contract. For example, the current price of a forward or futures contract on a commodity to be delivered in three months can be interpreted as the current expected value of the spot price of that commodity three months from now.[1] Furthermore, prices can contain information about other exogenous market determinants. For example, Roll (1984) documented that, as a result of the strong relation between orange juice production and weather, orange juice futures prices provide better information about weather forecasts than weather forecasts themselves.

CDS spreads are a type of market-determined price and, like other asset prices, contain potentially valuable information. In this section, we review the academic literature on the informational content of CDS spreads along three dimensions: (i) the information contained in CDS spreads about the credit risk of the underlying reference entity; (ii) the other economic variables that influence and are reflected in CDS spreads; and (iii) the use of CDS spreads to estimate the significance of

C. L. Culp et al., *Credit Default Swaps*, Palgrave Studies in Risk and Insurance, https://doi.org/10.1007/978-3-319-93076-3_9

firm-specific information releases (e.g., credit rating actions) and general market news announcements. The empirical research on these three issues can help us gain a better understanding of how well-connected single-name CDS spreads are to the credit risk of their underlying reference entities and other economically relevant variables and, hence, how well single-name CDSs and CDS indices can function as credit risk transfer and synthetic investment mechanisms.

9.1 Reference Entity Credit Risk

CDS spreads reflect important information about market participants' expectations concerning the future probability of default and the recovery rate (and, hence, LGD) for underlying reference entities. Before reviewing the empirical evidence in Sect. 9.2 of this chapter, a brief review of two anecdotal examples will help motivate the subsequent discussion.

9.1.1 CDS Spreads and the Greek Restructuring Event

Figure 9.1 shows single-name CDS spreads with one-, five-, and 10-year tenors on the Hellenic Republic from 2009 through March 9, 2012 (i.e., the date on which the EMEA DC declared that a restructuring event had occurred, as discussed in Sect. 2.2.2 of Chapter 2). For scaling purposes, the data are presented in two sub-figures: Fig. 9.1(a) presents Greek CDS spreads from 2009 through September 30, 2011; and Fig. 9.1(b) shows spreads from October 3, 2011, through March 9, 2012.

The Greek CDS spreads shown in Fig. 9.1 unsurprisingly and consistently track the major news events surrounding the Hellenic Republic's mounting fiscal crisis as explained in Chapter 2, Sect. 2.2.2. Tran (2013) confirms that sovereign CDS spreads on Greek debt provided a significant early warning to debt holders as much as three to six months in advance of the actual credit event determination. In Fig. 9.1(a), for example, the increase in CDS spreads is pronounced prior to the May 2010 E.U. bailout announcement, as is the subsequent retrenchment of

Fig. 9.1 Single-name CDS spreads for the Hellenic Republic: (a) 1/2/2009–9/30/2011 and (b) 10/3/2011–3/9/2012 (*Note* Spreads shown are the bid/ask midpoint for CDSs on senior Greek debt. *Source* Capital IQ and CMA subscribed data) ▶

(a)

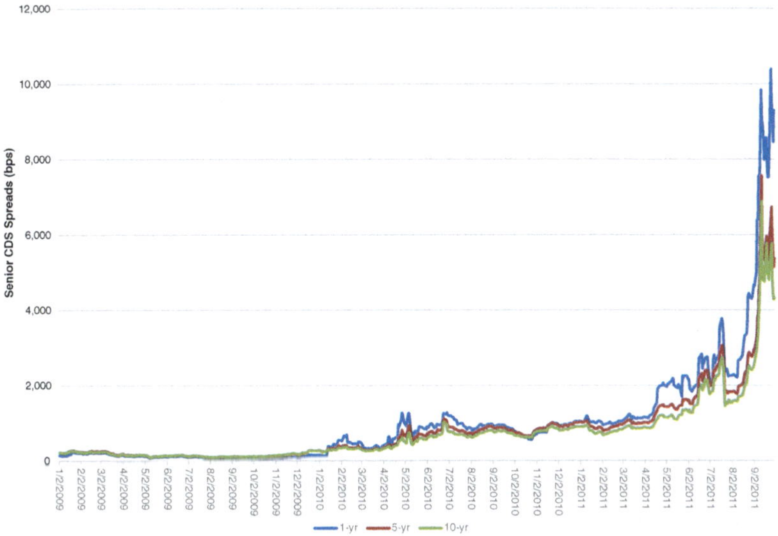
Senior CDS Spreads (bps)
12,000
10,000
8,000
6,000
4,000
2,000
0
1/2/2009
2/2/2009
3/2/2009
4/2/2009
5/2/2009
6/2/2009
7/2/2009
8/2/2009
9/2/2009
10/2/2009
11/2/2009
12/2/2009
1/2/2010
2/2/2010
3/2/2010
4/2/2010
5/2/2010
6/2/2010
7/2/2010
8/2/2010
9/2/2010
10/2/2010
11/2/2010
12/2/2010
1/2/2011
2/2/2011
3/2/2011
4/2/2011
5/2/2011
6/2/2011
7/2/2011
8/2/2011
9/2/2011
1-yr
5-yr
10-yr

(b)

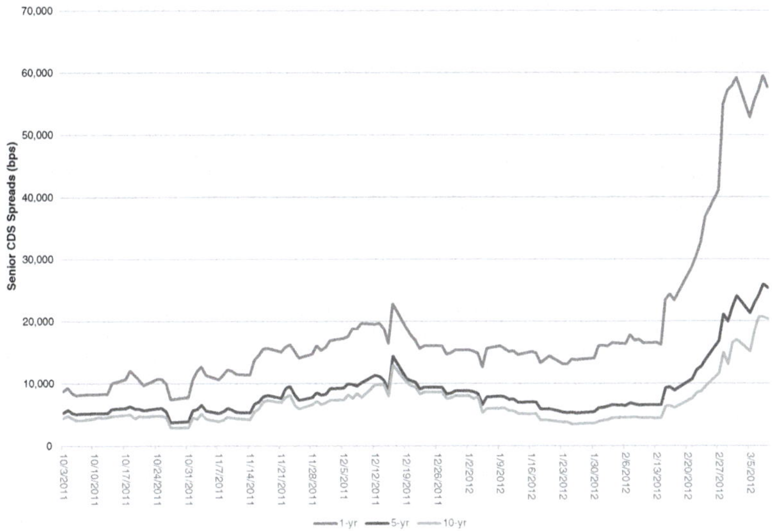
Senior CDS Spreads (bps)
70,000
60,000
50,000
40,000
30,000
20,000
10,000
0
10/3/2011
10/10/2011
10/17/2011
10/24/2011
10/31/2011
11/7/2011
11/14/2011
11/21/2011
11/28/2011
12/5/2011
12/12/2011
12/19/2011
12/26/2011
1/2/2012
1/9/2012
1/16/2012
1/23/2012
1/30/2012
2/6/2012
2/13/2012
2/20/2012
2/27/2012
3/5/2012
1-yr
5-yr
10-yr

spreads after the creation of the EFSF was announced (see Sect. 2.2.2 of Chapter 2). The significant increase in the volatility of credit spreads around the July 2011 E.U. summit is also apparent.

In Fig. 9.1(b), we can see that following the October 26, 2011, invitation by the Greek government for investors to engage in a voluntary debt exchange, credit spreads fell, albeit only briefly and from already exorbitant levels. As Fig. 9.1(b) further shows, moreover, spreads then generally rose through mid-December, with one-year spreads exceeding 20,000 basis points ("bps") per annum. A purchase of €1 million in notional credit protection on senior Greek debt in mid-December 2011 thus would have cost over €500,000 *per day*.

Also noteworthy from Fig. 9.1 is the relation between CDS spreads of different maturities, more generally known as the term structure of CDS spreads.[2] Beginning in mid-January 2010, one-year spreads rose above five-year spreads, and five-year spreads began to exceed 10-year spreads. That remained true more often than not through 2010 and was consistently true in 2011 and 2012. In other words, the cost of purchasing credit protection on Greek debt (on an annualized basis) was higher for a one-year tenor than for a five- or 10-year tenor. Indeed, the cheapest credit protection on Greek debt (on an annualized basis) was for the purchase of 10-year default protection.

Inversions in the term structure of credit spreads (known in futures parlance as "backwardation"[3]) are common for reference entities experiencing financial distress. In essence, market participants generally expect the firm or the sovereign either to fail in the short run or, if it survives, to experience a subsequent improvement in its financial condition and credit quality, which leads to lower conditional default probabilities and CDS spreads for more deferred maturities. We discuss the term structure of CDS spreads in more detail in Sect. 9.2.2 of this chapter.

9.1.2 CDS Spreads and the Lehman Credit Event

The one-, five-, and 10-year spreads on senior CDSs referencing Lehman Brothers presented in Fig. 9.2 tell a similar story for Lehman to that shown in Fig. 9.1 for Greece. The cost of purchasing credit protection on Lehman senior debt began to increase noticeably in August 2007, when what had previously been limited to a US subprime mortgage and

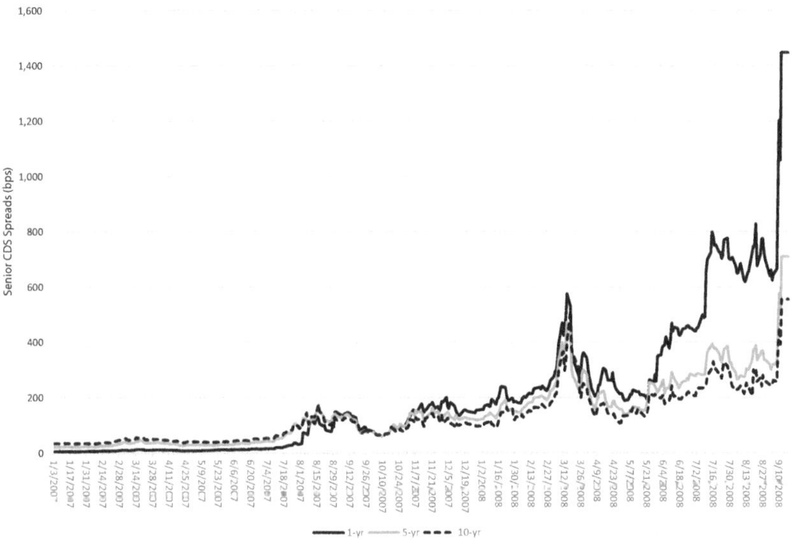

Fig. 9.2 CDS spreads for Lehman Brothers, 1/3/2007–9/15/2008 (*Note* Spreads shown are the bid/ask midpoint for CDSs on senior Lehman debt. *Source* Capital IQ and CMA subscribed data)

leveraged loan crisis suddenly erupted into a broader global credit crisis. Spreads then became relatively more volatile and increased through the March 14, 2008, announcement by the Federal Reserve Bank of New York that it would provide temporary liquidity to facilitate the sale of ailing investment bank Bear Stearns.

Beginning late May of 2008, as Fig. 9.2 indicates, the one-year single-name CDS spread for Lehman began to increase significantly. Five- and 10-year spreads also rose, but not nearly as much as one-year spreads. Although the slope of the term structure of Lehman CDS spreads had been mostly negative since late 2007, the extent of the inversion increased sharply in Lehman's final months. On July 15, 2008, for example, the cost of purchasing credit protection on Lehman's senior debt for one year was eight percent per annum as compared to 3.93 and 3.10% per annum for the cost of five- and 10-year protection, respectively.

9.2 Determinants of CDS Spreads

Although the CDS spreads and slopes of the CDS term structures on Greek and Lehman debt leading up to the two entities' credit events tell a plausible story that single-name CDSs reflect market participants' expectations of future credit events, the mere graphical depictions of spreads does not empirically substantiate that numerical default probabilities and recovery rates can be extracted with confidence from observed CDS spreads. To substantiate that notion, more rigorous econometric analyses are required. Such analyses are also required to determine which other economic variables may influence and be reflected in single-name CDS spreads.

Significant attention has been paid in the academic literature to the empirical determinants of CDS spreads. In other words, what actually determines the price that protection purchasers must pay to transfer their credit risk or initiate a new synthetic bond position on reference entities underlying and utilizing single-name CDSs?

At a broad level, the market-determined spread on a single-name CDS is comprised of two components. The first component is the expected credit loss associated with the underlying reference entity—i.e., the probability that the reference entity experiences a credit event over the life of the CDS contract, and the LGD if a credit event occurs (i.e., the expected loss less expected recoveries). Protection sellers demand a CDS coupon rate that compensates them for these expected credit-related losses. We review the empirical research on expected credit loss information reflected in CDS spreads in Sects. 9.2.1 and 9.2.2 of this chapter.

In addition to the expected credit loss component of CDS spreads, protection sellers also demand a risk premium from protection buyers to compensate the sellers for the risk that actual payouts on the single-name CDS protection sales they write may exceed expected credit losses (see, e.g., Pan and Singleton 2008). As we discuss in Sect. 9.2.3 of this chapter, the risk premium reflected in CDS spreads is not limited to a credit risk premium; protection sellers in single-name CDS appear also to require compensation for risks beyond the idiosyncratic credit risk of the reference entity.

Many of the economic variables discussed in the sections below have their theoretical roots in the classic characterization of corporate debt as a put option on the assets of a firm plus a risk-free loan originally pioneered by Merton (1974).[4] A large literature has evolved that expands and modifies the original lognormal Merton model, tests the original version of the model and many of its successors, and empirically examines the related issue of the "credit spread puzzle" (i.e., actual credit spreads are often much higher than those implied by the Merton model). Those theoretical and empirical studies are beyond the scope of this book, but interested readers are directed to the useful surveys by Jarrow (2009) and Sundaresan (2013).

9.2.1 CDS Spreads and Expected Credit Losses

A significant amount of research has investigated the forecasting power of CDS spreads with respect to the credit risk of underlying reference entities. The evidence indicates that CDS spreads (both spreads and changes in spreads) contain information that can be used to estimate the probability of future adverse credit events. Hull et al. (2004), Finnerty et al. (2013), and others confirm that CDS spreads contain information on future adverse credit events by looking at negative rating events (primarily reviews for downgrade). Jansen and Fabozzi (2017) show that implied ratings derived from CDS spreads and a selection of exogenous variables outperformed S&P ratings in terms of Gini-coefficients (i.e., a measure of statistical dispersion) but implied ratings were less stable than S&P ratings. Berndt et al. (2005), moreover, find that over 70% of the variation (across different reference entities) in five-year single-name corporate CDS spreads is explained by corresponding expected default frequencies ("EDFs") measured using the Moody's KMV model.[5] Other studies of CDS spreads have confirmed that a reference entity's credit risk (measured by credit rating or market-based measures like EDFs) is a primary determinant of credit spreads during normal market conditions—see, e.g., Aunon-Nerin et al. (2002), Abid and Naifar (2006), Fabozzi et al. (2007), Jakovlev (2007), Chen et al. (2008), Annaert et al. (2013), and Lin et al. (2017).

Some papers have focused specifically on the informational content of CDS spreads for banks or other financial institutions. Chiaramonte and Casu (2010) find that single-name CDS spreads on senior US bank debt reflect the same information as bank balance-sheet ratios and are a good proxy for banks' creditworthiness. The authors also deduce that the relationship between CDS spreads and balance-sheet ratios grew even stronger during the credit crisis. Norden and Weber (2012) find a similar result for CDSs on the senior debt of European banks and further document that CDSs on subordinated bank debt provide an early indication of bank default risk (which they measure using credit ratings and financial statement information). Not surprisingly, they show that CDSs on subordinated bank debt are more risk-sensitive than CDSs on senior debt.

Avino et al. (2016) examine the senior and subordinated CDS spreads of 60 European and US banks and confirm the results of earlier studies that changes in CDS spreads provide strong information about forthcoming financial distress at banks. The authors estimate that a one standard deviation increase in CDS spreads is associated with as much as a 15% increase in the probability of a reference bank's failure.

Single-name CDS spreads not only reflect the probability that the underlying reference entity will experience an event of default,[6] but also market participants' expectations about the recovery rate and LGD of the reference entity.[7] In a classic paper, Pan and Singleton (2008) estimate the nature of default arrivals and recovery rates implied by the term structure of sovereign CDS spreads using data from Mexico, Turkey, and Korea from 2001 to 2006. They show that the probability of default and LGD can be separately estimated from the term structure of sovereign CDS spreads. Christensen (2007), Schneider et al. (2010), Elkamhi et al. (2014), and Schläfer and Uhrig-Homburg (2014) also find that separate estimates of default probabilities and expected recovery rates or LGDs can be extracted from observed CDS spreads and that the risk of changes in expected recovery rates gives rise to a risk premium demanded by protection sellers as compensation for bearing that particular risk.

Spreads on CDX index tranches, moreover, appear to compensate investors for expected losses due to defaults, jump-to-default risk, and correlation risk in addition to reference entity and market-wide changes in credit conditions. Eckner (2010) decomposes the spreads on individual CDX index tranches to show that during the pre-crisis period from 2004 to 2006, the senior tranche carries a 9.9% compensation for systematic risk and a 0.2% compensation for reference entity-specific risk. In contrast, the residual tranche carries 81.7% of the compensation for reference entity risk but carries only 32% of the total compensation for systematic risk.

Scheicher (2008) compares the effect of the crisis on the pricing of CDX and iTraxx tranches for the period from 2004 through 2008 and shows that, despite similarities in the contract specifications of the US and European indices, spreads on US-based CDX tranches repriced relatively more frequently starting in July 2007. Seo and Wachter (2016) argue that the senior tranches of the tranched CDX index share characteristics with deep out-of-the money put options, which only reflect losses subsequent to the default of a large fraction of the underlying reference entities. The authors explain that spreads on senior tranches are closely related to the probability of extreme market-wide crisis events.

Not all empirical studies of implied default probabilities, however, have resulted in similar results as the above studies. For example, Stanton and Wallace (2011) analyze the ABX.HE index and conclude that index values during the crisis period were inconsistent with realized home equity loan default rates.

9.2.2 *The Term Structure of CDS Spreads*

The term structure of CDS spreads is normally upward-sloping. At least two different explanations have been posited for this phenomenon. The first and most obvious explanation for a positively sloped CDS term structure is that investors may perceive the firm's credit quality to be declining over time, resulting in rising costs of default protection and CDS spreads. Sometimes known as the expectations hypothesis, this explanation essentially adopts the view that current CDS spreads are good forecasts of future default probabilities and recovery rates.

A significant amount of theoretical research has been conducted to try and connect the slope of the term structure of CDS spreads to the expectations hypothesis. The idea is that the term structure of single-name CDS spreads should be upward-sloping for relatively high-quality, low-risk reference entities because of the direct link between CDS spreads and conditional default probabilities. To put it simply, the probability of a firm defaulting over the course of one year starting at time t—conditional on the firm having survived up to time t—is higher for larger values of t because expected future credit quality is perceived as lower than current credit quality. For example, the conditional probability of default from year five to year six for a firm that has survived to year five is lower than the conditional probability of default from year nine to year 10 for a firm that has survived to year nine, thus implying a higher one-year CDS spread at year nine than the one-year CDS spread at year five.

For relatively riskier, lower-quality firms—especially those experiencing financial distress—the opposite is true, and the term structure of CDS spreads is generally downward-sloping, as shown in Figs. 9.1 and 9.2 for

CDS spreads on Greece and Lehman Brothers, respectively. For such firms, the one-year conditional probability of default at time t is decreasing in t—i.e., a firm that survives the distressed short run is expected to have subsequent improvements in its credit quality, thus leading to lower conditional default probabilities and CDS spreads.

An alternative to the expectations hypothesis is that CDS spreads for different maturities reflect not only expected future credit losses but also a risk premium that investors require as compensation to bear the risk that future losses may be unexpectedly higher than the reference entity's future *expected* loss and for other non-credit risks to which protection sellers (and buyers) may be exposed. This explanation is known as the risk premium hypothesis. Like the expectations hypothesis, the risk premium hypothesis also implies a positively sloped term structure of CDS spreads on average for relatively low-risk firms—i.e., potential unexpected losses in excess of expected losses are perceived to be greater for dates further off in the future and lower for near-term risk horizons.

Both the expectations and risk premium theories of the CDS term structure have a common testable implication—i.e., the CDS term structure is upward-sloping for high-quality issuers and downward-sloping for the riskiest issuers. Using pre-crisis single-name CDS data from July 1999 through December 2003, Lando and Mortensen (2005) find that the data are consistent with the theoretical prediction. For example, reference entities whose five-year CDS spreads exceeded 1200 bps had downward-sloping term structures from the one-year tenor through the longest-dated tenor. The term structures of CDS spreads for issuers in the middle ground from a risk perspective tend to be hump-shaped. For example, reference entities whose five-year CDS spreads are above 600 bps but below 1200 bps had downward-sloping CDS term structures beginning with the three-year tenor and thereafter (Lando and Mortensen 2005). The impact of accounting information and associated uncertainties about reference entity credit risks on the CDS term structure has also been investigated by Duffie and Lando (2001), Das et al. (2009), Griffin (2014), and Trujillo-Ponce et al. (2014).

Han and Zhou (2011) analyze the relation between the slope of the CDS term structure (measured as five-year minus one-year single-name CDS spreads) and the expected returns on the stocks of those firms. Using North American corporate reference entities from 2002 through 2009, Han and Zhou find a negative relation between the slope of the CDS term structure and stock returns. Specifically, reference entities whose CDS term structures are steeply upward-sloping have negative abnormal stock returns on average, and firms with a mildly upward-sloping CDS term structures have positive abnormal returns. The abnormal returns, moreover, seem to persist for up to six months.

Da Fonseca and Gottschalk (2013) perform a joint analysis of the term structure of CDS and the equity-implied volatility surface between 2007 and 2011. The term structure of CDS spreads is measured as spreads on the CDX.IG and iTraxx indices of various maturities, and the implied volatility surface is derived from the S&P500 index (USA) and Euro Stoxx 50 index (E.U.). The authors perform a factor decomposition of each market to reduce the dimensionality to a parsimonious set of significant determinants. They find significant linkages between the credit and implied volatility components and deduce that information flows from the credit markets to the equity-based volatility markets drive their conclusions.

Calice et al. (2016) argue that the term premium, measured as the spread between the 10-year and five-year CDX indices, conveys information about macroeconomic conditions in the next five years. The authors show that sudden changes in the probability of default (based on aggregate economic developments) can lead to an inversion in the term premium. Their empirical results also illustrate the impact of monetary policy and the slope of the yield curve on the term premium of CDX index spreads, which they contend depends on the business cycle and is time-varying.

Calice et al. (2015) analyze the CDS term structure (measured as the difference between 10-year and five-year spreads) using sovereign CDSs on five European sovereign reference entities over the period from September 2007 through February 2012. As in similar studies of corporate single-name CDS term premiums, the authors find that the CDS yield curve slope is driven primarily by market liquidity, returns on local stock markets, and investor risk aversion. They also conclude that the sensitivity of the slope of the sovereign CDS term structure is regime-dependent and can be as much as 10 times higher during periods of unusually elevated market volatility.

The term structure of expected recovery rates implicit in CDS spreads exhibits opposite patterns from the term structure of CDS spreads, which is consistent with the testable implications of both the expectations and risk premium hypotheses. Doshi (2011) documented that the term structure of expected recovery rates is normally downward-sloping for healthy firms, but reverses and becomes upward-sloping when the reference entity is distressed. Doshi (2011) interprets the positively sloped term structure of recovery rates during distress as an indication of market participants' expectations that future expected recovery rates for the firm will be higher *provided* the firm survives its short-run distress.

Boudreault et al. (2013) develop a credit risk framework to analyze the sensitivity to a firm's leverage and use their proposed framework to construct firm-specific recovery rates—specifically the firm's term structure of recovery rates. For highly rated firms, the risk of a downgrade associated with a decreasing recovery rate leads to a downward-sloping term structure of recovery rates. In contrast, in the event that a risky firm survives, the term structure of recovery rates is upward-sloping because survival usually accompanies higher ratings and higher recovery rates.

9.2.3 Determinants of CDS Risk Premiums

As discussed previously, CDS spreads reflect both expected credit losses and a risk premium that compensates protection sellers for potential *unexpected* losses and other economically relevant variables. A significant literature has been developed that analyzes both single-name CDS risk premiums and the determinants of CDS spreads. The economic variables that influence CDS spreads can be classified into three categories: (i) reference entity-specific risks; (ii) risks related both to the reference entity and market-wide factors; and (iii) purely systematic or market-wide risks. We discuss these sources of risk to single-name CDS market participants in the next three subsections, respectively.

9.2.3.1 Reference Entity-Specific Risks

According to the Merton (1974) model, higher volatility of a firm's assets should lead to increases in the firm's credit spread (resulting from more asset value uncertainty as well as a higher probability of bankruptcy). Empirically, the literature confirms a strong relation between the volatility of a reference entity's equity price and that entity's single-name CDS spread. All else equal, the higher the volatility of a firm's equity price volatility, the larger will be the spread on that firm's single-name CDS contracts—see, e.g., Skinner and Townend (2002), Aunon-Nerin et al. (2002), Abid and Naifar (2006), Ericsson et al. (2009), Greatrex (2009a), Zhang et al. (2009), Cao et al. (2010), Tang and Yan (2010), Raunig and Scheicher (2011), Conrad et al. (2013), Doshi et al. (2017),

González and Naranjo (2014), Castellanos et al. (2015), Hasan et al. (2016), and Leccadito et al. (2015).[8] Gilchrist and Zakrajšek (2012) find that an adverse shock to the equity valuations of financial intermediaries leads to increases in those entities' CDS spreads that is both immediate and persistent. Longstaff and Rajan (2008) show that while most of the default risk is specific to the underlying reference entities, default risk in a particular industry or sector leads to an additional increase in CDS spreads. This finding has important implications for portfolios of credit-sensitive contracts including the constituents of CDX indices—i.e., their results suggest that a portion of corporate credit risk in such portfolios may not be diversifiable.

The Merton (1974) model also indicates that the greater a firm's leverage, the higher the credit spread. Empirical studies support the importance of leverage in determining corporate single-name CDS spreads—see, e.g., Aunon-Nerin et al. (2002), Ericsson et al. (2009), Di Cesare and Guazzarotti (2010), Gamba and Saretto (2013), and Hasan et al. (2016). Some studies have also examined the extent to which accounting information (e.g., earnings and accruals) helps explain corporate single-name CDS spreads. Such studies generally conclude that accounting numbers do have some explanatory power, but that accounting measures are at best noisy proxies for the default risks of the reference entities. See, e.g., Callen et al. (2009) and Batta (2011).

9.2.3.2 Both Reference Entity-Specific and Systematic Risk Factors

Berndt et al. (2007) compare single-name corporate CDS spreads on contracts that define restructuring as a triggering credit event *vis-à-vis* CDS contracts in which the counterparties exclude restructuring events. They estimate that the average risk premium demanded by protection sellers for bearing restructuring risk is six to eight percent of the no-restructuring CDS spread. The authors also find that the restructuring risk premium depends both on firm-specific balance-sheet variables and a systematic macroeconomic risk factor. Pelster and Vilsmeier (2018) studied determinants of CDS spreads using Bayesian Model Averaging which they applied to 336 reference entities for the period 2001 through September 2014. They find that co-movement of individual CDS with the market is the major determinant of CDS spreads.

CDS indices such as the iTraxx provide credit protection for index purchasers on the constituent names in the index. As discussed in Chapter 4, index CDSs continue trading even if a constituent reference entity experiences a credit event. Kajurová (2015) analyzes determinants of spreads for the iTraxx Europe Senior Financial CDS index. The author finds that market factors such as country stock indices, risk-free rates, and the term structure of sovereign debt yields have a significant impact on spreads vis-à-vis reference entity-specific factors during crisis periods. Chan and Marsden (2014) find similar results for the CDX.IG and CDX. HY indices.

The academic literature also empirically substantiates that market liquidity and liquidity risk are strong determinants of single-name CDS risk premiums. More specifically, single-name CDS risk premiums appear to include a risk premium for reference entity-specific liquidity risk and for market-wide liquidity risk.[9] As concerns the former, relative illiquidity and higher bid/ask spreads on both single-name CDSs and bonds issued by the reference entity have an impact on single-name CDS spreads. With respect to the latter, various measures of market liquidity risk have been shown to affect CDS spreads—namely, when market conditions deteriorate and market liquidity risk rises, protection sellers demand a higher CDS coupon to compensate for the risk that they may be unable to hedge or offset their CDS protection sales quickly and/or without a resulting adverse price impact precipitated by the hedge or offsetting transaction.

Studies that have documented the empirical relations between single-name CDS spreads and a liquidity risk premium include Düllmann and Sosinska (2007), Fabozzi et al. (2007), Tang and Yan (2007), Dunbar (2008), Remolona et al. (2008), Greatrex (2009a), Chen et al. (2010), Bongaerts et al. (2011), Pu et al. (2011), Chen et al. (2012), Coro et al. (2012), Eichengreen et al. (2012), Qiu and Yu (2012), Yeh (2012), Annaert et al. (2013), Bao and Pan (2013), Calice et al. (2013), Díaz et al. (2013), Gündüz et al. (2013), Mayordomo et al. (2014), Calice et al. (2015), Lin et al. (2017), Meine et al. (2015), and Pires et al. (2015).

Brigo et al. (2010) and van der Merwe (2015) present surveys of the different modeling methodologies proposed in the academic literature for measuring liquidity risk for CDSs. Junge and Trolle (2015) propose a tradeable, model-independent measure of CDS market illiquidity based on the theory of index-arbitrage. More specifically, the authors measure CDS market illiquidity as the deviation between spreads on the CDX and iTraxx and their respective underlying single-name CDS constituents. The analysis by Bhar et al. (2017) provides an additional insight that illiquidity has a bigger impact on CDS spreads for relatively longer periods of time than equity volatility, which they contend affects only the transitory component of CDS spread changes.

Liquidity risk is also a determinant of spreads on single-name CDSs with sovereign reference entities. Badaoui et al. (2013) analyze sovereign CDS spreads and estimate that default risk explains 55.6% of sovereign CDS spreads, but that market liquidity risk accounts for another 44.3% (The authors find that correlation risk explains the remainder.). Beber et al. (2009) also find that sovereign default risk and liquidity risk account for most variations in sovereign credit spreads, especially for relatively higher-risk countries. Marra (2015) compares the effects of market liquidity and funding risks on structured versus unstructured portfolios pre-crisis and during the 2007–2009 crisis period. Marra shows that increased market and funding liquidity risks give rise to wider spreads on indices such as the AAA-rated tranches of the Moody's Corporate Bond Index and the CDX.NA.IG. This study highlights the important role of time-varying liquidity on CDS spreads.

Collin-Dufresne et al. (2017) study the effect of the Dodd-Frank Act on transaction costs of the index CDS market in the dealer-to-customer ("D2C") versus the dealer-to-dealer ("D2D") markets. The authors show that for D2C trades, average transaction cost and price impacts are higher and increase with trade size, bid-offer spreads, and volatility. The high price impact of the average D2C trade suggests that clients trade on information, whereas the low permanent price impact of the average D2D trade suggests that dealers use the interdealer market to manage their inventory risk. The authors further show that D2C prices are typically favorable to the contemporaneous inside quotes on the main interdealer limit order book, thus suggesting that clients which value immediacy cannot get better execution by sending marketable orders to the interdealer market.

In the period following the 2008 Lehman default and prior to the implementation of the central clearing mandate for CDSs in September 2013 (see Chapter 6, Sect. 6.1.1)—and even after the clearing mandate for non-cleared CDSs—counterparty credit risk began to impact CDS spreads. Du et al. (2017) and Frei et al. (2017) examine how counterparty credit risk management affects CDS spreads. The authors show that counterparty credit risk had a negligible effect on CDS spreads, but counterparties with higher credit quality were a more frequent choice for executing trades in the bilateral over-the-counter market.

9.2.3.3 Systematic Risk Factors

Another important empirical determinant of CDS spreads is investor sentiment and risk aversion (often measured using the VIX index as a proxy). Irrespective of the perceived credit risk of the underlying reference entity, an increase in market-wide risk aversion leads to increases in CDS spreads, which Amato (2005), Remolona et al. (2008), Berndt and Obreja (2010), Tang and Yan (2010), Aizenman et al. (2013), Zinna (2013), Doshi et al. (2017), Calice et al. (2015), Leccadito et al. (2015), and others have all empirically substantiated for single-name CDSs. Alexander and Kaeck (2008), moreover, show that iTraxx index spreads are also more sensitive to changes in implied volatility during times of market distress but are more sensitive to stock market returns during calm times.

Macroeconomic variables are also important systematic risk factors that impact CDS spreads and risk premiums, especially when interaction effects are taken into account (e.g., the correlation between default rates and interest rates)—see, e.g., Hilscher and Nosbusch (2010), Chen et al. (2012), Fender et al. (2012), Gilchrist and Zakrajšek (2012), Doshi et al. (2013), González and Naranjo (2014), and Schläfer and Uhrig-Homburg (2014). The empirical evidence also indicates that uncertainty about macroeconomic conditions is a significant explanatory variable for CDS spreads (see, e.g., Baum and Wan 2010).

A significant amount of empirical research has been conducted to ascertain whether the primary driver of the term structure of sovereign CDS spreads is a global economic common factor or whether country-specific effects dominate. Through the end of the credit crisis and up to the beginning of the Eurozone sovereign debt crisis, most of the evidence indicates that strong co-movements in sovereign credit spreads were driven by a common global economic factor (generally thought to be changes in the US financial market conditions instead of domestic macroeconomic shocks)—see, e.g., Pan and Singleton (2008), Borri and Verdelhan (2012), Longstaff et al. (2011), and Ang and Longstaff (2013). For example, Longstaff et al. (2011) studied sovereign credit risk using sovereign CDS data for 26 countries over the 2000–2010 time period and found that sovereign CDS spreads had a significant common component that was more related to US financial market conditions than to local economic measures. They estimate that, on average, the default risk premium accounts for about one-third of the size of CDS spreads, and that the expected credit risk of the specific sovereign reference entity accounts for the remaining two-thirds of the credit spread.

Dieckmann and Plank (2012) and Eyssell et al. (2013) also find that the condition of the global financial system is an important determinant of sovereign CDS spreads. Other studies whose conclusions indicate that global risk factors dominate country-specific risk factors in explaining sovereign CDS spreads include Fender et al. (2012) and Sapriza et al. (2009).

Beginning with the advent of the Eurozone sovereign debt crisis, several studies have also found linkages between sovereign distress and domestic (rather than global) financial distress—see, e.g., Acharya et al. (2014) and Kallestrup et al. (2016). For example, Kallestrup et al. (2016) find that a 1 basis point ("bp") increase in domestic banks' risk-weighted exposures to foreign banks is associated with a 0.4 bp increase in five-year sovereign CDS spreads (see Chapter 12 for further discussion of the public–private connection between sovereign and commercial credit risk).

Augustin (2016) examines sovereign CDS spreads for tenors of one, two, three, five, seven, and 10 years on 44 countries in the EMEA region, as well as Latin America and Asia, from January 2001 through February 2012. His results indicate that both global and country-specific sources of risk are important drivers of sovereign CDS risk premiums and the term structures of sovereign CDS spreads. Specifically, he finds that local shocks to domestic economies and financial systems have a stronger impact on sovereign CDS spreads than global shocks for countries experiencing distress. For countries not experiencing any significant distress, shocks to the global economy and financial markets tend to dominate shocks to the local economy in their impact on sovereign CDS premiums and term structure slopes.

9.3 Single-Name CDS Event Studies

A standard tool in empirical financial economics is the event study.[10] The purpose of an event study is to analyze the informational impact of a significant event on the prices of an issuer's securities. Specifically, event studies can be used to answer two questions about a particular event: (i) Is there an "anticipation effect" in which the event and its impact on the price of the asset in question was anticipated in advance by market participants?; and (ii) Is there an "announcement effect" in which the event itself had a statistically significant impact on asset prices when and after it occurred?

Event studies are an important and large part of the broad financial economics and econometrics literatures. Most event studies have historically focused on examining abnormal stock returns. Abnormal returns are either higher or lower than the returns predicted by one or more common risk factors. For example, the classic and original version of an event study by Fama et al. (1969) uses the market model to compute predicted returns—i.e., a model in which the returns on a stock are driven by a measure of the broad market (e.g., the value-weighted index of stocks maintained by the Center for Research in Security Prices, the S&P 500 index).

Since the advent of single-name CDS trading, academic research began to utilize single-name CDSs in addition to or in lieu of equities and bonds to examine the informational content of announcements and events. To control for market-wide common factors influencing CDS spreads, CDS event studies generally examine spreads *relative to* an appropriate benchmark or index. The difference between the spread on a CDS for an individual reference entity and the most relevant CDS index is generally known as the adjusted or abnormal spread. Event studies then quantify the size and statistical significance of changes in adjusted spreads both before the event date (to ascertain an anticipation effect) and after (to estimate any announcement effects).

The anticipation and announcement effects of an event are interrelated. At the extreme, if an event is perfectly anticipated by market participants, the entire impact of that event on CDS spreads should result in strong abnormal spreads prior to the event (i.e., the anticipation effect) and virtually no abnormal changes following the actual event (i.e., the announcement effect). Conversely, if the event is a total surprise to market participants, we would expect to see no abnormal spreads prior to the event (i.e., no anticipation effect) and significant abnormal CDS spreads following the announcement (i.e., a strong announcement effect). When we observe significant abnormal spreads both before and after the event, we can infer both an anticipation and announcement effect. This often occurs when market participants anticipate only part of the information related to the announcement (e.g., the magnitude of the event but not its timing, the likelihood of the event but not its magnitude, the type of event (e.g., rating action) but not the exact event (e.g., unexpected downgrade as compared to expected negative watch listing)).

In this section, we review the literature on event studies involving CDSs. More specifically, we review the literature on what CDS spreads reveal about informational content of corporate credit rating actions, how adverse credit events at one reference entity may have spillover effects on other borrowers, the impact of corporate announcements on specific financial results, and more.

9.3.1 Credit Rating Actions

Hull et al. (2004) analyze the relationship between CDS spreads (primarily for five-year single-name CDSs on corporate, sovereign, and quasi-sovereign issuers) and ratings announcements over a period from 1998 through 2002. They find that rating agency reviews for downgrade (i.e., negative watch listing events) have a significant impact on CDS spreads, whereas actual downgrades and negative outlook listings do not. All three types of credit rating actions, moreover, are anticipated by market participants, although rating reviews are less anticipated than actual downgrades.

Like Hull et al. (2004) and Norden and Weber (2004) find that rating agency reviews for downgrades lead to significant abnormal changes in CDS spreads and that market participants anticipate rating actions before they occur, with reviews for downgrades being less anticipated than actual downgrades. Unlike Hull et al. (2004) and Norden and Weber (2004) find that actual downgrades do not seem to matter—i.e., the impact of actual downgrades is fully reflected in single-name CDS spreads prior to the downgrade itself. The results in Hull et al. (2004) and Norden and Weber (2004) regarding the anticipation and reaction effects for negative ratings announcements in the single-name corporate CDS market have been generally confirmed in other academic studies, including Daniels and Jensen (2005), Di Cesare (2006), Imbierowicz and Wahrenburg (2009), Brandstack (2010), Galil and Soffer (2011), Bedendo et al. (2013), Finnerty et al. (2013), Norden (2017), and Berg and Streitz (2016). Taking into account intra-industry effects, Cizel (2013) finds that S&P's negative announcements impact intra-industry CDS spreads but that Moody's and Fitch's negative announcements do not.

Most single-name corporate CDS event studies indicate that CDS market participants do not anticipate *positive* rating actions and only focus on negative rating actions. An exception is Finnerty et al. (2013), who find that positive credit rating events can have a significant positive impact on CDS spreads (i.e., causing them to narrow significantly), despite being less anticipated than downgrades.[11] The data sample in Finnerty et al. (2013), moreover, contains a significantly larger number of observations than most other research on this topic.

Other event studies involving single-name corporate CDSs have yielded additional insights on the informational content of CDS spreads. For example, Norden and Weber (2012) analyze abnormal price reactions around negative watch rating events for CDSs on both senior and subordinated European bank debt and find evidence that spreads on both CDS types react significantly to downgrade announcements and that, prior to the credit crisis, CDS spreads on subordinated debt reacted more than CDS spreads on senior debt. By contrast, the authors find that reactions of CDSs on senior and subordinated debt were comparable during the crisis.

Imbierowicz and Wahrenburg (2009) find that the size of the anticipation effect depends on the underlying reason for the rating agency action. In particular, the majority of the anticipation effect for negative rating announcements appears to depend on events related to issuers' operating performance.

Lehnert and Neske (2006) find evidence for an announcement effect—i.e., CDS spreads respond to rating actions and are informative. Their empirical results, however, are at odds with the rest of the literature on the anticipation effect in the single-name corporate CDS market. Specifically, they find that different types of rating announcements are *not* anticipated by market participants. Their sample size, however, is restricted to just 100 European firms and only covers the period from 2001 through 2003. Most papers on this topic published after 2006 confirm or extend the earlier results of Hull et al. (2004) and Norden and Weber (2004), suggesting that the results in Lehnert and Neske (2006) may be sample-specific.

Berndt and Ostrovnaya (2014) also find that CDS spreads reveal information about forthcoming adverse credit events. In addition, they find that equity options markets reveal anticipated negative news around the same time as CDS spreads but that equity markets do not respond to changes in option prices unless the anticipated adverse credit event is also already reflected in CDS spreads.

9.3.2 Spillover Effects from Adverse Credit Events

A slightly different branch of the CDS event study literature focuses on the impact that the downgrade of one reference entity may have on other entities. In the next two subsections, we review this literature based on single-name corporate and sovereign CDSs, respectively.

9.3.2.1 Corporate Reference Entities

Jorion and Zhang (2007) present a comprehensive analysis of intra-industry spillover effects. Specifically, they analyze single-name corporate CDS spreads to examine potential "contagion" or "spillover" effects—i.e., situations in which an adverse event at one firm causes CDS spreads to increase for other firms in the same industry—and potential "competitive effects" in which an adverse event at one firm benefits one or more competitors to that firm and thus causes the other firms' CDS spreads to decline. They find evidence of contagion effects following Chapter 11 bankruptcy filings and evidence of competitive effects following Chapter 7 filings. Huang and Cheng (2013) extend the analysis of Jorion and Zhang (2007) and find that inter-industry contagion effects are more pronounced for firms with higher "information uncertainty" (measured by the authors as dispersions in analyst forecasts).

In a later paper, Jorion and Zhang (2009) extend their earlier analysis and examine spillover effects on creditors arising from bankruptcy announcements through direct counterparty effects. They find that creditors to firms which announce bankruptcy filings exhibit negative abnormal equity returns and higher CDS spreads.

Huang et al. (2012) analyze the reactions of major companies to rival company defaults during the 2007 and 2008 credit crisis years. They investigate two competing hypotheses—i.e., the failure of a rival creates a crisis of confidence for all firms in the same industry (and, hence, a positive correlation between CDS spreads for single reference entities in the same industry), or the deterioration in the credit quality of one firm in a given industry results in higher investor confidence in the credit quality of its rivals, thereby causing a negative correlation between changes in CDS spreads for the downgraded firm and the credit spreads of its rivals. These hypotheses are comparable to the contagion and competitive effects analyzed in Jorion and Zhang (2007).

For financial firms with traded single-name CDSs, Huang et al. (2012) find support for the contagion hypothesis—i.e., spreads on single-name CDSs with financial firms as reference entities generally rise both before and after default events experienced by other financial firms. The authors also find support for earlier research that market participants react more to negative credit events than to positive ones, and that CDS market participants anticipate negative shocks. The authors further conclude that, to the extent there are any inter-dependencies in the CDS spreads of non-financial reference entities, those effects were competitive in the early period of the crisis and contagious later in the crisis.

9.3.2.2 Sovereign Reference Entities

For sovereign issuers, spillover effects have been examined primarily in response to rating agency actions using the event-study methodology. Ismailescu and Kazemi (2010) analyze single-name CDSs on 22 emerging market sovereigns around credit rating announcements. They find a strong anticipation effect for negative rating actions and no significant change in CDS spreads in the two days following the actual announcements, although some spillover effects can be observed. Positive rating announcements, however, lead to an immediate and significant reaction in CDS spreads and a strong spillover effect to other emerging market countries from the event country. The degree of the spillover effects of positive events is affected by the credit ratings of the non-event countries, and the spillover effect of negative events is affected by the credit rating of the event country.

Blau and Roseman (2014) adopt an approach similar to Ismailescu and Kazemi (2010) and estimate spillover effects on European sovereigns resulting from the downgrade of the USA on August 5, 2011. They estimate no significant change in US Government CDS spreads following the downgrade, which is consistent with the corporate CDS literature in which negative watch announcements impact CDS spreads but actual downgrades often do not. Their event-study methodology indicates, however, that European CDS spreads experienced significant increases following the US downgrade and that at least some aspect of the US downgrade was anticipated by sovereign CDS market participants.

Afonso et al. (2012) analyze 24 European sovereign issuers and the reactions of their CDS spreads to rating agency announcements. The results in Afonso et al. (2012) regarding the announcement effect are more consistent with the findings for corporate borrowers discussed in Sect. 9.2.1 in this chapter than for the sovereigns analyzed by Ismailescu and Kazemi (2010). Specifically, Afonso et al. (2012) estimate a significant reaction of credit spreads to negative rating announcements and only a minor reaction to positive announcements. They did not find a significant anticipation effect except within a week or two of the rating announcement date. Consistent with Ismailescu and Kazemi (2010), the authors document a spillover effect, especially from lower-rated to higher-rated countries.

9.3.3 Other Corporate Performance Announcements

Single-name corporate CDS spreads can also be used to examine what market participants anticipate regarding announcements related to specific corporate financial information. For example, the informational content of earnings announcements and "surprises" (i.e., deviations of announced earnings from expected earnings and earnings targets) is examined by Callen et al. (2009), Greatrex (2009b), Lok and Richardson (2011), Shivakumar et al. (2011), and Elkamhi et al. (2012) using an event-study framework. All of those studies find that earnings announcements are informative (i.e., CDS spreads respond to earnings announcements). Greatrex (2009b) finds that negative earnings announcements are anticipated, and Elkamhi et al. (2012) conclude that the impact of accounting information releases on CDS spreads is more than double the impact of credit-related news about reference entities.

Palmgren and Tamule (2009) study the reaction of single-name corporate CDS spreads to corporate dividend reduction announcements. The authors present some evidence of both anticipation and announcement effects, although their empirical analysis is based on a small sample of only seven firms and their paper does not indicate whether or not the results are statistically significant.

Sturm (2013/2014) analyzes the responses of single-name CDS spreads on bank reference entities related to losses of €1 million or more arising from operational risks, such as fraud. Although Sturm finds little evidence of a CDS market reaction to the first public announcements of operational risk-related losses, he does find evidence that CDS spreads rise on the settlement dates of such losses. He also documents that banks with relatively higher credit ratings experience greater increases in their CDS spreads following the settlements of operational risk-related losses and that, all else equal, the larger the loss, the larger the increase in the spread.

9.3.4 *Other Announcements and Information*

The event-study framework can also be used to examine the perceived impact of public policy initiatives, such as government interventions and bailouts. For example, using a novel methodology, Veronesi and Zingales (2010) rely on CDS spreads to estimate the costs and benefits of the US bank bailout plan announced on October 13, 2008. They find significant wealth transfers from taxpayers and stockholders of the banks to the bondholders of the banks receiving bailout funds. Other studies have also used event studies involving CDSs to estimate the benefits and/or costs of bank bailout programs—see, e.g., King (2009), Panetta et al. (2009), Balla et al. (2011), and Greatrex and Rengifo (2012).

Demirgüç-Kunt and Huizinga (2013) examine the influence of bank size and government deficits on bank stock prices and CDS spreads using a sample of banks in 20 countries over the 2001–2008 period. Under the belief that some banks may be too big to save ("TBTS"), the authors analyze the relations between bank equity valuations and the country's fiscal balance (which should be positive for TBTS banks) and CDS spreads and fiscal balances (which should be negative for TBTS banks). An alternative transmission channel is that large fiscal deficits associated with prior bank bailouts will tend to reduce banks' equity capital and increase bank CDS spreads. The authors find a significant inverse relation between the state of a country's finances and the valuation of systemically important banks—i.e., the less public funds are available to bail out the large banks, the lower are the amounts of those banks' equity capitalizations. For the same reason, they also concluded that bank CDS spreads were inversely related to a country's fiscal condition (although this finding is called into question in the authors' robustness checks).

Using an event-study framework, Bertoni and Lugo (2014) analyze the impact of investments by sovereign wealth funds in target investment companies and ascertain that CDS spreads of such target companies decline upon the investment announcement. Eisenthal et al. (2017) adopt the event-study methodology to examine how the announcements of LBOs impact the credit spreads of target firms. Using single-name CDS spreads as a measure of LBO target firms' credit spreads, the authors find that spreads rise significantly over the 22 days prior to the announcement (i.e., the anticipation effect) and during the two-day announcement period but remain stable thereafter (i.e., a short announcement effect). They also find that CDSs with longer-dated maturities exhibit larger changes in spreads, and that increases in spreads are more pronounced for investment-grade LBO targets.

The use of event studies to analyze the informational content of an event is not confined to announcements and can also be based on information provided by market-based events (e.g., severe credit deteriorations as indicated by significant changes in CDS spreads). The use of the event-study methodology to examine the implications of market-based events is often associated with studies of price discovery (see Sect. 11.1 of Chapter 11) or the analysis of contagion and spillover effects (see Chapter 12).

In addition, more complicated econometric models (as opposed to simple event studies) have been used to examine the impact of macroeconomic announcements on CDS spreads. For example, Dunbar and Amin (2012) employ a conditional heteroskedasticity model to examine how CDS spreads respond to unexpected changes in the Federal Funds target rate. Dunbar and Amin (2012) find that Federal Reserve policy influences short-term debt financing in both expansionary and contractionary monetary policy regimes.

Notes

1. Most of the empirical evidence indicates that futures prices are *unbiased* expectations of future spot prices. See, e.g., Working (1934, 1949, 1962), Telser (1958), Gray (1961), Dusak (1973), Fama and French (1987, 1988), and Ng and Pirrong (1994).
2. A true term structure of CDS spreads would typically include all available maturities and not just the three shown in Fig. 9.1.
3. Backwardation is a term used to describe futures markets for which prices of contracts for near-term expiration exceed prices of longer-dated contracts (see, e.g., Culp 2004). In the context of CDSs, this concept implies that coupon payments for the purchase of one-year credit protection on

a reference entity exceed the cost of credit protection for longer-dated tenors.

4. The Merton (1974) insight can be used as a nonparametric empirical benchmark for credit risk analyses, as discussed in Culp et al. (2018).
5. Moody's KMV model is based on the Merton (1974) structural model of credit spreads. EDFs are estimates of default probabilities specifically obtained from Moody's KMV model, and subsequent uses of the EDF acronym in this review refer to probabilities of default obtained or estimated by authors from Moody's KMV.
6. The probabilities of default extracted from the CDS term structure are known as "risk-neutral" probabilities—i.e., probabilities that a risk-neutral agent would perceive. Risk-neutral probabilities can be converted into "true" default probabilities by making some additional assumptions about investor risk aversion and systematic risk. See, e.g., J. H. Cochrane, *Asset Pricing*, rev. ed. (Princeton University Press, 2001).
7. CDS spread valuation models often assume a fixed-recovery rate. To the extent that recovery rates are not fixed, however, spreads estimated in fixed-recovery models may understate true CDS spreads. See, e.g., Singh and Spackman (2009).
8. Cao et al. (2010) present evidence that the relation between a reference entity's stock price volatility and CDS spread is significantly stronger when option-implied volatilities are used as forward-looking measures of a firm's equity price volatility (as opposed to historical measures of volatility).
9. For a detailed discussion of market liquidity risk generally, see van der Merwe (2015).
10. For reviews of the event-study methodology, see, e.g., MacKinlay (1997) and Binder (1998).
11. Micu, Remolona, and Wooldridge (2006) also detected an impact of positive rating announcements.

References

Abid, F., and N. Naifar. 2006. The Determinants of Credit Default Swap Rates: An Explanatory Study. *International Journal of Theoretical and Applied Finance* 9 (1).

Acharya, V., I. Drechsler, and P. Schnabl. 2014. A Pyrrhic Victory? Bank Bailouts and Sovereign Credit Risk. *Journal of Finance* 69 (6) (December).

Afonso, A., D. Furceri, and P. Gomes. 2012. Sovereign Credit Ratings and Financial Markets Linkages: Application to European Data. *Journal of International Money and Finance* 31 (3) (April).

Aizenman, J., M. Hutchison, and Y. Jinjarak. 2013. What Is the Risk of European Sovereign Debt Defaults? Fiscal Space, CDS Spreads and Market Pricing of Risk. *Journal of International Money and Finance* 34 (April).

Alexander, C., and A. Kaeck. 2008. Regime Dependent Determinants of Credit Default Swap Spreads. *Journal of Banking & Finance* 32 (6).

Amato, J.D. 2005. Risk Aversion and Risk Premia in the CDS Market. *BIS Quarterly Review* (December).

Ang, A., and F.A. Longstaff. 2013. Systemic Sovereign Credit Risk: Lessons from the U.S. and Europe. *Journal of Monetary Economics* 60 (5) (July).

Annaert, J., M. De Ceuster, P. Van Roy, and C. Vespro. 2013. What Determines Euro Area Bank CDS Spreads? *Journal of International Money and Finance* 32 (February).

Augustin, P. 2016. The Term Structure of CDS Spreads and Sovereign Credit Risk. Working Paper (April 21).

Aunon-Nerin, D., D. Cossin, T. Hricko, T., and Z. Huang. 2002. Exploring for the Determinants of Credit Risk in Credit Default Swap Transaction Data: Is Fixed-Income Markets'Information Sufficient to Evaluate Credit Risk? International Center for Financial Asset Management and Engineering Research Paper No. 65 (December).

Avino, D., T. Conlon, and J. Cotter. 2016. Credit Default Swaps as Indicators of Bank Financial Distress. UCD Geary Institute for Public Policy Discussion Paper Series No. WP2016/01 (January 7).

Badaoui, S., L. Cathcart, and L. El-Jahel. 2013. Do Sovereign Credit Default Swaps Represent a Clean Measure of Sovereign Default Risk? A Factor Model Approach. *Journal of Banking & Finance* 37 (7) (July).

Balla, E., R.E. Carpenter, and B.L. Robinson. 2011. Assessing the Effectiveness of the Paulson 'Teaser Freezer' Plan: Evidence from the ABX Index. *Journal of Economics and Business* 63 (5) (September–October).

Bao, J., and J. Pan. 2013. Bond Illiquidity and Excess Volatility. *Review of Financial Studies* 26 (12).

Batta, G. 2011. The Direct Relevance of Accounting Information for Credit Default Swap Pricing. *Journal of Business Finance & Accounting* 38 (9–10) (November–December).

Baum, C.F., and C. Wan. 2010. Macroeconomic Uncertainty and Credit Default Swap Spreads. *Applied Financial Economics* 20 (10).

Beber, A., M.W. Brandt, and K.A. Kavajecz. 2009. Flight-to-Quality or Flight-to-Liquidity? Evidence from the Euro-Area Bond Market. *Review of Financial Studies* 22 (3).

Bedendo, M., L. Cathcart, L. El-Jahel, and L. Evans. 2013. The Credit Rating Crisis and the Informational Content of Corporate Credit Ratings. Working Paper (March).

Berndt, A., and I. Obreja. 2010. Decomposing European CDS Returns. *Review of Finance* 14 (2).

Berndt, A., R. Douglas, D. Duffie, M. Ferguson, M., and D. Schranz. 2005. Measuring Default Risk Premia from Default Swap Rates and EDFs. BIS Working Papers No. 173 (March).

Berndt, A., R.A. Jarrow, and C. Kang. 2007. Restructuring Risk in Credit Default Swaps: An Empirical Analysis. *Stochastic Processes and Their Applications* 117 (11).

Berndt, A., and A. Ostrovnaya. 2014. Do Equity Markets Favor Credit Market News Over Options Market News? *Quarterly Journal of Finance* 4 (2) (June).

Berg, T., and D. Streitz. 2016. Determinants of the Size of the Sovereign Credit Default Swap Market. *Journal of Fixed Income* 25 (3) (Winter).

Bertoni, F., and S. Lugo. 2014. The Effect of Sovereign Wealth Funds on the Credit Risk of Their Portfolio Companies. *Journal of Corporate Finance* 27 (August).

Bhar, R., D. Colwell, and P. Wang. 2017. Component Structure of Credit Default Swap Spreads and their Determinants. Working Paper (October 4).

Binder, J.J. 1998. The Event Study Methodology Since 1969. *Review of Quantitative Finance and Accounting* 11 (2) (September).

Blau, B.M., and B.S. Roseman. 2014. The Reaction of European Credit Default Swap Spreads to the U.S. Credit Rating Downgrade. *International Review of Economics and Finance* 34 (November).

Bongaerts, D., F. De Jong, and J. Driessen. 2011. Derivative Pricing with Liquidity Risk: Theory and Evidence from the Credit Default Swap Market. *Journal of Finance* 66 (1) (February).

Borri, N. and A. Verdelhan. 2012. Sovereign Risk Premia. Working Paper (February).

Boudreault, M., G. Gauthier, and T. Thomassin. 2013. Recovery Rate Risk and Credit Spreads in a Hybrid Credit Risk Model. *Journal of Credit Risk* 9 (3) (Fall).

Brandstack, T. 2010. Do Credit Rating Announcements Matter? Master's Thesis Aalto University School of Economics (March 15).

Brigo, D., M. Predescu, and A. Capponi. 2010. Liquidity Modeling for Credit Default Swaps: An Overview. In *Credit Risk Frontiers: Suprime Crisis, Pricing and Hedging, CVA, MBS, Ratings, and Liquidity*, ed. T. R. Bielecki, D. Brigo, and F. Patras. Hoboken, NJ: Wiley.

Calice, G., J. Chen, and J. Williams. 2013. Liquidity Spillovers in Sovereign Bond and CDS Markets: An Analysis of the Eurozone Sovereign Debt Crisis. *Journal of Economic Behavior & Organization* 85 (January).

Calice, G., R. Mio, F. Štěrba, and B. Vašíček. 2015. Short-Term Determinants of the Idiosyncratic Sovereign Risk Premium: A Regime-Dependent Analysis

for European Credit Default Swaps. *Journal of Empirical Finance* 33 (September).
Calice, G., C. Ioannidis, and R. Miao. 2016. A Markov Switching Unobserved Component Analysis of the CDX Index Term Premium. *International Review of Financial Analysis* 44 (March).
Callen, J.L., J. Livnat, and D. Segal. 2009. The Impact of Earnings on the Pricing of Credit Default Swaps. *Accounting Review* 84 (5).
Cao, C., F. Yu, and Z. Zhong. 2010. The Information Content of Option-Implied Volatility for Credit Default Swap Valuation. *Journal of Financial Markets* 13 (3).
Castellanos, J., N. Constantinou, and W.L. Ng. 2015. The Signalling Properties of the Shape of the Credit Default Swap Term Structure. *Journal of Risk* 17 (4).
Chan, K.F., and A. Marsden. 2014. Macro Risk Factors of Credit Default Swap Indices in a Regime-Switching Framework. *Journal of International Financial Markets, Institutions &Money* 29 (March).
Chen, R.-R., X. Cheng, and B. Liu. 2008. Estimation and Evaluation of the Term Structure of Credit Default Swaps: An Empirical Study. *Insurance: Mathematics and Economics* 43 (3).
Chen, R.-R., X. Cheng, and L. Wu. 2012. Dynamic Interactions between Interest-Rate and Credit Risk: Theory and Evidence on the Credit Default Swap Term Structure. *Review of Finance* 17 (1).
Chen, R.-R., F.J. Fabozzi, and R. Sverdlove. 2010. Corporate Credit Default Swap Liquidity and Its Implications for Corporate Bond Spreads. *Journal of Fixed Income* 20 (2) (Fall).
Chiaramonte, L., and B. Casu. 2010. Are CDS Spreads a Good Proxy of Bank Risk? Evidence from the Financial Crisis. City University of London Cass Business School Centre for Banking Research Working Paper No. WP05/10.
Christensen, J.H.E. 2007. Joint Default and Recovery Risk Estimation: An Application to CDS Data. Working Paper (January).
Cizel, J. 2013. Are Credit Rating Announcements Contagious? Evidence on the Transmission of Information Across Industries in Credit Default Swap Markets. *Journal of Fixed Income* 23 (2).
Collin-Dufresne, P., B. Junge, and A.B. Trolle. 2017. Market Structure and Transaction Costs of Index CDSs. Working Paper (September 12).
Conrad, J., R.F. Dittmar, and A. Hameed. 2013. Cross-Market and Cross-Firm Effects in Implied Default Probabilities and Recovery Values. Working Paper (May 30).
Coro, F., A. Dufour, and S. Varotto. 2012. The Time Varying Properties of Credit and Liquidity Components of CDS Spreads. Working Paper (February 25).

Culp, C.L. 2004. *Risk Transfer: Derivatives in Theory and Practice*. Hoboken, NJ: Wiley.

Culp, C.L., Y. Nozawa, and P. Veronesi. 2018. Option-Based Credit Spreads. *American Economic Review* 108 (2) (February).

Da Fonseca, J., and K. Gottschalk. 2013. A Joint Analysis of the Term Structure of Credit Default Swap Spreads and the Implied Volatility Surface. *The Journal of Futures Markets* 33 (6) (June).

Daniels, K.N., and M.S. Jensen. 2005. The Effect of Credit Ratings on Credit Default Swap Spreads and Credit Spreads. *Journal of Fixed Income* 15 (3) (December).

Das, S.R., P. Hanouna, and A. Sarin. 2009. Accounting-Based Versus Market-Based Cross-Sectional Models of CDS Spreads. *Journal of Banking & Finance* 33 (4).

Demirgüç-Kunt, A., and H. Huizinga. 2013. Are Banks Too Big to Fail or Too Big to Save? International Evidence from Equity Prices and CDS Spreads. *Journal of Banking & Finance* 37 (3) (March).

Di Cesare, A., and G. Guazzarotti. 2010. An Analysis of the Determinants of Credit Default Swap Spread Changes Before and During the Subprime Financial Turmoil. Banca d'Italia Working Paper No. 749 (March).

Di Cesare, A. 2006. Do Market-Based Indicators Anticipate Rating Agencies? Evidence for International Banks. *Economic Notes* 35 (1).

Díaz, A., J. Groba, and P. Serrano, P. 2013. What Drives Corporate Default Risk Premia? Evidence from the CDS Market. *Journal of International Money and Finance* 37 (October).

Dieckmann, S., and T. Plank. 2012. Default Risk of Advanced Economies: An Empirical Analysis of Credit Default Swaps during the Financial Crisis. *Review of Finance* 16 (4) (October).

Doshi, H. 2011. The Term Structure of Recovery Rates. Working Paper (June).

Doshi, H., J. Ericsson, K. Jacobs, and S. Turnbull. 2013. Pricing Credit Default Swaps with Observable Covariates. *Review of Financial Studies* 26 (8).

Doshi, H., K. Jacobs, and V. Zurita. 2017. Economic and Financial Determinants of Credit Risk Premiums in the Sovereign CDS Market. *Review of Asset Pricing Studies* 7 (1) (June).

Du, W., S. Gadgil, M.B. Gordy, and C. Vega. 2017. Counterparty Risk and Counterparty Choice in the Credit Default Swap Market. Working Paper (August 7).

Duffie, D., and D. Lando. 2001. Term Structures of Credit Spreads with Incomplete Accounting Information. *Econometrica* 69 (3) (May).

Dunbar, K. 2008. US Corporate Default Swap Valuation: The Market Liquidity Hypothesis and Autonomous Credit Risk. *Quantitative Finance* 8 (3) (April).

Dunbar, K., and A.S. Amin. 2012. Credit Risk Dynamics in Response to Changes in the Federal Funds Target: The Implication for Firm Short-Term Debt. *Review of Financial Economics* 21 (3) (September).

Düllmann, K., and A. Sosinska. 2007. Credit Default Swap Prices as Risk Indicators of Listed German Banks. *Financial Markets and Portfolio Management* 21 (3).

Dusak, K. 1973. Futures Trading and Investor Returns: An Investigation of Commodity Market Risk Premiums. *Journal of Political Economy* 81 (6) (November–December).

Eckner, A. 2010. Risk Premia in Structured Credit Derivatives. Working Paper Department of Statistics, Stanford University (May 9).

Eichengreen, B., A. Mody, M. Nedeljkovic, and L. Sarno. 2012. How the Subprime Crisis Went Global: Evidence from Bank Credit Default Swap Spreads. *Journal of International Money and Finance* 31 (5) (September).

Eisenthal, Y., P. Feldhutter, and V. Vig. 2017. Leveraged Buyouts and Credit Spreads. Working Paper (February 20).

Elkamhi, R., K. Jacobs, and X. Pan. 2014. The Cross Section of Recovery Rates and Default Probabilities Implied by Credit Default Swap Spreads. *Journal of Financial and Quantitative Analysis* 49 (1) (February).

Elkamhi, R., K. Jacobs, H. Langlois, H., and C. Ornthanalai. 2012. Accounting Information Releases and CDS Spreads. Working Paper (March).

Ericsson, J., K. Jacobs, and R. Oviedo. 2009. The Determinants of Credit Default Swap Premia. *Journal of Financial and Quantitative Analysis* 44 (1) (February).

Eyssell, T., H.-G. Fung, and G. Zhang. 2013. Determinants and Price Discovery of China Sovereign Credit Default Swaps. *China Economic Review* 24 (1).

Fabozzi, F.J., X. Cheng, and R.-R. Chen. 2007. Exploring the Components of Credit Risk in Credit Default Swaps. *Finance Research Letters* 4 (1).

Fama, E.F. 1970. Efficient Capital Markets: A Review of Theory and Empirical Work. *Journal of Finance* 25 (2) (May).

Fama, E.F. 1991. Efficient Capital Markets II. *Journal of Finance* 46 (5) (December).

Fama, E.F., and K.R. French. 1987. Commodity Futures Prices: Some Evidence on Forecast Power, Premiums, and the Theory of Storage. *Journal of Business* 60 (1) (January).

Fama, E.F., and K.R. French. 1988. Business Cycles and the Behavior of Metals Prices. *Journal of Finance* 43 (5) (December).

Fama, E.F., L. Fisher, M.C. Jensen, and R. Roll. 1969. The Adjustment of Stock Prices to New Information. *International Economic Review* 10 (1) (February).

Fender, I., B. Hayo, and M. Neuenkirch. 2012. Daily Pricing of Emerging Market Sovereign CDS Before and During the Global Financial Crisis. *Journal of Banking & Finance* 36 (10) (October).

Finnerty, J.D., C.D. Miller, and R.-R. Chen. 2013. The Impact of Credit Rating Announcements on Credit Default Swap Spreads. *Journal of Banking & Finance* 37 (6) (June).

Frei, C., A. Capponi., and C. Brunetti. 2017. Managing Counterparty Risk in OTC Markets. *Finance and Economics Discussion Series 2017–083.*

Galil, K., and G. Soffer. 2011. Good News, Bad News and Rating Announcements: An Empirical Investigation. *Journal of Banking & Finance* 35 (11) (November).

Gamba, A., and A. Saretto. 2013. Firm Policies and the Cross-Section of CDS Spreads. Working Paper (August 7).

Gilchrist, S. and E. Zakrajšek. 2012. Credit Spreads and Business Cycle Fluctuations. *American Economic Review* 102 (4).

González, L., and L. Naranjo. 2014. Credit Risk Determinants of Insurance Companies. Working Paper (March).

Gray, R.W. 1961. The Search for a Risk Premium. *Journal of Political Economy* 69 (3) (June).

Greatrex, C.A. 2009a. Credit Default Swap Market Determinants. *Journal of Fixed Income* 18 (3) (Winter).

Greatrex, C.A., 2009b. The Credit Default Swap Market's Reaction to Earnings Announcements. *Journal of Applied Finance* 19 (1 & 2).

Greatrex, C.A., and E.W. Rengifo. 2012. Government Intervention and the CDS Market: A Look at the Market's Response to Policy Announcements During the 2007–2009 Financial Crisis. *Journal of Applied Finance* no. 1.

Griffin, P.A. 2014. The Market for Credit Default Swaps: New Insights into Investors' Use of Accounting Information? *Accounting & Finance* 54 (3).

Gündüz, Y., J. Nasev, and M. Trapp. 2013. The Price Impact of CDS Trading. Deutsche Bundesbank Discussion Paper No. 20/2013 (November 18).

Han, B., and Y. Zhou. 2011. Term Structure of Credit Default Swap Spreads and Cross-Section of Stock Returns. McCombs Research Paper Series No. FIN-01-11 (June).

Hasan, I., L. Liu, and G. Zhang. 2016. The Determinants of Global Bank Credit-Default-Swap Spreads. *Journal of Financial Services Research* 50 (3) (December).

Hayek, F.A. 1945. The Use of Knowledge in Society. *American Economic Review* 35 (4) (September).

Hilscher, J., and Y. Nosbusch. 2010. Determinants of Sovereign Risk: Macroeconomic Fundamentals and the Pricing of Sovereign Debt. *Review of Finance* 14 (2).

Huang, A.Y., and C.M. Cheng. 2013. Information Risk and Credit Contagion. *Finance Research Letters* 10 (3).

Huang, A.Y., C.-H. Shen, and C.-C. Chen. 2012. The Impact of Major Events from the Recent Financial Crisis on Credit Default Swaps. *Journal of Fixed Income* 21 (3) (Winter).

Hull, J., M. Predescu, and A. White. 2004. The Relationship between Credit Default Swap Spreads, Bond Yields, and Credit Rating Announcements. *Journal of Banking & Finance* 28 (11) (November).

Imbierowicz, B., and M. Wahrenburg. 2009. The Impact of Reasons for Credit Rating Announcements in Equity and CDS Markets. Working Paper (May 18).

Ismailescu, I., and H. Kazemi. 2010. The Reaction of Emerging Market Credit Default Swap Spreads to Sovereign Credit Rating Changes. *Journal of Banking & Finance* 34 (12) (December).

Jakovlev, M. 2007. Determinants of Credit Default Swap Spread: Evidence from European Credit Derivatives Market. Master's Thesis at Lappeenranta University of Technology (April 15).

Jansen, J., and F.J. Fabozzi. 2017. CDS Implied Credit Ratings. *The Journal of Fixed Income* 26 (2) (Spring).

Jarrow, R.A. 2009. Credit Risk Models. *Annual Review of Financial Economics* 1 (September).

Jorion, P., and G. Zhang. 2007. Good and Bad Credit Contagion: Evidence from Credit Default Swaps. *Journal of Financial Economics* 84 (3) (October).

Jorion, P., and G. Zhang. 2009. Credit Contagion from Counterparty Risk. *Journal of Finance* 64 (5) (October).

Junge, B., and A.B. Trolle. 2015. Liquidity Risk in Credit Default Swap Markets. Swiss Finance Institute Research Paper No. 13–65 (August).

Kallestrup, R., D. Lando, and A. Murgoci. 2016. Financial Sector Linkages and the Dynamics of Bank and Sovereign Credit Spreads. *Journal of Empirical Finance* 38, Part A (September).

Kajurová, V. 2015. CDS Spreads Determinants of Contracts Included in Markit iTraxx Europe Senior Financial Index. *Acta academica Karviniensia* (June).

King, M.R. 2009. Time to Buy or Just Buying Time? The Market Reaction to Bank Rescue Packages. BIS Working Papers No. 288 (September).

Lando, D., and A. Mortensen. 2005. Revisiting the Slope of the Credit Curve. *Journal of Investment Management* 3 (4) (Fourth Quarter).

Leccadito, A., R.S. Tunaru, and G. Urga. 2015. Trading Strategies with Implied Forward Credit Default Swap Spreads. *Journal of Banking & Finance* 58 (September).

Lehnert, T., and F. Neske. 2006. On the Relationship between Credit Rating Announcements and Credit Default Swap Spreads for European Reference Entities. *Journal of Credit Risk* 2 (2) (Summer).

Lin, M.-T., O. Kolokolova, and S.-H. Poon. 2017. Systematic and Firm-Specific Risks of CDS Spreads: Credit and Liquidity Under Scrutiny. Working Paper (August 3).

Lok, S., and S. Richardson. 2011. Credit Markets and Financial Information. *Review of Accounting Studies* 16 (3).

Longstaff, F.A., J. Pan, L.H. Pedersen, and K.J. Singleton. 2011. How Sovereign Is Sovereign Credit Risk? *American Economic Journal: Macroeconomics* 3 (2) (April).

Longstaff, F.A., and A. Rajan. 2008. An Empirical Analysis of the Pricing of Collateralized Debt Obligations. *The Journal of Finance* 63 (2) (April).

MacKinlay, A.C. 1997. Event Studies in Economics and Finance. *Journal of Economic Literature* 35 (1) (March).

Marra, M. 2015. The Impact of Liquidity on Senior Credit Index Spreads During the Subprime Crisis. *International Review of Financial Analysis* 37 (January).

Mayordomo, S., M. Rodríguez-Moreno, and J.I. Peña. 2014. Liquidity Commonalities in the Corporate CDS Market around the 2007–2012 Financial Crisis. *International Review of Economics and Finance* 31.

Meine, C., H. Supper, and G.N.F. Weiβ. 2015. Do CDS Spreads Move with Commonality in Liquidity? *Review of Derivatives Research* 18 (3) (October).

Merton, R.C. 1974. On the Pricing of Corporate Debt: The Risk Structure of Interest Rates. *Journal of Finance* 29 (2) (May).

Micu, M., E. Remolona, and P. Wooldridge. 2006. The Price Impact of Rating Announcements: Which Announcements Matter? BIS Working Papers No. 207 (June).

Ng, V.K., and S.C. Pirrong. 1994. Fundamentals and Volatility: Storage, Spreads, and the Dynamics of Metals Prices. *Journal of Business* 67 (2) (April).

Norden, L. 2017. Information in CDS Spreads. *Journal of Banking and Finance* 75 (February).

Norden, L., and M. Weber. 2004. Informational Efficiency of Credit Default Swap and Stock Markets: The Impact of Credit Rating Announcements. *Journal of Banking & Finance* 28 (11) (November).

Norden, L., and M. Weber. 2012. When Senior Meets Junior: Information in Credit Default Swap Spreads of Large Banks. Working Paper (July).

Palmgren, M., and H.B. Tamule. 2009. The Reaction of Credit Default Swap Prices to Corporate Dividend Reductions. Working Paper.

Pan, J., and K.J. Singleton. 2008. Default and Recovery Implicit in the Term Structure of Sovereign CDS Spreads. *Journal of Finance* 63 (5) (October).

Panetta, F., T. Faeh, G. Grande, C. Ho, M. King, A. Levy, F.M. Signoretti, M. Taboga, and A. Zaghini. 2009. An Assessment of Financial Sector Rescue Programmes. BIS Working Papers No. 48 (July).

Pelster, M., and J. Vilsmeier. 2018. The Determinants of CDS Spreads: Evidence from the Model Space. *Review of Derivatives Research* 21 (1) (April).

Pires, P., J.P. Pereira, and L.F. Martins. 2015. The Empirical Determinants of Credit Default Swap Spreads: A Quantile Regression Approach. *European Financial Management* 21 (3).

Pu, X., J. Wang, and C. Wu. 2011. Are Liquidity and Counterparty Risk Priced in the Credit Default Swap Market? *Journal of Fixed Income* 20 (4) (Spring).

Qiu, J., and F. Yu. 2012. Endogenous Liquidity in Credit Derivatives. *Journal of Financial Economics* 103 (3).

Raunig, B., and M. Scheicher. 2011. A Value-at-Risk Analysis of Credit Default Swaps. *Journal of Risk* 13 (4) (Summer).

Remolona, E., M. Scatigna, and E. Wu. 2008. The Dynamic Pricing of Sovereign Risk in Emerging Markets. *Journal of Fixed Income* (Spring).

Roll, R. 1984. Orange Juice and Weather. *American Economic Review* 74 (5) (December).

Sapriza, H., F. Zhao, and X. Zhou. 2009. Dose Limited Participation Make Sovereign CDS Markets Less Informative About Country-Specific Risks? Working Paper (September).

Schläfer, T., and M. Uhrig-Homburg. 2014. Is Recovery Risk Priced? *Journal of Banking & Finance* 40 (March).

Scheicher, M. 2008. How Has CDO Market Pricing Changed During the Turmoil? Evidence from CDS Index Tranches. European Central Bank Working Paper Series No. 910 (June).

Schneider, P., L. Sögner, and T. Veža. 2010. The Economic Role of Jumps and Recovery Rates in the Market for Corporate Default Risk. *Journal of Financial and Quantitative Analysis* 45 (6) (December).

Seo, S.B., and J.A. Wachter. 2016. Do Rare Events Explain CDX Tranche Spreads? NBER Working Paper 22723 (October).

Shivakumar, L., O. Urcan, F.P. Vasvari, and L. Zhang. 2011. The Debt Market Relevance of Management Earnings Forecasts: Evidence from Before and During the Credit Crisis. *Review of Accounting Studies* 16 (3).

Singh, M., and C. Spackman. 2009. The Use (and Abuse) of CDS Spreads during Distress. IMF Working Paper No. WP/09/62 (March).

Skinner, F.S., and T.G. Townend. 2002. An Empirical Analysis of Credit Default Swaps. *International Review of Financial Analysis* 11 (3).

Stanton, R., and N. Wallace. 2011. The Bear's Lair: Index Credit Default Swaps and the Subprime Mortgage Crisis. *The Review of Financial Studies* 24 (10) (October).

Sturm, P. 2013/2014. How Much Should Creditors Worry About Operational Risk? The Credit Default Swap Spread Reaction to Operational Risk Events. *Journal of Operational Risk* 8 (4) (Winter).

Sundaresan, S. 2013. A Review of Merton's Model of the Firm's Capital Structure with Its Wide Applications. *Annual Review of Financial Economics* 5 (November).

Tang, D.Y., and H. Yan. 2007. Liquidity and Credit Default Swap Spreads. Working Paper (September 4).

Tang, D.Y., and H. Yan. 2010. Market Conditions, Default Risk and Credit Spreads. *Journal of Banking & Finance* 34 (4) (April).

Telser, L.G. 1958. Futures Trading and the Storage of Cotton and Wheat. *Journal of Political Economy* 66 (3) (June).

Tran, H.Q. 2013. The Role of Markets in Sovereign Debt Crisis Detection, Prevention and Resolution. BIS Working Papers No. 72.

Trujillo-Ponce, A., R. Samaniego-Medina, and C. Cardone-Riportella. 2014. Examining What Best Explains Corporate Credit Risk: Accounting-Based versus Market-Based Models. *Journal of Business Economics and Management* 15 (2).

Van der Merwe, A. 2015. *Market Liquidity Risk*. Palgrave Macmillan.

Veronesi, P., and L. Zingales. 2010. Paulson's Gift. *Journal of Financial Economics* 97 (3).

Working, H. 1934. Price Relations Between May and New-Crop Wheat Futures at Chicago Since 1885. *Wheat Studies of the Food Research Institute* 10 (5) (February).

Working, H. 1949. The Theory of Price of Storage. *American Economic Review* 39 (6) (December).

Working, H. 1962. New Concepts Concerning Futures Markets and Prices. *American Economic Review* 52 (3) (June).

Yeh, A.J.-Y. 2012. Credit Default Swap Spreads, Fair-Value Spreads and Interest Rate Dynamics. *Journal of Credit Risk* 8 (4) (Winter).

Zhang, B.Y., H. Zhou, and H. Zhu. 2009. Explaining Credit Default Swap Spreads with the Equity Volatility and Jump Risks of Individual Firms. *Review of Financial Studies* 22 (12).

Zinna, G. 2013. Sovereign Default Risk Premia: Evidence from the Default Swap Market. *Journal of Empirical Finance* 21 (March).

CHAPTER 10

Implications of CDS Listings for Reference Entities and Creditors

The dominant view prior to the credit crisis was that financial innovations are beneficial to most market participants (see, e.g., Miller 1986, 1992; Kane 1988; Ross 1989; Finnerty 1992; Merton 1992, 1995). Useful surveys of financial innovation and economic activity can be found in Tufano (2003) and Frame and White (2004). Most credit markets (e.g., the market for CDOs backed by subprime ABS) broke down during the crisis. Although single-name CDS markets continued to function during the crisis, many market participants have nevertheless been critically reassessing their pre-crisis views of credit markets generally and products including single-name CDSs more specifically.

In this chapter, we review the empirical academic literature on the potential benefits and costs of single-name CDSs in the context of relations between CDS reference entities and their lenders. In Sect. 10.1, we consider how and why CDSs are used by bank lenders, whether bank CDS usage impacts banks' monitoring of borrower credit risk, whether the availability of CDSs changes the risk-taking behavior of banks, and how the availability of CDSs can impact the structure of syndicated loans to reference entities and the incentives and/or behavior of loan syndicate members. In Sect. 10.2, we examine the impact of single-name CDSs on the reference entities underlying traded CDSs—specifically, the relations between banks' usage of single-name CDSs and the availability and price of bank credit, and how the beginning of trading of single-name CDSs impacts the reference entities underlying the CDSs.

C. L. Culp et al., *Credit Default Swaps*, Palgrave Studies in Risk and Insurance, https://doi.org/10.1007/978-3-319-93076-3_10

10.1 The Impact of Single-Name CDSs on Bank Lenders

Firms are typically financed using equity and/or debt. Bank loans (both bilateral and syndicated), publicly traded commercial paper and bonds, and privately placed debt are the most prevalent types of banks' sources of debt financing. Single-name CDSs provide a mechanism through which lenders to corporate and sovereign borrowers can mitigate and transfer their credit risks to other firms more willing to bear such risks (including other hedgers as well as synthetic bond investors, as discussed in Chapter 7).

We begin this section with a discussion of the determinants of banks' credit risk transfer decisions—i.e., when and why banks use single-name CDSs. Related to that issue is whether or not the choice of single-name CDSs as a credit risk transfer mechanism has an impact on banks' monitoring of borrower credit risks. In the second subsection below, we consider the empirical evidence on whether single-name CDSs enable banks to achieve their desired risk/return profiles, or, alternatively, provide banks with a device to increase the risks of their lending activities without increasing their credit exposure to borrowers. Section 10.1.3 of this chapter then examines how the usage of CDSs by bank loan syndicate members can affect the design of syndicated loan facilities and the behavior of syndicate members.

10.1.1 Determinants of Bank Usage of Single-Name CDSs and Implications for Monitoring

Several papers have analyzed the economic factors that lead certain lenders to retain their ongoing credit exposures to borrowers *vis-à-vis* reducing or eliminating their ongoing credit risk. In the latter case, the literature analyzes the empirical determinants of banks' decisions whether to engage in loan sales (through primary syndications or on the secondary market as defined in Chapter 3), securitizations (as defined in Chapter 5), or hedging with single-name CDSs. As discussed in Chapter 8, a common concern about banks that utilize single-name CDSs for credit risk transfer is that such banks may face diminished incentives to monitor the credit quality of their borrowers once they have significantly reduced or eliminated their borrower credit exposures using CDSs. This is a testable hypothesis, and we review the relevant academic research in this section along with the related literature on how banks choose between competing credit risk transfer alternatives.

If a bank is willing to bear a small portion of its ongoing loan credit risk but prefers to eliminate the bulk of its exposure, the bank can either sell loans or loan participations through the syndication or securitization processes. Securitizing the loan (e.g., selling participants to CLOs), however, only mitigates *part* of the lender's credit risk.

Minton et al. (2009) examine the use of single-name CDSs by US bank holding companies with assets in excess of one billion dollars from 1999 to 2005. They find that only a few of the sample companies (i.e., 23 large banks out of a sample of 395) use CDSs and that those banks only use credit derivatives in their capacity as dealers rather than for hedging their own credit exposures. Their explanation for the apparent lack of single-name CDS usage for hedging is related to the relative benefits and costs of alternatives available to banks for credit risk transfer during their sample period—namely loan sales and securitizations.

As discussed in Chapter 5, bank sponsors of balance-sheet CLOs face potential moral hazard (i.e., incentives to engage in excessively risky lending or inadequate monitoring as a result of a planned securitization) and adverse selection (i.e., selling only the riskiest of its loans) issues that are of concern to loan investors. CLO investors thus advocate that banks which securitize loans to CLOs maintain the first-loss exposure and realize credit-related losses on the reference loan portfolio before external investors in those loans or notes backed by those loans. This arrangement—codified in the risk-retention regulation adopted in 2014 (see Chapter 5, Sect. 5.2.1)—ensures that the bank bears the first default-related losses on the underlying loan collateral (see, e.g., Duffee and Zhou 2001).

In addition to first-loss retentions, banks engaged in loan securitization can also utilize other mechanisms to align their incentives with investors in the securitization loans. For example, a bank can construct an ABS with a reserve account credit enhancement in which the sponsoring bank pre-funds a certain amount of potential losses with a cash deposit in an escrow account (see, e.g., Pagès 2013). Indeed, as explained in Sect. 5.2.1 of Chapter 5, funded reserve accounts can be used in lieu of explicit risk retentions to satisfy federal risk retention regulations in place since 2014.

Outright loan sales, moreover, are often accompanied by put-back provisions that enable investors to exchange a loan in the event that it is subsequently revealed to have had materially different risk characteristics than represented by the seller at the time of the loan conveyance to an SPE. Because put-back provisions obligate bank sellers to replace non-compliant loans or loans deemed to have had defective representations with compliant loans, such provisions further act to align the incentives of loan securitizers and investors.

Hedging individual loans or loan portfolios with single-name or portfolio CDSs (respectively), by contrast, enables a bank to transfer virtually *all* of its credit risk (with no first-loss retention) while keeping the loan portfolio on its balance sheet. Yet, banks using CDSs in turn bear counterparty and certain other risks to which loan sales and securitizations do not expose them. In addition, single-name CDSs include the CTD option for sellers, as discussed in Chapter 2. A physically or auction-settled single-name CDS hedge thus exposes a bank to the basis risk that the actual bonds and/or loans of the reference entity being hedged with the CDS do not experience similar price changes as the CTD bond or loan driving the pricing of the CDS. Especially for leveraged borrowers, the leveraged loan and high-yield bond spread can be very volatile, thus making this an important consideration for why banks might prefer to use LCDSs or engage in loan securitizations as opposed to hedging with single-name CDSs.

An implication of the analysis in Minton et al. (2009) is that a bank's preference—assuming it opts to engage in risk transfer rather than retain the credit risk of some or all of its loans—is generally to sell or securitize loans. All else equal, single-name CDSs are more likely to be used for credit risk transfer when they are more cost-effective than selling or securitizing loans. Indeed, during the 1999–2005 sample period studied by Minton, Stulz, and Williamson (2009), the appetite of CLOs for leveraged loans resulted in attractive spreads to loan sellers (Culp 2013). Between those low spreads and the basis risk of hedging a loan credit exposure with a single-name CDS, it is not surprising that banks did not make significant use of single-name CDSs to hedge their lending activities.

Beyhaghi et al. (2017) also analyze banks' risk management choices for their syndicated loan exposures. Specifically, the authors consider the characteristics of both lenders and borrowers to analyze when banks engaged in secondary market loan sales, CDS hedges, or retained borrower credit risk on their balance sheets. The authors determine that capital- and liquidity-constrained banks are more likely to engage in some form of credit risk transfer (as opposed to retaining the credit risks). For banks not facing capital or liquidity constraints, the authors contend that relationship bankers are more likely to retain credit risk from their loans on their balance sheets, whereas larger banks are more likely to engage in loan sales or hedging with CDS protection purchases. Beyhaghi et al. (2017) also find that of those loans whose lenders are engaged in credit risk transfer, loans to borrowers with higher perceived risks are more likely to be sold, whereas loans to relatively higher-quality borrowers are more likely to be hedged with CDSs.

Like Beyhaghi et al. (2017), Parlour and Winton (2013) find that loan sales are typically used by banks to manage their exposures to higher-risk credits and that CDS protection purchases are chosen for higher-quality loans and borrowers. The authors also conclude that the availability of loan sale and CDS credit risk management solutions leads to excessive monitoring by banks of high-risk credits and insufficient monitoring of lower-risk borrowers. Furthermore, the authors find that this effect is exacerbated for banks with higher costs of equity capital.

Norden et al. (2014) examine the extent to which banks use single-name CDSs to manage the credit risks of their loans and loan portfolios and/or to reduce economic or regulatory capital and how these uses of single-name CDSs were impacted by the credit crisis. The authors also consider the possibility that CDSs can increase borrower risk (putting upward pressure on spreads) if credit risk transfer by bank lenders leads to incentive problems regarding loan originations and monitoring. To disentangle these effects, they examine the banks' gross CDS positions, net CDS positions, and loan pricing. Their results provide evidence that banks use CDSs to manage their own credit exposures more effectively than if other credit risk transfer solutions were chosen, and that corporate borrowers benefit from banks' CDS hedging activities through lower spreads. The authors suggest that these benefits of single-name CDSs persisted through the crisis.

Shan et al. (2017) empirically study how banks utilize CDSs to reduce risk-weighted assets (i.e., a key component of risk-based capital requirements). Consistent with the notion that CDS usage can lessen the regulatory capital burden, they show that banks using CDSs essentially convert high-risk-weighted assets into low-risk-weighted assets, thereby enabling them to hold higher amounts of total assets. When compared to banks not using CDSs, CDS-using banks also earn higher returns on capital from their low-risk-weighted assets.

Martin and Roychowdhury (2015) analyze the extent to which the impact of single-name CDSs on lenders' monitoring incentives results in the conservatism of reference entities' financial reporting. The authors conclude that reference entities underlying traded CDSs do indeed adopt less conservative financial reporting. The authors also determine that less conservative reporting occurs when lenders face lower reputation costs from diminished borrower credit risk monitoring, covenants on reference entities' debt are more restrictive when CDSs are introduced, and lenders engage in more scrupulous monitoring prior to the introduction of CDSs and their use of those CDSs to hedge their credit exposures.

10.1.2 Single-Name CDSs and Risk-Taking by Banks and Insurers

As noted in Chapter 8, a widespread concern about single-name CDSs is that their usage by bank lenders can give rise to moral hazard in which banks make riskier loans and/or engage in suboptimal amounts of monitoring borrower credit risks. Yet, even the theoretical literature on bank usage of single-name CDSs is ambiguous on this point. For example, Chiesa (2008) describes various situations in which properly constructed credit risk transfer strategies (e.g., single-name CDS hedges) are commensurate with enhanced borrower credit risk monitoring. The issue of how the availability of single-name CDSs impacts banks' monitoring of borrower credit risks thus is an empirical question.

Shao and Yeager (2007) analyze the behavior of bank holding companies to evaluate whether or not banks use CDSs in a manner consistent with their risk/return preferences. Specifically, the authors examine whether the impact of their CDS activities (taken from Call Report data) on their risk and return, capital, and lending performance was consistent with whether the banks were protection buyers, sellers, or active users. Their findings indicate that credit protection buyers significantly reduced their total risk and increased their capital, which is consistent with using single-name CDSs to hedge the risk of their lending activities.

Yet, Shao and Yeager (2007) also find that credit protection sellers experience increases in their equity volatility, capital ratios, and returns. Active users of CDS with no apparent directional trend in their protection purchases and sales, moreover, are found to experience a small increase in risk, a small reduction in returns, and no significant impact on capital. The small reduction in returns, moreover, could be offset by revenues earned elsewhere in the bank—e.g., a bank may be willing to act as an intermediary for a customer at a small apparent loss to preserve its long-term fee-based customer relationship. On the whole, the research of Shao and Yeager (2007) indicates that banks are using CDSs in a manner consistent with their hedging and investment objectives.

In a similar study, González et al. (2012) investigate whether the use of single-name CDSs by European banks reduced or increased their respective risk profiles. Like Shao and Yeager (2007), they find that European banks using CDSs for hedging experienced an improvement in their level of financial stability, whereas those opting to use CDSs for synthetic bond investments experienced an increase in firm-specific risks.

Fung et al. (2012) conduct a study of how the use of single-name CDSs by US life and property/casualty insurers impacted the risk-taking decisions of those firms and their valuations. The authors conclude that such firms often use CDSs to generate income and not to hedge their credit exposures, and, as a result, their risk profiles became more aggressive. The paper further concludes that insurers' use of single-name CDSs was associated with reduced financial performance and lower firm valuations.

Although there are a number of articles in the academic literature that present theoretical models for how bank usage of CDSs can lead to increased bank risk-taking in their lending activities (e.g., Duffee and Zhou 2001; Morrison 2005), there is little *empirical* evidence in support of this. Exceptions are Le (2015) and Shan et al. (2014). Le (2015) presents empirical evidence that European banks that are more active in CDS markets tend to originate more risky assets and that increased risk-taking by banks is associated with larger CDS protection purchases. Shan et al. (2014) find that banks actively engaged in single-name CDS trading have significantly lower capital ratios and that such banks curtailed lending and raised capital during the credit crisis more than banks with little or no CDS usage, despite having higher pre-crisis operating performance and stock returns.

10.1.3 Single-Name CDSs and Loan Syndicates

The availability of single-name CDSs as instruments by which bank lenders can hedge their credit exposures to borrowers impacts bank lending and risk-taking behavior in a way that depends on the structure of the underlying loan facility. A bank loan facility (see Sect. 3.1 of Chapter 3) is typically "transactional" (i.e., akin to public debt issuance and involving one-off lender assessments of borrower credit risks) or "reputational" (i.e., loan facilities in which the borrower and lender have non-public information that materially impacts the terms of the loan and that is not observable to other market participants) (Boot and Thakor 2000). Syndicated loans are a hybrid of transactional and reputational loans in which a lead arranger conducts the initial credit risk assessment and engages in ongoing monitoring of borrower credit risk but underwrites or allocates portions of the loan to other syndicate members, whose sole function is to provide capital and purchase their allocated shares of the loan. Loan syndicate participants typically retain a relatively small total part of the loan facility in the form of pro rata tranches and then sell the remainder of the loan facility's institutional tranches in the primary or secondary market to asset managers or CLO sponsors and warehousing agents (see Chapter 3, Sect. 3.1 for a more detailed discussion).

In a typical syndicate, a lead arranger is responsible for both the original credit risk review of the borrower and the ongoing monitoring of borrower credit quality. Lee and Mullineaux (2004) find that loan syndicates have fewer participants when information about the credit risk of the borrower is more limited, thus suggesting that the membership and structure of a loan syndicate are driven at least in part by the need for enhanced monitoring of borrower credit risks. The authors also find that when syndicates place explicit limits on loan sales to non-syndicate members, larger and more diffuse syndicate structures result, which forces non-lead syndicate members to rely relatively more heavily on the lead arranger for the upfront and ongoing credit assessments of the borrower.

Because the actions of a lead arranger in a syndicate are generally not directly observable by other syndicate members whose primary role is to purchase allocated amounts of pro rata loans, lead arrangers typically must hold larger shares of syndicated pro rata loans than other syndicate members to mitigate the risk of moral hazard (Dennis and Mullineaux 2000; Sufi 2007). The ability of a lead arranger to lay off its credit exposure to the borrower using single-name CDSs without the knowledge of other syndicate members, however, limits the ability of the lead arranger to signal its greater monitoring efforts arising from larger pro rata loan allocations, and, indeed, defeats the purpose of such larger allocations (Parlour and Winton 2013).

Streiz (2016) analyzes how the availability of single-name CDSs impacts the structure of loan syndicates. Specifically, he compares syndicate structures before and after the introduction of single-name CDSs with syndicates that lend to borrowers with no actively traded single-name CDSs. The results of his empirical analysis indicate that lead arrangers sell on average three percent less of their pro rata loans after the introduction of CDSs and that the availability of single-name CDSs as hedging instruments is associated with more concentrated syndicates with fewer lender participants (Streiz 2016).

Song (2013) presents an interesting alternative to the more conventional moral hazard perspective on how CDSs can affect bank credit risk monitoring for syndicated loans. Specifically, Song (2013) suggests that if a lead arranger instead *sells* protection in a single-name CDS with the borrower as the reference entity, the lead arranger has essentially pre-committed to higher-quality monitoring. In other words, because a borrower default would impose losses on the lead arranger on its allocated share of the pro rata loans *and* its protection sales, the lead arranger has an incentive to engage in even greater upfront due diligence and ongoing monitoring. The incentive-aligning and signaling impacts are even more pronounced if the lead arranger sells protection *to other syndicate members* on the reference entity borrower.

The empirical results in Song (2013) support the hypothesis that lead arrangers selling CDS protection is a substitute for lead arrangers taking larger allocations of pro rata loans and loan participations.[1] In particular, Song's evidence shows that banks with larger amounts of CDS protection sales have smaller amounts of pro rata syndicated loan allocations. She also finds that active CDS dealers functioning as lead arrangers in loan syndicates are associated with larger syndicates and larger loans to borrowers. On the other hand, the presence of multiple active CDS participants or dealers in the same syndicate can attenuate this effect to the extent that non-lead syndicate members sell protection on the borrower to non-syndicate members.

10.2 The Impact of the Availability of Single-Name CDSs on Reference Entities

We now consider how the availability of single-name CDSs can impact the reference entities underlying those CDSs. In Sects. 10.2.1 and 10.2.2 of this chapter, we review the empirical evidence regarding the impact of the availability of single-name CDSs on the supply and cost of bank credit (both to reference entities and in general), respectively. In Sect. 10.2.3, we summarize the results of academic research concerning the impact of single-name CDS trading on the capital structure decisions of borrowers underlying CDS contracts. A fourth section below discusses evidence regarding the potential positive and negative externalities arising from the introduction of a single-name CDS. Section 10.2.5 concludes this section with a review of the literature regarding the impact of single-name CDSs and borrower hedging on the bankruptcy decisions of underlying reference entities.

10.2.1 Impact on the Supply of Credit

An often-cited benefit of single-name CDSs is their positive impact on the economy. Because single-name CDSs enable lenders to reduce their credit exposures and (potentially) monitoring costs, single-name CDSs should, in principle, lead to increased availability of credit and decreased borrowing costs for reference entities, which enables them to use those additional funds to finance productive investment opportunities, thereby increasing aggregate investment and economic growth (see, e.g., Jarrow 2011). Whether or not the availability of single-name CDSs actually does lead to an increase in the supply of credit to and reduced borrowing costs for reference entities is an empirical question, and the results are mixed.

Hirtle (2009) empirically analyzes whether increased CDS usage changed the amount of bank borrowing by CDS reference entities utilizing a comparison of US commercial bank holdings of CDSs and data on C&I loans issued by US banks for the period from 1997 to 2006. Hirtle's analysis shows that an increase in the use of CDSs is associated with an expansion in the supply of term loans to large borrowers. Hirtle (2009), however, found no increase in the volume of loan commitments or small-term loans. Hirtle's analysis also demonstrates that large firms (so-called named credits) are the primary beneficiaries of CDSs but that those benefits are limited to increases in the tenors and/or sizes of their term loans.[2]

Shan et al. (2014) empirically analyze the relation between the availability of single-name CDSs and bank lending. The authors find that banks actively engaged in single-name CDS trading extend more credit and make larger loans. Such banks, moreover, are more likely to extend larger loans to the reference entities underlying traded single-name CDSs.

Unlike Hirtle (2009) and Shan et al. (2014), Saretto and Tookes (2013) examine the impact of the introduction of single-name CDSs on all types of borrowings by reference entities. Their results indicate that the availability of single-name CDSs as hedging instruments leads to an increase in credit to reference entities, as well as longer debt maturities. The improved access to credit stems mostly from higher lending through the corporate bond market than the bank lending channel. They also find that the impact of CDS availability leads to greater increases in credit and debt maturities during periods in which credit supply is constrained or when unexpected shocks to local credit supplies occur (i.e., when the ability of lenders to hedge borrower credit exposures is the most important).

10.2.2 *Impact on Reference Entity Borrowing Costs*

The empirical literature indicates that the availability of CDSs as credit risk transfer mechanisms has an ambiguous overall impact on reference entity borrowing costs and that the net impact depends on the type of borrower.

Ashcraft and Santos (2009) find that the introduction of single-name CDS trading leads to improvements in the borrowing terms for safe and transparent firms in which banks' monitoring incentives are not likely to play a major role. In contrast, borrowing costs are higher for riskier and informationally opaque borrowers following the introduction of CDSs, which the authors attribute to the attenuated incentives of banks to engage in relatively costly borrower monitoring. Despite the ostensibly negative aspect of reduced bank monitoring of more opaque enterprises, the results in Ashcraft and Santos (2009) suggest that the introduction of single-name CDSs provides an important economic benefit by making it easier for lenders to identify creditworthy borrowers, thereby mitigating adverse selection problems in which "good" and "bad" borrowers cannot be distinguished and are charged a single price (Akerlof 1970; Rothschild and Stiglitz 1976). Hirtle (2009) also finds a separation effect in which the impact of CDS trading depends on the characteristics, reputation, and transparency/opacity of the reference entity.

Ismailescu and Phillips (2015) analyze the impact of CDS trading in sovereign debt markets and find that the informational role of CDSs is beneficial for closed economies with a high risk of default and for which relatively little financial information is available (absent the CDSs).

Ismailescu and Phillips (2015) also show that CDSs improve market liquidity and lower borrowing costs for investment-grade sovereigns, but that CDSs reduce market liquidity and increase borrowing costs for speculative-grade sovereign borrowers.

For large corporate borrowers, the evidence indicates that although the availability of credit and the size of loan facilities are higher after the introduction of single-name CDSs, the increased credit supply is accompanied by higher borrowing costs on loans by banks that actively hedge using single-name CDSs. For large banks that do not actively hedge, credits extended increase and borrowing costs for reference entities decline (Hirtle 2009; Shan et al. 2014).

The introduction of single-name CDS trading is also associated with an increase in the maturity of term loan facilities (Hirtle 2009; Saretto and Tookes 2013). Although a non-price term of bank credit facilities, borrowers often consider longer-term debt more desirable—especially large and transparent firms or firms that expect a deterioration in their credit ratings (see, e.g., Diamond 1991; Barclay and Smith 1995). In this sense, the impact of listing CDSs on the maturity structure of borrowers' debt may also be beneficial for certain borrowers.

Norden et al. (2014) analyze how and through which channel the use of single-name CDSs affect banks' hedging and how borrowers may benefit from any such hedging. They find that banks using single-name CDSs for credit risk transfer purposes do indeed pass the associated benefits and cost savings along to borrowers. They also determine that banks using CDSs to hedge exhibited smaller losses and a more stable supply of loans during the credit crisis.

The borrowing costs of reference entities underlying traded single-name CDSs are also affected by whether or not the corresponding loan facilities specify a credit spread (over a base floating rate like LIBOR) that is fixed or indexed to the borrower's CDS spread. As discussed in Chapter 9, the CDS spread is an observable measure of the reference entity's credit risk. Banks can thus use CDSs to monitor borrower credit quality.

Since 2008, moreover, banks have increasingly used single-name CDS spreads for reference entities over the term loans they have extended in order to calculate the interest payable by borrowers on such loans. The practice of incorporating CDS spreads explicitly into loan pricing is referred to as "market-based" loan pricing and is especially prevalent on revolving credit lines.

Ivanov et al. (2016) study how market-based pricing has impacted corporate borrowing costs. They ascertain that the borrowing cost on loans with market-based pricing is lower than on similar loans priced with fixed credit spreads, both at origination and over the lives of the loans. The authors attribute the lower cost on loans with market-based pricing to savings arising from reduced monitoring costs, which is supported by the evidence they present that market-based loans have more simplified covenants than loans with fixed credit spreads. Although the authors considered the possibility that loans with market-based pricing could lead to lower costs because such loans would be easier to hedge with the corresponding CDS, they did not find empirical support for that explanation and attributed the lower borrowing costs exclusively to savings realized by banks and passed on to borrowers arising from the replacement of costly credit monitoring with the information reflected in single-name CDS spreads.

The evidence and conclusions in Ivanov et al. (2016) raises concerns that greater reliance by banks on the information contained in CDS spreads could result in an excessive decline in loan and borrower credit monitoring by bank lenders, as discussed in Chapter 8 and Sect. 10.1.1 in this chapter. To the extent that the aggregated information of all market participants reflected in CDS spreads is higher quality than the credit information that a given lender would collect through an enhanced monitoring process; however, this concern is unfounded, and, in fact, CDS-based borrower credit monitoring is in that case preferable to bank-specific monitoring.

10.2.3 Impacts on Reference Entity Corporate Financing Decisions and Capital Structure

Perhaps the most important principle of corporate finance is the Modigliani-Miller ("M&M") proposition that the value of a firm is independent of its financing decisions—i.e., a firm cannot realize a higher valuation simply by altering its capital structure (Modigliani and Miller 1958). In contrast to actual financial markets, the M&M theory assumes that capital markets are "perfect" (e.g., no taxes, no costs of financial distress or bankruptcy, no transaction costs), information is equally shared by all market participants (i.e., information is "symmetric"), and that all securities issuers can access the capital markets on equal terms (Modigliani and Miller 1958; Fama 1978).

In an M&M world, the mere fact that a single-name CDS is available to trade for a given reference entity should have no impact on the corporate financing decisions (e.g., capital structure, leverage ratio, dividend policy, and hedging policies) of that firm or its cost of capital. With asymmetric information, market frictions and transaction costs, costs of financial distress and bankruptcy, and unequal access to financial markets, however, the existence of single-name CDSs can in principle impact the financial policies of the reference entities underlying those single-name CDSs. As Miller (1988) explained:

> [T]he view that capital structure is literally irrelevant or that "nothing matters" in corporate finance, though still sometimes attributed to us (and tracing perhaps to the very provocative way we made our point), is far from what we ever actually said about the real world applications of our theoretical propositions. Looking back now, perhaps we should have put more emphasis on the other, upbeat side of the "nothing matters" coin: showing what *doesn't* matter can also show, by implication, what *does.* (emphasis in original)[3]

In this section, we consider the empirical research on how the trading of a CDS on a particular reference entity may impact the corporate financing decisions and costs of capital for that reference entity. The results are ambiguous and sample-specific.

Saretto and Tookes (2013) consider how the trading of a single-name CDS affects the amount and maturity of a reference entity's debt. Even for firms with similar credit ratings, Saretto and Tookes (2013) find that firms with traded CDSs have higher leverage ratios and longer debt maturities. Their argument is that because CDSs enable lenders to hedge their exposure to the borrower more easily, lenders are willing to increase the amount of credit available to firms with traded CDSs. The findings of Saretto and Tookes (2013) thus support the importance of single-name CDSs as a credit risk transfer instrument for lenders.

Danis and Gamba (2018) developed a theoretical model to analyze how the onset of CDS trading would affect a firm's trade-offs between investment, equity financing, and debt financing. Their model incorporates real-world costs and frictions, such as equity issuance costs, bankruptcy costs, and debt renegotiation frictions. Danis and Gamba (2018) show that the initiation of CDS trading is associated with increases in the reference entity's leverage and investment but has no appreciable impact on its borrowing costs. In addition, the model shows that the existence of traded CDSs reduces the risk of strategic default but also increases the probability of bankruptcy. After calibrating the model to the underlying data, they find that the introduction of single-name CDSs on public US companies results in an average increase of 2.9% in firm value.

10.2.4 CDS Externalities

Externalities occur when the impact of a given activity (e.g., a CDS transaction) goes beyond the direct participants in the activity and conveys benefits or costs on other market participants that the original transacting parties cannot capture in the price of their transaction. In the classic microeconomics terminology, a positive externality exists when the marginal private benefit to the two counterparties of a transaction is less than the marginal social benefit (i.e., the benefit to all market participants). Conversely, a negative externality occurs when the private marginal cost of a transaction is less than the marginal social cost (see, e.g., Samuelson 1954; Bator 1958).[4] The difference between the marginal social benefit (cost) and marginal private benefit (cost) is known as the marginal external benefit (cost).

As the Nobel Prize-winning work of Ronald Coase (and the huge literature that followed) demonstrates, externalities almost always occur when some aspect of market structure, law, regulation, or institutions interfere with the definition or enforcement of property rights for the transacting parties (Coase 1960).[5] In particular, when the prices of transactions serve as a tangible benefit to parties that cannot be charged for the value those prices convey, a positive externality exists because the original parties do not have enforceable property rights in their prices (at least not in all senses).

For example, in 1991 a tunnel system underneath the Chicago Loop flooded, leading to the temporary closure of the Chicago Board of Trade ("CBOT"). During this time, grain elevators pulled down price quotes to farmers because they relied so heavily on futures prices to make their cash market quotes and did not repost those quotes until the futures markets re-opened (Kuserk and Locke 1994). Although exchanges routinely charge (and generate considerable revenues) for access to their real-time price feeds (especially in today's world in which high-frequency traders demand order book access down to the millisecond or microsecond), not *all* parties that benefit from those prices as signals of supply and demand can be charged for the value of the prices (Mulherin et al. 1991).

Studies of single-name CDSs contemplate both potential positive and negative externalities arising from the introduction of single-name CDS trading. One potential channel by which the trading of CDSs on a reference entity can generate externalities is through the information conveyed in CDS spreads. As discussed in Chapter 9, the empirical evidence confirms that single-name CDSs contain important information about reference entity credit risk and that CDS spreads reflect both anticipation and announcement effects regarding events that impact the financial conditions of reference entities. As we discuss later in Chapter 11, moreover, the empirical evidence overwhelmingly indicates that new information about reference entity credit is reflected in CDS spreads before credit spreads observed in the less liquid cash bond market. And, as discussed in Chapter 12, another potential positive externality of CDS spreads is their use in assisting regulators and policy makers in quantifying interconnectedness and potential system risks in the financial system.

The impact of the information contained in CDS spreads on other firms, however, is ambiguous as a matter of theory. On the one hand, this informational role of the CDS market could contribute to a reduction in the cost of a reference entity's debt by reducing the information premium that investors demand on bonds to compensate for their perceived informational disadvantage and, similarly, by reducing the rents that banks can extract from borrowers in connection with their informational advantage (Saretto and Tookes 2013). On the other hand, if the introduction of CDS trading on a reference entity increases the perceived likelihood of financial distress for that firm (as found in Subrahmanyam et al. 2014), the resulting negative signal could impact the financial decisions of counterparties and commercial or trade creditors with exposures to the firm that in turn could adversely impact the reference entity.

For example, Li and Tang (2016) postulate that commercial suppliers with trade and commercial exposures to the reference entity (and no listed CDSs on their own debt) may react to the perceived heightened financial distress risk of a reference entity customer through changes in their own leverage ratios. If a supplier's reaction to the seemingly higher distress probabilities at a customer conveyed by the information in its CDS spreads is a perceived increase in revenue risk from that customer, the supplier may react by decreasing its own leverage to absorb potentially higher expected credit losses. Yet, if the listing of a CDS on a particular reference entity enables the lender to cross-hedge its indirect exposure to the supplier (which has no listed CDSs), that could increase the supplier's debt capacity and access to funds, thereby leading to an increase in the supplier's leverage. As Li and Tang (2016) emphasize, the impact of single-name CDSs based on customers of suppliers and on the leverage of those suppliers is an empirical question.

Another possible source of positive externalities arising from CDS trading on a given reference name is improved pricing and compressed spreads for bond issuers resulting from enhanced cross-market integration. Specifically, because single-name CDSs involve both hedgers and speculators and trading frictions are relatively low for CDSs, CDS markets are generally more liquid than cash bond markets. To the extent that inter-market arbitrage keeps CDS spreads and corresponding cash bond prices tightly in line (a subject to which we return in Chapter 11), CDSs thus can help reduce spreads for issuers and improve access to and costs of financing (Oehmke and Zawadowski 2015). To the extent that the introduction of a single-name CDS attracts new traders and inter-market arbitrage volume, moreover, CDSs can promote additional bond market liquidity (Kim et al. 2017; Sambalaibat 2014; Shim and Zhu 2014).

10.2.5 The Empty Creditor and Negative Interest Problems

The "empty creditor" hypothesis and related issues were discussed in Chapter 8, Sect. 8.2. Because some models of the empty creditor hypothesis imply negative results for borrowers and other models have more constructive implications, it is unclear from first principles whether the existence of creditors hedged with single-name CDS protection purchases pose a net benefit or cost to reference entities. Likewise, the empirical evidence on the relation between the existence of empty creditors and the value of firms with traded CDSs is mixed.

Several studies report empirical results that support the negative implications of the empty creditor hypothesis for firms with traded single-name CDSs. Subrahmanyam et al. (2014) perform an empirical analysis of the effects of CDS trading on the credit risk of reference entities using CDS data on 901 North American firms with CDSs trading between 1997 and 2009. During this period, Standard & Poor's reported 3863 ratings downgrades and 1628 bankruptcy filings. The authors' analysis shows that both the likelihood of a rating downgrade and the likelihood of bankruptcy of reference entities increased after

CDSs started trading. On average, credit ratings decline by about half a notch within two years of the inception of CDS trading, and the probabilities of bankruptcy more than double (from 0.14 to 0.47%) over the two-year period after CDS trading begins. Subrahmanyam et al. (2014) also find that the negative effects of introducing CDSs on reference entities are more pronounced for firms with larger amounts of CDSs outstanding and when the CDSs do not include restructuring as a credit event. In their 2017 paper, Subrahmanyam, Tang, and Wang study the liquidity management and corporate risk of reference entities after the inception of CDS trading on their debt. They present empirical support for the empty creditor model—specifically, reference entities hold more cash after the launch of CDS trading on them as reference names.

Examining the period from 2001 through 2008, Peristiani and Savino (2011) find no systematic relation between the existence of CDS trading and bankruptcy events but did observe in the 2004–2008 period that firms with traded single-name CDSs were associated with higher estimated probabilities of default, which is consistent with the negative implications of the empty creditor hypothesis. Nevertheless, the authors also identified other explanations for their results that do not depend on misaligned incentives and empty creditors. Specifically, Peristiani and Savino (2011) find that firms with larger-than-normal exposures to institutional investors experience a greater incidence of defaults, which is consistent with institutional pressures on such firms to engage in fire-sale losses to cover funding liquidity needs (as suggested in the models of Brunnermeier and Pedersen (2009), Diamond and Rajan (2011), and Shleifer and Vishny (2011)).

Narayanan and Uzmanoglu (2018) analyze the relation between CDS activity and credit spreads empirically when creditors hedge using single-name CDSs. The authors conclude that hedged creditors have greater bargaining power in debt renegotiations that could deter firms from strategic default, but they also note that debt renegotiations in those situations could be costly and inefficient. The authors' empirical analysis found that on net, opposing forces resulting from the presence of hedged creditors, higher costs imposed by empty creditors, and the deferral of strategic default are all present but that the higher costs arising from empty creditors dominate the other effects. Narayanan and Uzmanoglu (2018) show that on average, firms with a higher net notional CDS outstanding have higher cost of debt. The authors also find that the costs imposed by empty creditors are even higher for firms with lower expected recovery rates.

Chakraborty et al. (2015) examine the relation between loan covenant violations and borrowers' investment expenditures, loan spreads, overall performance, and bankruptcy filings for firms with traded CDSs relative to firms without CDSs. They find some support for the empty creditor hypothesis—namely that firms with traded CDSs do not reduce their investment expenditures after covenant violations, but do pay higher loan spreads and experience more sluggish overall performance. Nevertheless, in contrast to the predictions of the empty creditor hypothesis, the authors also find that such firms do not file for bankruptcy at a higher rate than similar firms without traded CDSs.

Mengle (2009) observes a number of potential practical problems with the negative impacts of empty creditors and their impact on bankruptcy decisions. In particular, he notes that the real choice faced by hedged creditors is whether to opt for restructuring within a bankruptcy proceeding or an out-of-court restructuring. Restructurings outside of bankruptcy are not typically considered credit events because they are not binding on all debt holders, as discussed in Chapter 2. The empirical evidence suggests, moreover, that out-of-court restructurings can lead to higher recovery rates for lenders (Altman and Karlin 2009).

Mengle (2009) also concludes that restructuring within the confines of bankruptcy law has certain benefits—e.g., automatic stays, reduced conflicts among different security holders, and access to debtor-in-possession financing. Based on prior empirical corporate finance research, he infers that firms most likely to benefit from out-of-court restructurings are those firms with complex capital structures (and the security holder conflicts to which they give rise), significant pension liabilities, costly labor contracts, and substantial legacy contingent liabilities (e.g., catastrophic environmental clean-up costs or long-tailed liabilities arising from, say, asbestos or silicosis exposures).

Mengle (2009) contends that the impact of hedged creditors on a firm's bankruptcy decision—i.e., whether the existence of empty creditors leads to more bankruptcy filings even when out-of-court restructurings would be more efficient—is an empirical question. In that context, Altman and Karlin (2009) show that the number of restructuring events (as a percentage of default events) between 1984 and 2009 increased significantly after 2003 (when, as discussed in Chapter 2, a significant revision in the ISDA *Credit Derivatives Definitions* occurred). The correlation between the frequency of defaults and restructurings (as a percentage of total defaults), moreover, is nine percent over the whole sample period but jumped to 90% after 2003. Because the empty creditor theory implies a larger number of bankruptcies and a lower correlation between defaults and restructurings following the introduction of single-name CDS trading, the evidence summarized in Mengle (2009) and in Altman and Karlin (2009) calls into question (at least indirectly) the negative implications of the empty creditor hypothesis.

Colonnello et al. (2017) analyze publicly traded US firms (excluding utilities and financial institutions) in the period from 2001 through 2014 in order to examine the relation between "strong shareholders" and empty creditors. They conclude that debt holders purchase greater amounts of credit protection using single-name CDSs when strong shareholders have a larger degree of bargaining power in order to ensure a seat at the table during potential debt renegotiations. Following the inception of CDS trading, the authors estimate that the distance to default (a measure of probability of default) declines by 7.9% on average. They also find that firms' investments and market valuations decline by seven percent and 8.8%, respectively. The net impact of the availability of single-name CDSs for debt holders at firms with strong shareholders thus is ambiguous and depends on the channel through which the impact is viewed. Less ambiguously, Hong et al. (2017) show that outside shareholders exert power on CDS reference entities improving corporate governance and financial reporting quality subsequent to the onset of CDS trading.

Batta and Yu (2017) study the effect of CDS on investment for 554 North American firms which introduced CDS between 2001 and 2013. Similar to Saretto and Tookes (2013), Batta and Yu find an increase in debt capacity and investment expenditures (related, in particular, to merger and acquisition activities) during the CDS introduction year but smaller net debt issuance in subsequent years.

The Hovnanian controversy discussed in Sect. 2.2.4 of Chapter 2 also presents an interesting case study of strategic defaults. The Hovnanian case was not an empty creditor problem in which lenders had fully hedged their exposures to Hovnanian. On the contrary, Hovnanian involved a situation in which new lenders (i.e., Blackstone's GSO affiliate) seemingly used strategic default as a precondition for restructuring Hovnanian's debt and *avoiding* a bankruptcy filing. This is an even trickier situation than the simple empty creditor hypothesis because the benefits to Hovnanian from its restructuring must be compared to the net benefits to GSO as the new lender (which stands to profit significantly on its CDS protection sales) and the costs to non-lender CDS protection sellers that suffer from excessive payouts on their CDS protection sold. As discussed in Chapter 2, there is no obvious and easy answer to the question of whether the existence of creditors hedged with single-name CDS protection purchases is a net benefit or cost to reference entities in this case, given the incentive misalignment amongst some of the involved parties.

Notes

1. Song (2013) relies on CDS data regarding bank protection sales of the LCDX index.
2. Non-price terms in a loan—especially tenor—are often as important as the price in a loan.
3. Miller (1988, p. 100).
4. For a contrary perspective on the concept of "social efficiency," see Demsetz (1969).
5. See also Demsetz (1964, 1967) and the essays reprinted in T. Cowen, ed. *The Theory of Market Failure* (George Mason University Press, 1988).

References

Akerlof, G.A. 1970. The Market for 'Lemons': Quality Uncertainty and the Market Mechanism. *Quarterly Journal of Economics* 84 (3) (August).

Altman, E.I., and B. Karlin. 2009. The Re-Emergence of Distressed Exchanges in Corporate Restructurings. *Journal of Credit Risk* 5 (2) (Summer).

Ashcraft, A.B., and J.A.C. Santos. 2009. Has the CDS Market Lowered the Cost of Corporate Debt? *Journal of Monetary Economics* 56 (4) (May).

Barclay, M.J., and C.W. Smith, Jr. 1995. The Maturity Structure of Corporate Debt. *Journal of Finance* 50 (2) (June).

Bator, F.M. 1958. The Anatomy of Market Failure. *Quarterly Journal of Economics* 72 (3) (August).

Batta, G. and F. Yu. 2017. Credit Derivatives and Firm Investment. Claremont McKenna College Robert Day School of Economics and Finance Research Paper No. 2923236 (December 6).

Beyhaghi, M., N. Massoud, and A. Saunders. 2017. Why and How Do Banks Lay off Credit Risk? The Choice between Retention, Loan Sales, and Credit Default Swaps. *Journal of Corporate Finance* 42 (February).

Boot, A.W.A., and A.V. Thakor. 2000. Can Relationship Banking Survive Competition? *Journal of Finance* 55 (2) (April).

Brunnermeier, M.K., and L.H. Pedersen. 2009. Market Liquidity and Funding Liquidity. *Review of Financial Studies* 22 (6).

Chakraborty, I., S. Chava, and R. Ganduri. 2015. Credit Default Swaps and Moral Hazard in Bank Lending. Working Paper.

Chiesa, G. 2008. Optimal Credit Risk Transfer, Monitored Finance, and Banks. *Journal of Financial Intermediation* 17 (4) (October).

Coase, R.H. 1960. The Problem of Social Cost. *Journal of Law and Economics* 3 (October).

Colonnello, S., M. Efing, and F. Zucchi. 2017. Empty Creditors and Strong Shareholders: The Real Effects of Credit Risk Trading. Working Paper (October).

Culp, C.L. 2013. Syndicated Leveraged Loans During and After the Crisis and the Role of the Shadow Banking System. *Journal of Applied Corporate Finance* 25 (2) (Spring).

Danis, A., and A. Gamba. 2018. The Real Effects of Credit Default Swaps. *Journal of Financial Economics* 127 (1) (January).

Demsetz, H. 1964. The Exchange and Enforcement of Property Rights. *Journal of Law & Economics* 7 (October).

Demsetz, H. 1967. Toward a Theory of Property Rights. *American Economic Review* 57 (2) (May).

Demsetz, H. 1969. Information and Efficiency: Another Viewpoint. *Journal of Law & Economics* 12 (1) (April).

Dennis, S.A., and D.J. Mullineaux. 2000. Syndicated Loans. *Journal of Financial Intermediation* 9.

Diamond, D.W. 1991. Debt Maturity Structure and Liquidity Risk. *Quarterly Journal of Economics* 106 (3) (August).

Diamond, D.W., and R.G. Rajan. 2011. Fear of Fire Sales, Illiquidity Seeking, and Credit Freezes. *Quarterly Journal of Economics* 126 (2) (May).

Duffee, G.R., and C. Zhou. 2001. Credit Derivatives in Banking: Useful Tools for Managing Risk? *Journal of Monetary Economics* 48 (1) (August).

Fama, E.F. 1978. The Effects of a Firm's Investment and Financing Decisions on the Welfare of Its Security Holders. *American Economic Review* 68 (3) (June).

Finnerty, J.D. 1992. An Overview of Corporate Securities Innovation. *Journal of Applied Corporate Finance* 4 (4) (Winter).

Frame, W.S., and L.J. White. 2004. Empirical Studies of Financial Innovation: Lots of Talk, Little Action? *Journal of Economic Literature* 42 (1) (March).

Fung, H.-G., M.-M. Wen, and G. Zhang. 2012. How Does the Use of Credit Default Swaps Affect Firm Risk and Value? Evidence from US Life and Property/Casualty Insurance Companies. *Financial Management* 41 (4) (Winter).

González, L.O., L.I.R. Gil, S.C. Agra, and P.D. Santomil. 2012. Banking Risk and Credit Derivatives. Working Paper.

Hirtle, B. 2009. Credit Derivatives and Bank Credit Supply. *Journal of Financial Intermediation* 18 (2) (April).

Hong, H.A., J.W. Ryou, and A. Srivastava. 2017. Heightened Shareholder Interest in Firm Affairs Following the Inception of Credit Default Swap Trade. Tuck School of Business Working Paper No. 3094968 (December 31).

Ismailescu, I., and B. Phillips. 2015. Credit Default Swaps and the Market for Sovereign Debt. *Journal of Banking & Finance* 52 (March).

Ivanov, I.T., J.A.C. Santos, and T. Vo. 2016. The Transformation of Banking: Tying Loan Interest Rates to Borrowers' CDS Spreads. *Journal of Corporate Finance* 38 (June).

Jarrow, R.A. 2011. The Economics of Credit Default Swaps. *Annual Review of Financial Economics* 3.

Kane. E.J. 1988. Interaction of Financial and Regulatory Innovation. *American Economic Review* 78 (2) (May).

Kim, G.H., H. Li, and W. Zhang. 2017. The CDS-Bond Basis Arbitrage and the Cross Section of Corporate Bond Returns. *Journal of Futures Markets* 37 (8) (August).

Kuserk, G.J., and P.R. Locke. 1994. The Chicago Loop Tunnel Flood: Cash Pricing and Activity. *Review of Futures Markets.*

Le, T.N.P. 2015. The Use of Credit Derivatives and Bank's Risk Taking Behaviours. Working Paper (December 28).

Lee, S.W., and D.J. Mullineaux. 2004. Monitoring, Financial Distress, and the Structure of Commercial Lending Syndicates. *Financial Management* 33 (3) (Autumn).

Li, J.Y., and D.Y. Tang. 2016. The Leverage Externalities of Credit Default Swaps. *Journal of Financial Economics* 120 (3) (June).

Martin, X., and S. Roychowdhury. 2015. Do Financial Market Developments Influence Accounting Practices? Credit Default Swaps and Borrowers' Reporting Conservatism. *Journal of Accounting and Economics* 59 (1).

Mengle, D. 2009. The Empty Creditor Hypothesis. *ISDA Research Notes* (3) (November).

Merton, R.C. 1992. Financial Innovation and Economic Performance. Journal of Applied Corporate Finance 4 (4) (Winter).

Merton, R.C. 1995. A Functional Perspective of Financial Intermediation. Financial Management 24 (2) (Summer).

Miller, M.H. 1986. Financial Innovation: The Last Twenty Years and the Next. *Journal of Financial and Quantitative Analysis* 21 (4) (December).

Miller, M.H. 1988. The Modigliani-Miller Propositions after Thirty Years. *Journal of Economic Perspectives* 2 (4) (Autumn).

Miller, M.H. 1992. Financial Innovation: Achievements and Prospects. Journal of Applied Corporate Finance 4 (4) (Winter).

Minton, B.A., R. Stulz, and R. Williamson. 2009. How Much Do Banks Use Credit Derivatives to Hedge Loans? *Journal of Financial Services Research* 35.

Modigliani, F., and M.H. Miller. 1958. The Cost of Capital, Corporation Finance and the Theory of Investment. *American Economic Review* 48 (3) (June).

Morrison, A.D. 2005. Credit Derivatives, Disintermediation, and Investment Decisions. *Journal of Business* 78 (2) (March).

Mulherin, J.H., J.M. Netter, and J.A. Overdahl. 1991. Prices Are Property: The Organization of Financial Exchanges from a Transaction Cost Perspective. *Journal of Law and Economics* 34 (2), Pt. 2 (October).

Narayanan, R., and C. Uzmanoglu. 2018. Credit Insurance, Distress Resolution Costs, and Bond Spreads. *Financial Management.*

Norden, L., C.S. Buston, and W. Wagner. 2014. Financial Innovation and Bank Behavior: Evidence from Credit Markets. *Journal of Economic Dynamics and Control* 43 (June).

Oehmke, M., and A. Zawadowski. 2015. Synthetic or Real? The Equilibrium Effects of Credit Default Swaps on Bond Markets. *Review of Financial Studies* 28 (12) (August).

Pagès, H. 2013. Bank monitoring incentives and optimal ABS. *Journal of Financial Intermediation* 22 (1) (January).

Parlour, C.A., and A. Winton. 2013. Laying Off Credit Risk: Loan Sales Versus Credit Default Swaps. *Journal of Financial Economics* 107 (1).

Peristiani, S., and V. Savino. 2011. Are Credit Default Swaps Associated with Higher Corporate Defaults? Federal Reserve Bank of New York Staff Reports No. 494.

Ross, S.A. 1989. Institutional Markets, Financial Marketing, and Financial Innovation. *Journal of Finance* 44 (3) (July).

Rothschild, M., and J. Stiglitz. 1976. Equilibrium in Competitive Insurance Markets: An Essay on the Economics of Imperfect Information. *Quarterly Journal of Economics* 90 (4) (November).

Sambalaibat, B. 2014. CDS and Sovereign Bond Market Liquidity. Working Paper (April).

Samuelson, P.A. 1954. The Pure Theory of Public Expenditure. *Review of Economics and Statistics* 36 (4) (November).

Saretto, A., and H.E. Tookes. 2013. Corporate Leverage, Debt Maturity, and Credit Supply: The Role of Credit Default Swaps. *Review of Financial Studies* 26 (5) (May).

Shan, S.C., D.Y. Tang, and H. Yan. 2014. Did CDS Make Banks Riskier? The Effects of Credit Default Swaps on Bank Capital and Lending. Working Paper (June 7).

Shan, C., D.Y. Tang, and H. Yan. 2017. Credit Default Swaps and Bank Regulatory Capital. HKIMR Working Paper No. 20/2017 (September).

Shao, Y., and T.J. Yeager. 2007. The Effects of Credit Derivatives on U.S. Bank Risk and Return, Capital and Lending Structure. Working Paper (June).

Shim, I., and H. Zhu. 2014. The Impact of CDS Trading on the Bond Market: Evidence from Asia. *Journal of Banking & Finance* 40 (March).

Shleifer, A., and R. Vishny. 2011. Fire Sales in Finance and Macroeconomics. *Journal of Economic Perspectives* 25 (1) (Winter).

Song, W.-L. 2013. Do Credit Default Swaps Affect Lending Practices? Evidence from Syndicate Structures and the London Whale Incident. Working Paper (October).

Streiz, D. 2016. The Impact of Credit Default Swap Trading on Loan Syndication. *Review of Finance* 20 (1) (March).

Subrahmanyam, M.G., D.Y. Tang, and S.Q. Wang. 2014. Does the Tail Wag the Dog?: The Effect of Credit Default Swaps on Credit Risk. *Review of Financial Studies* 27 (10) (October).

Subrahmanyam, M.G., D.Y. Tang, and S.Q. Wang. 2017. Credit Default Swaps, Exacting Creditors and Corporate Liquidity Management. *Journal of Financial Economics* 124 (2) (May).

Sufi, A. 2007. Information Asymmetry and Financing Arrangements: Evidence from Syndicated Loans. *Journal of Finance* 62 (2) (April).

Tufano, P. 2003. Financial Innovation. In *Handbook of the Economics of Finance*, ed. G. Constantinides, M. Harris, and R. Stulz. Amsterdam: North-Holland.

CHAPTER 11

Inter-Market Basis Relations

In this chapter, we survey the significant academic literature on the relations between CDSs and the debt, equity, and equity options for reference entities underlying those CDSs. We begin in Sect. 11.1 by addressing the issue of price discovery—i.e., in which of the related markets is new information about the reference entity first reflected? In Sects. 11.2 and 11.3 of this chapter, we summarize the results from the empirical academic literature concerning the impacts of the introduction of single-name CDSs on liquidity and volatility in the reference entities' debt and equity securities, respectively. We conclude this chapter in Sect. 11.4 with a discussion of the determinants of the CDS-bond basis and the related empirical research.

11.1 Price Discovery

Price discovery is the process by which trading incorporates new information and market participants' expectations into asset prices. Thanks to the relatively low transaction costs and high market liquidity of many derivatives markets relative to their corresponding underlying cash markets, new information about assets (e.g., the perceived credit risk of the reference entity underlying a CDS contract) is often reflected in derivatives prices first.[1] In the discussion that follows, we refer to the market in which price discovery initially occurs—i.e., the market that first reflects new information about the underlying reference entity—as the primary price discovery market ("PPDM").

C. L. Culp et al., *Credit Default Swaps*, Palgrave Studies in Risk and Insurance, https://doi.org/10.1007/978-3-319-93076-3_11

11.1.1 CDSs vs. Bonds

The empirical evidence regarding the PPDM for *corporate* reference entities is consistent across different studies and data samples. Namely, essentially all of the studies we reviewed strongly indicate that single-name CDSs lead corporate bonds in price discovery. The result is unsurprising given the illiquidity in cash corporate bond markets, both on an absolute basis and relative to single-name CDSs. The studies that provide empirical evidence in support of single-name CDS markets as the PPDM for corporate reference entities include Longstaff et al. (2003), Blanco et al. (2005), Dötz (2007), Alexopoulou et al. (2009), Baba and Inada (2009), Forte and Peña (2009), Norden and Weber (2009, 2012), Delis and Mylonidis (2011), Coudert and Gex (2010a, 2013), Das et al. (2014), and Giannikos et al. (2013). Furthermore, Alexopoulou et al. (2009) and Coudert and Gex (2013) show that the price discovery role of single-name CDSs was even more pronounced after the onset of the credit crisis.

The results for *sovereign* reference entities are more ambiguous than the results for corporate borrowers and are sample-specific. The following studies empirically investigate the PPDM across sovereign CDS and corresponding sovereign debt markets:

- Chan-Lau and Kim (2004) estimate price discovery measures for emerging market economies and conclude that roughly equal price discovery occurs in CDS and bond markets in Bulgaria, Colombia, and Venezuela, but that the bond market leads the CDS market in Brazil and the CDS market leads the bond market in Russia;
- Ammer and Cai (2011) analyze the sovereign debt of Brazil, China, Colombia, Mexico, the Philippines, Russia, Turkey, Uruguay, and Venezuela and find that the cash bond market is the PPDM for the majority (but not for all) of the countries that the authors analyzed;
- Carboni and Carboni (2011) examine 14 European countries, three Asian countries, and the USA and find that the sovereign CDS market is the PPDM for most countries;
- Li and Huang (2011) evaluate 20 sovereign reference entities' CDS and bond spreads and concluded that the PPDM depends on the particular country but that, over time, sovereign CDS markets have become increasingly more common as the PPDM for sovereign reference entities' credit risks;

- Delatte et al. (2012) analyze European sovereign debt and CDS markets and ascertain that sovereign debt markets lead sovereign CDS markets for sovereigns experiencing little or no financial distress but that when sovereigns begin to come under pressure the sovereign CDS market becomes the PPDM (even for countries with relatively low-yield, low-risk bonds);
- O'Kane (2012) evaluates price discovery in European sovereign CDS and debt markets and concludes that the PPDM for Greece and Spain is the sovereign CDS market, the PPDM for France and Italy is the sovereign debt market, and Irish and Portuguese sovereign CDS and debt markets exhibit a feedback loop that makes the PPDM econometrically indeterminate for those countries;
- Alper et al. (2013) compare CDS spreads with relative asset swap spreads (i.e., spreads between benchmark sovereign debt yields and par interest rate swap rates) for developed, major economies in the 2008–2010 period and ascertain that sovereign CDS markets are the PPDMs primarily as a result of their greater relative liquidity;
- Coudert and Gex (2013) analyze both emerging market countries and developed countries in the Eurozone and conclude from their empirical analysis that the sovereign CDS market is the PPDM for emerging market countries but that the bond market leads the CDS market for Eurozone sovereigns;
- Gyntelberg et al. (2013) analyze intraday data on Eurozone sovereigns and find that the sovereign CDS market is the PPDM for the vast majority of sovereign borrowers;
- Hassan et al. (2015) investigate price discovery in several emerging markets and estimate that the bond market is the PPDM in Argentina, Colombia, Turkey, South Africa, and Brazil, and that the CDS market is the PPDM for Mexican and the Philippine sovereign debt; and
- Choi and Park (2017) analyze 18 sovereigns and find the bond market is the PPDM but the leadership role of the bond market depends significantly on several factors including credit rating events, funding costs, counterparty risks, risk appetites of counterparties, and the overall risk regime.

As the results in Coudert and Gex (2013) and Alper et al. (2013) indicate, price discovery in sovereign debt markets depends on the relative liquidity of cash markets and sovereign CDS markets. Sovereign

CDSs are more actively traded on lower-rated, higher-risk sovereign issuers and sovereigns experiencing financial distress and are less actively traded for higher-rated issuers for which there is less demand for credit protection and less uncertainty about the prospect of an adverse credit event. This result is also consistent with the findings of Delatte et al. (2012). The mixed results for sovereign debt thus are likely the result of differences in relative liquidity pools between sovereign debt and CDS markets and other sample- and country-specific considerations.

Lu et al. (2010) study the relation between the subprime asset-backed ABX index and the CDX and iTraxx CDS indices and between the CDS indices vis-à-vis underlying bond markets to determine the direction of information flow during the subprime mortgage crisis. Like the other results summarized in this section, Lu et al. (2010) demonstrate that the CDS indices lead the bond market in information processing and also that information in the ABX index was first reflected in ABX indices, particularly after the Lehman filed for bankruptcy. The effect was larger for lower-rated ABX index returns than for higher-rated ABX index returns.

11.1.2 CDSs vs. Equities

Several academic studies have investigated the price discovery role of single-name corporate CDSs compared to markets for equities and options on those equities issued by corporate reference entities underlying CDSs. In a significant and often-cited paper, Acharya and Johnson (2007) use equities as proxies for public information and examine potential insider trading by banks in the CDS market. They ascertain that significant incremental information is revealed in the CDS market in addition to the information already available in the equity market and thus conclude that the single-name CDS market is the PPDM. Acharya and Johnson (2007) also find that the new information reflected in single-name CDSs on corporate borrowers is only associated with negative credit news for borrowers that experience actual negative credit developments. The authors also determine that the relative magnitude of increased price discovery in the single-name CDS market is directly related to the strength of the relationships between reference entity borrowers with their banks, which provides support that asymmetric information is at least partially responsible for determining the PPDM.[2]

During the 2006 period when iTraxx was in its infancy, Byström (2006) shows high correlations between the stock market and iTraxx.

Calice (2014) performs a detailed analysis of the link between the iTraxx Europe and the CDX.NA indices and related equity markets for systemically important financial institutions ("SIFIs"). Despite the somewhat arbitrary and opaque designation of SIFIs by the US Financial Stability Oversight Council and comparable international regulators, their results indicate that large shocks in the CDX indices can destabilize the financial system. Specifically, they show that the CDX index predominates for US institutions while iTraxx predominates for European institutions.

Single-name CDSs are also found to be the PPDM by Zhu (2006), Flannery et al. (2010), Eyssell et al. (2013), and Berndt and Ostrovnaya (2014). Furthermore, Da Fonseca and Wang (2016) show that index CDS markets are the PPDMs.

Yet, other studies that have examined the role of single-name CDSs as compared to equity markets reach different conclusions. For example, although Forte and Peña (2009) and Norden and Weber (2009) confirm that the single-name CDS market is the PPDM when compared to corporate bonds, both studies also find that the equity markets of CDS reference entities are the PPDMs when compared to both single-name CDSs and corporate bonds. Byström (2005), Trutwein and Schiereck (2011), Marsh and Wagner (2012), and Hilscher et al. (2015) also find evidence that equity markets are the PPDMs when compared to single-name CDSs.

Several studies show that equity markets also dominate the price discovery process when compared to CDS indexes. Breitenfellner and Wagner (2012) and Schreiber et al. (2012) show that equity returns and corresponding implied volatility explain most of the variation in CDS swap spreads during the post-crisis period and global financial variables have significant influence before and during the crisis. Breitenfellner and Wagner (2012) further analyze the lead–lag relationship between iTraxx spread changes and stock returns and find that stock returns lead CDS spread changes during the crisis period, and they find a two-sided, bidirectional relationship during the post-crisis. Guo et al. (2011) analyze the contagion effects among the stock market, real estate market, CDS market, and energy market during the financial crisis over the period 2006 through 2009. They show that the CDX.IG index is most responsive to new information reflected in the stock market during the height of the crisis. Naifar (2011, 2012) confirms these results for the iTraxx CDS index and the Japanese and Australian stock markets and stock index volatility during the period 2005 through 2010. Fenech et al. (2014) also show a positive correlation between iTraxx and the Australian stock market during the financial crisis. Furthermore, Fung et al. (2008) and Ding and Pu (2012) find that the stock market leads changes in the CDX indices during the crisis. Hammoudeh and Sari (2011) confirm these results for the banking, financial services, and insurance sectors—viz., they find that the respective equity markets were a strong driver of CDS spreads during the financial crisis.

Some research indicates that the PPDM depends on market conditions. For example, Trutwein and Schiereck (2011) and Trutwein et al. (2011) analyze single-name CDS spreads and corresponding reference entity equity before and during the credit crisis, and Forte and Lovreta (2015) examine 92 non-financial European corporate issuers from 2002 through 2008. Both studies found that equity markets were informationally dominant and function as the PPDMs (compared to CDS markets) in periods of financial distress. Using the longer and larger sample of the two papers, Forte and Lovreta (2015) also conclude that the single-name CDS market is the PPDM during relatively stable periods. Coudert and Gex (2010c) reach similar conclusions that the CDS market is the PPDM during non-crisis periods but find that equity markets lead CDS markets in price discovery during market dislocations.

By contrast, Giannikos et al. (2013) find the opposite (based on an analysis of 39 US issuers over the period from 2005 through 2008). Specifically, they conclude from their empirical analysis that the equity market is the PPDM during stable periods but the single-name CDS market is informationally dominant and the PPDM during the crisis period of 2007 and 2008. Similarly, in a study of the 2008–2012 period of European sovereign debt, sovereign CDS, and equity markets located in those sovereign nations, Santamaría et al. (2014) find that broad-based equity markets were the PPDMs in the 2008–2009 period, but, when the sovereign debt crisis erupted in 2010, sovereign CDS markets became the PPDMs.

The apparent inconsistency between the findings of Giannikos et al. (2013) and Santamaría et al. (2014), on the one hand, and Forte and Lovreta (2015), on the other hand, suggests that the relation between equity and CDS markets differs between the USA and Europe. Given the differences in regulations and market microstructures in the USA and E.U. (see Chapter 6) and the resulting differential trading and regulatory costs faced by informed traders, this is a plausible explanation. Alternatively, the results may depend on the individual reference borrowers in the sample. For example, different cost structures for the acquisition of information may depend on characteristics of individual reference entities (e.g., small- and large-cap issuers sometimes have differing costs of information acquisition), which could also explain the distinct results in these studies.

Yet another possible explanation for these seemingly inconsistent results is that the PPDM varies depending on the type of new information the markets are processing. For example, Marsh and Wagner (2012) compare the speed of adjustment and lead/lag relations across single-name CDS and equity markets and ascertain that the equity market is the PPDM for new market-wide information and common risk factors but that the single-name CDS market is the PPDM (or that CDS spreads and equity prices reflect new information contemporaneously) for new information that is reference entity-specific. The authors also conclude from their empirical analysis that the CDS market is slower to process positive news than negative news about the underlying reference entity. Kryzanowski et al. (2017), however, show that no market has a price discovery advantage and that negative earnings announcements result in large relative increases of price discovery in the CDS market.

Episodic changes in relative market liquidity and depth also appear to impact the price discovery process. For example, Mayordomo et al. (2011) find that the single-name CDS market is the PPDM prior to the outbreak of the credit crisis, but that during the crisis the bond asset swap market becomes the PPDM. In both periods, the cash bond market is the slowest to incorporate new information.

Some research has also analyzed how options on the shares issued by firms that are reference entities underlying single-name CDSs process new information. For example, Berndt and Ostrovnaya (2014) find that equity markets do not respond to abnormal movements in option prices unless that information has already manifested itself in corresponding single-name CDS spreads.

11.2 Impacts of Single-Name CDS Trading on Bond Market Quality

As discussed in Chapter 8, one potential cost of the introduction of single-name CDSs for a reference entity is the possibility of adverse impacts on the cash bond market for debt issued by the reference entity. Those adverse impacts could include higher cash market volatility and/or reduced liquidity (to which we collectively refer as "market quality") that could potentially result in higher bid-ask spreads and execution costs in the underlying cash market.

Concerns that the introduction of derivatives in general precipitates increased cash market volatility—which is usually blamed on the presence of potentially destabilizing speculators—have been expressed for many decades. Yet, the evidence generally indicates the opposite—i.e., the introduction of derivatives results in a *reduction* in the volatility of underlying cash market volatility, both because the availability of derivatives enables commercial enterprises to manage better their price risks and such hedges promote stability in the market and because intermarket arbitrage helps keep prices of derivatives and cash markets in line through the execution of arbitrage trades on opposite sides of the market (e.g., long a futures contract and short the cash) which over time reduces fluctuations in the cash market.

For exchange-listed futures and options, Mayhew (2000) surveys the empirical literature over the 1896–2000 period and examines the impact of the introduction of commodity, fixed income, and stock index futures and individual equity options on the volatility of the underlying cash market products. In Table 11.1, the second column reports the number of research studies that he surveyed, and the third column reports the number of markets covered across all of those studies. For example, 13 academic analyses of commodity futures were produced over the time period that collectively examined 15 futures markets. (The markets often overlap in time across the studies.) The last three columns report

Table 11.1 Academic studies of the impact of the introduction of futures contracts on underlying cash market volatility, 1896–2000

Asset class	*# Studies*	*# Markets*	*Lower*	*No or mixed impact*	*Higher*
Commodities	13	15	10	4	1
Fixed income	11	12	4	7	1
Stock index	36	43	8	28	7
Equity options	17	17	16	11	1
Total	77	87	38	50	10
Total (%)			39	51	10

Source Mayhew (2000)

the number of markets for which the introduction of derivatives led to lower-cash market volatility, had no impact or a mixed impact, or led to higher volatility, respectively. As Table 11.1 indicates, the 77 studies indicate that only 11% of the 87 markets analyzed across four asset classes over a period of more than 100 years experienced higher cash market volatility after the introduction of futures and/or options on those products.

In the aftermath of the financial crisis in 2008 and the European sovereign debt crisis in 2011, regulators exhibited renewed interest in the impact of the introduction of CDSs on cash bond markets. For example, Securities and Exchange Commission Chairman Erik Sirri testified before the House Committee on Agriculture that:

> [t]he SEC has a great interest in the CDS market because of its impact on the debt and cash equity securities markets and the Commission's responsibility to maintain fair, orderly, and efficient securities markets. These markets are directly affected by CDS due to the interrelationship between the CDS market and the claims that compose the capital structure of the underlying issuers on which the protection is written.[3]

In this section, we summarize the academic research regarding the impact of the introduction of single-name CDSs on the quality of the markets for the bonds issued by the reference entities underlying those CDSs.

Using an extensive sample of single-name CDS and bond trades between 2002 and 2008, Das et al. (2014) show that the average trade size and average turnover (relative to the total outstanding) in corporate bond markets decline in the two-year period subsequent to the inception of single-name CDS trading. Because the CDS market involves active players and is dominated by financial institutions that typically are relatively better informed, it is not surprising that Das et al. (2014) also find evidence of large institutional traders migrating from corporate bond markets to single-name CDS markets after the latter were introduced. This exodus of institutional traders likely explains the apparent deterioration in bond market quality that the authors found following the introduction of single-name CDSs. Similar empirical results have been documented for equity options and equity markets—i.e., after options on a stock are listed for trading, the price discovery function increasingly occurs in the option market, particularly when the options are more liquid and/or options markets attract larger and better-informed traders (Easley et al. 1998; Pan and Poteshman 2006).

Nashikkar et al. (2011) study potential liquidity spillover effects from single-name CDSs to bonds and find that bonds with more liquid CDSs have lower yields than comparable bonds with less liquid CDSs. The seemingly adverse impact of the introduction of single-name CDSs on corporate bond markets reported by Das et al. (2014) thus may be a temporary phenomenon. Once liquidity in the single-name CDS market stabilizes, the results of Nashikkar et al. (2011) suggest that some of that liquidity will positively impact corporate bond market liquidity (either through inter-market arbitrage transactions or through other channels).

Despite the empirical evidence that the introduction of CDSs can have adverse impacts on bond market quality that may be deleterious to some cash bond market participants, there may be offsetting (or more than offsetting) benefits in the single-name CDS market such that there is a *net* benefit from the introduction of single-name CDSs across the two markets based on the same reference entity. For example, Oehmke and Zawadowski (2015) present a framework for analyzing the implications for corporate bond markets resulting from the introduction of CDSs. Oehmke and Zawadowski (2015) describe the role of CDSs as being similar to liquidity transformation—i.e., single-name CDSs are more liquid alternatives to relatively illiquid corporate bonds for trading and managing the credit risk of a reference entity.[4]

The introduction of single-name CDSs, however, creates opposing forces on bond demand. Assuming (realistically) that trading costs are lower for single-name CDSs than for corporate bonds, Oehmke and Zawadowski (2015) identify three possible impacts on corporate bond prices resulting from the introduction of single-name CDSs:

- Investors that previously held a long position in a bond may sell the bond and then sell CDS protection as a way of synthetically investing in the bond, which puts *downward pressure* on the cash bond price;
- Investors that previously shorted the bond may unwind their short sales and buy CDS protection because the relatively illiquid bond often trades at a discount to the CDS (see Sect. 11.4 of this chapter), which may reduce the amount of short selling and put *upward pressure* on the bond price; and

- When the CDS spread of a reference entity is lower than the credit spread on a bond issued by that reference entity (see Sect. 11.4 of this chapter), some investors will become negative basis traders that simultaneously buy the bond and purchase CDS protection; because the combined position of a negative basis trade is hedged, basis traders can usually take leveraged positions that put potentially significant *upward pressure* on the corporate bond price.

The impact from the introduction of single-name CDS trading on the prices of the reference entity's bonds thus is ambiguous as a matter of theory, although Oehmke and Zawadowski (2015) conclude that inter-market arbitrage and cross-market basis trades ultimately compress the CDS-bond basis (see Sect. 11.4 of this chapter) and mitigate the impact of new CDS transactions on cash bond prices.

Massa and Zhang (2012) consider the impact that an active single-name CDS market has on the corresponding corporate bond market from the perspective of large institutional investors such as insurance companies, banks, and pension funds. A drop in bond market value or a downgrade in bond ratings may force such institutions to raise additional equity or sell their bond investments to remain compliant with their risk-based capital requirements. Such forced bond sales can potentially create or exacerbate market liquidity risks for investors in corporate bonds. If those institutions purchase CDS protection, they could defer their sales of bonds until more stable market conditions prevail. The presence of single-name CDS may also induce arbitrageurs to enter the market. For example, if corporate bonds are temporarily underpriced because of market liquidity risks and shocks, inter-market arbitrage will result in greater liquidity in the bond market.

11.3 Impacts of Single-Name CDS Trading on Equity Market Quality

Because of the economic near-equivalence of single-name CDS protection sales and purchases of bonds issued by the reference entity underlying the CDS, the results summarized in the previous section that document the impacts from the introduction of CDS trading on corresponding corporate bond markets are unsurprising. Why the introduction of a single-name CDS could impact the liquidity and volatility (i.e., quality) of the market for the stock issued by the reference entity is less obvious.

The classic insight of Merton (1974) laid the theoretical foundation for our understanding of the relationship between a firm's debt and equity in an options framework. Equity can be viewed as a call option on the firm's assets with a strike price equal to the face value of the firm's debt ("*FV*"), whereas zero-coupon debt can be viewed as a short put option on the firm's assets with a strike price of *FV* plus a riskless loan of *FV*. Culp et al. (2018) analyze the empirical relations between credit spreads of "pseudo firms" that hold actual, traded securities as assets and document numerous similarities between the credit spreads on the debt of such pseudo firms and actual, observed credit spreads on both the single-name CDSs and cash bonds issued by comparable securities issuers.

Any relative mispricing across the debt and equity securities issued by the same firm gives rise to potential capital structure arbitrage opportunities. Single-name CDSs are relatively low-cost, liquid, and attractive instruments with which firms can conduct capital structure arbitrage. As long as the gains from arbitraging the mispricing exceed transaction costs, such arbitrage activities help eliminate any relative mispricing of a reference entity's debt and equity and enhance the firm's capital structure efficiency, which can lead to a lower cost of capital for the firm.[5]

Yet, if single-name CDSs are predominantly traded by informed traders with complex and/or opaque strategies, the information reflected by single-name CDS trades may not be discernible to relatively less-informed traders (Boehmer et al. 2015). In that case, market makers may perceive themselves to be at a relative informational disadvantage to informed traders, which will lead them to widen their quoted bid/ask spreads as compensation for providing liquidity to relatively better-informed traders (Glosten and Milgrom 1985). Those higher transaction costs may in turn discourage capital structure arbitrage and allow perceived relative mispricings to persist.

Using a sample of NYSE stocks during the period from 2003 through 2007, Boehmer et al. (2015) investigate the impact of the introduction of CDSs on equity markets and ascertain that equity markets become less liquid and equity prices become less informationally efficient after a market for a single-name CDS emerges. The authors note an increased presence of informed institutional investors following the introduction of CDS trading, as well as a heightened price impact resulting from informed equity trades. The adverse impact of single-name CDS trading is more pronounced for firms that are closer to default and facing greater market uncertainty.

Conversely, the authors also find that the introduction of single-name CDSs has a less negative (and sometimes a positive) role for healthy firms. They conjecture that their results may be driven by the fact that there is more speculative trading in CDSs for firms in distress and when market conditions are volatile and that the activities of hedgers are more dominant during stable market conditions.

Haas and Reynolds (2017) reach somewhat similar conclusions. They find that as liquidity in CDS markets tightens, equity market makers that rely on CDS spreads as important sources of information about the credit quality of reference entities reduce their liquidity provision in response to the reduction of information from the CDS market, thereby resulting in a spillover of any market illiquidity from single-name corporate CDS markets to the corresponding equity markets.

Liu et al. (2017) study the role of CDSs in revealing information about management to investors that do not have alternative avenues for knowing when management withholds bad news about the firm. The authors analyze 761 CDS reference entities between 1997 and 2014. They conclude that the onset of CDS trading has had a stabilizing effect on the stock prices of sample firms—i.e., CDS markets *do* reveal useful information to such traders.

11.4 The CDS-Bond Basis

The CDS-bond basis is the difference in the credit spread for a given reference entity reflected in single-name CDS spreads and corporate bond spreads. Although the basis can be measured either way, the traditional measure of the CDS-bond basis is to subtract the corporate bond credit spread from the CDS spread. When the CDS-bond basis is negative, an arbitrageur can buy protection on the reference entity and contemporaneously purchase the corporate bond.[6] The arbitrageur in a negative basis trade profits by receiving the relatively higher bond yield and paying the cheaper CDS coupon to hedge the credit exposure of the combined position.

In a frictionless market with no impediments to trade and no transaction costs, inter-market arbitrage keeps the prices of bonds and related CDS spreads in line and gives rise to a mean-reverting CDS-bond basis. During normal market conditions, the CDS-bond basis is close to zero, although various institutional details (discussed in Sect. 11.4.2) generally prevent the basis from being exactly zero. Because CDSs and bonds are often used in dynamic hedging or basis trading strategies—both of which depend on the convergence of CDS spreads and bond yield spreads—understanding the factors driving the CDS-bond basis and the related empirical evidence highlights the risks associated with these types of strategies.

11.4.1 Measuring the CDS-Bond Basis

In any empirical examination of the CDS-bond basis, care must be taken to properly define the basis so that credit spreads on bonds and CDSs are expressed consistently on an apples-to-apples basis. To assess the relative value and credit risk of a bond and CDS based on the same reference entity, several different measures of the CDS-bond basis have been developed. The most common such measures are as follows[7]:

- *Asset swap/CDS basis*: This measure of the CDS-bond basis is the difference between the observed CDS spread and the asset swap spread on a bond issued by the reference entity underlying the CDS. The advantage of this measure is that it reflects the carrying cost (possibly negative) of the trade—i.e., the actual cash cost of holding the bond and buying protection on it. For bonds trading well away from par, however, this measure of the basis can be unreliable.
- *z-Spread/CDS basis*: The *z*-spread on a bond is the spread which, when added to maturity-specific rates on the zero-coupon swap curve at all maturities, reprices the bond to par. Because this is a zero-coupon-equivalent rate, the actual CDS spread must also be adjusted to a zero-coupon-equivalent rate (e.g., by bootstrapping the par CDS curve). Although this measure of the basis does not reflect the cash carrying costs of a basis trade, it is generally considered to be a more economically informative measure of the *true value* of the basis than the asset swap/CDS basis for bonds trading at a discount to par.
- *Adjusted z-spread/CDS basis*: In this measure of the basis, default risk is explicitly incorporated into the potential cash flows on the bond, and the basis is defined as the difference between the *z*-spread of a bond whose price has been calculated using CDS

spreads and the *z*-spread of the actual bond. This is the most direct comparison of theoretical and actual bond spreads.

- *Repo/CDS basis*: This measure of the basis is essentially the same as the adjusted *z*-spread except that the spread is expressed as a difference in yields rather than zero-coupon rates. Specifically, the yield is calculated on a hypothetical bond priced off the CDS curve and then compared to the observed yield on the actual cash bond in the repo market.
- *Arbitrage-Pricing Difference ("APD")*: The APD measure uses the CDS curve to derive a CDS-implied theoretical bond price,[8] which then is compared to the market price of the actual bond. The APD is a very robust measure of the basis that does not suffer the limitations identified in the other measures and can be used to identify relative value opportunities. For example, when the CDS-implied bond price exceeds the market price of the bond, the bond is cheap relative to the CDS, and it can make sense for arbitrageurs or investors to buy the bond and purchase CDS protection to exploit the negative basis. Conversely, a positive basis occurs when the market price of the bond exceeds the CDS-implied bond price and suggests a sale of CDS protection and sale of the bond.[9]

11.4.2 Economic Factors Affecting the Basis

Credit spreads on corporate and sovereign bonds and the single-name CDS contracts for the same reference entities reflect the same underlying reference entity-specific credit risks. In principle, differences in the design of the products or differences in the risk premiums across the two products for *non-credit* risks should explain any situations where the CDS-bond basis is not zero (i.e., does not reflect "parity" between the CDS- and bond-implied credit spreads for the same reference entity).

In other words, no-arbitrage requirements stipulate that whenever the CDS-bond basis is sufficiently different from zero, it is theoretically possible to implement a basis arbitrage trade, selling (buying) credit risk in the bond market and buying (selling) credit risk in the CDS market. For the basis trading strategy to be profitable, markets should be relatively liquid with narrow bid-ask spreads, funding for bond purchases should be readily available, and the interbank market should function efficiently. Even under these conditions, this arbitrage strategy is still imperfect as a result of product design differences such as the CTD option owned by protection purchasers in physically settled single-name CDSs and the practical challenges involved with short-selling cash bonds, both of which tend to render the basis slightly positive during normal market conditions (see, e.g., Duffie 1999).

Gyntelberg et al. (2017) analyze the relation between arbitrage trading and arbitrage costs and the size of the CDS-bond basis for European sovereigns. Arbitrage trades are more profitable when the CDS-bond basis exceeds a certain level and results in faster adjustment to the long-run equilibrium once this level is breached. Fontana and Scheicher (2016) examine Eurozone sovereign debt markets using a weekly dataset from 2007 to 2012 and find that a persistence of positive basis deviations can be explained by short-selling frictions, whereas the persistence of negative basis deviations, which are observed for countries with weak public finances, can be explained by funding frictions. Further, they show that a key driver of the large positive basis of better-rated countries is the "flight-to-quality/liquidity" phenomenon in bond markets.

One simple reason that the CDS-bond basis may not be exactly zero is that the no-arbitrage relation between single-name CDSs and bonds for the same reference entity only holds strictly for floating-rate notes (Duffie 1999). As Hull and White (2000) observe, "[t]he difference between the spread on par yield floaters and par yield fixed rate instruments is very small for flat term structures, but noticeable for non-flat term structures."[10]

A second significant reason for divergences of the CDS-bond basis from parity is relative differences in liquidity across single-name CDSs and corresponding cash bonds. In particular, the relatively greater illiquidity in the corporate bond market can give rise to a non-zero CDS-bond basis (see, e.g., Gârleanu and Pedersen 2011). In fact, this belief is so deeply ingrained in the academic literature that the CDS-bond basis is sometimes used as a *measure* of the market liquidity risk premium in corporate bonds. Although the relative simplicity of that measure of the bond liquidity risk premium is appealing, it ignores other factors that could also affect the CDS-bond basis and thus can lead to biased estimates of bond market liquidity risk premiums.

In addition to relative differences in single-name CDS and bond market liquidity risks, other factors that may impact the CDS-bond basis include the following: (i) the impact of the value of the CTD option owned by protection purchasers in physically settled single-name CDSs; (ii) different treatments of accrued interest in CDSs and bonds;

(iii) short sale restrictions in either or both markets; and (iv) counterparty risk in the CDS market.[11] The relative importance of these factors, moreover, is not constant over time. For example, Andritzky and Singh (2006) find that the CTD option in sovereign CDSs is significant for sovereign debt trading well below par but is insignificant for relatively low-risk sovereign debt with prices near their par amounts.

The Lehman Brothers credit event in September 2008 and the subsequent global financial crisis introduced a new era in financial markets in which counterparty risks began to affect derivatives prices. Prior to the Lehman Brothers default, derivatives were priced "as if" the credit quality of counterparties was AAA.[12] For counterparties rated below AAA, collateral requirements brought the credit risk of the transaction to a AAA-equivalent rating. Subsequent to the Lehman Brothers default, however, most derivatives are now priced to reflect the credit risk of the two counterparties.[13] Following the implementation of the CDS clearing mandate in 2013, this counterparty risk component of CDS pricing disappeared for mandatorily cleared CDS index products but persists for uncleared single-name CDSs.

In particular, if the occurrence of a credit event at the reference entity coincides with the default of the CDS protection seller, the CDS buyer is at risk not to receive the full contractually required payment from the CDS protection selling counterparty. CDS buyers facing counterparties with non-trivial perceived credit risk thus will pay less for credit protection than if they were facing otherwise-similar counterparties with lower-perceived credit risk. The typical mitigating factors for this type of counterparty risk are the posting of collateral on non-cleared CDSs and the clearing of certain CDSs by CCPs. The empirical evidence confirms that spreads on uncollateralized CDSs reflect counterparty credit risk and gives rise to a non-zero CDS-bond basis[14] (see, e.g., Bongaerts et al. 2011).

Adler and Song (2010) analyze the theoretical impacts on the CDS-bond basis of economic factors. Table 11.2 summarizes those factors and the direction of the impact of those factors on the CDS-bond basis.

11.4.3 Empirical Examinations of the CDS-Bond Basis

Virtually all empirical investigations into deviations of the CDS-bond basis from the theoretical parity relationship are based on institutional frictions that interfere with the inter-market arbitrage trading strategies

Table 11.2 Factors influencing the CDS-bond basis

Direction of basis	*Effect*	*Description*
Positive (i.e., CDS spread exceeds bond spread)	CTD option in CDSs	The protection buyer in a physically settled CDS can choose to deliver any eligible bond and receive par value
	Issuance of new bonds	Pushes up demand for insurance, resulting in a higher price of protection
	Bond short-selling abilities	If the reference entity's credit deteriorates, CDS spreads react more quickly than bonds as the demand for credit protection increases
	Repo specialness	Repurchase agreements on certain bonds that are deliverable into physically settled CDSs put upward pressure on CDS spreads due to limited availability of bonds
Negative (i.e., bond spread exceeds CDS spread)	Counterparty risk	Premium compensating CDS protection buyer for the risk that the protection seller defaults
	Bond illiquidity	Although the effect can be ambiguous, illiquid bonds trade at higher spreads and therefore reduce the basis
	Funding risk	The protection seller's funding risk is different than what would be incurred if, instead of entering into a CDS, it replicated the CDS by buying the underlying bond with funds borrowed at the risk-free rate

Source Adler and Song (2010)

that normally would eliminate perceived violations in the law of one price across single-name CDS and related bond markets. For example, De Wit (2006), Bai and Collin-Dufresne (2013), and Mayordomo and Peña (2014) empirically confirm that the institutional issues discussed in the previous section (e.g., trading liquidity, funding costs and constraints, counterparty risk, and margin requirements) explain a significant amount of the variation in the CDS-bond basis prior to, during, and after the credit crisis.

Longstaff et al. (2003) compare credit spreads in corporate bonds to corresponding single-name CDS credit spreads and find that CDS spreads are lower than corporate bond credit spreads for all firms in their sample—i.e., they document a systematically negative CDS-bond basis in the cross section of their data. They suggest that tax-related and liquidity components reflected in corporate bond spreads explain the higher credit spreads on corporate bonds. In a follow-up to their 2003 paper, Longstaff et al. (2005) decompose the CDS-bond basis into default and non-default components and find that the non-default component varies over time and is correlated with bond market illiquidity.[15] Cossin and Lu (2005), Levy (2009), Küçük (2010), and Badaoui et al. (2015) also find that illiquidity is a significant explanatory variable for deviations of the CDS-bond basis from parity.

Houweling and Vorst (2005) and Adler and Song (2010) show that the spread on a par fixed-coupon bond over a par default risk-free fixed-coupon bond only equals the CDS premium if the payment dates on the CDS and bond coincide and recovery on default is a constant fraction of face value. These studies thus confirm the parity relation established by Duffie (1999) and show that it only holds exactly for par bonds.

Blanco et al. (2005) and Zhu (2006) confirm that the parity relation between CDSs and bonds is an equilibrium condition but that substantial deviations from parity can arise in the short run if, for example, the cost of shorting a bond in the repo market is significant. A non-zero CDS-bond basis can also arise from combinations of imperfections in the contract specification of CDSs and measurement errors in computing credit spreads. For example, with no restructuring event specified in the ISDA master agreements, as much as 6–8% of the CDS spread is a premium paid to protection sellers for bearing restructuring risk (Berndt et al. 2007).

As discussed in Sect. 2.1.6 of Chapter 2, protection buyers are entitled to choose from a basket of eligible deliverable obligations to be delivered to the protection seller in a physically settled single-name CDSs in exchange for receiving the cash value of the par amount of the delivered bond. Bonds of a defaulted obligor with different coupon rates, maturities, and depths of subordination do not trade at the same price following a default. As such, the CTD option owned by single-name CDS protection buyers entitles them to deliver any eligible bond, and rational market participants thus will deliver a bond with the lowest price—i.e., the bond with the lowest expected recovery rate. Jankowitsch et al. (2008) find that recovery rates can span a wide range, varying between 8 and 47% across ratings classes and across industries. As such, the CTD option can be a significant determinant of deviations of the CDS-bond basis from parity (Singh 2003; Cossin and Lu 2005; Jankowitsch et al. 2008).

Bühler and Trapp (2009) show that the CDS-bond basis is sensitive to credit- and liquidity risk considerations associated with the underlying reference entity. Several studies document a CDS "basis smile" in which issuers with single-A credit ratings have lower CDS spreads than issuers with AA or BBB rated entities. Relatively low CDS spreads for very high-grade firms suggest a greater likelihood of a positive basis, whereas for higher-risk firms other factors (e.g., the CTD option) are relatively more important determinants of the CDS-bond basis.

Coudert and Gex (2010b) consider the relation between secondary market bond prices following credit events at large reference entities and the recovery rates determined through the corresponding auction settlement process (see Sect. 2.2 of Chapter 2). Their empirical analysis of large entities that experienced credit events from 2005 through 2009 includes the Lehman Brothers, Washington Mutual, Fannie Mae, and Freddie Mac credit events. The authors conclude from their empirical analysis that the major drivers of a non-zero CDS-bond basis are counterparty risk (which is magnified when credit events are correlated across protection sellers) and the capital outlay required to support CDS-bond inter-market arbitrage transactions. Brigo and Chourdakis (2009), Morkoetter et al. (2012), and Haerri et al. (2015) also find that counterparty credit risk impacts the CDS-bond basis. Arora et al. (2012), however, present evidence that the effect of counterparty risk is economically small due to the widespread use of collateral in the CDS market.

Market participants commonly use the difference between the interest rates on Treasury bills and Eurodollar time deposits (a.k.a. the "TED" spread) as an indicator of default risk in the interbank market. Understanding the dynamics of the relationship between the TED spread and CDS, which is often used to hedge against default risk, is important and studied by Wu and McMillan (2013). The authors find that the correlation between the TED and CDS spreads varies over time and peaked at the height of the financial crisis.

As discussed in more detail in Sect. 11.1 of this chapter, information about a reference entity's credit risk is generally reflected in the CDS market before the bond market. Short-lived deviations from parity can thus also arise purely as a result of single-name CDS spreads reflecting new information earlier than bond-based credit spreads (Blanco et al. 2005).

Gârleanu and Pedersen (2011) study the negative CDS-bond basis observed for several months during the credit crisis. The authors attribute the persistently negative basis to differences in margin requirements on corporate bonds and CDSs. For example, with a 5% cost of capital and an initial margin requirement of 2% on the CDS and 20% on the repo of an investment-grade corporate bond (all of which were typical during the crisis period), the margin differential between single-name CDSs and bond repos would have been 0.9% (i.e., 5% × (20% − 2%) = 0.9%), which is close to what was observed at the time.

In the event that financing and margin costs become prohibitively expensive for would-be inter-market arbitrageurs, basis trades will not be executed even in the face of obvious relative mispricings, which can cause a non-zero CDS-bond basis to persist for extended periods of time and by possibly significant amounts. This dynamic was at work particularly during the 2008 phase of the credit crisis when the CDS-bond basis was substantially negative across broad portfolios of both investment-grade and high-yield bonds. During that period of the crisis, the costs of financing inter-market arbitrage became prohibitively expensive for typical arbitrageurs. According to J. P. Morgan, initial margin on corporate bonds and repos increased from 5% in June 2007 to 10% in June 2008. In October 2008, margin increased to 20–25%, and financing for many hedge funds (potential basis arbitrageurs) was simply not available at any cost (Mitchell and Pulvino 2012). Various other academic studies have confirmed the role of binding funding constraints as a significant determinant of the persistent negative CDS-bond basis during the crisis—see, e.g., Fontana (2011), Augustin (2012), and Bhanot and Guo (2012).

Regulatory and economic capital constraints also contributed to the sustained negative CDS-bond basis during the crisis. Specifically, market making in CDS basis trades is balance-sheet intensive and requires a substantial amount of capital. In market making for CDS basis trades involving single-name CDS and cash bond transactions, a dealer acts as an intermediary for both transactions.[16] The dealer's trades involving cash bonds affect its total bond inventory holdings and capital requirements. (Dealers hold surplus inventories of securities for which they make markets. Low dealer inventories therefore have a negative impact on their ability to intermediate markets.) The dealer also faces two different counterparties in two different but related markets (i.e., the bond and the related single-name CDS). These economic considerations for dealers translate into costs for inter-market arbitrageurs that are higher when bank intermediaries face higher funding and capital costs to support such arbitrage activities.

Dealer banks experienced severe capital shortages during the financial crisis, which was exacerbated by dislocations in the repurchase market (see, e.g., Gorton and Metrick 2012). As dealers faced binding economic and regulatory capital constraints during the crisis, CDS-bond arbitrage activities were impeded, which reinforced the persistence of a negative CDS-bond basis (Duffie 2010; Fontana 2011; Choi et al. 2017). The CDS-bond basis reverted to more normal levels in 2009 subsequent to an improvement in general market conditions and dealers' balance-sheet capacities.

The non-zero CDS-bond basis during the financial crisis is also confirmed by the CDS index literature. For instance, Ben Dor and Guan (2017) compared the hedging effectiveness of the CDS indices (CDX and iTraxx) versus equity index derivatives such as S&P500 index futures on protecting a high-yield credit portfolio against systematic risk. The authors show that equity index futures are better hedges. Although CDSs mimicked cash market dynamics in calm periods, they underperformed during periods of distress, indicating increased CDS-Bond basis risk during the crisis. Cana and Cinca (2017) find the basis risk remains if a global credit portfolio is hedged using only index CDS such as CDX or iTraxx.

Choi and Park (2017) analyze the relationship between sovereign debt and CDS for 18 sovereign reference entities for the period November 2005 through December 2016. During normal market conditions, liquidity, funding cost, counterparty risk, country-specific, and risk appetite are significant drivers of the basis but these factors are overshadowed by global sentiments on risk appetite and counterparty risk during turbulent regimes.

For sovereign CDSs, Foley-Fisher (2010) documents violations between the CDS and bond parity relation in the 2008–2009 period and attributes those deviations primarily to constraints on credit protection sales (e.g., the E.U. ban on naked shorting using sovereign CDSs) and heterogeneous beliefs among CDS traders. Janus et al. (2013) also conclude that sovereign CDS trading is driven in part by the disparate expectations of investors.

Notes

1. See, e.g., Van der Merwe (2015).
2. Separate and apart from price discovery comparisons of corporate debt and equity markets, some research focuses instead on extracting implied information about equities from traded single-name CDSs—see, e.g., Byström (2016).
3. E. Sirri, *Testimony Concerning Credit Default Swaps before the House Committee on Agriculture* (October 15, 2008).
4. Recent proposals of bond standardization as a way of improving bond market liquidity overlook the benefits provided by a liquid CDS market. See, e.g., BlackRock, "Setting New Standards: The Liquidity Challenge II," *BlackRock Investment Institute* (May 2013).
5. Regulatory capital requirements, however, could rise as a result of such arbitrage strategies and thereby limit the amount of arbitrage.
6. Alternatively, if the basis becomes materially positive, arbitrageurs sell credit default swap protection and simultaneously short the corporate bond.
7. See, e.g., O'Kane and Sen (2005) and Choudhry (2006).
8. See, e.g., Lando (1998), Duffie (1999), and Duffie and Singleton (1999).
9. See H. Haworth, C. Schwarz, and W. Porter, "Understanding the Negative Basis," *Credit Suisse* (March 6, 2009).
10. Hull and White (2000, p. 36). For a discussion on CDSs and counterparty risk, see "Credit Default Swaps and Counterparty Risk," *European Central Bank* (August 2009).
11. M. Choudhry, *The Credit Default Swap Basis* (Bloomberg Press, 2006), and Choudhry (2006).
12. See, e.g., D. Duffie and K. J. Singleton, *Credit Risk: Pricing, Measurement, and Management* (Princeton University Press, 2003).
13. See, e.g., P. Veronesi, "Discounting and Derivative Pricing Before and After the Financial Crisis: An Introduction," in *Handbook of Fixed-Income Securities*, ed. P. Veronesi (Hoboken, NJ: Wiley, 2016).
14. See also Johannes and Sundaresan (2007) for an analysis of similar pricing implications in the interest rate swap market.

15. The authors assumed no liquidity premium in the CDS market; all liquidity effects enter through the cash side of the market.
16. CDS-bond basis trades involving single-name CDSs and asset swaps on related bonds are less capital intensive and costly than arbitrage transactions involving cash bond transactions. Asset swaps, however, do not provide default protection.

References

Acharya, V.V., and T.C. Johnson. 2007. Insider Trading in Credit Derivatives. *Journal of Financial Economics* 84 (1).

Adler, M., and J. Song. 2010. The Behavior of Emerging Market Sovereigns' Credit Default Swap Premiums and Bond Yield Spreads. *International Journal of Finance & Economics* 15.

Alexopoulou, I., M. Andersson, and O.M. Georgescu. 2009. An Empirical Study on the Decoupling Movements Between Corporate Bond and CDS Spreads. ECB Working Paper No. 1085 (August).

Alper, C.E., L. Forni, and M. Gerard. 2013. Pricing of Sovereign Credit Risk: Evidence from Advanced Economies During the Financial Crisis. *International Finance* 16 (2) (Summer).

Ammer, J., and F. Cai. 2011. Sovereign CDS and Bond Pricing Dynamics in Emerging Markets: Does the Cheapest-To-Deliver Option Matter? *Journal of International Financial Markets, Institutions and Money* 21 (3) (July).

Andritzky, J., and M. Singh. 2006. The Pricing of Credit Default Swaps During Distress. IMF Working Paper No. 254 (November).

Arora, N., P. Gandhi, and F.A. Longstaff. 2012. Counterparty Credit Risk and the Credit Default Swap Market. *Journal of Financial Economics* 103 (2).

Augustin, P. 2012. Squeezed Everywhere: Can We Learn Something New from the CDS-Bond Basis? Working Paper (September 13).

Baba, N., and M. Inada. 2009. Price Discovery of Subordinated Credit Spreads for Japanese Mega-Banks: Evidence from Bond and Credit Default Swap Markets. *Journal of International Financial Markets, Institutions and Money* 19 (4) (October).

Badaoui, S., L. Cathcart, and L. El-Jahel. 2015. Implied Liquidity Risk Premium in the Term Structure of Sovereign Credit Default Swap and Bond Spreads. *European Journal of Finance* (January).

Bai, J., and P. Collin-Dufresne. 2013. The CDS-Bond Basis. Working Paper (November).

Ben Dor, A., and J. Guan. 2017. Hedging Systematic Risk in High Yield Portfolios with a Synthetic Overlay: A Comparative Analysis of Equity Instruments vs. Credit Default Swaps. *The Journal of Fixed Income* 26 (4) (Spring).

Berndt, A., R.A. Jarrow, and C. Kang. 2007. Restructuring Risk in Credit Default Swaps: An Empirical Analysis. *Stochastic Processes and Their Applications* 117 (11) (November).

Berndt, A., and A. Ostrovnaya. 2014. Do Equity Markets Favor Credit Market News Over Options Market News? *Quarterly Journal of Finance* 4 (2) (June).

Bhanot, K., and L. Guo. 2012. Types of Liquidity and Limits to Arbitrage—The Case of Credit Default Swaps. *Journal of Futures Markets* 32 (4).

Blanco, R., S. Brennan, and I. W. Marsh. 2005. An Empirical Analysis of the Dynamic Relation Between Investment-Grade Bonds and Credit Default Swaps. *Journal of Finance* 60 (5) (October).

Boehmer, E., S. Chava, and H.E. Tookes. 2015. Related Securities and Equity Market Quality: The Case of CDS. *Journal of Financial and Quantitative Analysis* 50 (3) (June).

Bongaerts, D., F. De Jong, and J. Driessen. 2011. Derivative Pricing with Liquidity Risk: Theory and Evidence from the Credit Default Swap Market. *Journal of Finance* 66 (1) (February).

Breitenfellner, B., and N. Wagner. 2012. Explaining Aggregate Credit Default Swap Spreads. *International Review of Financial Analysis* 22 (April).

Brigo, D., and K. Chourdakis. 2009. Counterparty Risk for Credit Default Swaps: Impact of Spead Volatility and Default Correlation. *International Journal of Theoretical and Applied Finance* 12 (7) (November).

Bühler, W., and M. Trapp. 2009. Explaining the Bond-CDS Basis—The Role of Credit Risk and Liquidity. Centre for Financial Research Working Paper No. 9–12.

Byström, H.N.E. 2005. Using Credit Derivatives to Compute Marketwide Default Probability Term Structures. *Journal of Fixed Income* 15 (3) (December).

Byström, H. 2006. CreditGrades and the iTraxx CDS Index Market. *Financial Analysts Journal* 62 (6) (November–December).

Byström, H. 2016. Stock Prices and Stock Return Volatilities Implied by the Credit Market. *Journal of Fixed Income* 25 (4) (Spring).

Calice, G. 2014. CDX and iTraxx and Their Relation to the Systemically Important Financial Institutions: Evidence from the 2008–2009 Financial Crisis. *Journal of International Financial Markets, Institutions and Money* 32 (September).

Cana, A.C., and A.N. Cinca. 2017. Basis Risk When Hedging a Global Credit Portfolio. Working Paper (November 3).

Carboni, A., and A. Carboni. 2011. The Cash-CDS Basis for Sovereign Countries: Market Strategy, Price Discovery and Determinants. Working Paper (February).

Chan-Lau, J.A., and Y.S. Kim. 2004. Equity Prices, Credit Default Swaps, and Bond Spreads in Emerging Markets. IMF Working Paper No. 27 (February).

Choi, J., O. Shachar, and S.S. Shin. 2017. Dealer Liquidity Provision and the Breakdown of the Law of One Price: Evidence from the CDS-Bond Basis. Working Paper (October 21).

Choi, S.J. and S. Park, 2017. Regime Dependency of Credit Risk Discrepancy: Evidence of the Sovereign CDS and Bond Markets. Working Paper (April 27).

Choudhry, M. 2006. Revisiting the Credit Default Swap Basis: Further Analysis of the Cash and Synthetic Credit Market Differential. *Journal of Structured Finance* 11 (4) (Winter).

Cossin, D., and H. Lu. 2005. Are European Corporate Bond and Default Swap Markets Segmented? FAME—International Center for Financial Asset Management and Engineering Research Paper No. 133 (March).

Coudert, V., and M. Gex. 2010a. Credit Default Swap and Bond Markets: Which Leads the Other? *Banque de France Financial Stability Review* (14) (July).

Coudert, V., and M. Gex. 2010b. The Credit Default Swap Market and the Settlement of Large Defaults. *Economie Internationale* 3 (123).

Coudert, V., and M. Gex. 2010c. Disrupted Links between Credit Default Swaps, Bonds, and Equities during the GM and Ford Crisis in 2005. *Applied Financial Economics* 20 (November).

Coudert, V., and M. Gex. 2013. The Interactions Between the Credit Default Swap and the Bond Markets in Financial Turmoil. *Review of International Economics* 21 (3).

Culp, C.L., Y. Nozawa, and P. Veronesi. 2018. Option-Based Credit Spreads. *American Economic Review* 108 (2) (February).

Da Fonseca, J., and P. Wang. 2016. A Joint Analysis of Market Indexes in Credit Default Swap, Volatility and Stock Markets. *Applied Economics* 48 (19).

Das, S., M. Kalimipalli, and S. Nayak. 2014. Did CDS Trading Improve the Market for Corporate Bonds? *Journal of Financial Economics* 111 (2).

De Wit, J. 2006. Exploring the CDS-Bond Basis. National Bank of Belgium Working Paper No. 104 (November).

Delatte, A.-L., M. Gex, and A. López-Villavicencio. 2012. Has the CDS Market Influenced the Borrowing Cost of European Countries during the Sovereign Crisis? *Journal of International Money and Finance* 31 (3) (April).

Delis, M.D., and N. Mylonidis. 2011. The Chicken or the Egg? A Note on the Dynamic Interrelation Between Government Bond Spreads and Credit Default Swaps. *Finance Research Letters* 8 (3) (September).

Ding, L., and X. Pu. 2012. Market Linkage and Information Spillover: Evidence from Pre-Crisis, Crisis, and Recovery Periods. *Journal of Economics and Business* 64 (2) (March–April).

Dötz, N. 2007. Time-Varying Contributions by the Corporate Bond and CDS Markets to Credit Risk Price Discovery. Deutsche Bundesbank Discussion Paper Series 2: Banking and Financial Studies No. 08/2007.

Duffie, D. 1999. Credit Swap Valuation. *Financial Analysts Journal* (January/ February).

Duffie, D. 2010. Is There a Case for Banning Short Speculation in Sovereign Bond Markets? *Banque de France Financial Stability Review* (14) (July).

Duffie, D., and K. J. Singleton. 1999. Modeling Term Structures of Defaultable Bonds. *Review of Financial Studies* 12 (4).

Easley, D., M. O'Hara, and P.S. Srinivas. 1998. Option Volume and Stock Prices: Evidence on Where Informed Traders Trade. *Journal of Finance* 53 (2) (April).

Eyssell, T., H.-G. Fung, and G. Zhang. 2013. Determinants and Price Discovery of China Sovereign Credit Default Swaps. *China Economic Review* 24 (1).

Fenech, J.-P., H. Vosgha, and S. Shafik. 2014. Modelling the Dependence Structures of Australian iTraxx CDS Index. *Applied Economics* 46 (4).

Flannery, M.J., J.F. Houston, and F. Partnoy. 2010. Credit Default Swap Spreads as Viable Substitutes for Credit Ratings. *University of Pennsylvania Law Review* 158 (7) (June).

Foley-Fisher, N. 2010. Explaining Sovereign Bond-CDS Arbitrage Violations during the Financial Crisis 2008–09. Working Paper (October).

Fontana, A. 2011. The Negative CDS-Bond Basis and Convergence Trading during the 2007/09 Financial Crisis. Swiss Finance Institute Occasional Paper Series No. 11–41 (September).

Fontana, A., and M. Scheicher. 2016. An Analysis of Euro Area Sovereign CDS and Their Relation with Government Bonds. *Journal of Banking and Finance* 62 (January).

Forte, S., and L. Lovreta. 2015. Time-Varying Credit Risk Discovery in the Stock and CDS Markets: Evidence from Quiet and Crisis Times. *European Financial Management* 21 (3).

Forte, S., and J.I. Peña. 2009. Credit Spreads: An Empirical Analysis on the Informational Content of Stocks, Bonds, and CDS. *Journal of Banking & Finance* 33 (11) (November).

Fung, H.-G., G.E. Sierra, J. Yau, and G. Zhang. 2008. Are the U.S. Stock Market and Credit Default Swap Market Related? Evidence from the CDX Indices. *Journal of Alternative Investments* (Summer).

Gârleanu, N., and L.H. Pedersen. 2011. Margin-Based Asset Pricing and Deviations from the Law of One Price. *Review of Financial Studies* 24 (6).

Giannikos, C., H. Guirguis, and M. Suen. 2013. The 2008 Financial Crisis and the Dynamics of Price Discovery Among Stock Prices, CDS Spreads, and Bond Spreads for U.S. Financial Firms. *Journal of Derivatives* 21 (1) (Fall).

Glosten, L.R., and P.R. Milgrom. 1985. Bid, Ask and Transaction Prices in a Specialist Market with Heterogeneously Informed Traders. *Journal of Financial Economics* 14 (1) (March).

Gorton, G., and A. Metrick. 2012. Securitized Banking and the Run on Repo. *Journal of Financial Economics* 104.

Guo, F.C.R. Chen, and Y.S. Huang. 2011. Markets Contagion During Financial Crisis: A Regime-Switching Approach. *International Review of Economics and Finance* 20 (1) (January).

Gyntelberg, J., P. Hördahl, K. Ters, and J. Urban. 2013. Intraday Dynamics of Euro Area Sovereign CDS and Bonds. BIS Working Papers No. 423 (September).

Gyntelberg, J., P. Hördahl, K. Ters, and J. Urban. 2017. Arbitrage Costs and the Persistent Non-Zero CDS-Bond Basis: Evidence from Intraday Euro Area Sovereign Debt Markets. BIS Working Paper No. 631 (April).

Haas, M., and J. Reynolds. 2017. Illiquidity Contagion and Information Spillover from CDS to Equity Markets. Working Paper (November 6).

Haerri, M., S. Morkoetter, and S. Westerfeld. 2015. Sovereign Risk and the Pricing of Corporate Credit Default Swaps. *Journal of Credit Risk* 11 (1) (March).

Hammoudeh, S., and R. Sari. 2011. Financial CDS, Stock Market and Interest Rates: Which Drives Which? *North American Journal of Economics and Finance* 22 (3) (December).

Hassan, M.K., G.M. Ngene, and J.-S. Yu. 2015. Credit Default Swaps and Sovereign Debt Markets. *Economic Systems* 39 (2) (June).

Hilscher, J., J.M. Pollet, and M. Wilson. 2015. Are Credit Default Swaps a Sideshow? Evidence that Information Flows from Equity to CDS Markets. *Journal of Financial and Quantitative Analysis* 50 (3) (June).

Houweling, P., and T. Vorst. 2005. Pricing Default Swaps: Empirical Evidence. *Journal of International Money and Finance* 24 (8).

Hull, J., and A. White. 2000. Valuing Credit Default Swaps I: No Counterparty Default Risk. NYU Working Paper No. FIN-00-021.

Jankowitsch, R., R. Pullirsch, and T. Veža. 2008. The Delivery Option in Credit Default Swaps. *Journal of Banking & Finance* 32 (7) (July).

Janus, T., Y, Jinjarak, and M. Uruyos. 2013. Sovereign Default Risk, Overconfident Investors and Diverse Beliefs: Theory and Evidence from a New Dataset on Outstanding Credit Default Swaps. *Journal of Financial Stability* 9 (3) (September).

Johannes, M., and S. Sundaresan. 2007. The Impact of Collateralization on Swap Rates. *Journal of Finance* 62 (1) (February).

Kryzanowski, L., S. Perrakis, and R. Zhong. 2017. Price Discovery in Equity and CDS Markets. *Journal of Financial Markets* 35 (September).

Küçük, U. 2010. Non-Default Component of Sovereign Emerging Market Yield Spreads and Its Determinants: Evidence from the Credit Default Swap Market. *Journal of Fixed Income* 19 (4) (Spring).

Lando, D. 1998. On Cox Processes and Credit Risky Securities. *Review of Derivatives Research* 2 (2–3) (December).

Levy, A. 2009. The CDS Bond Basis Spread in Emerging Markets: Liquidity and Counterparty Risk Effects. Working Paper (April 6).

Li, N., and A.Y. Huang. 2011. Price Discovery Between Sovereign Credit Default Swaps and Bond Yield Spreads of Emerging Markets. *Journal of Emerging Market Finance* 10 (2).

Liu, J., J. Ng, D.Y. Tang, and R. Zhong. 2017. CDS Trading and Stock Price Crash Risk. Working Paper (December 12).

Longstaff, F.A., S. Mithal, and E. Neis. 2003. The Credit-Default Swap Market: Is Credit Protection Priced Correctly. Working Paper (August).

Longstaff, F.A., S. Mithal, and E. Neis. 2005. Corporate Yield Spreads: Default Risk or Liquidity? New Evidence from the Credit Default Swap Market. *Journal of Finance* 60 (5) (October).

Lu, Y.-C., H. Fang, and R.-G. Lue. 2010. Shocks from the Subprime Crisis to Bond Indices in the U.S., the EU and Emerging Markets via CDS Indices. Working Paper (August 23).

Marsh, I.W., and W. Wagner. 2012. Why is Price Discovery in Credit Default Swap Markets News-Specific? Bank of Finland Research Discussion Paper No. 6/2012 (February).

Massa, M., and L. Zhang. 2012. CDS and the Liquidity Provision in the Bond Market. INSEAD Working Paper No. 2012/114/FIN (November).

Mayhew, S. 2000. The Impact of Derivatives on Cash Markets: What Have We Learned? Working Paper (February 3).

Mayordomo, S., and J.I. Peña. 2014. An Empirical Analysis of Dynamic Depencences in the European Corporate Credit Markets: Bonds Versus Credit Derivaives. *Applied Financial Economics* 24 (9).

Mayordomo, S., J.I. Peña, and J. Romo. 2011. The Effect of Liquidity on the Price Discovery Process in Credit Derivatives Markets in Times of Financial Distress. *European Journal of Finance* 17 (9–10) (October–November).

Merton, R.C. 1974. On the Pricing of Corporate Debt: The Risk Structure of Interest Rates. *Journal of Finance* 29 (2) (May).

Mitchell, M., and T. Pulvino. 2012. Arbitrage Crashes and the Speed of Capital. *Journal of Financial Economics* 104.

Morkoetter, S., J. Pleus, and S. Westerfeld. 2012. The Impact of Counterparty Risk on Credit Default Swap Pricing Dynamics. *Journal of Credit Risk* 8 (1) (Spring).

Naifar, N. 2011. What Explains Default Risk Premium During the Financial Crisis? Evidence from Japan. *Journal of Economics and Business* 63 (5) (September–October).

Naifar, N. 2012. Modeling the Dependence Structure Between Default Risk Premium, Equity Return Volatility and the Jump Risk: Evidence from a Financial Crisis. *Economic Modelling* 29 (2) (March).

Nashikkar, A., M.G. Subrahmanyam, and S. Mahanti. 2011. Liquidity and Arbitrage in the Market for Credit Risk. *Journal of Financial & Quantitative Analysis* 46 (3) (June).

Norden, L., and M. Weber. 2009. The Co-movement of Credit Default Swap, Bond and Stock Markets: An Empirical Analysis. *European Financial Management* 15 (3).

Norden, L., and M. Weber. 2012. When Senior Meets Junior: Information in Credit Default Swap Spreads of Large Banks. Working Paper (July).

Oehmke, M., and A. Zawadowski. 2015. Synthetic or Real? The Equilibrium Effects of Credit Default Swaps on Bond Markets. *Review of Financial Studies* 28 (12) (August).

O'Kane, D. 2012. The Link between Eurozone Sovereign Debt and CDS Prices. EDHEC-Risk Institute (January).

O'Kane, D., and S. Sen. 2005. Credit Spreads Explained. *Journal of Credit Risk* 1 (2) (Spring).

Pan, J., and A.M. Poteshman. 2006. The Information in Option Volume for Future Stock Prices. *Review of Financial Studies* 19 (3) (Autumn).

Santamaría, M.T.C., J.G. Biscarri, and L.L. Benito. 2014. Financial Crises and the Transfer of Risk Between the Private and Public Sectors: Evidence from European Financial Markets. *Spanish Review of Financial Economics* 12 (1) (January–June).

Schreiber, I., G. Müller, C. Klüppelber, and N. Wagner. 2012. Equities, Credits and Volatilities: A Multivariate Analysis of the European Market During the Subprime Crisis. *International Review of Financial Analysis* 24 (September).

Singh, M. 2003. Are Credit Default Swap Spreads High in Emerging Markets? An Alternative Methodology for Proxying Recovery Value. IMF Working Paper No. WP/03/242 (December).

Trutwein, P., and D. Schiereck. 2011. The Fast and the Furious—Stock Returns and CDS of Financial Institutions Under Stress. *Journal of International Financial Markets, Institutions and Money* 21 (2) (April).

Trutwein, P., S. Ramchander, and D. Schiereck. 2011. Jumps in Credit Default Swap Spreads and Stock Returns. *Journal of Fixed Income* 20 (3) (Winter).

Van der Merwe, A. 2015. *Market Liquidity Risk.* Palgrave Macmillan.

Wu, W., and D. McMillan. 2013. Dynamic Linkages in Credit Risk: Modeling the Time-Varying Correlation between the Money and Derivatives Markets over the Crisis Period. *Journal of Risk* 16 (2) (December).

Zhu, H. 2006. An Empirical Comparison of Credit Spreads Between the Bond Market and the Credit Default Swap Market. *Journal of Financial Services Research* 29 (3).

CHAPTER 12

Interconnectedness and Systemic Risk

In Chapter 9, we reviewed the empirical literature that documents the valuable information provided by CDS prices and spreads vis à-vis the credit risk of underlying reference name(s). In this chapter, we review the literature on the information reflected by CDS spreads about the informational content regarding the nature and magnitude of interconnectedness between financial institutions that buy and sell CDS protection and the potential systemic risks to which such interconnectedness may give rise through counterparty credit exposures and other transmission channels.

We review the empirical results from the academic literature on the sources and nature of interconnectedness across firms to which CDSs give rise. Our discussion in this chapter is not primarily concerned with whether CDSs create or exacerbate systemic risk. Instead, we focus on the informational content of CDS spreads as harbingers of potential systemic issues. Some of the papers that analyze interconnectedness through CDS channels can be interpreted to support conclusions that single-name CDSs result in heightened cross-firm interconnectedness, but other papers reviewed in this chapter can be interpreted as evidence against any systemic interconnectedness resulting from CDS activities (see, e.g., Duffie 2010; Stulz 2010; Tran 2013).

In Sect. 12.1 of this chapter, we review the volatilities of CDS spreads and the correlations between volatilities of credit spreads implied by CDSs, cash bonds, and equities. The Sect. 12.2 reviews literature discussing sources of interconnectedness. Section 12.3 of this chapter then discusses the empirical evidence on spillovers in sovereign CDS markets.

C. L. Culp et al., *Credit Default Swaps*, Palgrave Studies in Risk and Insurance, https://doi.org/10.1007/978-3-319-93076-3_12

Specifically, we review the empirical record for both the US post-Lehman and the Eurozone sovereign debt crisis, followed by a review of the significant empirical academic studies that examine the interplay between sovereign CDSs and foreign exchange markets. Finally, Sect. 12.4 concludes this chapter with an overview on the literature on regarding the interrelation between sovereign and banking/corporate credit risk.

12.1 Credit Default Swap Volatility and Correlation

Many CDS underlying reference entities have securities that are actively traded in the single-name CDS, corporate bond, and stock markets at the same time. Many of these firms, moreover, are constituents in major CDS indices such as the CDX.HY or CDX.IG indices. Volatilities of CDS spreads, bond yield spreads, and stock prices can provide a three-dimensional view of the financial condition of reference entities underlying outstanding single-name CDSs and CDS indices. Another useful and related measure is the co-movement of volatilities (i.e., estimated covariance or correlation coefficients) of credit spreads implied by CDSs, cash bonds, and equities. The relative magnitudes of these empirical indicators of co-movements in asset prices across related markets based on the same common reference entities indicate how these different markets are affected by common economic shocks.

Increased risk and greater uncertainty during crises are reflected in elevated volatilities of CDS spreads, bond spreads, and stock prices relative to normal market conditions. For example, Belke and Gokus (2011) analyzed the CDS spreads of four large US banks from 2006 to 2009 and found (not surprisingly) that CDS spread volatilities rose significantly during the crisis and that correlations across CDS spreads also became higher during the crisis (see also Coudert and Gex 2010a).

Correlations and covariances are not constant over time and often exhibit elevated levels during times of market-wide uncertainty such as when Lehman Brothers failed. Covariances tend to be higher (lower) in times of high (low) volatility, but variability in covariance has been documented to exist beyond what can be explained only by volatility. Some (e.g., Belke and Gokus 2011) argue that increased correlations between single-name CDSs and local equity markets during the financial crisis indicate contagion effects, particularly in the banking sector in which different banks are often connected (see Sect. 12.4 below for a further discussion). Nevertheless, causality is not implied by correlation, and more robust analyses are required to identify statically significant cross-market contagion and interconnectedness channels (see, e.g., Sect. 12.2 of this chapter).

Javadi et al. (2017) propose that correlations in daily CDS spreads capture the time-varying correlation in default probabilities and then proceed to calculate the rolling one-month correlations of daily CDS spreads to measure time-varying correlated default risk, which they call the aggregate default correlation. The authors show that a 0.5 increase in correlated default risk of US corporate bonds is associated with a 13 basis point ("bp") increase in credit spreads during normal market conditions and as much as 22 basis points ("bps") for speculative issues during the periods of financial distress.

Calice et al. (2012) and Calice and Ioannidis (2012) analyze the propagation of shocks between the CDS market (using spreads on the iTraxx and CDX indices) and the banking sector (using equity prices of large complex financial institutions). The study provides evidence that the CDX index seems to be a conduit for the propagation of shocks across large financial institutions and also that volatility between equity and CDS indices were correlated during the financial crisis because many large banks had large exposures to securitized products, which are in turn exposed to a widening of credit spreads. Billio et al. (2012a) show that credit risk is correlated between the industrial sectors using 18 US industrial sector CDS indices, but that the relation varies over time. They show that systemic risk dominated credit risk rendering typical portfolio diversification strategies ineffective during periods of market-wide distress. Using CDX and CDO tranche spreads, Feldhütter and Nielsen (2012) show that systematic default risk has low volatility but is subject to sudden jump risks, whereas idiosyncratic default risk is less volatile and not as vulnerable to explosive jumps.

Almer et al. (2008) analyze the dynamic behavior of the slope of the CDS term structure and correlations between short-term (six-month) and long-term (five-year) CDS spreads of banks from 2001 to 2007. The authors show that this correlation exhibits large variations over time. During periods of market distress, spreads tend to co-move, whereas such co-movements subside during normal market conditions. An interesting finding by Almer et al. (2008) is that five-year single-name CDS spreads (which, as noted in Chapter 2, is typically the most actively traded CDS tenor) are correlated with the borrower distress proxies contained in the Merton (1974) model (e.g., firm value volatility, stock prices, and interest rates) but are not sensitive to cross-market liquidity risk factors.[1] As discussed in Chapters 9 and 11, their finding of the insensitivity of single-name CDS spreads to CDS and/or bond market liquidity risk is at odds with the rest of the literature.

12.2 Measuring Interconnectedness Using CDSs

Coudert and Gex (2010a, b) analyze how the financial distress at General Motors ("GM") and Ford in May 2005 affected single-name CDS spreads on GM and Ford. Specifically, spreads on both firms' CDSs increased significantly prior to their rating downgrades in May 2005. More interestingly, CDS spreads for longer-dated tenors also rose during this period for US and European corporates. The authors estimated correlation coefficients across markets that rose appreciably following the auto manufacturers' credit downgrades, thereby confirming a strong degree of international cross-market integration and market participants' expectations about potential spillover effects.

Especially since the outbreak of the credit crisis in 2007 and the highly publicized failures of firms like Lehman Brothers, the academic literature on the estimation of interconnectedness has burgeoned. Interest in this literature has been fueled by enhanced regulatory scrutiny of systemic risk and the creation of "systemically important financial institutions" as defined by the Financial Stability Board ("FSB") and Financial Stability Oversight Council ("FSOC") for international and US institutions, respectively.

Much of the academic literature on systemic risk today focuses on efforts to quantify the riskiness of specific financial institutions in an interconnected world (see, e.g., Acharya et al. 2017; Billio et al. 2012b; Adrian and Brunnermeier 2016). Bisias et al. (2012) present a useful survey of various measures of systemic risk as of 2012. Such measures of systemic risk (ranging from simple examinations of market data to complex econometric models of financial networks) often utilize CDS spreads as inputs to the analysis of interconnectedness.

Some examples of academic studies that utilize single-name CDS spreads to analyze cross-firm interconnectedness include the following[2]:

- Jacoby et al. (2009) study spillovers of liquidity shocks across single-name CDS, corporate bond, and equity markets and find no evidence of a liquidity spillover effect from bonds to CDSs and a time lag between the reflection of liquidity shocks on single-name CDS spreads vis-à-vis both bond and equity markets;
- Kim et al. (2010) analyze CDS spreads and EDFs on 38 corporate names from the Asia-ex-Japan area over the period from January 2005 through January 2009 and find that "knock-on" effects from the global (mainly Western) credit crisis had some impact on higher EDFs for Asian firms but that the majority of the adverse impacts felt by the Asian companies was attributable to increases in investor risk aversion following the outbreak of the credit crisis;
- Eichengreen et al. (2012) examine the CDS spreads of the largest 45 financial institutions in the USA, UK, Germany, Switzerland, France, Italy, Spain, the Netherlands, and Portugal as measures of their interconnectedness and conclude from their empirical work that a strong common factor explained CDS spreads even before the credit crisis, and that the common factor driving CDS spreads became more pronounced following the outbreak of the crisis;
- Giglio (2011) analyzes bond and CDS spreads to differentiate correlated systemic credit risks from the firm-specific credit risks of individual reference entities;
- Nijskens and Wagner (2011) analyze the 38 banks that began to use CDSs from June 1998 through June 2006 and determine that the introduction of CDSs was commensurate with increases in the banks' equity betas—i.e., after decomposing the beta increase into volatility and correlation effects, the authors conclude that increased interconnectedness is almost entirely a correlation effect, which indicates evidence linking CDS usage with systemic interconnectedness;
- Chen et al. (2013) analyze CDS spreads and stock prices from 2001 through 2011 in the insurance sector and find strong evidence of interconnectedness between banks and insurers;
- Conrad et al. (2013) estimate joint default probabilities and LGDs for corporate reference entities using both CDS spreads and equity option-implied volatilities and find evidence that increases in default probabilities at systemically important financial institutions precipitate increases in the default probabilities and LGDs of other companies that are reflected in single-name CDS spreads;

- Rodríguez-Moreno and Peña (2013) compare market-based measures of systemic risk using CDS spreads, interbank rates, and stock prices and conclude that systemic risk measures based on CDSs outperform measures based on the other two candidates;
- Yang and Zhou (2013) analyze interconnectedness and spillover effects across 43 large international financial institutions and use CDS spreads to characterize a network comprised of "prime senders, exchange centers and prime receivers of credit risk information"[3];
- Getmansky et al. (2016) analyze the ostensible interconnectedness of CDS exposures across multiple swap dealers and find that the network of dealers was highly concentrated for a variety of CDSs;
- Peltonen et al. (2014) construct a network from the bilateral notional CDS exposures across 642 sovereign and financial reference entities and identify a center of the network consisting of 14 dealers, at which a significant concentration of CDS protection sales is apparent;
- Oh and Patton (2017) develop a dynamic model to analyze CDS spreads for US corporates from 2006 to 2012 and find that systemic risks arising from CDS interconnectedness were the highest in 2008 and 2009 and remained above pre-crisis levels from 2010 through 2012;
- Zareei (2015) analyzes single-name CDS data and concludes that firms with less interconnectedness and systemic importance are more likely to experience credit-related jumps in their CDS spreads and are more likely to fail, whereas firms with greater systemic importance exhibit lower failure rates and bankruptcy probabilities;
- Abbassi et al. (2016) rely on market-based CDS spreads to measure market-based measures of bank interconnectedness and find a strong relation between CDS-based interconnectedness measures and banks' actual risk exposures in wholesale funding, securities investment, and loan markets;
- Cetina et al. (2018) use CDSs as proxies for the risk in banks' trading books in the annual Comprehensive Capital Analysis and Review ("CCAR") stress tests performed annually by the Federal Reserve;
- Paddrik et al. (2016) analyze the effect of a shock, modeled using the CCAR shocks on CDS contracts and the variation margin owed through a network of counterparty exposures. The network amplifies the effect of increases in margin but the CCP contributes less to contagion than some of the CCP members;

- D'Errico et al. (2018) follow a network structure approach to analyze risk transfers across a network utilizing CDSs. Their empirical analysis, using data between 2011 and 2014, shows that flows of risk originate from hedge funds and end up in non-banks such as asset managers; and
- Kanno (2016) employs network measures of systemic risk to examine interconnectedness in CDS markets and draws the conclusion that the risks of contagious defaults spreading from single-name CDS markets to cash bond, equity, and equity options markets are relatively low.

Further academic studies examining contagion effects using CDS indices include the following[4]:

- Bhansali et al. (2008) quantify the relative contributions of idiosyncratic company-level credit risk, sector-wide risk at companies within an industry, and systemic risk of the iTraxx and the CDX. HY and CDX.IG indices during the credit crisis. They show that systemic risk dominated idiosyncratic and sector-specific credit risks during the period, thus suggesting that typical portfolio diversification strategies are ineffective during the periods of market-wide distress;
- Fang and Lee (2011) use a variance decomposition methodology to identify the directionality of risk spillover effects during the 2006 through 2009 period. Their study shows two directional effects involving the CDX index: (i) contagion effects are larger from lower-rated ABX tranches to the CDX indices than from higher-rated ABX tranches to the CDX indices and (ii) contagion effects are larger from the CDX and from equity markets in high-risk countries (including the USA and E.U.) than in low-risk countries, such as Peru, Mexico, and Indonesia;
- Rodríguez-Moreno and Peña (2013) show that CDSs, measured using CDX and iTraxx indices, were superior indicators of systemic risk during the financial crisis, outperforming measures based on interbank markets or stock market prices; and
- Tamakoshi and Hamori (2014) show significant dependence between insurance sector CDS indices using five-year CDS indices of several insurance sectors (including the E.U. and UK).

12.3 Sovereign CDSs and Spillover Effects

Much of the academic literature that has analyzed sovereign CDS spreads has focused on the relation between macroeconomic fundamentals, financial market conditions, and sovereign credit risk and the transmission channels for financial and macroeconomic shocks across countries. For example, Ang and Longstaff (2013) undertake a comparative analysis of interconnectedness and systemic sovereign risk within the USA (i.e., across different individual US states and the US Treasury) and within Eurozone countries to investigate whether systemic sovereign risk is based primarily on financial market disruptions or macroeconomic shocks. Their conclusion is that the systemic interconnectedness of sovereign credit risk is driven primarily by the financial sector and not by macroeconomic shocks. Similarly, De Boyrie and Pavlova (2016) find not only that spillover effects across emerging market sovereigns are driven primarily by shocks in the financial market sector, but also that the interconnectedness arises primarily from *global* financial market shocks.

Yet, as the discussions below of the Eurozone sovereign debt crisis and the US financial crisis following the failure of Lehman suggest, inferences about financial versus macroeconomic drivers of interconnectedness often depend significantly on sample-specific variables, such as the market (i.e., financial or real economy) from which the primary original shock emanated, the size and international interconnectedness of a country, and the relative sovereign credit risk of a country. We review the empirical evidence below for both the Eurozone sovereign debt crisis and the US post-Lehman financial crisis, and we conclude the section with a review of the significant articles that empirically examine the interplay between sovereign CDS and foreign exchange markets.

12.3.1 Evidence from the Eurozone Crisis

The Eurozone sovereign debt crisis from 2010 through 2012 provides the basis for most academic studies that have analyzed the sovereign CDS-bond basis (see Chapter 11), and these studies have produced a range of often-disparate results. Broto and Pérez-Quirós (2015) analyzed sovereign CDS spreads for the 10 members of the Organisation for Economic Co-operation and Development ("OECD") and found a significant variation in the co-movement of cross-country CDS spreads during the

Eurozone crisis period as compared to non-crisis periods. The authors also find that specific contagion effects in the sovereign CDS market vary on a country-by-country basis. Dieckmann and Plank (2012), Kalbaska and Gątkowski (2012), Calice et al. (2013), Gündüz and Kaya (2013), Blasques et al. (2016), Doshi et al. (2017), Glover and Richards-Shubik (2014), Huang et al. (2014), Galariotis et al. (2016), and Ters and Urban (2016) present comparable empirical findings that contagion in sovereign CDS markets varies in both direction and magnitude on a country-specific basis.[5] Antón et al. (2017), moreover, document that sovereign CDS spreads for single-name sovereign CDSs that are most often quoted by a common set of swap dealers tend to exhibit higher correlations.

Caporin et al. (2018) find that the spillover effects across sovereign CDSs in the Eurozone were not dependent on the size of the underlying shocks. Although the authors documented a change in the size of the propagation of shocks across Eurozone countries in the 2003–2006 and 2008–2011 periods, the degree to which shocks from one country were transmitted to another actually declined in the post-Lehman period. The authors interpret their results as indicating that post-Lehman transmission mechanisms of shocks across sovereign CDS markets to private bank funding markets were the result of larger shocks and not a series of similar, correlated shocks across multiple countries.

Kirschenmann et al. (2017) show that sovereign CDS spreads exhibit a larger co-movement with other European sovereign CDS spreads if domestic banks have large, undercapitalized foreign sovereign bond exposures which implies that the severity of spillovers within the European Union is affected by capital buffers of banks.

Groba et al. (2013) examine spillover effects from peripheral Eurozone countries to central EU members in the period from January 2008 through July 2012. In contrast to the conventional view that shocks were transmitted from central European countries to the periphery, the authors find that shocks were transmitted in the opposite direction, thus indicating a common global shock that propagated through Eurozone sovereign debt markets at an uneven pace. A significant conclusion (in line with Pan and Singleton 2008) from this study is that a major component of risk premiums on sovereign CDSs is based on market-wide, systematic risks and is not merely a market-based revision of expected country-specific credit risks (see Sect. 9.2 of Chapter 9).

Dockner et al. (2013) and Consiglio et al. (2017) also show that sovereign CDS spreads are driven mainly by global factors, but that country-specific risks still explain some variations in CDS returns (in magnitudes that differ depending on the country).

Significant evidence also suggests that observed co-movements in sovereign credit spreads across different countries were not primarily the result of contagion *within the financial market* but rather were the product of transmissions of country-specific *macroeconomic shocks* (see, e.g., Aizenman et al. 2013; Manasse and Zavalloni 2013; Shoesmith 2014). Using spreads on sovereign CDSs and long-term sovereign debt (as well as ratings for those debt instruments), Beirne and Fratzscher (2013) show that the main explanation for the rise in sovereign debt yields and CDS spreads during the Eurozone crisis was the deterioration of country-specific macroeconomic fundamentals and the transmission of macroeconomic shocks across countries and was not the result of regional spillover effects or financial market contagion.

Kim et al. (2015) find a similar result by analyzing the impact of macroeconomic news from the USA, Eurozone countries, and China on sovereign CDS spreads. Not surprisingly, they find that macroeconomic news has a significant impact on sovereign credit spreads. Better than expected news reduces sovereign CDS spreads, and vice versa. News regarding the three major economies that the authors studied also has significant macroeconomic spillover effects on sovereign CDS spreads for other countries.

Stamatopoulos et al. (2016) study the effects of downgrade announcements and sovereign debt holdings on CDS spreads, in particular the risk of default priced into CDS. The authors show that debt downgrade announcements had a bigger effect on CDS spreads during the pre-crisis period (2008–2010), but country-specific debt holdings had a bigger effect post-crisis (2011–2013).

The literature also attributes the co-movements in sovereign credit spreads across different countries to other factors. For example, Sgherri and Zoli (2009), Caceres et al. (2010), Revoltella et al. (2010), Longstaff et al. (2011), and Heinz and Sun (2014) conclude that spreads on sovereign CDSs during the Eurozone crisis were more the result of global investor sentiment and risk aversion than country-specific macroeconomic problems. Similarly, Aretz and Pope (2013) find that sovereign credit risk reflected in CDS spreads is explained primarily by global and industry risk factors and not country-specific risks.

12.3.2 Lehman Brothers and the Credit Crisis

Sovereign CDS spreads have also been used to analyze the diffusion effects of the US subprime crisis through other global financial markets. Dooley and Hutchison (2009) analyze the spillover effects from single-name CDSs on distressed reference names during the credit crisis vis-à-vis sovereign CDS spreads for emerging-market economies. The authors conclude that emerging markets were somewhat insulated from the crisis before the Lehman Brothers failure in 2008, but were infected by the deteriorating situation of the US financial system and global credit markets thereafter (Dooley and Hutchison 2009). This evidence contradicts the prevalent view before the crisis that emerging markets were well insulated from adverse financial sector shocks in the rest of the world.

Dumontaux and Pop (2013) rely on single-name CDS and equity market data to examine the spillover effect of the Lehman Brothers' failure on other financial institutions. They provide evidence of significant abnormal jumps in CDS spreads following the collapse of Lehman in September 2008 and conclude that those jumps reflect upward revisions in market participants' assessments of the future credit risks of surviving firms that had characteristics similar to Lehman.

Wang and Moore (2012) study the extent to which the sovereign CDS markets of 38 developed and emerging countries became integrated with the US market during the credit crisis. Their evidence reveals that the Lehman shock strengthened cross-market integration interaction effects, especially across developed markets. Wang and Moore (2012) attribute the shift in the relations between developed and emerging market economics to the low absolute levels of US interest rates.

12.3.3 Sovereign CDSs and Currency Market Linkages

Carr and Wu (2007) find that sovereign CDS spreads for both Brazil and Mexico are significantly affected by the level of implied volatility and the slope of the implied volatility curve derived from currency options markets. Some studies have investigated the transmission mechanisms between sovereign credit risk and currencies in more detail. For example, Hui and Chung (2011) examine information flows between sovereign CDSs and foreign exchange options for 11 countries in the Eurozone during the European sovereign debt crisis. Employing a methodology similar to the price discovery analyses reviewed in Chapter 9, the authors find that from September 2009 through April 2010, at the height of the Eurozone sovereign debt crisis, significant and strong flows of information occurred between sovereign debt and foreign exchange markets. In a broader sample from 2006 through 2010, such flows were less pronounced and no clear direction of information transmission could be identified. Hui and Fong (2011) find similar results.

Huang and MacDonald (2014) analyze the relation between sovereign CDS spreads and returns on foreign exchange "carry trades"—i.e., speculative strategies in which investors borrow in a currency with a low interest rate and invest the proceeds of that loan in a higher-yielding currency in order to try and exploit deviations from uncovered interest parity. Although popular with many investors, the seemingly regular and positive excess returns that such trades generate are regarded as an anomaly (see, e.g., Hansen and Hodrick 1980; Fama 1984). Huang and MacDonald find that sovereign CDS premiums together with a market liquidity risk premium explain over 90% of cross-sectional variation in excess returns on carry trades.[6]

De Santis (2015) investigates quanto sovereign CDS spreads (i.e., spreads on sovereign CDSs that incorporate price differences between Euros and US dollars) and finds that sovereign yields of French, Italian, and Spanish sovereign bonds are significantly affected by the perceived risk that those countries could exit the Eurozone and have their debt redenominated in a devalued legacy currency after controlling for exchange rate, global, regional, and liquidity shocks. Like other papers, De Santis (2015) also finds evidence of spillover effects in which shocks to domestic economies arising from foreign redenomination risk are larger than the domestic shocks in some European countries. Pu and Zhang (2012) also examine the spreads between Euro- and dollar-denominated sovereign CDSs and found a significant increase in those spreads during the European sovereign debt crisis.

12.4 Interrelated Sovereign and Banking/Corporate Credit Risks

A number of studies have empirically analyzed the relations between financial distress in a country's banking sector and the sovereign credit risk of the country. Such relations can run in both directions causally, especially if sovereign bailouts of banks or the banking sector are associated with the crisis. In that case, such bailouts of a distressed national banking sector can lead to higher sovereign debt costs that can put fiscal pressure on the sovereign, thereby resulting in increased sovereign credit risk. Evidence that bank bailout programs by governments lead to increased sovereign credit risk and sovereign CDS spreads is presented in Attinasi et al. (2009), Sgherri and Zoli (2009), Alter and Schüler (2012), Ejsing and Lemke (2011), Mody and Sandri (2012), and Demirgüç-Kunt and Huizinga (2013).

Increased sovereign credit risk also puts pressure on the national banking sector by reducing government bond values (which, all else equal, decline when sovereign credit risk is higher, as shown in Gennaioli et al. 2014), thereby reducing the value of future government guarantees, and jeopardizing the sovereign rating assigned to the country by the major rating agencies.[7] Acharya et al. (2014) describe the bi-directional impacts of sovereign interventions in the banking sector as the "sovereign-bank loop."

Based on bank and sovereign CDS spread data from January 2007 through April 2011 for all Eurozone countries (as well as Denmark, Norway, Sweden, Switzerland, and the UK), Acharya et al. (2014) report that bank bailouts did in fact shift credit risk from national banks to sovereigns, which caused an increase in sovereign credit risk and CDS spreads. The authors also find that the resulting increase in sovereign credit risk caused an increase in national bank credit risk and bank CDS spreads, even after controlling for common risk factors across banks and bank-specific risk attributes. Alter and Schüler (2012), Alter and Beyer (2014), Billio et al. (2013), Gerlach-Kristen (2013), Battistini et al. (2014), Li and Zinna (2017), Gątarek and Wojtowicz (2015), and Haerri et al. (2015) find similar evidence supporting the sovereign-bank risk loop.

Erce (2015) finds for 10 Eurozone countries that the sovereign risk feeds back more strongly into banking system risk than vice versa. Gross and Kok (2013) study 23 sovereign and 41 bank reference entities in Europe, Japan, and the USA and conclude that credit risk was generally spread from banks to sovereigns in 2008 but that contagion moved in the opposite direction from sovereigns to banks during the Eurozone sovereign debt crisis. Ohno (2013) finds evidence of the sovereign-bank loop within European countries that received bailout funds but does not find significant evidence that those shocks were transmitted to peripheral

Eurozone countries not experiencing fiscal crises. Billio et al. (2013) and Gross and Kok (2013) use network and interconnectedness measures like those summarized in Sect. 12.2 of this chapter to propose a measure of the systemic sovereign-bank loop.

Yu (2017) shows that correlations between sovereign and bank CDS vary over time and increase during periods of market distress such as the subprime crisis and during the Greek default crisis. The price discovery role of bank CDS during the subprime crisis (when bank CDS spreads led sovereign CDS spreads) was reversed during the E.U. sovereign debt crisis, when sovereign CDSs began to lead bank-specific CDS spreads. Hui et al. (2013) document the inter-dependence among financial and corporate sectors markets during the European debt crisis by looking at the iTraxx Europe CDS index option-implied correlation.

Increased sovereign risk also leads to increased borrowing costs for non-financial corporations (although, unlike banks, the causation appears to be unidirectional). For example, Augustin et al. (2017) analyze the spillover effects following the first Greek bailout announcement on the corporate sector and ascertained that a 10% increase in sovereign credit risk led to a 1.1% increase in reference entity corporate credit risk. Bedendo and Colla (2015) similarly find that heightened sovereign risk results in higher corporate spreads and borrowing costs with a more pronounced effect for non-financial borrowers that depend directly on government support, firms whose sales are primarily in the domestic market, and firms that are dependent on bank financing. Haerri et al. (2015) report empirical evidence of similar relations.

Avino and Cotter (2014) analyze the information conveyed by both bank and sovereign single-name CDS spreads in the 2004–2013 period for six major European economies from a price discovery perspective (as discussed in Sect. 11.1 of Chapter 11). By examining both the informational efficiency of bank and sovereign CDS spreads and the relative speeds of adjustment in the two markets, the authors conclude that both markets play important price discovery roles. For developed economies that were relatively healthy during the sample period, the authors conclude that bank CDSs were the PPDMs. For distressed economies (e.g., Portugal and Spain), however, sovereign CDS markets tended to be the PPDMs during both the credit crisis and Eurozone sovereign debt crisis.

De Bruyckere et al. (2013) analyze the linkage between bank and sovereign credit risk at a more granular level in the 2007–2012 period. The authors ascertain that banks with relatively less capital, more limited accesses to funding, and a more limited focus on traditional banking activities are more vulnerable to risk spillover effects. The authors also found that the connection between sovereign and banking shocks depends on the nature of government bailout programs vis-à-vis the banking sector.

Notes

1. Almer et al. (2008) use systematic proxies for liquidity such as bid-ask spreads of three-month deposits, the bid-ask spread for the overnight money market segment, the government bond swap spread, the amount of ECB tenders, and the number of bidders.
2. These examples are not intended to be exhaustive.
3. Yang and Zhou (2013).
4. These examples are not intended to be exhaustive.
5. See also Chen et al. (2011) for a paper that finds similar conclusions in Latin America around the Argentine debt crisis.
6. Pavlova and De Boyrie (2015) also examined the relation between carry trade returns and sovereign CDS spreads.
7. As a general rule, a private corporation cannot have a higher credit rating than the country rating. For example, the downgrade of a country from A− to BBB+ would cause the contemporaneous downgrade of A−rated private corporate debt to BBB+.

References

Abbassi, P., C. Brownlees, C. Hans, and N. Podlich. 2016. Credit Risk Interconnectedness: What Does the Market Really Know? Deutsche Bundesbank Discussion Paper No. 09/2016.

Acharya, V., I. Drechsler, and P. Schnabl. 2014. A Pyrrhic Victory? Bank Bailouts and Sovereign Credit Risk. *Journal of Finance* 69 (6 (December).

Acharya, V., L.H. Pedersen, T. Philippon, and M. Richardson. 2017. Measuring Systemic Risk. *The Review of Financial Studies* 30 (1) (January 1).

Adrian, T., and M.K. Brunnermeier. 2016. CoVaR. *American Economic Review* 106 (7).

Aizenman, J., M. Hutchison, and Y. Jinjarak. 2013. What Is the Risk of European Sovereign Debt Defaults? Fiscal Space, CDS Spreads and Market Pricing of Risk. *Journal of International Money and Finance* 34 (April).

Almer, T., T. Heidorn, and C. Schmaltz. 2008. The Dynamics of Short- and Long- Term CDS-Spreads of Banks. Frankfurt School of Finance & Management Working Paper Series No. 95 (April).

Alter, A., and A. Beyer. 2014. The Dynamics of Spillover Effects During the European Sovereign Debt Turmoil. *Journal of Banking & Finance* 42 (May).

Alter, A., and Y.S. Schüler. 2012. Credit Spread Interdependencies of European States and Banks During the Financial Crisis. *Journal of Banking & Finance* 36 (12) (December).

Ang, A., and F.A. Longstaff. 2013. Systemic Sovereign Credit Risk: Lessons from the U.S. and Europe. *Journal of Monetary Economics* 60 (5) (July).

Antón, M., S. Mayordomo, and M. Rodriguez-Moreno. 2017. Dealing with Dealers: Sovereign CDS Comovements. Banco de Espana Working Paper No. 1723 (July 7).

Aretz, K., and P.F. Pope. 2013. Common Factors in Default Risk across Countries and Industries. *European Financial Management* 19 (1).

Attinasi, M.-G., C. Checherita, and C. Nickel. 2009. What Explains the Surge in Euro Area Sovereign Spreads During the Financial Crisis of 2007–09? ECB Working Paper No. 1131 (December).

Augustin, P., H. Boustanifar, J. Breckenfelder, and J. Schnitzler. 2017. Sovereign to Corporate Risk Spillovers. Working Paper (September 19).

Avino, D., and J. Cotter. 2014. Sovereign and Bank CDS Spreads: Two Sides of the Same Coin? *Journal of International Financial Markets, Institutions & Money* 32 (September).

Battistini, N., M. Pagano, and S. Simonelli. 2014. Systemic Risk, Sovereign Yields and Bank Exposures in the Euro Crisis. *Economic Policy* (April).

Bedendo, M., and P. Colla. 2015. Sovereign and Corporate Credit Risk: Evidence from the Eurozone. *Journal of Corporate Finance* 33.

Beirne, J., and M. Fratzscher. 2013. The Pricing of Sovereign Risk and Contagion During the European Sovereign Debt Crisis. *Journal of International Money and Finance* 34 (April).

Belke, A., and C. Gokus. 2011. Volatility Patterns of CDS, Bond and Stock Markets Before and During the Financial Crisis: Evidence from Major Financial Institutions. Ruhr Economic Papers No. 243 (February).

Bhansali, V., Gingrich, R., and F.A. Longstaff. 2008. Systemic Credit Risk: What Is the Market Telling Us? *Financial Analysts Journal* 64 (4).

Billio, M., M. Caporin, L. Pelizzon, and D. Sartore. 2012a. CDS Industrial Sector Indices, Credit and Liquidity Risk. Working Paper No. 09/WP/2012, Department of Economics, Ca' Foscari University of Venice.

Billio, M., M. Getmansky, A.W. Lo, and L. Pelizzon. 2012b. Econometric Measures of Connectedness and Systemic Risk in the Finance and Insurance Sectors. *Journal of Financial Economics* 104.

Billio, M., M. Getmansky, D. Gray, A.W. Lo, R.C. Merton, and L. Pelizzon. 2013. Sovereign, Bank and Insurance Credit Spreads: Connectedness and System Networks. Working Paper (June 30).

Bisias, D., M. Flood, A.W. Lo, and S. Valavanis. 2012. A Survey of Systemic Risk Analytics. Office of Financial Research Working Paper No. 1 (January 5).

Blasques, F., S.J. Koopman, A. Lucas, and J. Schaumburg. 2016. Spillover Dynamics for Systemic Risk Measurement Using Spatial Financial Time Series Models. *Journal of Econometrics* 195 (2 (December).

Broto, C., and G. Pérez-Quirós. 2015. Disentangling Contagion Among Sovereign CDS Spreads During the European Debt Crisis. *Journal of Empirical Finance* 32 (June).

Caceres, C., V. Guzzo, and M. Segoviano. 2010. Sovereign Spreads: Global Risk Aversion, Contagion or Fundamentals? IMF Working Paper No. WP/10/120 (May).

Calice, G., and C. Ioannidis. 2012. An Empirical Analysis of the Impact of the Credit Default Swap Index Market on Large Complex Financial Institutions. *International Review of Financial Analysis* 25 (December).

Calice, G., C. Ioannidis, and J. Williams. 2012. Credit Derivatives and the Default Risk of Large Complex Financial Institutions. *Journal of Financial Services Research* 42 (1–2) (October).

Calice, G., J. Chen, and J. Williams. 2013. Liquidity Spillovers in Sovereign Bond and CDS Markets: An Analysis of the Eurozone Sovereign Debt Crisis. *Journal of Economic Behavior and Organization* 85 (January).

Caporin, M., L. Pelizzon, F. Ravazzolo, and R. Rigobon. 2018. Measuring Sovereign Contagion in Europe. *Journal of Financial Stability* 34 (February).

Carr, P., and L. Wu. 2007. Theory and Evidence on the Dynamic Interactions Between Sovereign Credit Default Swaps and Currency Options. *Journal of Banking & Finance* 31 (8) (August).

Cetina, J., M. Paddrik, and S. Rajan. 2018. Stressed to the Core: Counterparty Concentrations and Systemic Losses in CDS Markets. *Journal of Financial Stability* 35 (April).

Chen, Y.-H., K. Wang, and A.H. Tu. 2011. Default Correlation at the Sovereign Level: Evidence from Some Latin American Markets. *Applied Economics* 43 (11).

Chen, H., J.D. Cummins, K.S. Viswanathan, and M. Weiss. 2013. Systemic Risk and the Interconnectedness Between Banks and Insurers: An Econometric Analysis. *Journal of Risk and Insurance* 81 (3).

Conrad, J., R.F. Dittmar, and A. Hameed. 2013. Cross-Market and Cross-Firm Effects in Implied Default Probabilities and Recovery Values. Working Paper (May 30).

Consiglio, A., S. Lotfi, and S.A. Zenios. 2017. Portfolio Diversification in the Sovereign Credit Swap Markets. *Annals of Operations Research*.

Coudert, V., and M. Gex. 2010a. Contagion Inside the Credit Default Swaps Market: The Case of the GM and Ford Crisis in 2005. *Journal of International Financial Markets, Institutions and Money* 20 (2) (April).

Coudert, V., and M. Gex. 2010b. Disrupted Links Between Credit Default Swaps, Bonds, and Equities During the GM and Ford Crisis in 2005. *Applied Financial Economics* 20.

De Boyrie, M.E., and I. Pavlova. 2016. Dynamic Interdepence of Soverign Credit Default Swaps in BRICS and MIST Countries. *Applied Economics* 48 (7).

De Bruyckere, V., M. Gerhardt, G. Schepens, and R. Vander Vennet. 2013. Bank/Sovereign Risk Spillovers in the European Debt Crisis. *Journal of Banking & Finance* 37 (12) (December).

D'Errico, M., S. Battiston, T. Peltonen, and M. Scheicher. 2018. How Does Risk Flow in the Credit Default Swap Market? *Journal of Financial Stability* 35 (April).

De Santis, R.A. 2015. A Measure of Redenomination Risk. ECB Working Paper No. 1785 (April).

Demirgüç-Kunt, A., and H. Huizinga. 2013. Are Banks Too Big to Fail or Too Big to Save? International Evidence from Equity Prices and CDS Spreads. *Journal of Banking & Finance* 37 (3) (March).

Dieckmann, S., and T. Plank. 2012. Default Risk of Advanced Economies: An Empirical Analysis of Credit Default Swaps During the Financial Crisis. *Review of Finance* 16 (4).

Dockner, E.J., M. Mayer, and J. Zechner. 2013. Sovereign Bond Risk Premiums. Center for Financial Studies Working Paper No. 2013/28 (May), Goethe University Frankfurt.

Dooley, M., and M. Hutchison. 2009. Transmission of the U.S. Subprime Crisis to Emerging Markets: Evidence on the Decoupling–Recoupling Hypothesis. *Journal of International Money and Finance* 28 (8) (December).

Doshi, H., K. Jacobs, and V. Zurita. 2017. Economic and Financial Determinants of Credit Risk Premiums in the Sovereign CDS Market. *Review of Asset Pricing Studies* 7 (1) (June).

Duffie, D. 2010. Is There a Case for Banning Short Speculation in Sovereign Bond Markets? Banque de France Financial Stability Review No. 14 (July).

Dumontaux, N., and A. Pop. 2013. Contagion Effects in the Aftermath of *Lehman*'s Collapse: Evidence from the US Financial Services Industry. Banque de France Working Paper No. 427 (March).

Eichengreen, B., A. Mody, M. Nedeljkovic, M., and L. Sarno. 2012. How the Subprime Crisis Went Global: Evidence from Bank Credit Default Swap Spreads. *Journal of International Money and Finance* 31 (5) (September).

Ejsing, J., and W. Lemke. 2011. The Janus-Headed Salvation: Sovereign and Bank Credit Risk Premia During 2008–2009. *Economics Letters* 110 (1).

Erce, A. 2015. Bank and Sovereign Risk Feedback Loops. Globalization and Monetary Policy Institute Working Paper No. 227 (February), Federal Reserve Bank of Dallas.

Fama, E.F. 1984. Forward and Spot Exchange Rates. *Journal of Monetary Economics* 14 (3).

Fang, H., and Y.-H. Lee. 2011. The Impact of the Subprime Financial Crisis on Stock Index Returns for High- and Low-Risk Countries Via CDS Indices. *Investment Management and Financial Innovations* 8 (4).

Feldhütter, P., and M.S. Nielsen. 2012. Systematic and Idiosyncratic Default Risk in Synthetic Credit Markets. *Journal of Financial Econometrics* 10 (2) (March).

Galariotis, E.C., P. Makrichoriti, and S. Spyrou. 2016. Sovereign CDS Spread Determinants and Spill-Over Effects During Financial Crisis: A Panel VAR Approach. *Journal of Financial Stability* 26 (October).

Gątarek, L., and M. Wojtowicz. 2015. The Relation Between Sovereign Credit Default Swap Premium and Banking Sector Risk in Poland. Narodowy Bank Polski Working Paper No. 222.

Gennaioli, N., A. Martin, and S. Rossi. 2014. Banks, Government Bonds, and Default: What Do the Data Say? IMF Working Paper No. WP/14/120 (July).

Gerlach-Kristen, P. 2013. Euro Area CDS Spreads in the Crisis: The Role of Open Market Operations and Contagion. Working Paper No. 449 (February), Economic and Social Research Institute.

Getmansky, M., G. Girardi, and C. Lewis. 2016. Interconnectedness in the CDS Market. *Financial Analysts Journal* 72 (4) (July/August).

Giglio, S. 2011. Credit Default Swap Spreads and Systemic Financial Risk. Working Paper (February).

Glover, B., and S. Richards-Shubik. 2014. Contagion in the European Sovereign Debt Crisis. NBER Working Paper No. 20567 (October).

Groba, J., J.A. Lafuente, and P. Serrano. 2013. The Impact of Distressed Economies on the EU Sovereign Market. *Journal of Banking & Finance* 37 (7) (July).

Gross, M., and C. Kok. 2013. Measuring Contagion Potential among Sovereigns and Banks Using a Mixed-Cross-Section GVAR. ECB Working Paper No. 1570 (August).

Gündüz, Y., and O. Kaya. 2013. Sovereign Default Swap Market Efficiency and Country Risk in the Eurozone. Deutsche Bundesbank Discussion Paper No. 08/2013.

Haerri, M., S. Morkoetter, and S. Westerfeld. 2015. Sovereign Risk and the Pricing of Corporate Credit Default Swaps. *Journal of Credit Risk* 11 (1) (March).

Hansen, L.P., and R.J. Hodrick. 1980. Forward Exchange Rates as Optimal Predictors of Future Spot Rates: An Econometric Analysis. *Journal of Political Economy* 88 (5) (October).

Heinz, F.F., and Y. Sun. 2014. Sovereign CDS Spreads in Europe – The Role of Global Risk Aversion, Economic Fundamentals, Liquidity, and Spillovers. IMF Working Paper No. WP/14/17 (January).

Huang, H., and R. MacDonald. 2014. Currency Carry Trades, Position-Unwinding Risk, and Sovereign Credit Premia. Working Paper (January 23).

Huang, A.Y., C.-C. Chen, and C.-H. Shen. 2014. Dynamics of Sovereign Credit Contagion. *Journal of Derivatives* 22 (1) (Fall).

Hui, C.-H., and T.-K. Chung. 2011. Crash Risk of the Euro in the Sovereign Debt Crisis of 2009–2010. *Journal of Banking & Finance* 35 (11) (November).

Hui, C.-H., and T. Fong. 2011. Information Flow Between Sovereign CDS and Dollar-Yen Currency Option Markets in the Sovereign Debt Crisis of 2009–2011. HKIMR Working Paper No. 40/2011 (December).

Hui, C.-H., C.-F. Lo, and C.-S. Lau. 2013. Option-Implied Correlation Between iTraxx Europe Financials and Non-Financials Indexes: A Measure of Spillover Effect in European Debt Crisis. *Journal of Banking & Finance* 37 (9) (September).

Jacoby, G., G.J. Jiang, and G. Theocharides. 2009. Cross-Market Liquidity Shocks: Evidence from the CDS, Corporate Bond, and Equity Markets. Working Paper (August 30).

Javadi, S., S. Kim, T. Krehbiel, and A. Nejadmalyeri. 2017. Measuring Correlated Default Risk: A New Metric and Validity Tests. *Journal of Fixed Income* 27 (2) (Fall).

Kalbaska, A., and M. Gątkowski. 2012. Eurozone Sovereign Contagion: Evidence from the CDS Market (2005–2010). *Journal of Economic Behavior & Organization* 83 (3) (August).

Kanno, M. 2016. Interconnectedness and Systemic Risk in the US CDS Market. Working Paper.

Kim, D.H., M. Loretan, and E.M. Remolona. 2010. Contagion and Risk Premia in the Amplification of Crisis: Evidence from Asian Names in the Global CDS Market. *Journal of Asian Economics* 21.

Kim, S.-J., L. Salem, and E. Wu. 2015. The Role of Macroeconomic News in Sovereign CDS Markets: Domestic and Spillover News Effects from the U.S., the Eurozone and China. *Journal of Financial Stability* 18 (June).

Kirschenmann, K., J. Korte, and S. Steffen. 2017. The Zero Risk Fallacy? Banks' Sovereign Exposure and Sovereign Risk Spillovers. ZEW Discussion Paper No. 17–069 (August 28).

Li, J., and G. Zinna. 2017. How Much of Bank Credit Risk Is Sovereign Risk? Evidence from Europe. Working Paper (June).

Longstaff, F.A., J. Pan, L.H. Pedersen, and K.J. Singleton. 2011. How Sovereign Is Sovereign Credit Risk? *American Economic Journal: Macroeconomics* 3 (2) (April).

Manasse, P., and L. Zavalloni. 2013. Sovereign Contagion in Europe: Evidence from the CDS Market. Quaderni DSE Working Paper No. 863 (February 14).

Merton, R.C. 1974. On the Pricing of Corporate Debt: The Risk Structure of Interest Rates. *Journal of Finance* 29 (2) (May).

Mody, A., and D. Sandri. 2012. The Eurozone Crisis: How Banks and Sovereigns Came to be Joined at the Hip. *Economic Policy* 27 (70) (April).

Nijskens, R., and W. Wagner. 2011. Credit Risk Transfer Activities and Systemic Risk: How Banks Became Less Risky Individually But Posed Greater Risks to the Financial System at the Same Time. *Journal of Banking & Finance* 35 (6) (June).

Oh, D.H., and A.J. Patton. 2017. Time-Varying Systemic Risk: Evidence from a Dynamic Copula Model of CDS Spreads. *Journal of Business & Economic Statistics* 36 (2).

Ohno, S. 2013. European Sovereign Risk: The Knock-On Effects of Default Risk Across the Public and Financial Sectors. *Public Policy Review* 9 (1) (January).

Paddrik, M., S. Rajan, and H.P. Young. 2016. Contagion in the CDS Market. Office of Financial Research Working Paper 16-12 (December 1).

Pan, J., and K.J. Singleton. 2008. Default and Recovery Implicit in the Term Structure of Sovereign *CDS* Spreads. *Journal of Finance* 63 (5) (October).

Pavlova, I., and M.E. De Boyrie. 2015. Carry Trades and Sovereign CDS Spreads: Evidence from Asia-Pacific Markets. *Journal of Futures Markets* 35 (11).

Peltonen, T.A., M. Scheicher, and G. Vuillemey. 2014. The Network Structure of the CDS Market and Its Determinants. *Journal of Financial Stability* 13 (August).

Pu, X., and J. Zhang. 2012. Can Dual-Currency Sovereign CDS Predict Exchange Rate Returns? *Finance Research Letters* 9 (3).

Revoltella, D., F. Mucci, and D. Mihaljek. 2010. Properly Pricing Country Risk: A Model for Pricing Long-Term Fundamental Risk Applied to Central and Eastern European Countries. *Financial Theory and Practice* 34 (3).

Rodríguez-Moreno, M., and J.I. Peña. 2013. Systemic Risk Measures: The Simpler the Better? *Journal of Banking & Finance* 37 (6) (June).

Sgherri, S., and E. Zoli. 2009. Euro Area Sovereign Risk During the Crisis. IMF Working Paper No. WP/09/222 (October).

Shoesmith, G.L. 2014. A Time-Series Postmorten on Eurozone Financial Integration and the Debt Crisis: Modeling and Policy Implications. *International Journal of Business* 19 (2).

Stamatopoulos, T.V., S.E. Arvanitis, and D.M. Terzakis. 2016. The Risk of the Sovereign Debt Default: The Eurozone Crisis 2008–2013. *Applied Economics* 49 (38).

Stulz, R.M. 2010. Credit Default Swaps and the Credit Crisis. *Journal of Economic Perspectives* 24 (1) (Winter).

Tamakoshi, G., and S. Hamori. 2014. The Conditional Dependence Structure of Insurance Sector Credit Default Swap Indices. *North American Journal of Economics and Finance* 30 (November).

Ters, K., and J. Urban. 2016. Credit Risk Contagion Before and During the Euro Area Sovereign Debt Crisis: Evidence from Central Europe. Working Paper (October 24).

Tran, H.Q. 2013. The Role of Markets in Sovereign Debt Crisis Detection, Prevention and Resolution. BIS Working Papers No. 72.

Wang, P., and T. Moore. 2012. The Integration of the Credit Default Swap Markets During the US Subprime Crisis: Dynamic Correlation Analysis. *Journal of International Financial Markets, Institutions & Money* 22 (1) (February).

Yang, J., and Y. Zhou. 2013. Credit Risk Spillovers Among Financial Institutions Around the Global Credit Crisis: Firm-Level Evidence. *Management Science* 59 (10).

Yu, S. 2017. Sovereign and Bank Interdependencies—Evidence from the CDS Market. *Research in International Business and Finance* 39, Part A (January).

Zareei, A. 2015. Network Centrality, Failure Prediction and Systemic Risk. *Journal of Network Theory in Finance* 1 (4).

Appendix A: Research Methodology

Sample Universe

Our review of the relevant academic empirical literature on CDSs was based on several objective considerations. First, we only surveyed academic and research-oriented articles and papers. Our review covers articles published in peer-reviewed academic journals, quasi-academic/trade journals with largely academic editorial boards (e.g., the *Journal of Fixed Income*), and working papers distributed through the Social Science Research Network ("SSRN"), universities, and the research divisions of financial regulators (e.g., the Bank for International Settlements, European Central Bank, and Federal Reserve System). Our review did not include a survey of industry research (e.g., bank research publications or analyst reports), articles in industry and trade magazines or journals, and mainstream media publications.[1]

Second, our literature review is focused on *empirical* research involving single-name, multi-name, and asset-backed CDSs. The theoretical academic literature comprises an important part of CDS research as well, and a large such body of research exists that presents a range of theoretical models of various issues involving CDSs. That literature, however, is beyond the scope of this review (except in a few specific instances in which theoretical papers play an important role in guiding empirical research).

C. L. Culp et al., *Credit Default Swaps*, Palgrave Studies in Risk and Insurance, https://doi.org/10.1007/978-3-319-93076-3

Third, although many of the issues we discuss touch on the credit crisis, we do not include in this book a systematic review of the empirical credit crisis issues. (See, e.g., Culp (2018) for a survey of those articles.)

Given the extensive amount of academic research on CDSs, it is likely that we have missed some working papers or publications that fall within the criteria defined above. If so, we apologize to the authors that we have left out in advance. In no case did we exclude any article for deliberate reasons.

Citation Style

Throughout this book, we adopt a parenthetical citation style for the academic studies we reference. In other words, we cite the research we review using a reference style such as Smith (2012), which corresponds to a citation in the References section for each chapter to a publication by Smith dated 2012. When one or more of the same authors have multiple publications in the same year, we note the references using lower-case letters.

In many situations throughout our book, we also cite non-academic publications, corporate filings and industry press releases, and books (both by trade and academic publishers) for background purposes. In those cases, we provide full citations in the End Notes for each chapter but do not include those citations in the References for each chapter.

Sample Data Underlying Surveyed Articles

For expositional simplicity, we omit the details of the sample data underlying the empirical studies reviewed in the book in most cases. All empirical studies cited in Part III of the book, however, are summarized in Table B.3 that appears in Appendix B. That table summarizes the nature of the underlying data samples on which authors relied to draw their conclusions. The information presented in that table for all of the empirical studies we reference includes the sample period (i.e., dates over which the analysis was performed), type of reference entity, sample size, region(s) in which reference entities included by authors are located, CDS tenors reviewed in the studies, and the authors' CDS-related data sources.

Note

1. Research produced by industry and distributed by financial institutions—as well as other trade literature—is often very high quality and informative. We excluded such publications purely for reasons of tractability and limitations of scope.

Reference

Culp, C.L. 2018. A Review of the Academic Literature on the Causes and Evolution of the Credit Crisis. *Johns Hopkins Institute for Applied Economics, Global Health, and the Study of Business Enterprise—Studies in Applied Finance* (24) (April).

Appendix B: Additional Tables

C. L. Culp et al., *Credit Default Swaps*, Palgrave Studies in Risk and Insurance, https://doi.org/10.1007/978-3-319-93076-3

Table B.1 Single-Name CDS event determinations and Auctions, April 2009–December 2017

Region/Determinations Committee	*Reference name*	*Key dates*		
		Event determination	*Auction*	*Auction settlement*
Americas	Bowater Inc.	4/16/2009	5/12/2009	5/19/2009
EMEA (Europe)	JSC BTA Bank	4/29/2009	6/10/2009	6/15/2009
Americas	Syncora Guarantee Inc. (fka XL Capital Assurance Inc.)	5/1/2009	5/27/2009	6/3/2009
EMEA (Europe)	JSC Alliance Bank	5/15/2009	6/18/2009	6/25/2009
Americas	R. H. Donnelley Corp.	5/18/2009	6/11/2009	6/18/2009
Americas	Visteon Corp.	5/28/2009	6/23/2009	7/1/2009
Americas	General Motors Corp.	6/1/2009	6/12/2009	6/18/2009
Americas	Six Flags, Inc.	6/15/2009	7/9/2009	7/16/2009
Americas	Lear Corp.	7/2/2009	7/21/2009	7/28/2009
EMEA (Europe)	Bradford & Bingley plc	7/9/2009	7/30/2009	8/6/2009
EMEA (Europe)	Thomson SA	8/10/2009	10/22/2009	10/29/2009
EMEA (Europe)	NJSC Naftogaz of Ukraine	10/6/2009	12/16/2009	12/23/2009
Americas	Cemex S.A.B. de C.V.	10/9/2009	2/18/2010	2/25/2010
Americas	CIT Group Inc.	11/2/2009	11/20/2009	12/1/2009
EMEA (Europe)	Hellas Telecom (Luxembourg) II	11/18/2009	12/15/2009	12/18/2009
EMEA (Europe)	Thomson	12/1/2009	12/10/2009	12/17/2009
Americas	Financial Guaranty Insurance Co.	12/2/2009	1/7/2010	1/14/2010
Japan	AIFUL Corp.	12/24/2009	3/25/2010	3/30/2010
Japan	Japan Airlines Corp.	1/19/2010	4/22/2010	4/27/2010
Americas	Ambac Assurance Corp.	3/25/2010	6/4/2010	6/11/2010
EMEA (Europe)	Truvo Subsidiary Corp.	7/1/2010	7/15/2010	7/22/2010
Japan	Takefuji Corp.	9/29/2010	10/28/2010	11/2/2010
Americas	Ambac Financial Group, Inc.	11/9/2010	12/10/2010	12/15/2010

(continued)

Table B.1 (continued)

Region/Determinations Committee	*Reference name*	*Key dates*		
		Event determination	*Auction*	*Auction settlement*
EMEA (Europe)	Anglo Irish Bank Corporation Ltd	11/23/2010	12/9/2010	12/14/2010
EMEA (Europe)	Anglo Irish Bank Corporation Ltd (Restructuring)	12/23/2010	2/2/2011	2/7/2011
EMEA (Europe)	Allied Irish Banks plc	6/20/2011	6/30/2011	7/5/2011
EMEA (Europe)	Irish Life & Permanent plc	7/4/2011	7/29/2011	8/5/2011
EMEA (Europe)	The Governor and Company of the Bank of Ireland	7/11/2011	7/28/2011	8/2/2011
EMEA (Europe)	Irish Life & Permanent plc (Restructuring)	8/25/2011	10/5/2011	10/12/2011
Japan	Victor Company of Japan, Ltd	8/26/2011	11/9/2011	11/16/2011
Americas	Dynegy Holdings, LLC	11/8/2011	11/29/2011	12/6/2011
Americas	The PMI Group, Inc.	11/23/2011	12/13/2011	12/23/2011
Americas	AMR Corp.	11/29/2011	12/15/2011	12/23/2011
EMEA (Europe)	Seat Paginegialle SpA	12/1/2011	12/9/2011	12/14/2011
EMEA (Europe)	Northern Rock (Asset Management) plc	12/15/2011	2/2/2012	2/9/2012
Americas	Eastman Kodak Co.	1/19/2012	2/22/2012	2/29/2012
Japan	Elpida Memory, Inc.	2/27/2012	3/22/2012	3/29/2012
EMEA (Europe)	*The Hellenic Republic*	*3/9/2012*	*3/19/2012*	*3/26/2012*
EMEA (Europe)	ERC Ireland Finance Ltd	3/16/2012	3/29/2012	4/5/2012
Asia Ex-Japan	Sino-Forest Corp.	4/2/2012	5/9/2012	5/16/2012
Americas	Residential Capital, LLC	5/14/2012	6/6/2012	6/13/2012
Americas	Houghton Mifflin Harcourt Publishing Co.	5/21/2012	5/30/2012	6/6/2012

(continued)

Table B.1 (continued)

Region/Determinations Committee	*Reference name*	*Key dates*		
		Event determination	*Auction*	*Auction settlement*
Americas	Overseas Shipholding Group, Inc.	11/14/2012	12/6/2012	12/12/2012
Americas	Edison Mission Energy	12/17/2012	1/16/2013	1/23/2013
EMEA (Europe)	SNS Bank NV	2/4/2013	4/4/2013	4/11/2013
EMEA (Europe)	Bankia, S.A.	4/24/2013		
Americas	Urbi Desarrollos Urbanos, S.A.B. de C.V.	5/20/2013	6/6/2013	6/13/2013
Americas	Cengage Learning Acquisitions, Inc.	7/9/2013		
Americas	Desarrolladora Homex, S.A.B. de C.V.	7/12/2013		
EMEA (Europe)	Codere Finance (Luxembourg) S.A.	9/17/2013	10/9/2013	10/16/2013
Americas	OGX Petroleo e Gas Participacoes S.A.	11/4/2013	12/4/2013	12/9/2013
Americas	EFIH Finance, Inc.	4/29/2014	5/21/2014	5/29/2014
Americas	Energy Future Intermediate Holding Co., LLC	4/29/2014	5/21/2014	5/29/2014
Americas	Texas Competitive Electric Holdings Co., LLC	4/29/2014	5/21/2014	5/29/2014
Americas	Energy Future Holdings Corp.	4/29/2014	5/21/2014	5/29/2014
Americas	*Argentine Republic*	*7/31/2014*	*9/3/2014*	*9/8/2014*
Americas	Caesars Entertainment Operating Co.	1/15/2015	2/19/2015	2/24/2015
Americas	RadioShack Corp.	2/6/2015	3/5/2015	3/10/2015
Americas	Sabine Oil & Gas Corp.	5/28/2015	6/23/2015	6/26/2015

(continued)

Table B.1 (continued)

Region/Determinations Committee	*Reference name*	*Key dates*		
		Event determination	*Auction*	*Auction settlement*
Americas	Alpha Appalachia Holdings, Inc. (f/k/a Massey Energy Co.)	8/3/2015	9/17/2015	9/23/2015
EMEA (Europe)	*Republic of Ukraine*	*10/5/2015*	*10/6/2015*	*10/13/2015*
EMEA (Europe)	Abengoa S.A.	12/10/2015	1/14/2016	1/21/2016
Americas	Pacific Exploration & Production Corp.	3/7/2016	4/6/2016	4/11/2016
Americas	Peabody Energy Corp.	4/13/2016	5/4/2016	5/9/2016
Americas	Commonwealth of Puerto Rico	7/8/2016	8/17/2016	8/22/2016
EMEA (Europe)	Grupo Isolux Corsan Finance B.V.	8/2/2016	8/24/2016	8/30/2016
Americas	iHeart Communications, Inc.	12/20/2016	2/2/2017	2/7/2017
Americas	GenOn Energy, Inc	6/14/2017	7/11/2017	7/14/2017
Americas	Puerto Rico Electric Power Authority	7/12/2017	8/2/2017	8/7/2017
Americas	Toys "R" Us, Inc.	9/19/2017	10/11/2017	10/16/2017
Americas	Petróleos de Venezuela, S.A.	11/15/2017	12/13/2017	12/18/2017
Americas	*Bolivarian Republic of Venezuela*	*11/15/2017*	*12/12/2017*	*12/15/2017*

Notes Italicized entries indicate sovereign reference names. Blanks for both the auction and auction settlement dates indicate either that no auction was held or there was zero net open interest and the inside market midpoint based on round one initial bids and offers was the final price in lieu of a final auction price. A blank in only the auction settlement date column indicates that the settlement date is not available
Source ISDA

Table B.2 Single-Name LCDS event determinations and auctions, March 2009–December 2017

Region/Determinations Committee	*Reference name*	*Key dates*		
		Event determination	*Auction*	*Auction settlement*
Americas	Charter Communications	3/27/2009	4/24/2009	
Americas	General Growth Properties, Inc.	4/16/2009	5/13/2009	
Americas	Georgia Gulf Corp.	5/19/2009	6/10/2009	
Americas	Visteon Corp.	5/28/2009	6/23/2009	
Americas	R.H. Donnelley Corp.	5/29/2009	6/24/2009	7/1/2009
Americas	General Motors Corp.	6/1/2009	6/12/2009	6/18/2009
Americas	Six Flags, Inc.	6/15/2009	7/9/2009	7/16/2009
Americas	Lear Corp.	7/2/2009	7/21/2009	7/28/2009
EMEA (Europe)	McCarthy & Stone	4/6/2010	4/15/2010	
EMEA (Europe)	Truvo USA	7/1/2010	9/9/2010	
Americas	Boston Generating, LLC	8/19/2010	9/21/2010	9/28/2010
EMEA (Europe)	Panrico	11/21/2011	11/23/2011	
EMEA (Europe)	Seat Pagine SpA	1/16/2012	1/17/2012	
EMEA (Europe)	Financière Gaillon 7 ELCDS Credit Event	3/27/2012	3/28/2012	
EMEA (Europe)	Eircom ELCDS Credit Event	3/29/2012	5/2/2012	
Americas	Hawker Beechcraft Acquisition Co., LLC	4/5/2012	4/26/2012	5/3/2012
EMEA (Europe)	Yell Ltd.	11/9/2012	11/15/2012	
EMEA (Europe)	Mediannuaire	1/29/2013	1/31/2013	
Americas	SuperMedia, Inc. / Dex Media West, Inc	3/26/2013	4/24/2013	

(continued)

Table B.2 (continued)

Region/Determinations Committee	*Reference name*	*Key dates*		
		Event determination	*Auction*	*Auction settlement*
Americas	Cengage Learning Acquisitions, Inc.	7/9/2013	8/6/2013	8/13/2013
Americas	Momentive Performance Materials, Inc	4/14/2014		
Americas	Texas Competitive Electric Holdings Co., LLC	4/29/2014	5/21/2014	5/29/2014
EMEA (Europe)	Pages Jaunes	6/19/2014	8/19/2014	
Americas	Caesars Entertainment Operating Co., Inc.	1/15/2015	2/19/2015	2/24/2015
Americas	iHeart Communications, Inc.	12/20/2016	2/2/2017	2/7/2017
Americas	Avaya, Inc.	1/27/2017	3/1/2017	3/6/2017
Americas	Toys "R" Us – Delaware, Inc.	9/20/2017	10/11/2017	10/16/2017

Notes Blanks for both the auction and auction settlement dates indicate either that no auction was held or there was zero net open interest and the inside market midpoint based on round one initial bids and offers was the final price in lieu of a final auction price. A blank in only the auction settlement date column indicates that the settlement date is not available

Source ISDA

Table B.3 Data sources for empirical studies reviewed

Article	*Sample period*	*Type of reference entities*[a]	*Reference entity notes*	*Region(s) of reference entities*[b]	*CDS tenor(s) (years)*	*CDS data source(s)*
Abbassi, Brownlees, Hans, and Podlich (2016)	1/2006–12/2013	Financial Institutions (13)	Financial Institutions Sample Restricted to Banks	Germany	1, 2, 3, 5, 7, 10	Markit
Abid and Naifar (2006)	5/2000–5/2001	Corporates (73)		Global	N/A	UBS
Acharya and Johnson (2007)	1/2001–10/2004	Corporates (79)		North America	5	CreditTrade
Acharya, Drechsler, and Schnabl (2014)	1/2007–4/2011	Financial Institutions (36), Sovereigns (15)	Financial Institutions Sample Restricted to Banks	Austria, Belgium, Denmark, France, Germany, Great Britain, Greece, Ireland, Italy, Netherlands, Norway, Portugal, Spain, Sweden, Switzerland	N/A	Bloomberg, Datastream, Markit
Acharya, Pedersen, Philippon, and Richardson (2017)	6/2006–7/2007	Financial Institutions (40)		U.S.	N/A	Bloomberg
Adler and Song (2010)	1998–1/2006	Sovereigns (16)		Argentina, Brazil, Chile, China, Colombia, Korea, Mexico, Malaysia, Panama, Peru, Philippines, Poland, Russia, Turkey, Venezuela, South Africa	1, 3, 5, 10	JP Morgan
Afonso, Furceri and Gomes (2012)	1/2003–10/2010	Sovereigns (24)		Austria, Belgium, Bulgaria, Czech Republic, Denmark, Finland, France, Germany, Greece, Hungary, Ireland, Italy, Latvia, Lithuania, Malta, Netherlands, Poland, Portugal, Romania, Slovakia, Slovenia, Spain, Sweden, United Kingdom	5	Datastream

(continued)

Table B.3 (continued)

Article	*Sample period*	*Type of reference entities*[a]	*Reference entity notes*	*Region(s) of reference entities*[b]	*CDS tenor(s) (years)*	*CDS data source(s)*
Aizenman, Hutchinson, and Jinjarak (2013)	2005–2010	Sovereigns (50)		Global	3, 5, 10	CMA Datavision
Alexander and Kaeck (2008)	6/2004–6/2007	iTraxx Europe Indices (5)		Europe	5	Bloomberg, Datastream, iTraxx
Alexopoulou, Andersson, and Georgescu (2009)	1/2004–10/2008	Corporates (29)		Europe	5	Datastream
Almer, Heidorn, and Schmaltz (2008)	1/2001–12/2007	Financial Institutions (58)		Global	0.5, 5	Markit
Alper, Forni, Gerard (2013)	1/2008–10/2010	Sovereigns (18)		Australia, Austria, Belgium, Denmark, Finland, France, Germany, Greece, Ireland, Italy, Japan, Netherlands, Norway, Portugal, Spain, Sweden, United Kingdom., U.S.	5	Markit
Alter and Beyer (2014)	10/2009–7/2012	Sovereigns (11), Financial Institutions (38), Index (4)	Financial Institutions Sample Restricted to Banks, Sovereign Sample includes Austria, Belgium, Finland, France, Germany, Greece, Ireland, Italy, Netherlands, Portugal, Spain	Austria, Belgium, Finland, France, Germany, Greece, Ireland, Italy, Netherlands, Portugal, Spain, United Kingdom	5	CMA, Datastream, Bloomberg
Alter, Schüler (2012)	6/2007–5/2010	Sovereigns (7), Financial Institutions (14)	Financial Institutions Sample Restricted to Banks	France, Germany, Italy, Ireland, the Netherlands, Portugal, Spain	5	Datastream

(continued)

Table B.3 (continued)

Article	*Sample period*	*Type of reference entities*[a]	*Reference entity notes*	*Region(s) of reference entities*[b]	*CDS tenor(s) (years)*	*CDS data source(s)*
Amato (2005)	5/2002–9/2005	Corporates (125)	Corporates Sample are those included in CDX.NA.IG.4	North America	1, 5, 10	Markit
Ammer and Cai (2011)	2/2001–3/2005	Sovereigns (9)		Brazil, China, Colombia, Mexico, Philippines, Russia, Turkey, Uruguay, Venezuela	5	Markit
Andritzky and Singh (2006)	7/2002–1/2003	Sovereigns (1)	Brazil	Latin America	1, 3, 5	Bloomberg, CreditTrade, Datastream, quotes directly provided by traders
Ang, Longstaff (2013)	5/2008–1/2011	Sovereigns (12), States (10)	States include California, Florida, Illinois, Massachusetts, Michigan, Nevada, New Jersey, New York, Ohio, Texas	Austria, Belgium, Finland, France, Germany, Greece, Ireland, Italy, the Netherlands, Portugal, Spain, U.S.	1, 2, 3, 4, 5	Bloomberg
Annaert, De Ceuster, Van Roy, and Vespro (2013)	12/2003–9/2010	Financial Institutions (32)	Financial Institutions Sample Restricted to Banks	Europe	5	Datastream
Antón, Mayordomo, and Rodriquez-Moreno (2017)	1/2008–10/2011	Sovereigns (11)	For Robustness Checks: additional non-EMU Sovereign (39)	Austria, Belgium, Finland, France, Germany, Greece, Ireland, Italy, Netherlands, Portugal, Spain	5	CMA
Arce, Mayordomo, and Peña (2013)	1/2004–2/2012	Sovereigns (11)		Austria, Belgium, Finland, France, Germany, Greece, Ireland, Italy, Netherlands, Portugal, Spain	5	CMA

(continued)

Table B.3 (continued)

Article	*Sample period*	*Type of reference entities*[a]	*Reference entity notes*	*Region(s) of reference entities*[b]	*CDS tenor(s) (years)*	*CDS data source(s)*
Aretz and Pope (2013)	2006–2008	Corporates (N/A)		Global	N/A	Old Mutual Asset Management
Arora, Gandhi, and Longstaff (2012)	3/2008–1/2009	Corporates (125)	CDX index constituents	North America	5	Bloomberg
Ashcraft and Santos (2009)	Q1/2001–Q2/2005	Corporates (111/152)	111 firms in bond analysis; 152 firms in loan analysis	N/A	5	Markit
Attinasi, Checherita, and Nickel (2009)	7/2007–3/2009	Sovereigns (11), Index (1)	Index Sample consists of the iTraxx Financials Senior	Austria, Belgium, Finland, France, Germany, Greece, Ireland, Italy, Netherlands, Portugal, Spain	N/A	Bloomberg
Augustin (2012)	1/2004–9/2010	Corporates (177)		U.S.	5	CMA Datavision
Augustin (2014)	5/2003–8/2010	Sovereigns (38)		Americas, Europe, Africa, the Middle East and Asia	1, 2, 3, 5, 7, 10	Markit
Augustin (2016)	1/2001–2/2012	Sovereigns (44)		Global	1, 2, 3, 5, 7, 10	Markit
Augustin, Boustanifar, Breckenfelder, and Schnitzler (2017)	2/2010–6/2010	Corporates (226)		Global	5	CMA Datastream
Aunon-Nerin, Cossin, Hricko, Huang (2002)	1/2008–2/2000	Corporates (323), Sovereigns (69)		Global		London Interdealer Broker

(continued)

Table B.3 (continued)

Article	*Sample period*	*Type of reference entities*[a]	*Reference entity notes*	*Region(s) of reference entities*[b]	*CDS tenor(s) (years)*	*CDS data source(s)*
Avino, Conlon and Cotter (2016)	2004–2012	Financial Institutions (60)	Financial Institutions Sample Includes Banks, Diversified Banks, and Financial Services	Europe	5	Markit
Avino, Cotter (2014)	1/2004–3/2013	Financial Institutions (28), Sovereigns (6)	Financial Institutions Sample Restricted to Banks	Europe	5	CMA, Datastream, Thomson Reuters
Baba and Inada (2009)	4/2004–12/2005	Financial Institutions (4)	Financial Institutions Sample Restricted to Banks	Japan	5	Bloomberg
Badaoui, Cathcart, El-Jahel (2013)	11/2005–9/2010	Sovereigns (9)		Chile, Korea, Mexico, Colombia, Peru, Brazil, Philippines, Indonesia, Turkey	5	Thomson Reuters
Badaoui, Cathcart, El-Jahel (2015)	11/2005–9/2010	Sovereigns (3)		Brazil, Turkey, Philippines	1, 3, 5, 7, 10	Thomson Reuters
Bai, Collin-Dufresne (2013)	1/2006–12/2011	Corporates (487)		U.S.	5	Markit
Bao, Pan (2013)	1/2004–9/2010	Corporates (N/A)	Sample Size Varies Each Year; Average of 303 Companies	N/A	5	CMA
Batta (2011)	6/1997–5/2004	Corporates (242)		N/A	5	CreditTrade
Batta, and Yu (2017)	1/2001–12/2013	Corporates (554)		North America	5	Markit
Battistini, Pagano, Simonelli (2014)	4/2010–3/2013	Countries (15)		Global	5	Bloomberg

(continued)

Table B.3 (continued)

Article	*Sample period*	*Type of reference entities*[a]	*Reference entity notes*	*Region(s) of reference entities*[b]	*CDS tenor(s) (years)*	*CDS data source(s)*
Beber, Brandt, Kavajecz (2009)	4/2003–12/2004	Countries (10)	Corporate Sample Restricted to Entities in European Union Member States	Europe	3, 5, 7, 10	Lombard Risk
Bedendo, Cathcart, El-Jahel, Evans (2013)	2/2004–1/2010	Corporates (249)		U.S.	5	CMA Datavision
Bedendo, Colla (2015)	1/2008–12/2011	Corporates (118), Sovereigns (8)	Sovereign Sample Includes Belgium, Finland, France, Germany, Italy Netherlands, Portugal, Spain	Europe	5	Markit
Beirne and Fratzscher (2013)	9/2008–9/2011	Sovereigns (31)		Euro area (10), Other Advanced (7), Latin America EME (5), other EME (9)	N/A	Bloomberg
Belke and Gokus (2011)	1/2006–12/2009	Financial Institutions (4)		U.S.	5	CMA, Datastream, Thomson Reuters
Bella, Carpenter, and Robinson (2011)	3/2007–6/2008	ABX Index (06-1, 06-2, 07-1, and 07-2 vintages)		U.S.	N/A	Markit
Ben Dor and Guan (2017)	9/2004–10/2015	CDX.HY, iTraxx XO		North America and Europe	N/A	Bloomberg, Barclays
Berg and Streitz (2016)	7/2010–7/2012	Sovereigns (57)		Worldwide	N/A	DTCC
Berndt, Douglas, Duffie, Ferguson, Schranz (2005)	9/2000–8/2003	Corporates (69)		U.S.	5	CIBC

(continued)

Table B.3 (continued)

Article	*Sample period*	*Type of reference entities*[a]	*Reference entity notes*	*Region(s) of reference entities*[b]	*CDS tenor(s) (years)*	*CDS data source(s)*
Berndt, Jarrow, Kang (2007)	7/1999–6/2005	Corporates (1521)	60 CDSs in the study are index products	U.S. (929), Non-U.S. (532)	5	ValuSpread, Lombard Risk
Berndt, Obreja (2010)	1/2003–12/2008	Corporates (150)	Corporate Sample Restricted to Euro-denominated CDSs	Europe	5	Bloomberg
Berndt, Ostrovnaya (2014)	1/2002–11/2006	Corporates (144)	Corporate Sample Includes Companies from 9 Different Industries	U.S.	5	Markit
Bertoni and Lugo (2014)	1/2003–12/2010	Corporates (1429)		Global (52 Countries)	1, 3, 5	Datastream
Bertoni, Lugo (2014)	1/2003–10/2010	Corporates (1429)		N/A	5	CMA, Datastream
Beyhaghi, Massoud, Saunders (2017)	1/2003–12/2007	Corporates (323)		U.S.	5	Markit
Bhanot, Guo (2012)	6/2008–9/2009	Corporates (35)		U.S.	N/A	Bloomberg
Bhansali, Gingrich, and Longstaff (2008)	3/2007–12/2007	Indices (3)	CDX.NA.IG, CDX.NA.HY, and iTraxx IG	U.S. and Europe	5, 7, 10	PIMCO and JPMorgan Chase & Co.
Bhar, Colwell, and Wang (2017)	6/2004–5/2007	Indices (3)	Indices include iTraxx Europe, iTraxx Europe HiVol, and iTraxx Europe Crossover	Europe	5, 10	The International Index Company
Billio, Caporin, Pelizzon, and Sartore (2012)	1/2004–12/2011	Indices (18)	Indices include 18 sector indices such as Automobile, Banking, Basic Resources, etc.	U.S.	5	Datastream

(continued)

Table B.3 (continued)

Article	*Sample period*	*Type of reference entities*[a]	*Reference entity notes*	*Region(s) of reference entities*[b]	*CDS tenor(s) (years)*	*CDS data source(s)*
Billio, Getmansky, Gray, Lo, Merton, Pelizzon (2013)	1/2001–3/2012	Sovereigns (17)		Austria, Belgium, Germany, Spain, France, Greece, Ireland, Italy, Netherland, Portugal, Denmark, Sweden, United Kingdom, Norway, Switzerland, U.S., Japan	5	Bloomberg
Blanco, Brennan, Marsh (2005)	1/2001–6/2002	Corporates (33)	Corporate Sample Restricted to Investment-Grade Companies	Europe and U.S.	5	CreditTrade and JP Morgan
Blasques, Koopman, Lucas, and Schaumburg (2016)	2/2009–5/2014	Sovereigns (8)		Belgium, France, Germany, Ireland, Italy, Netherlands, Portugal, Spain	N/A	Bloomberg
Blau and Roseman (2014)	7/2011–9/2011	Sovereigns (31)		Asia, Europe, U.S.	5	Bloomberg
Bongaerts, De Jong, Driessen (2011)	1/2004–12/2008	Corporates (595)		U.S.	5	CMA, Datastream
Boudreault, Gauthier, and Thomassin (2013)	12/2007–1/2012	Corporates (210)	Corporates Sample are those included in CDX.NA.IG and CDX.NA.HY	North America	1, 2, 3, 4, 5, 7, 10	Markit
Brandstack (2010)	1/2000–6/2009	Corporates (160)	Corporate Sample Restricted to Investment-Grade Companies	U.S.	5	Bloomberg

(continued)

Table B.3 (continued)

Article	*Sample period*	*Type of reference entities*[a]	*Reference entity notes*	*Region(s) of reference entities*[b]	*CDS tenor(s) (years)*	*CDS data source(s)*
Breitenfellner and Wagner (2012)	6/2004–8/2010	iTraxx Europe (first 13 series)	Data includes the benchmark index as well as the subindices of the iTraxx Europe universe, namely the iTraxx High- Vol, the iTraxx Senior Financials, the iTraxx Subordinated Financials and the iTraxx Non-Financials index	Europe	5	Open Bloomberg
Broto and Pérez-Quirós (2015)	1/2007–12/2012	Sovereigns (10)		Belgium, France, Germany, Greece, Ireland, Italy, Portugal, Spain, United Kingdom, U.S.	10	CMA, Datastream, Thomson Reuters
Bühler and Trapp (2009)	6/2001–6/2007	Corporates (155)	Corporate Sample Restricted to Euro-denominated CDSs	N/A	5	Bloomberg
Byström (2016)	1/2004–1/2013	Corporates (22)	Corporate Sample Restricted to USD-denominated CDSs	U.S.	1, 5, 10	Datastream
Byström (2005)	3/2005–9/2005	Corporates (125)	Corporates Sample are those included in the iTraxx Europe CDS index and iTraxx Europe HiVol index	Europe	iTraxx Europe: 5, 10; iTraxx Europe HiVol: 3, 5, 7, 10	N/A

(continued)

Table B.3 (continued)

Article	*Sample period*	*Type of reference entities*[a]	*Reference entity notes*	*Region(s) of reference entities*[b]	*CDS tenor(s) (years)*	*CDS data source(s)*
Byström (2006)	6/2004–3/2006	Indices (7)	Indices sample includes 7 sector indices in the iTraxx Europe Index plus iTraxx Europe Crossover Index	Europe	5	International Index Company
Caceres, Guzzo, Segoviano (2010)	6/2005–1/2010	Sovereigns (10)		Europe	N/A	Datastream
Calice (2014)	1/2005–6/2011	Corporates (250)	Corporates Sample includes constituents of CDX NA IG and iTraxx Europe	U.S. and Europe	5	Bloomberg
Calice and Ioannidis (2012)	1/2005–11/2008	Indices (2)	DJ CDX.NA and iTraxx Europe Main Index	U.S. and Europe	5	Morgan Stanley
Calice, Chen, and Williams (2013)	8/2005–10/2010	Sovereigns (10)		Austria, Belgium, France, Germany, Greece, Ireland, Italy, Netherlands, Portugal, Spain	5, 10	CMA, Datastream, Thomson Reuters
Calice, Ioannidis, and Miao (2016)	9/2004–7/2009	North America CDX IG indices		North America	5, 10	Markit
Calice, Ioannidis, and Williams (2012)	10/2003–4/2009	Indices (2)	CDX.NA.IG and iTraxx IG	U.S. and Europe	5	Thomson Reuters Datastream
Calice, Mio, Štěrba, Vašíček (2015)	9/2007–2/2012	Sovereigns (5)		Spain, Portugal, Ireland, Czech Republic, Poland	5, 10	Bloomberg
Callen, Livnat and Segal (2009)	2002–2005	Corporates (508)	Corporate Sample Restricted to USD-denominated CDSs	N/A	1, 3, 5, 7, 10	Lombard Risk

(continued)

Table B.3 (continued)

Article	*Sample period*	*Type of reference entities*[a]	*Reference entity notes*	*Region(s) of reference entities*[b]	*CDS tenor(s) (years)*	*CDS data source(s)*
Cana and Cinca (2017)	2006–2012	Corporates (722), iTraxx Europe, iTraxx Europe Crossover, HiVol iTraxx, CDX.NA.IG, CDX.NA.IG Japan Main Index		Europe, North America, and Asia	5	Markit
Cao, Yu, and Zhong (2010)	1/2001–12/2006	Corporates (301)	Corporate Sample Restricted to USD-denominated CDSs	N/A	5	Markit
Caporin, Pelizzon, Ravazzolo, Rigobon (2018)	11/2008–9/2011	Sovereigns (8)		France, Germany, Greece, Ireland, Italy, Portugal, Spain, United Kingdom	5	Datastream
Carboni and Carboni (2011)	9/2008–9/2010	Sovereigns (18)		Europe (14), Asia-Pacific (3), U.S. (1)	5	CMA, Merrill Lynch
Carr and Wu (2007)	1/2002–3/2005	Sovereigns (2)		Mexico and Brazil	1, 3, 5	Bloomberg
Castellanos, Constantinou, Ng (2015)	1/2007–2/2011	Corporates (20)		U.S.	0.5, 1, 2, 3, 4, 5, 7, 10	HSBC
Cetina, Paddrik, Rajan (2018)	2012–2015	Corporates (3173-4297)	4,297 (as of 11/09/12), 3,651 (as of 10/11/13), and 3,173 (as of 10/3/14)	N/A	N/A	Bloomberg, DTCC, Markit
Chakraborty, Chava, and Ganduri (2015)	1994–2012	Corporates (507)		U.S.	N/A	Markit, CMA Datavision, and Bloomberg

(continued)

Table B.3 (continued)

Article	*Sample period*	*Type of reference entities*[a]	*Reference entity notes*	*Region(s) of reference entities*[b]	*CDS tenor(s) (years)*	*CDS data source(s)*
Chan and Marsden (2014)	11/2003–7/2011 (IG), 3/2006–7/2011 (HY)	Indices (2)	CDX.NA.IG, CDX.NA.HY	North America	5	Markit
Chan-Lau and Kim (2004)	3/2001–5/2003	Sovereigns (8)		Brazil, Bulgaria, Colombia, Mexico, the Philippines, Russia, Turkey, Venezuela	5	CreditTrade, Deutsche Bank
Chen, Cheng, Liu (2008)	4/2003–5/2004	Corporates (44)		Global	1, 2, 3, 5, 7, 10	JP Morgan
Chen, Cheng, Wu (2012)	5/2003–10/2007	Corporates (310), Financial Institutions (90)	Number of reference entities reported are averages	N/A	1, 2, 3, 5, 7, 10	Investment Bank
Chen, Cummins, Viswanathan, Weiss (2013)	2/2002–5/2008	Financial Institutions (33)	Financial Institutions Sample Includes Banks and Insurance Companies	Global	5	Markit
Chen, Fabozzi, Sverdlove (2010)	2/2000–4/2003	Corporates (584)		U.S.	5	Creditex
Chernov, Gorbenko, Makarov (2013)	1/2006–12/2011	Auctions (26)		Global	N/A	Creditfixings
Chiaramonte and Casu (2010)	1/2005–3/2009	Financial Institutions (57)	Financial Institutions Sample Restricted to Banks	U.S. (7), Europe (43), Asia (7)	5	Datastream
Choi and Park (2017)	11/2005–12/2016	Sovereign (18)		South Korea, China, Indonesia, Malaysia, Philippines, Thailand, Colombia, Mexico, Chile, France, Germany, Italy, Spain, Portugal, South Africa, Belgium, Austria, and Denmark	5	Bloomberg

(continued)

Table B.3 (continued)

Article	*Sample period*	*Type of reference entities*[a]	*Reference entity notes*	*Region(s) of reference entities*[b]	*CDS tenor(s) (years)*	*CDS data source(s)*
Choi, Shachar, and Shin (2017)	3/2005–6/2009	Financial Institutions (35)		U.S.	All	DTCC, Markit
Christensen (2007)	3/2001–6/2005	Corporates (1)	Corporate Sample Limited to Ford Motor Co.	U.S.	1, 3, 5, 7, 10	Markit
Cizel (2013)	1/2003–3/2011	Corporates (169)		U.S.	5	CMA, Thomson Reuters
Collin-Dufresne, Junge, and Trolle (2017)	10/2013–10/2015	Indices (2)	CDX.NA.IG, CDX.NA.HY	North America	N/A	Bloomberg Swap Data Repository, Depository Trust Clearing Corporation Data Repository, and the Intercontinental Exchange Trade Vault
Colonnello, Efing, Zucchi (2017)	1/2001–12/2014	Corporates (5843)	Corporate Sample Includes Companies with and without CDS Trading and excludes financial institutions	U.S.	All	DTCC, Markit
Conrad, Dittmar, Hameed (2013)	7/2006–10/2010	Corporates (119)		Global	5	CMA, Bloomberg
Consiglio, Lotfi, and Zenios (2016)	10/2008–3/2016	Sovereigns (N/A)		Europe	5	Datastream

(continued)

Table B.3 (continued)

Article	*Sample period*	*Type of reference entities*[a]	*Reference entity notes*	*Region(s) of reference entities*[b]	*CDS tenor(s) (years)*	*CDS data source(s)*
Coro, Dufour, and Varotto (2012	1/2006–7/2009	Corporates (135)		Europe	5	GFI Group
Cossin and Lu (2005)	1/2002–7/2003	Corporates (39)		Europe	5	Bloomberg, Morgan Stanley
Coudert and Gex (2010a)	1/2004–2/2007	Corporates (224)		U.S. and Europe	5	Bloomberg, Datastream
Coudert and Gex (2010b)	2005–2009	Corporate (26), Sovereign (1)	CDS Auction Data	Global	N/A	Bloomberg, Creditex, ISDA, Markit
Coudert and Gex (2010d)	6/2004–12/2005	Corporates (120)	Corporate Sample Restricted to Entities in the CDX.NA.IG, iTraxx Europe Main, CDX.NA.HY, iTraxx Europe Crossover	U.S.	5	Bloomberg, Datastream
Coudert and Gex (2013)	1/2007–3/2010	Financial Institutions (17), Sovereigns (18)	Financial Institutions Sample Restricted to Banks	Argentina, Austria, Belgium, Brazil, Denmark, Finland, France, Lithuania, Mexico, the Netherlands, Greece, Ireland, Italy, the Philippines, Poland, Portugal, Spain, Turkey	5	Bloomberg, Datastream
Da Fonseca and Gottschalk (2013)	1/2007–12/2011	CDX.NA.IG, iTraxx Europe Indices (2)		U.S. and Europe	0.5, 1, 2, 3, 5, 7, 10	Markit
Da Fonseca and Wang (2016)	10/2004–2/2012		CDX.NA.IG, CDX.NA.IG.HVOL	North America	5	Bloomberg
Daniels and Jensen (2005)	2000–2002	Corporates (72)		U.S.	5	JP Morgan

(continued)

Table B.3 (continued)

Article	*Sample period*	*Type of reference entities*[a]	*Reference entity notes*	*Region(s) of reference entities*[b]	*CDS tenor(s) (years)*	*CDS data source(s)*
Danis and Gamba (2016)	1994–2013	Corporates (N/A)		U.S.	N/A	N/A
Das, Hanouna, and Sarin (2009)	Q3/2001–Q1/2005	Corporates (230)	Sample Restricted to USD-denominated CDSs and excludes Financial Institutions	N/A	1, 2, 3, 5, 10	Bloomberg
Das, Kalimipalli, Nayak (2014)	8/2001–12/2008	Corporates (350)		U.S.	5	Bloomberg
De Boyrie and Pavlova (2016)	1/2010–7/2014	Sovereigns (14)		Brazil, Russia, India, China, South Africa, Mexico, Indonesia, South Korea, Turkey, United States, Portugal, Italy, Ireland, Spain	5	Thomson Reuters
De Bruyckere, Gerhardt, Schepens, Vander Vennet (2013)	2007–2012	Financial Institutions (40), Sovereigns (15)	Financial Institutions Sample Restricted to Banks	Sovereigns are Austria, Belgium, Denmark, Finland, France, Germany, Greece, Ireland, Italy, Norway, Portugal, Spain, Sweden, the Netherlands, United Kingdom	5	Bloomberg, CMA
De Santis (2015)	9/2011–11/2013	Sovereigns (4)		Italy, Spain, France, Germany	3, 5	Thomson Reuters
De Wit (2006)	1/2004–12/2005	Corporates (92), Sovereigns (11)		Global	3, 5, 10	Bloomberg
Delatte, Gex, López-Villavicencio (2012)	1/2008–7/2010	Sovereigns (10)		Austria, Belgium, Denmark, France, Greece, Ireland, Italy, Netherlands, Portugal, Spain	5	Datastream
Delis, Mylonidis (2011)	7/2004–5/2010	Sovereigns (4)		Greece, Italy, Portugal, Spain	10	Bloomberg

(continued)

Table B.3 (continued)

Article	*Sample period*	*Type of reference entities*[a]	*Reference entity notes*	*Region(s) of reference entities*[b]	*CDS tenor(s) (years)*	*CDS data source(s)*
Demirgüç-Kunt and Huizinga (2013)	2001–2008	Financial Institutions (62 in CDS Sample and 1045 in Market-to-Book Sample)	Financial Institutions Sample Restricted to Banks	Worldwide	5	Markit
D'Errico, Battiston, Peltonen, and Scheicher (2018)	3/2011, 4/2012, 12/2012, 10/2014	Financial Institutions and Sovereigns (162)	Most traded 162 reference entities, including all G20 sovereigns, emerging markets sovereigns, and global financials	Global	N/A	DTCC
Di Cesare (2006)	8/2001–7/2005	Financial Institutions (42)	Financial Institutions Sample Restricted to Banks	U.S. (11), Europe (27), Japan (4)	5	Bloomberg
Di Cesare and Guazzarotti (2010)	1/2002–3/2009	Corporates (167)		U.S.	5	Bloomberg
Díaz, Groba and Serrano (2010)	6/2006–3/2010	Corporates (85)		Europe	1, 3, 5	Markit
Dieckmann and Plank (2011)	1/2007–4/2010	Sovereigns (18)		Belgium, Czech Republic, Denmark, Finland, France, Germany, Greece, Hungary, Ireland, Israel, Italy, the Netherlands, Poland, Portugal, Slovenia, Spain, Sweden, United Kingdom	10	Markit
Ding and Pu (2012)	1/2004–12/2009	Index (1)	CDX.NA.IG	North America	5	Reuters

(continued)

Table B.3 (continued)

Article	*Sample period*	*Type of reference entities*[a]	*Reference entity notes*	*Region(s) of reference entities*[b]	*CDS tenor(s) (years)*	*CDS data source(s)*
Dockner, Mayer and Zechner (2013)	1/2006–2/2012	Sovereigns (10)		Austria, Belgium, France, Greece, Ireland, Italy, Netherlands, Portugal, Slovakia, Spain	1, 3, 5, 7, 10	Bloomberg and Datastream
Dooley and Hutchinson (2009)	1/2007–2/2009	Sovereigns (14)		Argentina, Brazil, Chile, Colombia, Mexico, China, South Korea, Malaysia, Czech Republic, Poland, Hungary, Russia, South Africa, Turkey	5	N/A
Doshi (2011)	1/2001–3/2008	Corporates (46)	Corporate Sample Restricted to USD-denominated CDSs	N/A	3, 5, 7	CRSP & Compustat
Doshi, Ericsson, Jacobs, Turnbull (2013)	1/2011–12/2010	Corporates (95)	Corporate Sample Restricted to Entities in the DJ.CDX.NA.IG	North America	1, 3, 5, 7, 10	Markit
Doshi, Jacobs and Zurita (2017)	1/2001–6/2012	Sovereigns (25)		Brazil, Colombia, Mexico, Peru, Austria, Belgium, Finland, France, Germany, Ireland, Italy, Portugal, Slovenia, Spain, Hong Kong, Japan, Malaysia, Philippines, South Korea, Thailand, Czech Republic, Poland, Russia, South Africa, Turkey, United Kingdom	1, 3, 5, 7, 10	Markit
Dötz (2007)	1/2004–10/2006	Corporates (36)	Corporates Sample is based on iTraxx Europe constituents	Europe	5	Bloomberg, Thomson Financial Datastream

(continued)

Table B.3 (continued)

Article	*Sample period*	*Type of reference entities*[a]	*Reference entity notes*	*Region(s) of reference entities*[b]	*CDS tenor(s) (years)*	*CDS data source(s)*
Dötz (2007)	1/2004–10/2006	Corporates (36)	Corporate Sample Restricted to Entities in the iTraxx Europe	Europe	5	Bloomberg, Thomson Financial Datastream
Du, Gadgil, Gordy, and Vega (2017)	1/2010–12/2013	Financial Institutions (N/A)	Corporates sample restricted to FRB regulated entities	Global	5	Markit
Düllmann and Sosinska (2007)	2/2002–6/2005	Financial Institutions (3)	Financial Institutions Sample Restricted to Banks	Germany	3, 5, 10	Bloomberg
Dumontaux and Pop (2013)	1/2008–12/2008	Financial Institutions (85)		U.S.	1, 5, 10	Thomson Reuters
Dunbar (2008)	1/2004–8/2006	Corporates (41)	Corporate Sample Restricted to USD-denominated CDSs	U.S.	1, 3, 5, 7, 10	Bloomberg, JP Morgan
Dunbar and Amin (2012)	3/2003–9/2008	Indices (2)	CDX.NA.IG, CDX.NA.HY	North America	5, 10	Markit
Eckner (2010)	9/2004–11/2006	CDX.NA.IG		North America	5	Citi, Morgan Stanley, and Markit
Eichengreen, Mody, Nedeljkovic, Sarno (2012)	7/2002–11/2008	Corporates (45)	Corporate Sample Restricted to Banks and Insurers and USD-denominated CDSs	Global	5	Bloomberg
Eisenthal, Feldhutter, and Vig (2017)	2001–2015	Corporates (43)	US corporations; only CDS on unsecured debt	U.S.	5	Markit

(continued)

Table B.3 (continued)

Article	*Sample period*	*Type of reference entities*[a]	*Reference entity notes*	*Region(s) of reference entities*[b]	*CDS tenor(s) (years)*	*CDS data source(s)*
Ejsing and Lemke (2011)	1/2008–6/2009	Corporates (10)		Austria, Belgium, Germany, Spain, France, Greece, Ireland, Italy, the Netherlands, Portugal	5	Datastream
Elkamhi, Jacobs, Pan (2014)	10/2004–6/2007	Corporates (152)	Corporate Sample Restricted to Entities in the CDX Index	North America	1, 3, 5	Markit
Elkhami, Jacobs, Langlois, Ornthanalai (2012)	1/2002–3/2008	Corporates (87)	Corporate Sample Restricted to Entities in the CDX Index	North America	5	Markit
Erce (2015)	9/2005–1/2014	Financial Institutions (48), Sovereigns (10)	Financial Institutions Sample Restricted to Banks	Germany, Italy, France, Spain, Ireland, Greece, Portugal, Belgium, Netherlands, Austria	5	Bloomberg, Datastream
Ericsson, Jacobs, and Oviedo (2009)	1/1999–12/2002	Corporates (N/A)		Global	5	CreditTrade
Eyssell, Fung, and Zhang (2013)	1/2001–12/2010	Sovereigns (1)	Sovereign Sample Restricted to USD-denominated CDSs	China	5	Markit
Fabozzi, Cheng, Chen (2007)	2/2000–4/2003	Corporates (562)		Europe, U.S.	1, 2, 3, 4, 5	Creditex
Fang and Lee (2011)	1/2006–9/2009	ABX.HE 1, ABX.HE 2, ABX.HE 3, ABX.HE 4. and CDX.NA.IG		North America	5	Reuters (ABX), Bloomberg (CDX)
Feldhütter and Nielsen (2012)	3/2006–9/2006	Index (1)	Index sample consists of CDX.NA.IG	North America	5	Markit

(continued)

Table B.3 (continued)

Article	*Sample period*	*Type of reference entities*[a]	*Reference entity notes*	*Region(s) of reference entities*[b]	*CDS tenor(s) (years)*	*CDS data source(s)*
Fender, Hayo, Neuenkirch (2012)	4/2002–12/2011	Sovereigns (12)		Bulgaria, Russia, Turkey, Brazil, Colombia, Peru, Venezuela, China, Malaysia, the Philippines, Thailand, South Africa	5	Markit
Fenech, Vosgha, and Shafik (2014)	2004–8/2012	Index (1)	iTraxx	Australia	N/A	N/A
Flannery, Houston, Partnoy (2010)	1/2006–3/2009	Corporates (302)		North America	5	Markit
Foley - Fisher (2010)	12/2007–3/2010	Sovereigns (10)		Greece, Ireland, Spain, Portugal, Italy, France, Netherlands, Belgium, Finland, Austria	5, 10	Bloomberg, CMA
Fontana (2011)	1/2006–8/2009	Corporates (37)		U.S.	5	Thomson Financial Datastream
Fontana and Scheicher (2016)	1/2007–12/2012	Sovereigns (10)	Sovereign Sample Restricted to USD- and EUR-denominated CDSs	Austria, Belgium, France, Germany, Greece, Ireland, Italy, Netherlands, Portugal, Spain	10	Markit
Forte and Lovreta (2015)	1/2002–12/2008	Corporates (92)	Corporate Sample Excludes Financial Institutions	Europe	5	GFI
Forte and Peña (2009)	9/2001–6/2003	Corporates (17)	Corporate Sample Excludes Financial Institutions	Europe (15), U.S. (2)	5	Banco Santander
Frei, Capponi, and Brunetti (2017)	N/A–12/2011	Financial Institutions (N/A)	Financial Institutions Sample Restricted to Banks	N/A	N/A	DTCC

(continued)

Table B.3 (continued)

Article	*Sample period*	*Type of reference entities*[a]	*Reference entity notes*	*Region(s) of reference entities*[b]	*CDS tenor(s) (years)*	*CDS data source(s)*
Fung, Sierra, Yau, and Zhang (2008)	1/2001–4/2004	Indices (3)	Index sample includes self-created CDS index using 125 IG firms and 100 HY firms, CDX.NA.IG, CDX.NA.HY	North America	5	Markit
Galariotis, Makrichoriti, Spyrou (2016)	11/2008–4/2014	Sovereigns (10)		Germany, Austria, Belgium, France, Greece, Ireland, Italy, Netherlands, Portugal, Spain	5	Bloomberg, Datastream International, DTCC
Galil and Soffer (2011)	1/2002–6/2006	Corporates (N/A)		N/A	5	Markit
Gamba and Saretto (2013)	1/2002–12/2010	Corporates (276)		U.S.	5	Bloomberg
Gârleanu and Pedersen (2011)	9/2005–12/2009	Corporates (N/A)		U.S.	N/A	"A major broker-dealer"
Gątarek and Wojtowicz (2015)	1/2004–6/2014	Sovereigns (15)		Poland, Netherlands, France, Belgium, Denmark, Finland, Sweden, Austria, Switzerland, United Kingdom, Ireland, Italy, Spain, Portugal, Greece, Germany	5	CMA, Datastream, Thomson Reuters
Gerlach-Kristen (2013)	8/2005–8/2012	Financial Institutions (12), Sovereigns (6)	Financial Institutions Sample Restricted to Banks	Sovereigns include Germany, Greece, Ireland, Italy, Portugal, Spain	5	Datastream

(continued)

Table B.3 (continued)

Article	*Sample period*	*Type of reference entities*[a]	*Reference entity notes*	*Region(s) of reference entities*[b]	*CDS tenor(s) (years)*	*CDS data source(s)*
Getmansky, Girardi, and Lewis (2016)	1/2012–12/2012	Corporates & Sovereigns (20)	Sample Restricted to Contracts with U.S. Counterparties or Affiliated with U.S. Entities or U.S. Reference Entities	Global	N/A	DTCC
Giannikos, Guirguis, and Suen (2013)	1/2005–12/2008	Financial Institutions (39)		U.S.	5	CMA
Giglio (2011)	1/2004–6/2010	Financial Institutions (15)	Financial Institutions Sample Restricted to Banks	Europe, U.S.	5	Bloomberg, CMA
Glover and Richards-Shubik (2014)	Q3/2005–Q3/2011	Sovereigns (13)		Europe	5	CMA
González and Naranjo (2014)	7/2002–6/2012	Corporates (20)		U.S.(12), Europe(8)	5	Bloomberg, Compustat and official regulatory filings
González, Gil, Agra, Santomil (2012)	2006–2010	Corporates (134)		Europe	All	Financial Statements
Greatrex (2009a)	1/2001–3/2006	Corporates (333)		U.S.	5	Markit
Greatrex (2009b)	1/2001–4/2006	Corporates (476)		U.S.	5	Markit
Greatrex, Rengifo (2012)	7/2006–12/2009	Corporates (348)		U.S.	5	N/A

(continued)

Table B.3 (continued)

Article	*Sample period*	*Type of reference entities*[a]	*Reference entity notes*	*Region(s) of reference entities*[b]	*CDS tenor(s) (years)*	*CDS data source(s)*
Groba, Lafuente and Serrano (2013)	1/2008–7/2012	Sovereigns (14)		Austria, Belgium, Germany, Finland, France, Greece, Ireland, Italy, Netherlands, Portugal, Spain, Denmark, Sweden, United Kingdom	1, 3, 5	Datastream
Gross and Kok (2013)	1/2008–4/2013	Financial Institutions (41), Sovereigns (23)	Financial Institutions Sample Restricted to Banks	Austria, Belgium, Bulgaria, Czech Republic, Germany, Denmark, Spain, France, Greece, Hungary, Ireland, Italy, Japan, Lithuania, Latvia, Netherlands, Poland, Portugal, Sweden, Slovenia, Slovakia, United Kingdom, U.S.	5	N/A
Gündüz and Kaya (2013)	1/2004–10/2011	Sovereign (10)		Austria, Belgium, France, Germany, Greece, Ireland, Italy, Netherlands, Portugal, Spain	10	Markit
Gündüz, Nasev and Trapp (2013)	1/2009–6/2011	Corporates (7[illegible])		Germany	5	DTCC
Guo, Chen, and Huang (2011)	10/2003–3/2009	Index (1)	CDX.NA.IG	North America	5	Bloomberg
Gupta and Sundaram (2015b)	11/2006–12/2013	Auctions (73)		U.S.	N/A	Creditex, Markit, DTCC
Gyntelberg, Hördahl, Ters, and Urban (2017)	1/2008–12/2011	Sovereign (7)		France, Germany, Greece, Ireland, Italy, Portugal, and Spain	5, 10	CMA Datavision
Gyntelberg, Hördahl, Ters, Urban (2013)	10/2008–5/2011	Sovereigns (7)		France, Germany, Greece, Ireland, Italy, Portugal, Spain	5, 10	CMA
Haas and Reynolds (2017)	1/2008–12/2013	Corporates (463)		U.S.	5	GFI, Thomson Reuters

(continued)

Table B.3 (continued)

Article	*Sample period*	*Type of reference entities*[a]	*Reference entity notes*	*Region(s) of reference entities*[b]	*CDS tenor(s) (years)*	*CDS data source(s)*
Haerri, Morkoetter and Westerfeld (2015)	1/2009–2011	Companies (107)		Europe	5	Bloomberg
Hammoudeh and Sari (2011)	1/2004–4/2009	Indices (3)	Index sample includes sector indices for financial services, banking, and insurance	U.S.	5	Datastream
Han and Zhou (2011)	8/2002–12/2009	Corporates (695)		North America	1, 2, 3, 5, 7, 10	Markit
Hasan, Liu, and Zhang (2016)	2001–2011	Financial Institutions (161)	Financial Institutions Sample Restricted to Banks	Global	5	Markit
Hassan, Ngene, and Yu (2015)	N/A–11/2013	Sovereigns (7)		Argentina, Brazil, Mexico, Colombia, Philippines, South Africa, Turkey	5	Bloomberg, Datastream, Thomson Reuters
Heinz and Sun (2014)	1/2007–12/2012	Sovereigns (24)		Bulgaria, Croatia, Czech Republic, Estonia, Hungary, Latvia, Lithuania, Poland, Romania, Russia, Slovak Republic, Slovenia, Turkey, Ukraine, Greece, Italy, Ireland, Portugal, Spain, Austria, Belgium, France, Germany, Netherlands	5	Bloomberg, Datastream
Helwege, Maurer, Sarkar, Wang (2009)	1/2005–3/2009	Auctions (43)		U.S.	N/A	ISDA, Creditex, Markit

(continued)

Table B.3 (continued)

Article	*Sample period*	*Type of reference entities*[a]	*Reference entity notes*	*Region(s) of reference entities*[b]	*CDS tenor(s) (years)*	*CDS data source(s)*
Hilscher, Pollet, Wilson (2015)	1/2001–12/2007	Corporates (783)		U.S.	5	Datastream, DTCC, Markit
Hirtle (2009)	Q2/1997–Q4/2006	Financial Institutions (57)	Financial Institutions Sample Restricted to Banks			Call Reports
Hong, Ryou, and Srivastava (2017)	1983–2014	Corporates (520), Corporates (610)	Hypothesis 1, Hypothesis 2	U.S.	All	Markit
Houweling and Vorst (2005)	5/1999–1/2001	Corporates/Sovereigns (225)	Corporate Sample Restricted to USD and Euro-denominated CDS; Quotes on Euro denominated CDS are only observed from 3/2000–1/2001	Global	0.08, 0.5, 1, 2, 3, 4, 5, 7, 10	creditex, CreditTrade, and quotes from commercial and investment banks
Huang and Cheng (2013)	1/2004–12/2010	Corporates (200)		U.S.	5	Thomson Datastream
Huang and MacDonald (2014)	9/2005–1/2013	Sovereigns (26)		Europe	5	Bloomberg, Datastream, Markit, CMA Datavision
Huang, Chen, and Shen (2014)	9/2005–5/2010	Sovereigns (≤7)		Global	5	Thomson Reuters, Datastream

(continued)

Table B.3 (continued)

Article	*Sample period*	*Type of reference entities*[a]	*Reference entity notes*	*Region(s) of reference entities*[b]	*CDS tenor(s) (years)*	*CDS data source(s)*
Huang, Shen, and Chen (2012)	1/2007–12/2008	Financial Institutions (73)/ Corporates (395)		U.S.	5	Thomson Reuters, Datastream
Hui and Chung (2011)	1/2006–4/2010	Sovereigns (11)		Austria, Belgium, Finland, France, Germany, Greece, Ireland, Italy, Netherlands, Portugal, Spain	5	Bloomberg
Hui and Fong (2011)	12/2007–8/2011	Sovereigns (N/A)		U.S. & Japan	0.08, 0.25, 5	Bloomberg
Hui, Lo, and Lau (2013)	1/2009–1/2013	Indices (3)	Index sample consists of iTraxx Europe Main index and and financials and non-financial compositions of iTraxx Europe	Europe	5	JP Morgan DataQuery
Hull, Predescu and White (2004)	1/1998–5/2002	Corporates (1502), Sovereigns (60), Quasi-Sovereign (37)		North America (798), Europe (451), Asia (330), Other (20)	5	GFI
Imbierowicz and Wahrenburg (2009)	1/2001–12/2007	Corporates (472)		North America (185), Europe (153), Asia (133), Latin America (1)	5	Bloomberg, Datastream
Ismailescu and Phillips (2015)	1/2001–9/2010	Sovereigns (41)		Global	5	Datastream, Markit, Thomson Reuters

(continued)

Table B.3 (continued)

Article	*Sample period*	*Type of reference entities*[a]	*Reference entity notes*	*Region(s) of reference entities*[b]	*CDS tenor(s) (years)*	*CDS data source(s)*
Ivanov, Santos, and Vo (2016)	2005–2012	Corporates (62)		N/A	5	Markit
Jacoby, Jiang, and Theocharides (2009)	1/2001–12/2008	Corporates (N/A)	Corporate Sample Restricted to USD-denominated CDSs	U.S.	5	Bloomberg, Markit
Jakovlev (2007)	1/2003–12/2006	Corporates (50)	Corporate Sample Excludes Financial Institutions	Europe	5	Datastream
Jankowitsch, Pullirsch, Veža (2008)	1/2003–1/2005	Corporates (12)		Europe	All	Thomson Reuters
Jansen and Fabozzi (2017)	1/2001–6/2014	Corporates (N/A)		U.S.	1	Markit
Janus, Jinjarak and Uruyos (2013)	2010–2011	Sovereigns (50)		Global	5	CMA
Javadi, Kim, Krehbiel, and Nejadmalyeri (2017)	7/2002–8/2013	Corporates (864)		U.S.	5	Markit
Jorion and Zhang (2007)	1/2001–12/2004	Corporates (820)		North America	5	Markit
Jorion and Zhang (2009)	1/2001–12/2005	Corporates (178)	Corporate Sample Restricted to USD-denominated CDSs	North America	5	Markit
Junge and Trolle (2015)	9/2006–2/2012	CDX.NA.IG, CDX.NA.HY, iTraxx Europe, iTraxx Xover		North America and Europe	5	Markit
Kajurová (2015)	9/2007–1/2015	iTraxx Europe Senior Financial Index		Europe	5	Bloomberg

(continued)

Table B.3 (continued)

Article	*Sample period*	*Type of reference entities*[a]	*Reference entity notes*	*Region(s) of reference entities*[b]	*CDS tenor(s) (years)*	*CDS data source(s)*
Kalbaska and Gątkowski (2012)	8/2005–9/2010	Sovereigns (9)		Portugal, Ireland, Italy, Greece, Spain, France, Germany, United Kingdom, U.S.	5	Datastream
Kallestrup, Lando, Murgoci (2016)	Q1/2004–Q4/2010	Corporates (33), Sovereigns (17)	Corporate Sample Restricted to USD- or Euro-denominated CDSs	Sovereigns are Austria, Australia, Belgium, Switzerland, Germany, Denmark, Spain, France, United Kingdom, Greece, Ireland, Italy, Japan, the Netherlands, Portugal, Sweden, the United States	5	CMA, Fitch
Kim (2013)	2/2001–3/2008	Corporates (136)		U.S.	5	Markit
Kim, Li, Zhang (2017)	1/2001–12/2008	Corporates (N/A)	Sample Restricted to USD-denominated CDSs and Sample Size Varies by Period	N/A	All	Markit
Kim, Loretan, and Remolona (2010)	1/2005–1/2009	Corporates (38), Indices (5)	Indices include IG and HY iTraxx Asia-ex-Japan, IG and HY DJ CDX NA, and iTraxx Europe	Asia, excluding Japan	N/A	Markit
Kim, Salem, and Wu (2015)	11/2007–3/2012	Sovereigns (19)		Australia, China, Indonesia, Japan, Korea, France, Germany, Greece, Italy, Portugal, Russia, Spain, South Africa, Turkey, United Kingdom, Argentina, Brazil, Mexico, U.S.	5	Thomson Reuters

(continued)

Table B.3 (continued)

Article	*Sample period*	*Type of reference entities*[a]	*Reference entity notes*	*Region(s) of reference entities*[b]	*CDS tenor(s) (years)*	*CDS data source(s)*
King (2009)	1/2008–1/2009	Financial Institutions (28)	Financial Institutions Sample Restricted to Banks	Europe, U.S.	5	Markit
Kirschenmann and Steffen (2017)	Q4/2010–Q4/2012	Sovereign (25), iTraxx		Europe	5	Bloomberg, Thomson Reuters Datastream
Kryzanowski, Perrakis, and Zhong (2017)	8/2009–12/2014	Corporates (97)	Including financials	U.S.	5	Markit
Küçük (2010)	1/2004–5/2008	Sovereigns (21)		Emerging Markets	5	CMA
Lando and Mortensen (2005)	7/1999–12/2003	Sovereigns (65), Other (1,425)		Global	1, 3, 5, 7, 10	Lombard Risk Systems Limited
Le (2015)	1/2005–12/2009	Financial Institutions (179)	Financial Institutions Sample Restricted to Banks with assets greater or equal to USD 3 billion	U.S.	All	Uniform Bank Performance Report
Leccadito, Tunaru, Urga (2015)	1/2001–11/2006 and 6/2008–3/2013	Corporates (198-207 and 626-647)	Sample Sizes Depend on Methodology and Sample Period	N/A	0.5, 1, 2, 3, 4, 5, 7, 10, 15, 20, 30	Markit
Lee, Oh, and Yermack (2017)	2001–2015	Corporates (N/A)		U.S.	All	Markit
Lehnert and Neske (2006)	8/2000–8/2003	Corporates (100)	Corporate Sample Restricted to entities in the TRAC-X Europe index	Europe	5	JP Morgan

(continued)

Table B.3 (continued)

Article	*Sample period*	*Type of reference entities*[a]	*Reference entity notes*	*Region(s) of reference entities*[b]	*CDS tenor(s) (years)*	*CDS data source(s)*
Levy (2009)	1/2000–5/2008	Sovereigns (16)	Sovereign Sample Restricted to entities in the Lehman Brothers MSCI Emerging Market Index	Brazil, Chile, China, Colombia, Malaysia, Mexico, Panama, Peru, Philippine, Poland, Russia, South Africa, South Korea, Turkey, Ukraine, Venezuela	5	Bloomberg
Li and Huang (2011)	1/2004–7/2008	Sovereigns (20)	Sovereign Sample Restricted to USD-denominated CDSs	China, Korea, Czech Republic, Israel, Malaysia, Poland, Hungary, Russia, Mexico, Colombia, Egypt, Morocco, Peru, Brazil, Indonesia, Philippines, Turkey, Venezuela, Argentina, Pakistan	5	Thomson Reuters
Li and Tang (2016)	6/1997–4/2009	Corporates (N/A)	Sample Sizes Depend on Methodology and Sample Period	North America	N/A	CreditTrade, GFI
Li and Zinna (2017)	1/2008–12/2015	Financial Institutions (54)	Financial Institutions Sample Restricted to Banks	Europe	1, 3, 5, 7, 10	CMA
Lin, Kolokolova, Poon (2017)	2002–2011	Corporates (286)	Corporate Sample Excludes Financial Institutions	U.S.	5	Markit
Liu, Ng, Tang, and Zhong (2017)	1997–2014	Corporates (761)		U.S.	All	Markit, CredtTrade, and GFI Group
Longstaff and Rajan (2008)	10/2003–10/2005	CDX.NA.IG		North America	5	Citigroup
Longstaff, Mithal, and Neis (2003)	3/2001–10/2002	Corporates (68)		U.S	5	Citigroup

(continued)

Table B.3 (continued)

Article	*Sample period*	*Type of reference entities*[a]	*Reference entity notes*	*Region(s) of reference entities*[b]	*CDS tenor(s) (years)*	*CDS data source(s)*
Longstaff, Mithal, and Neis (2005)	3/2001–10/2002	Corporates (68)		U.S.	5	Citigroup
Longstaff, Pan, Pedersen, and Singleton (2011)	10/2000–1/2010	Sovereigns (26)		Global	5	Bloomberg
Lu, Fang, and Lue (2010)	1/2006–6/2009	CDX.NA.IG, emerging markets CDX index, iTraxx Europe, iTraxx Asia		North America, Europe, Asia, emerging markets	5	Bloomberg
Manasse and Zavalloni (2013)	1/2006–3/2012	Sovereigns (15)		Germany, France, Italy, Spain, Belgium, Greece, Portugal, Ireland, Netherland, Austria, Finland, Sweden, Norway, United Kingdom, Northern Ireland, Denmark	N/A	Thomson Reuters
Marra (2015)	9/2006–5/2009	CDX.NA.IG		North America	5	Bloomberg
Marsh and Wagner (2012)	1/2004–10/2008	Corporates (193)		U.S.	5	Anonymous Credit-Oriented Hedge Fund
Martin and Roychowdhury (2015)	1/2002–12/2009	Corporates (529)	Corporate Sample Excludes Financial Institutions	U.S.	N/A	CMA
Massa and Zhang (2012)	1/2001–12/2009	Corporates (N/A)	158122 bond-month observations	U.S.	5	Markit

(continued)

Table B.3 (continued)

Article	*Sample period*	*Type of reference entities*[a]	*Reference entity notes*	*Region(s) of reference entities*[b]	*CDS tenor(s) (years)*	*CDS data source(s)*
Mayordomo and Peña (2014)	11/2005–4/2011	Corporates (38)	Corporate Sample Excludes Financial Institutions	Europe	1, 2, 3, 4, 5	GFI
Mayordomo, Rodriguez-Moreno, and Peña (2014)	1/2005–3/2012	Corporates (401)	Corporate Sample Excludes Financial Institutions	Global	5	CMA
Meine, Supper, and Weiβ (2015)	1/2004–9/2010	Corporates (228)		U.S.	5	CMA
Micu, Remolona, and Wooldridge (2006)	1/2001–3/2005	Corporates (439)		U.S. (246), Europe (114), Japan (79)	5	Markit
Minton, Stulz, and Williamson (2009)	1/1999–12/2005	Financial Institutions (395)	Financial Institutions Sample Restricted to Banks		All	FR Y-9C filings
Morkoetter, Pleus, and Westerfeld (2012)	9/2004–12/2009	Reference (198)		Europe, North America	5	Bloomberg
Naifar (2011)	3/2006–11/2009	Index (1)	iTraxx Japan	Japan	5	Markit
Naifar (2012)	3/2005–8/2010	Indices (2)	iTraxx Japan and Australia	Japan and Australia	5	Markit
Narayanan and Uzmanoglu (2018)	10/2008–12/2012	Corporates (303)		U.S.	All	CMA
Nashikkar, Subrahmanyam, and Mahanti (2011)	7/2002–6/2006	Corporates (1,167)		U.S.	All	CMA, GFI
Ni and Pan (2011)	8/2008–11/2016	Corporates (395)		N/A	N/A	CMA

(continued)

Table B.3 (continued)

Article	*Sample period*	*Type of reference entities*[a]	*Reference entity notes*	*Region(s) of reference entities*[b]	*CDS tenor(s) (years)*	*CDS data source(s)*
Nijskens and Wagner (2011)	6/1998–6/2006	Financial Institutions (38)	Financial Institutions Sample Restricted to Banks	Europe (9), North-America (25), Asia (2), Australia (2)	N/A	US FDIC Call Reports
Norden (2017)	1/2000–1/2006	Corporates (95)		Europe, U.S.	5	CreditTrade and anonymous European bank
Norden and Weber (2004)	7/1998–12/2002	Corporates (90)		Europe (58), U.S. (24), Asia (8)	5	Anonymous European Bank
Norden and Weber (2009)	7/1998–12/2002	Corporates (58)		Europe (35), U.S. (20), Asia (3)	5	CreditTrade and anonymous European bank
Norden and Weber (2012)	1/2001–12/2008	Financial Institutions (20)	Financial Institutions Sample Restricted to Banks	Europe	5	Bloomberg, CreditTrade
Norden, Buston, and Wagner (2014)	1/1997–12/2009	Financial Institutions (1046)	Financial Institutions Sample Restricted to Banks (918 Banks had CDS Positions)		All	Call Reports
Oehmke and Zawadowski (2017)	8/2010–12/2012	Corporates (123)		U.S.	All	DTCC
Oh and Patton (2017)	1/2006–4/2012	Corporates (100)	Corporate Sample Restricted to Entities in the CDX.NA.IG Series 17		5	Markit
Ohno (2013)	7/2007–10/2011	Financial Institutions (21), Sovereigns (8)		Sovereigns are Belgium, France, Germany, Italy, Ireland, Spain, Portugal, Greece	N/A	Markit
O'Kane (2012)	1/2008–9/2011	Sovereigns (7)		Portugal, Ireland, Italy, Greece, Spain, France, Germany	5	Bloomberg

(continued)

Table B.3 (continued)

Article	*Sample period*	*Type of reference entities*[a]	*Reference entity notes*	*Region(s) of reference entities*[b]	*CDS tenor(s) (years)*	*CDS data source(s)*
Paddrik, Rajan, and Young (2016)	N/A	Corporates (52)	ICE Clear Credit's 26 members, and largest 26 non-members	U.S.	N/A	DTCC, Markit
Palmgren and Tamule (2009)	1989–2007	Corporates (7)		U.S.	1, 3, 5, 7, 10	Research Insight
Pan, Singleton (2008)	3/2001–8/2006	Sovereigns (3)		Mexico, Turkey, Korea	1, 2, 3, 5, 10	CreditTrade
Pavlova and De Boyrie (2015)	9/2008–8/2013	Sovereigns (10)	Sovereign Sample Restricted to Entities in the Markit iTraxx SovX Asia Pacific Index	Australia, Japan, Thailand, Malaysia, New Zealand, China, Indonesia, Korea, Philippines, Vietnam	5	Datastream
Pelster and Vilsmeier (2018)	1/2001–9/2014	Corporates (277)	Corporates Sample are those included in CDX.NA.IG and CDX.NA.HY	North America	5	Markit
Peltonen, Scheicher, Vuillemey (2014)	12/30/2011	Financial Institutions (602), Sovereigns (40)		Sovereign Sample Includes 18 G20 Sovereigns and 22 European Sovereigns	5	DTCC
Peristiani and Savino (2011)	2001–2008	Corporates (N/A)		U.S.	N/A	Bloomberg, DTCC, Markit
Pires, Pereira, and Martins (2015)	8/2002–2/2007	Corporates (260)		Europe, U.S.	5	Bloomberg
Pu and Zhang (2012a)	1/2008–12/2010	Sovereigns (10)		Austria, Belgium, Finland, France, Germany, Portugal, Ireland, Italy, Greece, Spain	5	Bloomberg

(continued)

Table B.3 (continued)

Article	*Sample period*	*Type of reference entities*[a]	*Reference entity notes*	*Region(s) of reference entities*[b]	*CDS tenor(s) (years)*	*CDS data source(s)*
Pu and Zhang (2012b)	10/2000–4/2011	Sovereigns (54)		Africa, Asia, Europe, Middle East, South America	5	Bloomberg
Pu, Wang, annd Wu (2011)	1/2001–12/2007	Corporates (523)	Corporate Sample Restricted to USD-denominated CDSs	U.S.	5	Markit
Qiu and Yu (2012)	2001–2008	Corporates (732)		North America	5	Markit
Raunig and Scheicher (2011)	3/2003–10/2006	Corporations (86)	Corporate Sample Restricted to Entities in the iTraxx Europe and iTraxx Crossover	Europe	N/A	N/A
Remolona, Scatigna, and Wu (2008)	1/2002–5/2006	Sovereigns (24)		Latin America, Central and Eastern Europe, Asia, Middle East, Africa	5	Markit
Revoltella, Mucci and Mihaljek (2010)	2000–2009	Sovereigns (14)		Bulgaria, Czech Republic, Estonia, Hungary, Latvia, Lithuania, Poland, Romania, Slovakia, Croatia, Turkey, Serbia, Kazakhstan, Russia	5	Bloomberg
Rodríguez-Moreno and Peña (2013)	1/2004–11/2009	Financial Institutions (33), Indices (2)	Index sample includes CDX.IG 5Y and iTraxx Europe 5 year	U.S. (13) and Europe (20)	5	Reuters, Datastream
Rodríguez-Moreno and Peña (2013)	1/2004–11/2009	Corporates (33), Index (2)	Corporate Sample Restricted to Banks, Index Sample Includes CDX IG 5y and iTraxx Europe 5y	Western Europe (20), U.S. (13)	5	Datastream, Markit, Thomson Reuters

(continued)

Table B.3 (continued)

Article	*Sample period*	*Type of reference entities*[a]	*Reference entity notes*	*Region(s) of reference entities*[b]	*CDS tenor(s) (years)*	*CDS data source(s)*
Salomao (2017)	1/2008–3/2011	Sovereigns (1)		Greece	5	Datastream
Sambalaibat (2014)	1/2004–1/2012	Sovereigns (65)		N/A	5	CMA, DTCC
Santamaría, Biscarri, and Benito (2014)	1/2008–6/2012	Sovereigns (13)		Spain, Portugal, Italy, France, Ireland, United Kingdom., Greece, Germany, Austria, Belgium, Netherlands, Finland, Denmark	5	CMA
Sapriza, Zhao, and Zhou (2009)	10/2000–12/2007	Sovereigns (13)		Argentina, Brazil, Colombia, Mexico, Panama, Peru, Venezuela, Bulgaria, Poland, Russia, Turkey, Ukraine, Philippines	5	Bloomberg
Saretto and Tookes (2013)	2002–2010	Corporates (122)		U.S.	N/A	Bloomberg
Scheicher (2008)	8/2004–1/2008	iTraxx Europe Main CDX index		Europe and North America	5	JP Morgan Securities
Schläfer and Uhrig-Homburg (2014)	1/2001–12/2007	Corporates (17)	Corporate Sample Restricted to USD-denominated CDSs and Excludes Financial Institutions	U.S.	5	Markit
Schneider, Sögner, and Veža (2010)	1/2/2001–5/30/2008	Corporates (278)		U.S.	1, 3, 5, 7, 10	Markit

(continued)

Table B.3 (continued)

Article	*Sample period*	*Type of reference entities*[a]	*Reference entity notes*	*Region(s) of reference entities*[b]	*CDS tenor(s) (years)*	*CDS data source(s)*
Schreiber, Müller, Klüppelber, and Wagner (2012)	6/2004–4/2009	Index (1)	iTraxx Europe	Europe	5	N/A
Seo and Wachter (2016)	10/2005–9/2008	CDX.NA.IG	Series 5 to 10 (excluding super-senior)	North America	5	Markit
Sgherri and Zoli (2009)	1/2003–3/2009	Sovereigns (11)		Austria, Belgium, Finland, France, Germany, Greece, Italy, Ireland, Netherlands, Portugal, Spain	10	Datastream
Shan, Tang, and Winton (2014)	6/1997–4/2009	Corporates (921)		U.S.	N/A	CreditTrade, GFI, Markit
Shan, Tang, and Yan (2014)	6/1997–4/2009	Financial Institutions (43)	Financial Institutions Sample Restricted to Banks	U.S.	N/A	FR Y-9C filings, OCC reports
Shan, Tang, and Yan (2017)	1997–2014	Financial Institutions (38–85)	Financial Institutions Sample Restricted to Banks	U.S.	All	FR Y-9C and OCC
Shao and Yeager (2007)	1/1997–12/2005	Financial Institutions (2,246)	Financial Institutions Sample Restricted to Bank Holding Companies; Maximum Sample Size is Shown	U.S.	All	FR Y-9C filings
Shim and Zhu (2014)	1/2003–6/2009	Corporates (116)		Hong Kong, SAR, Japan, Korea, Malaysia, Singapore	5	Markit
Shivakumar, Urcan, Vasvari, Zhang (2011)	2001–2008	Corporates (710)		U.S.	5	Markit

(continued)

Table B.3 (continued)

Article	*Sample period*	*Type of reference entities*[a]	*Reference entity notes*	*Region(s) of reference entities*[b]	*CDS tenor(s) (years)*	*CDS data source(s)*
Shoesmith (2014)	4/2007–3/2012	Sovereigns (8)		France, Italy, Spain, Netherlands, Belgium, Austria, Finland, Portugal	N/A	Bloomberg
Silva, Vieira and Vieira (2016)	1/2008–12/2015	Sovereigns (84)		Global	3, 5, 7, 10	Bloomberg, DTCC, Thomson Reuters
Skinner and Townend (2002)	9/1997–2/1999	Sovereigns (29)		Global	N/A	CDS trade tickets
Song (2013)	2006–2008	Financial Institutions (40)	Financial Institutions Sample Restricted to Banks	U.S.	All	FR Y-9C filings
Stamatopoulos, Arvanitis, and Terzakis (2016)	Q1/2008–Q1/2013	Sovereign (16)		Austria, Belgium, Cyprus, Estonia, Finland, France, Germany, Malta, the Netherlands, Slovakia, Slovenia, Greece, Italy, Spain, Portugal, and Ireland	5	Thomson Reuters / Eikon
Stanton and Wallace (2011)	7/2007–7/2010	ABX.HE 2006-1, ABX.HE 2006-2, ABX.HE 2007-1, ABX.HE 2007-2		N/A	N/A	CTSlink, Bloomberg, Lewtan ABSNet

(continued)

Table B.3 (continued)

Article	*Sample period*	*Type of reference entities*[a]	*Reference entity notes*	*Region(s) of reference entities*[b]	*CDS tenor(s) (years)*	*CDS data source(s)*
Streitz (2016)	2000–2010	Corporates (327)		U.S.	All	Bloomberg, CMA
Sturm (2013/14)	1/2004–9/2010	Financial Institutions (33)	Financial Institutions Sample Restricted to Banks	Europe	5	CMA
Subrahmanyam, Tang, and Wang (2014)	6/1997–4/2009	Corporates (901)		North America	All	CreditTrade, GFI, Markit
Subrahmanyam, Tang, and Wang (2017)	6/1997–4/2009	Corporates (901)		North America	All	CreditTrade and GFI Group
Tamakoshi and Hamori (2014)	1/2004–6/2013	Indices (3)	Index sample includes CDX index for the US, EU, and UK insurance sectors	U.S., E.U., and U.K.	5	Thomson Reuters Datastream
Tang and Yan (2007)	6/1997–3/2006	Corporates (120)	Sample Size is Averaged	U.S.	5	CreditTrade
Tang and Yan (2010)	6/1997–11/2006	Corporates (176)		U.S.	5	CreditTrade, GFI
Ters and Urban (2016)	1/2008–12/2011	Sovereign (12)		Greece, Ireland, Italy, Portugal, Spain, Czech Republic, Hungary, Poland, Slovakia, Austria, France, and Germany	5	CMA Datavision
Trujillo-Ponce, Samaniego-Medina, Cardone-Riportella (2014)	2002–2009	Corporates (51)	Corporate Sample Restricted to Entities in the FTSEuroFirst 100 Index	France, Germany, Italy, Netherlands, Spain, United Kingdom	All	Markit

(continued)

Table B.3 (continued)

Article	*Sample period*	*Type of reference entities*[a]	*Reference entity notes*	*Region(s) of reference entities*[b]	*CDS tenor(s) (years)*	*CDS data source(s)*
Trutwein and Schierek (2011)	1/2007–12/2008	Financial Institutions (13)	Financial Institutions Sample Restricted to Banks	U.S.	5	Markit
Trutwein, Ramchander, and Schiereck (2011)	4/2005–3/2008	Corporates (295)		North America	5	Markit
Veronesi and Zingales (2010)	1/2007–10/2008	Financial Institutions (9)	Financial Institutions Sample Restricted to Banks	U.S.	5	Datastream
Wang and Moore (2012)	1/2007–12/2009	Sovereigns (38)		Global	5, 7	Datastream
Wu and McMillan (2013)	1/2004–12/2009	Index (1)	Datastream CDX index for UK banking sector	U.K.	N/A	Datastream
Yang and Zhou (2013)	1/2007–9/2008	Financial Institutions (43)		U.S., United Kingdom, Germany, Switzerland, France, Italy, Netherlands, Spain, Portugal	5	Bloomberg, CMA
Yeh (2012)	2001–2008	Corporates (N/A)		North America	5	Markit
Yu (2017)	1/2006–12/2012	Sovereigns (11), Banks (26)		Austria, Belgium, Denmark, France, Germany, Greece, Ireland, Italy, Netherlands, Portugal, and Spain	5	Datastream, Bloomberg
Zareei (2015)	1/2010–12/2012	Corporates (50)		U.S.	N/A	N/A

(continued)

Table B.3 (continued)

Article	*Sample period*	*Type of reference entities*[a]	*Reference entity notes*	*Region(s) of reference entities*[b]	*CDS tenor(s) (years)*	*CDS data source(s)*
Zhang, Zhou, and Zhu (2009)	1/2001–12/2003	Corporates (307)		U.S.	5	Markit
Zhu (2006)	1/1999–12/2002	Financial Institutions (8), Corporates (16)	Financial Institutions Sample Restricted to Banks	U.S. (19), Europe (3), Asia (2)	5	CreditTrade
Zinna (2013)	4/2003–11/2007	Sovereigns (8)		Brazil, Colombia, Malaysia, Mexico, Peru, Philippines, Russia, Turkey	1, 2, 3, 5, 10	JP Morgan

Notes [a]The number in parentheses indicates the number of reference entities in a particular sample. For studies that analyze the impact of CDS usage on certain corporations, the number in parentheses indicates the number of corporations in the sample—e.g., for studies which analyze the impact of CDS usage on bank lending behavior, the number in parentheses indicates the number of banks in the sample.

[b]The numbers in parentheses indicate the numbers of reference entities per region in studies that analyze more than one region (when available)

Index

C. L. Culp et al., *Credit Default Swaps*, Palgrave Studies in Risk and Insurance, https://doi.org/10.1007/978-3-319-93076-3

D

The manufacturer's authorised representative in the EU is Springer Nature Customer Service Centre GmbH, Europaplatz 3, 69115 Heidelberg, Germany. If you have any concerns regarding our products, please contact ProductSafety@springernature.com

Printed and bound by CPI Group (UK) Ltd, Croydon, CR0 4YY
25/09/2026
02222852-0001